On the Order of Chaos

ON THE ORDER OF CHAOS
Social Anthropology and the Science of Chaos

Edited by Mark S. Mosko and Frederick H. Damon

Berghahn Books
New York • Oxford

First published in 2005 by

Berghahn Books

www.BerghahnBooks.com

Berghahn Books and the editors would like to thank Penguin USA
and James Gleick for the use of Figures 1.1–1.6 in the Introduction.

Library of Congress Cataloging-in-Publication Data

On the order of chaos : social anthropology & the science of chaos/edited by Mark S.
Mosko and Frederick H. Damon.
    p. cm.
Includes bibliographical references.
ISBN 1-84545-023-X (alk. paper) -- ISBN 1-84545-024-8 (pbk.)
 1. Ethnology--Philosophy. 2. Ethnology--Methodology. 3. Chaotic behavior in systems
I. Mosko, Mark S., 1948-   II. Damon, Frederick H.

GN345.O5 2005
306'.01--dc22   2005043636

British Library Cataloguing in Publication Data

A catalogue record for this book is available
from the British Library.

Printed in the United States on acid-free paper.

CONTENTS

FIGURES AND TABLES

Figures

Table

LIST OF CONTRIBUTORS

Frederick H. Damon
Department of Anthropology
University of Virginia

José Antonio Kelly
"Amazonian Center for Research and Control of
Tropical Diseases", Amazonas, Venezuela

Jack Morava
Department of Mathematics
Johns Hopkins University

Mark S. Mosko
Department of Anthropology
Research School of Pacific and Asian Studies
The Australian National University

Charles Piot
Department of Cultural Anthropology
Duke University

Marilyn Strathern
Department of Social Anthropology
Cambridge University

Christopher C. Taylor
Anthropology Department
University of Alabama at Birmingham

Roy Wagner
Department of Anthropology
University of Virginia

PREFACE AND ACKNOWLEDGMENTS

There was a time when sociocultural anthropology as a discipline was considered to be unique due to its holistic integration of elements from the social sciences, the natural sciences, and the humanities. Over the past two decades, though, the combination of postmodern challenges to anthropology from both within and without and vigorous denunciations of the postmodern critique have seemingly shattered any such pretensions to disciplinary coherence.

This is not to say that anthropology's current predicament lacks structure or pattern entirely. During recent years, particularly in North America, much debate in anthropology has focused on the issue of *science*, particularly whether or not anthropology is, or should be a science, social or otherwise. As in the "Science Wars" that ran concurrently through the 1990s, however, anthropological arguments put forward by both defenders and critics of science have presupposed definitions of "science" that have been demonstrably obsolete for at least a quarter of a century; that is, since the development of "chaos theory"—the analysis of complex dynamical systems—across nearly all scientific fields. In our view, as long as both humanist and scientific perspectives in anthropology fail to take sufficient stock of the revolutionary implications of chaos theory for comprehending human social life, their judgments over the "scientific" merits of the discipline or of "science" itself must be regarded as tentative, if not irrelevant.

But the issue of chaos theory's relevance to social anthropology in particular is an issue interesting in itself. To the best of our knowledge, this volume constitutes the discipline's first attempt at a sustained and comprehensive treatment of chaos theory. By now, however, all of the natural sciences and most other social sciences and humanities have sustained numerous such examinations. Why has anthropology, particularly with its preexisting connections to the sciences and the humanities, been among the last to be drawn to reflect on the merits of chaos theory? Perhaps because, as the contributions to this volume amply attest, many of the key ingredients of chaos theory have for long been stock and trade social anthropological theory. Ironically, it may be that anthropologists have displayed seemingly little conscious interest in chaos theory because many of its tenets have struck them intuitively as all too familiar! Alternatively, it may be that those same anthropological precursors to chaos theory were first brought to conscious light through the discipline's engagements with postmodernism and the humanities—which thus could have precluded their recognition as possibly "scientific."

Be that as it may, serious consideration of the implications of chaos theory for social anthropological analysis is long overdue. Accordingly, the chapters of this volume explore a wide range of aspects of chaos theory—sensitivity to initial conditions, nonlinearity, complexity, fractal self-similarity, self-organization, universality—from a variety of anthropological and empirical perspectives. As editors, we are particularly pleased to include among the contributors to this volume the two scholars who probably more than all others have helped bring chaos theory to the attention of the anthropological community: Roy Wagner and Marilyn Strathern. We are greatly indebted as well to the several authors of the volume's remaining chapters who have provided such stimulating and exemplary illustrations of the potentiality of chaos theory for anthropological applications. There are also friends and colleagues too many to name in full who, over the past ten years, have supported this endeavor with their thoughts and curiosities. We offer special thanks to Chris Gregory, Steve Gudeman, Roger and Valerie Green, Margaret Jolly, Emiko Ohnuki-Tierney, Jane Goodale, and Claude Lévi-Strauss. Finally, for our cover we thank Kaze design, Washington, DC, and Luke Hambly, our research assistant, who must be credited for the superb copyediting and for, several times, keeping our common effort from spiraling into true disorder.

MSM
FHD

PROLOGUE

Marilyn Strathern
Cambridge, 1 November 2003

Words exist in complex relations with one another. One aspect of Mosko and Damon's extraordinary endeavor, of the words that follow, deserves an initial glance.

The capacity to replicate not-quite similar forms allows us—anyone—to move around a social world that manages to remain familiar to the senses. It also allows us to differentiate kinds of people and their manifold interactions, so that the very act of moving may be registered as travel across distinct spheres or domains of activity. That in turn feeds the capacity to perceive the world as different and connected at the same time. The capacity is so close to that of procreation, the parent producing a not-quite similar child, one might imagine it was born there. Regardless of the answer, we might ask where this capacity lodges.

Of course it does not have to lodge anywhere in particular. Once it has generated its effects, those effects will take on a life of their own, and all one need do is to keep producing them. I speak of effects since what I am calling a capacity is nothing but an ability or capability inferred from sights seen, action acted, effort expended. A capacity of sorts may be deduced from how it is that anthropologists feel able to describe such activities (I subsume analysis and theorization under "description"). Now a discipline is no more and no less than the effort to describe, and the genius of anthropology has always been its descriptive engagement with the fact of description, with how people generate accounts of themselves. Far from being a surprise, it is surely a matter of demonstration, as the reader of this book will find, that the anthropological project participates in the same exercise as its subjects of study. But whereas the anthropolog-

---

ical capacity to replicate the not-quite similar is an effect of descriptive practice, their subjects of study often act it out in other registers. A social encounter becomes a procreative moment. Insofar as relationships are the condition of persons in communication with one another, we could say that relationships create persons in not-quite similar states to one another. All one needs (to keep the world going round on this particular axis) is to learn how to "do" relationships.

For description to have an effect, one has to learn how to "do" words— the complexity of their interrelations seems to come of its own accord. Take the example of Lorenz's so-called strange attractor, which makes its first appearance quite early in the Introduction. Its initial graphic description of seven loops took Lorenz 500 successive computer calculations. Gleick adds that Lorenz could see more than he drew. In words, "These loops and spirals were infinitely deep, never quite joining, never intersecting. Yet they stayed inside a finite space" (1987: 140). The words both are and are not sufficient to describe the phenomenon, both falling short and recursively adding layers of reference (depth, join, intersection) that build up an image—even though the image itself can be grasped all at once.

Originally expounded for phenomena apprehended in nonverbal (e.g., mathematical) form, such verbal expositions take off on their own trajectories. When the patterns created by dense mathematical equations are translated (via graphics) into words, their origins still evident, they lodge in language as metaphors or similes. Or language seems to lodge in them. So the strange attractor is described as "highly sensitive to initial conditions."[1] This condenses a series of observations into a verbal phrase which, by virtue of being a description, draws on and is drawn into other domains of verbalized experience. Responsiveness, priority, givens of existence, even the notion that relationships are the condition of persons in communication with one another: "sensitivity to initial conditions" now belongs to a semantic field that has its own character and impetus. It has entered that field as a (new) metaphor for experiences or perceptions already conceptualized in other terms. One of the interesting questions broached in this book is when such metaphors also become analogies that can be laid out as models of conceptual relationships .

In this particular example, there is in fact a succession of translations or redescriptions going on: the convection of hot and cold air currents Lorenz[2] had to reduce to mathematical formulae were subject to computer operations and then rendered as a graph[3] before being converted to a text. At each translation information is both lost and gained. Moreover, these final verbal formulae summon images that have their own complex character in outrunning and falling short of the words, even as the words themselves will be both more encompassing (summoning other words) and less encompassing (never overcoming the ineffable) than their referents.[4] The point of interest to an anthropologist is that, at the moment at which these mathematical operations get written about, they enter a domain of social description. They both take on values already available in how language is used and make available other ways of thinking about social phenomena. So they appear apposite for (re)describing the effects and outcomes of human relationships.

This sense of the apposite may well draw on the reflexivity offered by the language of chaos, coming as that does from a cultural-linguistic universe in the first place ("order," "instability," "attraction"). What can seem impossibly impoverished or even weird to the mathematician (the verbal renderings) can be reabsorbed by a language that sees a new use for their descriptive power. But now what is being described are seemingly quite other phenomena altogether—social and cultural processes—obtained through quite different computational steps. An example would be the observation that order and disorder are created simultaneously or appear mutually constitutive. "Mutual constitution" points to a perfectly feasible analysis of the interdigitation of social activity; the difference is made in how the concepts of stability and instability are being brought together, given the kinds of sociological presumptions ordinarily made of them as antagonistic or contradictory forces.[5] However, I see a more general point here.

After years of thinking that the way to grow was to castrate, or to cast off the ancestors, or to sneer at other people's essentialisms, in short, to shed the embarrassing, perhaps it is exhilarating for anthropology to go over what it already has. So a discipline whose conversations are coming to seem more and more like everyone else's finds new life in recognition, in realizing the scope of social extension, and its many scales, already in its repertoire. This is one of the dazzling effects of reading this book.

Of course chaos theory provides figures of speech. It does so precisely to the extent that it points to the way figures of speech behave, or for that matter the way descriptions of social life behave. The only surprising thing is that it has taken anthropologists so long to hold up the not-quite similar form of chaos theory to itself. It challenges us—anyone—to know how it is that we can move around the objects in our world, including anthropologists' objects of study (cultures, societies), and at the same time keep them familiar to the senses.

Notes

1. E.g., Kauffman (1993: 178), Coveney and Highfield (1995: 174).
2. He "replaced the correct time evolution in infinite dimension by a time evolution in three dimensions, which he could study on a computer" (Ruelle 1993: 62). Ruelle adds: "The Lorenz time evolution is not a realistic description of atmospheric convection, but its study nevertheless gave a very strong argument in favor of unpredictability of the

motions of the atmosphere" (1993: 63). [It was Ruelle, with Takens, who gave the strange attractor its name.]

3. Each stage in turn may contain several operations. Gleick (1987: 142) describes the problems of mapping three-dimensional pictures of attractors in two dimensions, e.g., removing one dimension by turning a continuous line into a collection of points.

   Making pictures of strange attractors was not a trivial matter. Typically, orbits would wind their ever-more-complicated paths through three dimensions or more, creating a dark scribble in space that could not be seen from the outside. To convert these three-dimensional skeins into flat pictures, scientists first used the technique of projection, in which a drawing represented the shadow that an attractor would cast on a surface... [Or took] a slice from the tangled heart of the attractor, removing a two-dimensional section just as a pathologist prepares a section of tissue for a microscope slide.

4. In other registers nonlinear descriptions abound. Apropos ritualization, to take one instance, Humphrey and Laidlaw write that "actors both are and are not authors of their acts" (1994: 133).

5. As in the title of Coveney and Highfield's book. The vocabulary of stability / instability (chaos / order) is not without baggage. One should be suspicious of invitations to think with concepts that rely on an intuitive sense of life inherently taking after one or the other, and especially so when once "discovered" chaos (instability) comes to have the stronger voice. In fact it is a great pity that, outside mathematics and physics, complexity thinking got drawn into an order-disorder axis, a function of language-use. It bought too readily into the fragmented / subversive / hybridized language of the latter part of the twentieth century where, in descriptions of society, the ostensibly fragmented, unstable regime came to have a privileged place.

1

INTRODUCTION: A (RE)TURN TO CHAOS

Chaos Theory, the Sciences, and Social Anthropological Theory

Mark S. Mosko
The Australian National University

Over the past two decades, the natural sciences have been revolutionized by the development of "chaos theory," a new approach to kinds of order previously hidden within the stochastic, seemingly disorderly phenomena of complex dynamical systems. This volume is an attempt to evaluate critically the potential contributions that chaos theory can make both to anthropological analyses of social, cultural, and historical phenomena and to recent methodological and theoretical debates in anthropology and beyond.

Chaos theory, heralded as the "New Science" (Prigogine and Stengers 1984; Briggs and Peat 1989; Gleick 1987; Nicolis and Prigogine 1989; Stewart 1989), constitutes a revolutionary paradigm of scientific analysis and theorizing that has fundamentally transformed many areas of physics, chemistry, biology, meteorology, physiology, and mathematics. Through the lens of chaos, a wide range of seemingly random and disparate phenomena—weather patterns, fluid turbulence, traffic jams, population changes, chemical solutions, the building of termite nests, cardiovascular and neural rhythms, biological evolution and natural selection—which previously were regarded as beyond conventional modes of scientific explanation have been shown to exhibit properties of deterministic order within apparent disorder.

On the basis of these successes and certain perceived parallels between the natural and human domains, numerous social scientists and humanist scholars have recently begun to explore comprehensively the applicability of chaos theory to phenomena distinctive to human activity and experience (Hayles 1990; 1991a; Kiel and Elliot 1997; McClure 1998).

Disciplinary examples would include economics (Drucker 1989; Rosser 1997), political science (Brown 1997; Sapperstein 1997), criminology (Arrigo and Young 1998; Milovanovic 1997), cognitive science (A. Jones 1998), ecology (Goerner 1994), psychology (Mainzer 1994; Butz 1997; Guastello, Hyde, and Odak 1998; Arrigo and Williams 1999), sociology (Young 1991a; 1991b; 1992; Eve, Horsfall, and Lee 1997; Byrne 1998; McClure 1998), and literature (Hayles 1990; 1991a; 1991b).

In recent years, a number of influential social anthropologists have also drawn on chaos theory for inspiration (e.g., Wagner 1986a; 1986b; 1986c; 1991; 2001; Abrahams 1990; Strathern 1991a; 1991b; 1995; 1999; 2000; 2001; Appadurai 1996; Schlee 2002). These, however, have tended to focus only on selected *parts* of chaos theory as it has been developed in the natural sciences (e.g., sensitive dependence on initial conditions, fractal or holographic self-scaling, nonlinearity; see below). Contrary to developments in sister social sciences and the humanities, in social anthropology there has been as yet no comprehensive, systematic attempt to evaluate the applicability of the new science to anthropology's distinctive ethnographic, comparative, methodological and theoretical materials.

Such an anthropological undertaking is particularly timely in respect of one key issue that has animated the disciplinary debates for the past two decades; namely, the relative merits and appropriateness of scientific as distinct from humanistic approaches to the study of human affairs, particularly in an increasingly globalizing world. At a critical early juncture, for example, Marcus and Fischer (1986) proclaimed "a crisis of representation" in anthropology and other social sciences involving "intense concerns with the way social reality is to be presented" (1986: 165). This "crisis" was supposedly marked by two countervailing yet complementary tendencies. On the one hand, Marcus and Fischer argued that most of the established, generalizing paradigms of social-scientific objectivist empirical research that had till then informed much anthropological research and publication had become untenable in light of the emergence of literary postmodernism, poststructuralism, interpretivism, cultural criticism, radical feminism, and other critiques (see also Asad 1973; Said 1979; Fabian 1983; Clifford 1988). On the other, they recognized a growing tendency among humanist scholars to transcend disciplinary boundaries and to explore and borrow one another's ideas and methods. Particularly noteworthy at this "experimental moment" (Marcus and Fischer 1986: 8) were the influences of various humanist disciplines—literary criticism, postmodernism, deconstructivism, and cultural studies—where a wide variety of fresh inquiries over the writing of ethnographic accounts and other genres of documentation and exposition were celebrated (e.g., Rabinow 1977; Geertz 1980a; Clifford and Marcus 1986).

One consequence of this crisis of representation over the intervening years has been a series of animated debates over the appropriateness in anthropology of scientifically "objectivist" epistemological and theoretical paradigms and their possible replacement by humanistic, interpretivist, "subjectivist" approaches. However, the portrayals of science in these anthropological discussions by both its defenders and its detractors have for the most part employed classical, *prechaos* formulations quite as though the revolutionary changes attendant to the emergence of chaos theory had not taken place. The series of "Science versus Humanities" commentaries in *Anthropology Newsletter* over the period 1995 to 1996, for instance, overwhelmingly dwelt on conventional prechaos characterizations of science; and despite a few allusions to chaos theory in these exchanges, virtually none of the relevant implications are heeded or elaborated. Similarly, the "Objectivity and Militancy" debate between D'Andrade (1995), Schepper-Hughes (1995) and others in *Current Anthropology* was conducted with reference exclusively to prechaos representations of science (for additional anthropological examples of this neglect, see Spiro 1986; 1996; Friedman 1987; Kuper 1994; Singleton and Reyna 1995; O'Meara 1997; Harris 1997; Kuznar 1997; A. Jones 1998; Fujimura 1998; Guille-Escuret 1999; Hamel 1999; Godelier 2000; Shankland 2001; Tresch 2001; cf. A. Jones 1998: 62-63; Anderson 2000). A few practitioners, however, have perceived that chaos theory's successes in the natural sciences can be partly explained as responses to many of classical science's limitations which in the humanities and social sciences have led to postmodernism, poststructuralism, and the other critiques constituting Marcus and Fischer's "experimental moment" (1986: 8; see Hayles 1991b; 1996; Young 1991a; Downey and Rogers 1995: 271; Harvey and Reed 1997: 296; Byrne 1998).

These anthropological wranglings have coincided with the "Science Wars" of the 1990s waged between "objectivist," "positivist" scientists on one front and "postmodernists," "culturalists," "social constructionists," "humanists," and practitioners of "science studies" on the other (Gross and Levitt 1994; Ross 1996; Sokol 1996; Sokol and Bricmont 1998; Segerstråle 2000). And as in anthropology, most of those battles have been fought over prechaos models of science—that is, independent of any novel implications that might arise from chaos theory as distinct from more conventional understandings of science—even though chaos theory's emergence and success in the natural sciences are arguably due to its transcendence of many of the same limitations that defined Marcus and Fischer's experimental moment for the social sciences.

Nonetheless, there have been a few junctures in the Science Wars when scientists and humanists contended directly over chaos theory. Perceiving epistemological similarities between chaos theory and their own positions, some of the humanist protagonists ironically proclaimed chaos theory for themselves as "postmodern science" (Hayles 1990; 1991b; Best 1995; Hart 1996: 275-277; Levine 1996: 133-134; Price 1997; cf. Lyotard 1984: 60; Young 1991a; Gross and Levitt 1994: 99). In much the same spirit, Appadurai (1996), as one example of a postmodern-oriented social anthropologist, has appropriated chaos theory to address the apparent lack of linear ordering among processes of globalization. The objectivist science warriors, however, dismissed the humanists' and postmodernists' applications of chaos theory as "vaporous," "confused," "grotesque," etc. In response, the humanists accused the defenders of science of systematically distorting and misrepresenting their positions and thus failing to engage with many of their arguments, including those focused on chaos theory (Gross and Levitt 1994; Ruelle 1993; Sokol and Bricmont 1998: 128-136; Bricmont 1996; A. Jones 1998; Koertge 1998; cf. Best 1995; Hayles 1991b; 1996; Jardine and Frasca-Spada 1997: 232; Labinger 1997; Byrne 1998; Robbins 1998; Van Peer 1998; Segerstråle 2000: 83-84). So even during those rare moments when the science warriors on both sides have invoked chaos theory directly, the wider polemical field has tended to subvert a more balanced appraisal of the convergences between chaos theory and contemporary analytical practices in the humanities and social sciences.

Although most social anthropologists are thus by now probably aware that something new has emerged in the natural sciences having to do with "chaos" and that scientists and humanists have recently fought vigorous battles over science itself, few practitioners have been in a position to consider fully the implications that chaos theory might have for social anthropology's current ruminations over epistemology, methodology, comparison, and theory. This volume's ostensible purpose, therefore, is to reorient the recent debates over science in anthropology away from outdated prechaos notions to the dominant paradigm of late twentieth and early twenty-first century science—the science of chaos. The contributors to this volume thus proclaim a second experimental moment for contemporary social anthropology. A key irony emphasized throughout the chapters of this volume is that, while social anthropologists have been arguing their cases both for and against science largely in terms of outmoded epistemologies, they have been pursuing a variety of discernible disciplinary approaches unaware of the many long-standing conceptual convergences between their own theories and the basic tenets of chaos theory. This is not a mere matter of nomenclature, however, for it is the recognition and fuller appreciation of the heretofore unrecognized conceptual linkages and correspondences that may well guide future social anthropologists to new theoretical insights not possible otherwise.

Chaos Theory and Social Anthropology

According to James Gleick, authoritative chronicler of the development of chaos theory, "twentieth-century science will be remembered for just three things: relativity, quantum mechanics, and chaos" (1987: 6). While this claim might betray a degree of hyperbole, there is nonetheless a certain appropriateness for social anthropologists. Relativity and quantum mechanics emerged early in the last century when social anthropology was maturing as a social science. As suggested above, it is no coincidence either that the natural sciences have been revolutionized by chaos theory at roughly the same time that the social sciences, and social anthropology in particular, have been informed by postmodern critiques of all grand narratives. Unlike the other two revolutions of the twentieth century, as Gleick notes,

> the revolution in chaos applies to the universe we see and touch, to objects at human scale. [In the chaos sciences,] everyday experience and real pictures of the world have become legitimate targets for inquiry. There has long been a feeling, not always expressed openly, that theoretical physics has strayed far from human intuition about the world (Gleick 1987: 6).

And for social anthropologists who had previously seen themselves caught in the natural scientists' predicament, there is hope. "Some of those who thought physics might be working its way into a corner now look to chaos as a way out" (Gleick 1987: 6).

This does not mean to imply, however, that social anthropologists are being asked again to depend solely on the natural sciences for their future theoretical or methodological inspiration. Quite the contrary, for I argue here that most of the critical concepts and applications of chaos theory in the natural sciences possess clear analogues in both conventional and contemporary social anthropological thinking: for example, indeterminacy and lack of predictability of complex social processes; the dynamic relations of social forms to historical processes; partial connections between discrete phenomena, homologous structuring of conceptual and interactive patterns at a diversity of levels or scales, and so on. As a major portion of this Introduction and several of the chapters of this volume seek to demonstrate, many of the tenets of the revolution in the chaos sciences are, and for long have been, conventional social anthropological theory and practice.

But even the more abstract formulations of chaos theory in the natural sciences present social anthropology with something more valuable than merely formal descriptions of seemingly analogous cultural phenomena. Chaos theory, in other words, offers a way to integrate an otherwise heterogeneous collection of many of social anthropology's most provocative and far-reaching theories and postulates of recent decades, among them: Evans-Pritchard's analysis of the dynamics of segmentary opposition (1940); Lévi-Strauss's canonic formula for myth (1963c; 1988; 1995; Mosko 1991a; Maranda 2001); the widely acknowledged indeterminacy of historical events; Leach's (1954) model of societies in "moving equilibrium"; homologous structural replications across cultural domains; Fortes's (1970) formulation of the developmental cycle in domestic groups; the unpredictable influence of individual personalities on historical events;

the structural pervasiveness of binary constructions in sociocultural systems; structural analyses of history (e.g., Sahlins 1981; 1985; 1991; Lévi-Strauss 1995); Dumont's (1980) theory of religious and political hierarchy; Wagner's "obviation" theory, and particularly his grasp of representation in symbols standing for themselves (1986a; 1986c; 2001); Marilyn Strathern's portrayal of Melanesian sociality (1988; 1992a; 1995; 1999) and her discussions of scale and proportion (1991a; 1991b; 2000; 2001); and Appadurai's (1996) perception of the patterns shaping current processes of globalization. The current developments in chaos theory necessitate, therefore, not so much a new departure for social anthropology as a consolidation and appreciation of a disciplinary coherence until now only dimly and incompletely perceived.

Nonetheless, it can be assumed that most social anthropologists possess till now only a faint understanding of the core elements of chaos theory as it has developed in the natural sciences or, more importantly for my purposes, how the seemingly dissimilar features or aspects of dynamical chaotic systems articulate together within a coherent unified body of theory. It is in this latter regard that the contributions of chaos theory to social anthropology are likely to have their greatest value. Correspondingly, in the next section of this Introduction I attempt to outline in turn the main elements of chaos theory, deliberately aiming to excite the responsive chords of informed social anthropological readers. This should not be taken as a primer on chaos theory as it is strictly understood in the natural sciences, but as a guide and inducement to social anthropologists and cognate social scientists that they might gain considerably by paying attention to the implications that a knowledge of chaotic dynamical systems might have for their own theory and practice. Beginning with the main features that distinguish chaos theory from the prechaos formulations of conventional science, a few exemplary instances of chaos in the natural sciences will be examined for the sake of the new light they might shed onto a wide range of contemporary anthropological issues. As this discussion proceeds, I shall have increasing opportunity to note the impressive number and scope of both classic and contemporary anthropological theories and interpretive perspectives which already resonate with, if not incorporate, major elements of chaos theory. I shall focus particularly on several of the convergent ways in which complex dynamic processes are addressed by chaos scientists, on the one hand, and in anthropological treatments of history and social change, on the other.

This Introduction's final section will summarize the remaining chapters of this volume where fuller discussions of the relevance of chaos theory to social anthropology are developed and demonstrated. Several of these consist in detailed empirical exemplifications of key elements of chaos theory with cultural and historical materials from Africa, Melanesia, and Amazonia. The others develop more philosophically critical views of the limitations of chaos theory for social anthropology from the perspectives of mathematics and culture theory itself. Altogether, then, the volume seeks to cover a wide range of views of the potential utility of chaos theory for contemporary social anthropological theory.

Chaos Theory—The Science of Complex Dynamical Systems

The word "chaos" in present-day science has come to refer to deterministic kinds of order—*not* "disorder" as the term is understood popularly—arising from the generalized properties of complex dynamical systems; or, simply, order within apparent disorder. Chaos theory has enabled mathematicians, physicists, chemists, biologists, meteorologists, and others to identify new islands of pattern and order amidst what previously appeared to be seas of random, stochastic phenomena. With a few relatively simple formulae, chaos scientists can now account for a wide and disparate range of seemingly irregular phenomena formerly eluding explanation. In recent years, as noted above, practitioners in other social sciences and the humanities have begun to explore the implications of chaos theory for their disciplines. To the extent that sociocultural and historical phenomena—subjects at the center of anthropological investigation—can also be seen as complex dynamic systems, the possibility exists that they too may contain order where previously only disorder, randomness, and unpredictability were presumed to exist.

In the natural sciences, chaotic phenomena have been shown to exhibit six basic interrelated characteristics: (1) sensitive dependence on initial conditions, (2) complex, unstable relations among variables, (3) fractal or self-similar patterning on different scales, (4) dynamical transformations in accordance with nonlinear (rather than linear) equations, (5) self-organization or "dissipative structures," and (6) universality or previously undetected numerical constants (Prigogine 1980; Prigogine and Stengers 1984; Gleick 1987; Stewart 1989; Nicolis and Prigogine 1989).

To appreciate the possibilities that these features of chaos theory offer to contemporary social anthropology, it is necessary to grasp the chief differences between chaos theory and the antecedent explanatory frameworks of orthodox Newtonian science. Here I shall follow the excellent summaries of Gleick (1987), Stewart (1989), Briggs and Peat (1989) and Nicolis and Prigogine (1989).

The science on which much of twentieth-century social science including social anthropology has been premised is the classical model of Newtonian mechanics. According to this formulation, with sufficient knowledge of each independent body (the planets, for example), it should be possible to determine and predict the movements of all bodies in a given system indefinitely. Thus hypothetically entire systems in the Newtonian view are reducible to the discrete mechanics of their individual parts. However, this degree of scientific explanation and predictability has proven to be obtainable only so long as it has involved closed, two-body mechanics, or so-called "simple systems." The solar system and virtually the rest of the universe, however, consist in open complex systems of three or more interacting bodies.

On the basis of calculations by Poincare at the turn of the nineteenth century (Gleick 1987: 145-146), it was discovered that in complex systems predictability is greatly limited, at best approximate, and achievable for only relatively short spans of time. This means that as the cherished measure of scientific validity, predictability can only hold true for a radically narrow range of phenomena. The overwhelming proportion of reality investigated by natural as well as social scientists, because it consists in complex dynamical systems, will forever reside in the realm of instability, randomness, and disorder—at least from the perspective of classical Newtonian mechanics.

In the unpredictable operations of complex systems lie several of the central elements of chaos theory: extreme sensitivity to initial conditions, nonlinearity, and fractal geometry or self-similarity. Before I go further into them specifically, it is worth stressing that the plight of prechaos natural science was not unlike the predicament of much modernist social anthropology. To many analysts' great disappointment, Marxist, functionalist, structuralist, developmental, and many other models have turned out to possess predictive value only in the most vague and general sense and a very limited ability to account for the apparent randomness of given historical sequences of events. While many anthropologists have abandoned all brands of overarching, totalizing determinism and turned toward more reflexive, critical, anti-deterministic, and highly particularistic perspectives (literary criticism, postmodernism, historicism, deconstructionism, feminism, existentialist philosophy), at the analogous juncture natural scientists have turned to radically different nonmechanistic kinds of determinism, or chaos. Nonetheless, the views of reflexivist anthropologists and chaos scientists do intersect in celebrating a type of acumen that was explicitly lacking in the old, exhausted mechanistic paradigms, viz. intuition, whether as pronounced subjectivity and relativity or as the sensitive perception of pattern. In this regard, chaos theory has enabled scientists to recapture the study of "sensible qualities" and "expressive modes" which were forsaken early in science's development for the sake solely of "intelligibility" (Gleick 1987: 6; Clifford 1988: 5; Lévi-Strauss 1988: 111-112).

Sensitive Dependence on Initial Conditions

Of course, social anthropology of all the social sciences has long been acknowledged (and often dismissed) for its emphasis upon qualitative as distinct from quantitative methods and models—or what Lévi-Strauss (1963a), for example, termed "mechanical" and "statistical" models, respectively. It is in this space between qualitative and quantitative approaches that three of the distinctive features of chaos science can be preliminarily considered: extreme sensitivity to initial conditions, complexity, and nonlinearity.

In the models of classical Newtonian science, phenomena of nature were analyzed to measure quantitatively the mechanisms at play. Any natural system thus consisted in the numerically cumulative effects and interactions of its parts. Since the models that were employed to describe these phenomena presumed simple rather than complex interactions (i.e., few rather than many bodies) and closed rather than open systems, the goal was to characterize the relevant mechanisms in terms of quantitatively linear equations. More will be said below of the distinction between linear and nonlinear formulations. For now, it is enough to appreciate that linear equations are of the sort which are strictly proportional and allow for only a single numerical solution. Two *nearly but not exactly identical* initial states of a given system, according to projections from linear equations, would be predicted to reach *nearly but not quite identical* future states. In the Malthusian calculation of population increase, for example, two populations of the same species in nearly identical environments should naturally increase or decrease at the same rate so that, assuming no extraneous factors are involved, they will at any future moment arrive at population levels proportional to the slight difference between their initial states. Small changes produce small effects. It is a commonplace occurrence in observed populations, however, that such linear or proportional outcomes are rarely realized. Typically, such disjunctions are traced either to greater-than-previously appreciated differences in initial conditions or to the differential impact of external influences.

This predicament should be familiar to every social anthropologist. Well before the relatively recent turn to history, there has been a long-standing and deep-seated suspicion of all formulations of cultural and social systems which were closed rather than open (e.g., Leach 1954; Evans-Pritchard 1962; Gluckman 1964; Thomas 1989). This is one of the main sources of suspicion behind the rejection of most functionalist, structuralist, and other totalizing approaches even prior to the announced crisis of the 1980s and 1990s. No matter how identical two neighboring communities with the same language, culture, and social organization might appear to be, they can be expected to differ and diverge because they can never actually be *the same in every respect*. Similarly, a single community can be expected to follow detectably different courses of action at different historical junctures no matter how much the two historical moments might appear to be the same or similar. Of course, when dealing with human beings and human systems, anthropologists along with other social scientists have typically attributed differences of this order to the effects of the "individual," "human will," "subjectivity," "agency," "choice," and so on. Particularly in recent years, accordingly, the closer anthropologists have looked, the less overt order they have been able to discern.

These all-too-familiar observations by social scientists are known among chaos scientists as *extreme sensitivity to initial conditions*. Here, even hypothetically closed systems can behave in seemingly random, unpredictable ways. This is because in complex systems of many interacting parts, minute differences between initial conditions can ultimately produce great differences for those systems at later stages. Small changes produce large effects. Two systems starting on nearly but not quite identical initial conditions may closely follow one another's behavior at first, but eventually their behaviors will progressively diverge to the point that there may be no indication that they ever departed from nearly identical conditions. Moreover, no two systems in nature can ever be considered to possess truly *identical* initial conditions since it is impossible to ascertain their respective initial conditions with infinite accuracy. The classic visual analogue of this sensitivity to initial conditions is Smale's "horseshoe" (Figure 1.1, from Gleick 1987: 51).

> Pick two nearby points in the original space, and you cannot guess where they will end up. They will be driven arbitrarily far apart by all the folding and stretching. Afterward, two points that happen to lie nearby will have begun arbitrarily far apart (Gleick 1987: 52).

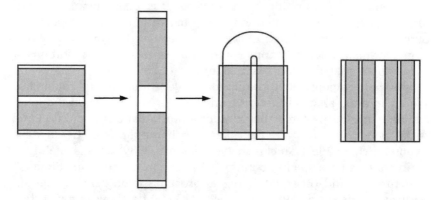

Figure 1.1: Smale's horseshoe

For anthropologists, the sensitivity to initial conditions of chaotic systems would appear to have the most obvious relevance in the commonplace observation of the unpredictability of historical events. History's unpredictability, in other words, might involve aspects of discernable chaotic processes rather than mere manifestations of contingency or accident. I discuss this important possibility more fully below, and it is developed much further in several of the volume's later chapters, especially those by Piot, Taylor, and Mosko.

Nonlinearity

Sensitive dependence on initial conditions in the complex systems of nature is partly a manifestation of *nonlinearity*. In classical mathematics and the natural sciences prior to the development of chaos theory, equations and formulas employed to explain the world were predominantly linear: "The classical procedure is to linearize the nonlinear by throwing away all awkward terms in the equation ... It's tacitly assumed that since the neglected terms in the equations are small—which is true—the difference between the solution of the linearized equation and that of the true equation must also be small" (Stewart 1989: 82; see also Nicolis and Prigogine 1989: 58-60). Mathematically speaking, the difference between linear and nonlinear equations is that, with the former but not the latter, the sum of two solutions produces another single solution (Stewart 1989: 81). This means that with linear equations, relationships are proportional—outputs are proportional to inputs—and the equations can be added up to yield a single solution. With nonlinear equations, however, relationships are not strictly proportional. Outputs are not proportional to inputs, and two or more such equations cannot be simply added up to produce a single solution (Gleick 1987: 23-24; Stewart 1989: 82-84; see also Nicolis and Prigogine 1989). A change in the value of one variable does not produce a constant or proportional change in the value of related variables. Rather, the relationship between variables is itself variable in unpredictable ways even though the relationship is deterministic.

In an illustration from physics, for example, friction and its effects cannot be specified linearly, that is, as a constant, for the amount of friction depends on the speed of an object; but the speed of an object depends on the amount of friction. Hence the relation of friction to speed, while deterministic, is a nonlinear one. Each temporal change in the one is dependent upon the temporal state of the other. As Gleick has characterized it, "the act of playing the game has a way of changing the rules" (1987: 24). A given nonlinear system is thus capable of displaying a wide range of complex behaviors.

The linear/nonlinear distinction is important inasmuch as, more often than not, the phenomena of nature—and almost by definition, sociocultural systems—are nonlinear. "[Chaos] science shows that nature is relentlessly *non*linear" (Stewart 1989: 83, original emphasis). As Stewart, one of the key mathematical theorists of chaos, argues, "Linearity is a trap. The behavior of linear equations like that of choirboys—is far from typical" (1989: 84). Much of the inability of classical Newtonian science to account adequately for the behavior of complex systems, in other words, is due to a reliance on a mathematical form ill-suited to its subject (Briggs and Peat 1989: 110; Nicolis and Prigogine 1989). While prechaos scientists' equations were predominantly linear, the world they were devised to explain is nonlinear.

Quite likely, therefore, any truly valuable contribution to social anthropological thinking from chaos theory will depend on a firm grasp of the implications of nonlinearity. And for social anthropologists these are potentially substantial.

Apparently, the simplest nonlinear equation is the logistic mapping or logistic difference equation, $x_{next} = rx(1-x)$. This formula is important in chaos theory for a number of reasons: it is supposedly the simplest of all nonlinear equations; it describes the sensitivity to initial conditions as illustrated in the example of Smale's horseshoe (see previous section); it was with respect to the logistic mapping equation that chaos theory had its first empirical applications (Gleick 1987: 63-77; Stewart 1989: 154-156); and it is the nonlinear counterpart to the familiar linear Malthusian equation for population growth. In physical systems, r would correspond to "the amount of heating, or the amount of friction, or the amount of some other messy quantity. In short, the amount of nonlinearity" (Gleick 1987: 63). In the example of animal populations, the parameter r corresponds with the rate of growth, which can vary. This formula is important for social anthropologists also, I argue, because it illustrates in a comprehensive way how pockets of order typically appear in diverse complex dynamical systems—pockets of order that otherwise would be dismissed as "aberrations" or "disorder"—and because it has discernible analogues in many commonplace social processes.

Following Gleick's (1987: 166-168; see also Stewart 1989: 154-164) discussion, the logistic difference equation $x_{next} = rx(1-x)$ is nonlinear, first of all, inasmuch as the relation between parameter r and variable x is not proportional but iterative or recursive, that is, each subsequent ("next") value of x is dependent upon the numerical outcome of the previous run of the equation in a feedback loop. But also the equation eventually generates qualitatively as well as quantitatively different solutions depending on the value of the parameter r, or rate of growth. Set at any value between $r = 0$ to $r = 3$, after numerous runs the value of x settles upon a single numerical value, a "point attractor" or steady state, traced as a point along the single curved line in the central portion of the graph in Figure 1.2. Between $r = 0$ and 3.0, the system will settle into a state of equilibrium so that further iterations continue to produce the same value of x. As the parameter r is moved to values above 3.0, however, the system begins to depart from equilibrium (see discussion of Prigogine's "dissipative structures" or systems "far from equilibrium," below). With r set slightly higher than 3.0, the fixed point x becomes unstable and alternates between two points on the curve of the parabola. This is known as a "bifurcation," of which more will be noted below. What this means so far in the case of population growth, for example, is that between $r = 0$ and $r = 3$, populations increase in a fairly regular or steady fashion through time until they reach equilibrium. But as the parameter r is increased slightly above the value of 3.0—meaning that the rate of growth increases beyond a certain point—the system becomes unstable. It is no longer in equilibrium and gross population sizes oscillate between high and low values every other year, say—the typical "boom or bust" pattern with which population biologists are familiar. This pattern—a "period two cycle," or "period two attractor"—will emerge from recursive application of the formula for any number of r between 3.0 and about 3.5.

At about 3.5, however, the period two cycle itself becomes unstable once more, eventually doubling or bifurcating again to produce a "period four cycle." As the value of parameter r is increased further to 3.56, the period doubles again to produce a "period eight cycle." And at 3.567 it doubles yet again to produce cycles of 16 values, etc (Figure 1.3).

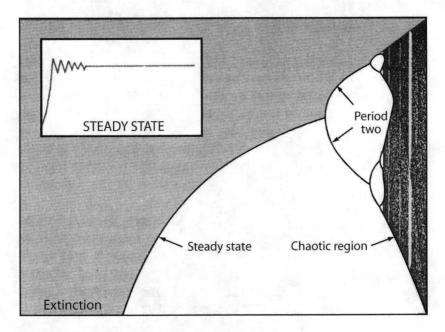

Figure 1.2: Bifurcation diagram i (after Gleick 1987: 71)

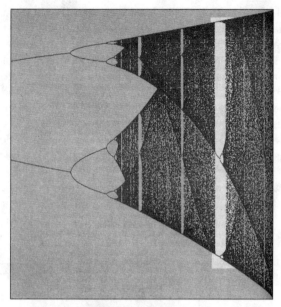

Figure 1.3: Bifurcation diagram ii (after Gleick 1987: 74)

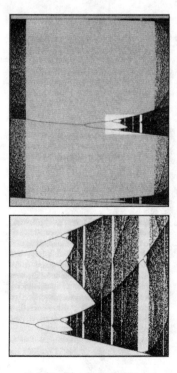

Figure 1.4: Bifurcation diagram iii (after Gleick 1987: 75)

As the numerical value of parameter *r* is raised higher than 3.58, other period-doubling arises—not just additional doubling, but cascades. At *r* = 3.739, a "period five cycle" arises which initiates at slightly higher values of *r* a further cascade of bifurcations of 10, 20, 40, 80, etc. Then at *r* = 3.835 a "period three cycle" emerges, followed at slightly higher values of *r* by periods of 6, 12, 24, 48, and so on (Figure 1.4). Complete randomness or disorder, apparently, is not achieved until the value of *r* reaches its mathematical maximum of 4. As Gleick notes,

> If you were following an animal population governed by this simplest of non-linear equations, you would think the changes from year to year were absolutely random, as though blown about by environmental noise. Yet in the middle of this complexity, stable cycles suddenly return. Even though the parameter [*r*] is rising, meaning that the nonlinearity is driving the system harder and harder, a window will suddenly appear with a regular period: an odd period, like 3 or 7. The pattern of changing population repeats itself on a three-year or seven-year cycle. Then the period-doubling bifurcations begin all over at a faster rate, rapidly passing through cycles of 3, 6, 12 …or 7, 14, 28 … , and then breaking off once again to renewed chaos (Gleick 1987: 73).

For later reference with respect to self-organization and dissipate structures, note that increasing the value of *r* above 3.0 consists in "driving the system harder and harder," that is, generating states of the system that are farther and farther away from equilibrium. Chaos theorists and scientists in recent years have demonstrated how many widely disparate phenomena seem to obey or conform with these cascades of bifurcations arising from the nonlinear logistical difference equation (Gleick 1987: 68-80; Briggs and Peat 1989: 143-146; Stewart 1989: 156-164, 321-324).

In the example I have just summarized, it can be appreciated how extreme sensitivity to initial conditions arises. Very slight increases in the value of *r* above 3 can produce quantitatively and qualitatively dramatic changes, or bifurcations. Moreover, the patterning of those changes as doubling, trebling, etc., are systematic. Changes in systems which previously appeared to be unexplainable or the result of disorder and contingency can now be appreciated as containing within themselves pockets of ordered transformations. Very importantly, the logistic mapping equation indicates how the relation of order to disorder in complex systems can be much more subtle than simply a matter of either/or; rather, complete order and complete disorder are interconnected through a complex but structured series of ordering patterns which is itself nonlinear. Disorder, therefore, is not merely an abrupt rupture from order but part and parcel of a process of structured, sequential bifurcations.

Many social anthropologists, of course, will recognize a strong resemblance between this formulation of nonlinear bifurcation in chaos theory and the binary dualism of much classic and contemporary structuralist anthropology. While Durkheimian theory has been often criticized for its seeming emphasis upon stability, cohesion, and synchrony, Durkheim's (1915) original analysis of Aboriginal Australian society and religion consisted in a dynamic process much more closely akin to dynamic nonlinearity, that is, temporal phase-two alternation or bifurcation between antithetical contexts, the sacred and the profane. Many of the most highly regarded theoretical progeny of Durkheim exhibit similar traces of chaotic nonlinearity, from Mauss's (1979 [1906]) analysis of seasonality among the Eskimo/Inuit and Hertz's (1960 [1909]) treatment of right-left asymmetry to Van Gennep's (1960) and V. Turner's (1969) analysis of rites of passage (see also below). Hegel's dialectic of thesis, antithesis, and synthesis is in essence nonlinear and recursive—qualities, of course, which were retained and elaborated in Marx's adaptation of Hegelian metaphysics to historical materialism. Many analyses of the variation among Australian Aboriginal marriage and section/subsection systems (Radcliffe-Brown 1931; Lévi-Strauss 1969 [1949]) and also the kinship and marriage systems of many parts of precolonial North and South America, Asia, and the Pacific from Morgan onward exhibit similar properties of elaborated recursive dualism and bifurcation (Durkheim and Mauss 1963; Bourdieu 1973; Fox 1973; 1975; 1989; Sahlins 1976: 25-44; Allen 2000; R. Needham 1962; J. Needham 1970; Mosko 1985; 1991a; 1995). In a notable departure from conventional Durkheim on religion, Dumont's theory of hierarchy (1980) still retains the quality of nonlinearity; that is, the relation of purity to impurity in India does not consist in a linear series of inequalities but in a series of recursive and reversible inclusions. Sahlins's (1981; 1985; 1991) relatively recent analyses of structural historical processes, partly inspired by Dumont's theory of hierarchical organization, include at a crucial juncture conceptual revaluations in the culture-as-constituted that closely resemble nonlinear bifurcations. Topology, which Edmund Leach (1961a; Abrahams 1990) used to model the flexibility of networks of social relationships, is a branch of nonlinear mathematics (Stewart 1989: 57-72). Also, the source of the dynamic alternation in Leach's model of political relations in Highland Burma was a basically nonlinear formulation: the inherently contradictory rule of *mayudama* alliance. Leach's (1954) view of the dynamic "moving equilibrium" linking *gumsa* and *gumlao* societal forms for the same system entailed as well a nonlinear bifurcation in accordance with a period two cycle. Lévi-Strauss's (1963c) canonic formula for myth, discussed more fully below and elsewhere in the volume (see chapters by Morava, Damon, Piot, Mosko, and Wagner), can likewise be characterized as nonlinear for various reasons: it cannot be reduced to orthodox (i.e., linear) analogical formulations, its internal relations between terms and functions are not proportional, for any one myth it is generative of many versions or transformations, and in the view of one of its chief interpreters (Racine 2001) it conforms formally with one of the classic instances of nonlinearity, Thom's (1975) "catastrophe theory."

In short, the greater share of British and French social anthropological theory can be seen as founded on understandings closely akin to those of chaotic nonlinearity. With the advent of chaos theory in social anthropological theorizing, analysts are offered the option of trying to explain the crosscultural similarities observed so far as consequences of the inherent nonlinearity characteristic of complex systems generally rather than to speculate on such qualities as the psychic unity of humankind or deep structures of the Human Mind.

The above illustration of the nonlinearity of the logistic difference equation bears on three additional aspects of chaos discussed at further length below that should be of particular interest to comparative-minded social anthropologists: "fractal self-similarity," "universality," and "self-organization." For the graph of the logistic difference equation (Figures 1.2, 1.3, and 1.4 above), sequential bifurcations are "nested" and "self-similar." Each bifurcation has within it at higher values of *r* further bifurcations that resemble it. This is the aspect of chaos theory known most widely in terms of "fractals," "self-similarity," or "holography." Also, as Stewart describes, the numerical sequencing of ordered bifurcations arising from increases in the parameter *r* of the logistic mapping equation (1, 2, 4, 8 ...) itself follows a certain numerical ordering regardless of the empirical character of the system at issue. This means that "some of the patterns of chaos might be *universal*, that is, not specific to individual examples but representative of entire classes of systems" (Stewart 1989: 161, original emphasis). Following a rather different route of analysis, Prigogine has argued that it is at the chaotic juncture of such transitions between prebifurcated to bifurcated systems that natural systems achieve self-organization at higher and higher levels of complexity. Thus the numerical universality, the fractal self-similarity of cascading bifurcations, and the tendency for self-organization in nature which are discussed separately below, are intimately connected with the nonlinearity of complex, chaotic systems.

Nonlinearity, Complexity, and "Attractors"

The properties of nonlinearity as illustrated by the logistic difference and other nonlinear equations have been successfully employed in the natural sciences to model a great variety of complex phenomena, "richly organized patterns, sometimes stable and sometimes unstable, sometimes finite and sometimes infinite" (Gleick 1987: 43).

Uniting much of this variety is the notion of "attractor." An attractor is some portion of a system's movement (its "phase space") "such that any point which starts nearby gets closer and closer to it" (Stewart 1989: 110). With each bifurcation or periodic doubling (1, 2, 4, 8, etc.) in the logistic difference equation, for example, each point on the parabolic curve of the graph at a given value of *r* is a "point attractor" (see Figure 1.2). A period two cycle thus has two attractor points which alternate in recursive runs of the formula. A period four cycle has four such attractors, and so on.

Now in some of the nonlinear formulations which have been devised for many complex physical phenomena, there is a special type of attractor, a "strange attractor." Unlike the attractors of the logistic mapping example, strange attractors are nonperiodic. With a nonperiodic strange attractor, the movements of a system never repeat or cross themselves so the system itself never returns to exactly the same state that it has been in before. The first such strange attractor was identified by Edward Lorenz (1963) in attempting to characterize convection in fluids and weather dynamics. Because of the strong affinity of Lorenz's strange attractor and processes familiar to social anthropologists, it is worthwhile to repeat Gleick's elegant description of the former (Figures 1.5 and 1.6):

> ... a picture with just two curves on the right, one inside the other, and five on the left. To plot just these seven loops required 500 successive calculations on the computer. A point moving along this trajectory in phase space, around the loops, illustrated the slow, chaotic rotation of a fluid as modeled by Lorenz's three equations for convection. Because the system had three independent variables, this attractor lay in a three-dimensional phase space. Although Lorenz drew only a fragment of it, he could see more than he drew: a sort of double spiral, like a pair of butterfly wings interwoven with infinite dexterity. When the rising heat of his system pushed the fluid around in one direction, the trajectory stayed on the right wing; when the rolling motion stopped and reversed itself, the trajectory would swing across to the other wing.
>
> The attractor was stable, low-dimensional, and nonperiodic. It could never intersect itself, because if it did, returning to a point already visited, from then on the motion would repeat itself in a periodic loop. That never happened—that was the beauty of the attractor. Those loops and spirals were infinitely deep, never quite joining, never intersecting. Yet they stayed inside a finite space, confined by a box (Gleick 1987: 139-140).

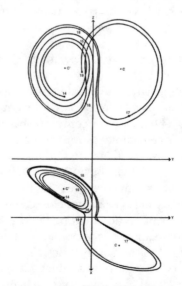

Figure 1.5: The first strange attractor (after Gleick 1987: 140)

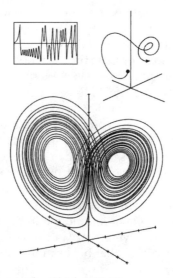

Figure 1.6: The Lorenz attractor (after Gleick 1987: 28)

Lorenz's strange attractor involves: (1) a complex system of more than two variables; (2) nonlinear, hence recursive, relations among those variables; and (3) a pattern of reversal, or alternations and oscillations between states of the system which never exactly repeat one another. These criteria should be of particular interest to social anthropologists. Societies with formal marriage rules, for example, whether by the relations of moieties or sections, or positions, say mbd marriage, clearly specify dynamics that are like those of a strange attractor. Certain rules are specified, and while organizing clear patterns they never exactly repeat themselves. I shall illustrate the pertinence of strange attractors for social anthropology by drawing once more upon a few well-established anthropological theories. The classic Durkheimian (1915) characterization of ritual process as sacred/profane alternation conforms closely with the behavior of a strange attractor. While temporal oscillations between profane and sacred conditions may in general appear as repetitions, in actuality the specific events comprising a series of profane phases (or two or more sacred phases) of the system never perfectly repeat themselves. No analogous moments in the performance of any one sacred rite are experienced as exactly the same any more than the analogous moments of two distinct historical performances of "the same" rite. Van Gennep's (1960) model for rites of passage, a well-known elaboration of the Durkheimian sacred/profane formula, illustrates particularly clearly how in sociocultural systems strange attractors, on the one hand, and the cascading of bifurcations, on the other, might be connected—which would be expected inasmuch as both are results of recursion and nonlinearity. Most renditions of Van Gennep's model for ritual process emphasize the three sequential phases of separation, transition, and reincorporation (Van Gennep 1960; V. Turner 1969). Leach (1961b) early on noted, however, that the complete formulation is comprised of a fourfold temporal sequence involving two oppositions: profane time versus sacred (transitional) time, and sacralizing (separation) time versus desacralizing (reincorporation) time. Elsewhere (Mosko 1985: 6-7) I have suggested that the second opposition might be usefully construed as a second or recursive instance of the first one. The full model of ritual process would thus include the one principal opposition (sacred vs. profane) as well as its nonlinear iteration (profane-ing or desacralizing vs. sacred-ing or sacralizing). In terms of chaos theory, therefore, it can be argued that the fuller formulation of rites of passage consists of a "period four cycle" comprised of two nonperiodic strange attractors which have undergone bifurcation to produce activity corresponding with a system of four nonperiodic strange attractors.

It should be noted, however, that Van Gennep's original formulation hinted at the possibility of further bifurcations and strange attractors by means of what he termed the "pivoting of the sacred" (1960: 12-13; T. Turner 1977). Within a single sequence of separation, transition, and incorporation, Van Gennep posited that a person arriving at a ritually sacred condition might then consider his/her condition to be relatively profane from which to seek further sacralization. From there, of course, additional bifurcations (i.e., further pivoting or recursive separation) might be possible, ultimately requiring additional bifurcating discriminations of sacred/profane in the process of returning to the world of profane social experience.

In another context, I have suggested as well (Mosko 1994b) that Dumont's notion of religious hierarchy partially corresponds in structural terms with Van Gennep's pivoting of the sacred. If so, this would further imply that the key dynamics of many African, South and Southeast Asian, and Oceanic systems which have been analyzed in terms of Dumontian hierarchy might correspond with nonlinear processes involving strange attractors (e.g., Sahlins 1976: 24-46; 1985; Geertz 1980b; Valeri 1985; 1991; Tcherkezoff 1987; de Coppet 1985; Iteanu 1983; 1985; Jamous 1981; Barraud et al. 1994; Mosko 1985; 1989; 1991a; 1991b; 1994a; 1994b; 1995; Lévi-Strauss 1995: 225-242).

Chaos, Conflict, and Contradiction

Several of the examples of anthropological theorizing I have cited thus far fall within the broadly Durkheimian tradition, which has usually been noted for its emphasis upon continuity and cohesion (Kuper 1992). Strange attractors and nonlinear processes of bifurcation, however, also imply movements or moments of discontinuity, contradiction, conflict, inversion, and reversibility which have their counterparts as well in several areas of established anthropology theory. Reversal and inversion, for example, figure centrally in many of the variants of Durkheimian social anthropology (functionalism, structure-functionalism, structuralism, symbolism), and the alternation between sacred and profane conditions can be easily seen as signifying discontinuity and even contradiction and conflict as regards conceptualization. Following Hegel, as noted above, Marx specifies contradictions between variable and constant capital in their complementary roles in producing surplus value. The continuous interaction of these variables, according to Marx, generates the ebbs, flows, and transformations of the capitalist mode of production. The crises lead to regular reorganization and expansion of the system. His model embodies a clear analogue of nonlinearity and the behavior of strange attractors. Although Bateson's (1958 [1936]) notion of schizmogenesis could be regarded as a model of the eventual achievement of social cohesion, it is posited on showing how solidarity relationships set off in a trajectory of escalating strain, conflict, and distancing, until one of two outcomes is achieved: either exogenous factors intervene before bifurcating relationships reach crisis points so that they return to a relationship of mutual support; or beyond the crisis point the relationships are severed and the parties separate to establish new independent relations of harmony and cohesion.

Perhaps the definitive example of a nonlinear thinking in prechaos social anthropology is Lévi-Strauss's canonic formula for the structure of myth: $F_x(a) : F_y(b) \quad F_x(b) : F_{a-1}(y)$ (Lévi-Strauss 1963c; see also Leach 1970: 62-86; Mosko 1991a; Maranda 2001). The canonic formula has, of course, been subjected to considerable critical comment and interpretation in a wide range of contexts over the years, and in his more recent writings Lévi-Strauss (1988; 1995) has developed it in a number of novel ways. Inasmuch as several of the contributors to this volume examine the chaotic implications of the formula in much greater detail than I can attempt in this Introduction (see especially chapters by Morava, Damon, Piot, Mosko, and Wagner), here I will merely point to those properties of the formula which seem to be clearly analogous to key aspects of chaos theory. First, it can be seen in Lévi-Strauss's own paraphrasing of the formula that it is nonlinear to the extent that relations between elements are not proportional:

> Here, with two terms, *a* and *b*, being given as well as two functions, *x* and *y*, of these terms, it is assumed that a relation of equivalence exists between two situations defined respectively by an inversion of *terms* and *relations*, under two conditions: (1) that one term be replaced by its opposite (in the above formula, *a* and *a-1*); (2) that an inversion be made between the *function value* and the *term value* of two elements (above, *y* and *a*) (Lévi-Strauss 1963c: 228).

Here, changes to either term or function are not proportional to changes in the other term or function, as relations between terms and functions in the first half of the equation are inverted in the second half. Moreover, the second half of the equation contains a second inversion—the so-called "additional twist" (Maranda 2001)—which gives the formula its spiraling possibilities. Now by this process, categories at the myth's beginning, through inversion and reversal, effectively undergo bifurcation as relations with other elements of the myth are transformed. Due, on the one hand, to the "additional twist"—the spiraling of one myth into alternate versions and alternate myths—and on the other to the ways in which certain relations and themes seem to recur across widely varying myths, the nonlinearity of myth seems to involve what in the terms of chaos theory could only be regarded as strange attractors: complex systems of binarily opposed and bifurcating categories which, in this case, never quite repeat themselves exactly from one myth or version of a myth to another but which are nonetheless linked in iterative nonperiodic dynamic relations within and between related cultures. One does not have to be a devotee to either chaos theory or Lévi-Strauss's structuralist theory of myth to appreciate at least their formal convergence. Several of the following chapters exploit this potentiality in their handling of empirical materials. On the evidence of certain varying spatial references across the Massim region of Papua New Guinea, for example, Damon (this volume) argues that the members of Lévi-Strauss's equation are effectively strange attractors, the formula itself then being a statement about relations between strange attractors. Piot (this volume) describes how the recursiveness of numerous cultural categories and structural oppositions in several domains of Kabre culture corresponds with the iterative behavior of strange attractors as well as fractals. The transformations Kelly (this volume) develops in his comparisons of several Amerindian groups (Araweté, Wari', and Tupinamba) strongly imply the presence of analogous dynamics.

Also, if Lévi-Strauss's formula and Van Gennep's classic schema of rites of passage can both be shown to be isomorphic with the analogous processes of chaotic nonlinear systems generally, then social anthropologists would have additional grounds for explaining the long-acknowledged but problematic relation of myth to ritual and other nonmythic domains (Mosko 1985: 6-7; 1991a). Moreover, if the mythical corpus of entire continents, as illustrated by Lévi-Strauss's Amerindian examples, can be regarded as the product of millennia of historical elaboration and communication, then the variations among myths and mythical traditions can be regarded in chaos terms as instances of extreme sensitivity to initial conditions. Simply put, two communities which may have begun with only the slightest of differences in their cosmologies might well diverge as their respective histories unfold, a result as much of chaotic processes inherent in complex systems as of diffusion or differential experiences of external influence.

Considering myth from this perspective draws me to one of the more fundamental dilemmas in social anthropology: the relation between discrete enactments of cultural categories by acting agents and the reification of those culture categories in actors' (and anthropologists') models of those category systems—what Sahlins (1991) has portrayed as "events" composed of a relation between a "happening" and a category of "structure." Here the notion of strange attractor from chaos theory helps in breaking through an otherwise most intractable problem. Every nonrepeatable happening (to follow Sahlins's terminology) can only be interpreted in respect of its relation to a category (i.e., an attractor) defined in terms of reciprocal relations with other categories of structure. This structure can only be posited to exist (since it is never itself completely instantiated at one moment) to the extent that happenings tend, imperfectly in each event or performance, to approximate and reproduce the categories (attractors) of which it is composed. Of particular interest are cases where the meaning values of particular actions or signs suddenly shift in historical interaction; where, as in the case of Lorenz's strange attractor, there is a sudden bifurcation and switch in the performance of the system whereby relations of actions and categories are reversed, as when, for example, in Sahlins's case of Polynesian chiefs being "male," then "female," or vice-versa (Sahlins 1985: xvi, 102-103; see Piot, Mosko, this volume) or in Taylor's (this volume) perceptions of the horrific processural order underlying the recent massacres in Rwanda. Moments of such categorical transition might well be explained in terms of the randomness or disorderliness of history, but they might also be appreciated in terms of a strange attractor of phase-two alteration. Historical shifts in the relations among culture categories thus bear the traces characteristic of strange attractors in dynamic nonlinear systems.

Further implications of chaos theory for the anthropological grasp of historical process will be discussed in a subsequent section of this chapter with reference to "self-organization" and in the chapters by Piot, Taylor, and Mosko.

This is a suitable juncture to consider one of the more compelling reasons for social anthropologists to pay close attention to chaos theory: it provides a perspective from which relations among a wide variety of anthropology's theoretical formulations, heretofore regarded as unrelated, can be identified. The various anthropological illustrations of sensitivity to initial conditions, nonlinearity, and strange attractors that have been mentioned in the foregoing discussion can now be viewed through the lens of chaos as possible manifestations of the same or related processes. Aspects of the alternation between sacred and profane conditions, processes of reversal, inversion, and recursion, binary modes of thought and action, historical shifts between seemingly "stable" and "unstable" conditions, the inescapable contingencies of history, and the patterning of myth can thus be appreciated as related in ways previously unsuspected. While these and many other of the most sophisticated theoretical formulations of social anthropology have been developed in parallel with the chief components of chaos theory, it has not always been possible to discern their possible compatibilities with one another. The discernible connections between the main elements of chaos theory thus provide an analogy or map for tracing new links across anthropology's rich, already familiar theoretical landscape.

The other main reason for social anthropologists to heed developments in chaos theory, of course, is that they may lead to theoretical insights for which there are no analogues or antecedents, as parts of the following sections illustrate.

Fractal Geometry

Of all the discoveries made by chaos scientists, "fractals" have undoubtedly received the most public attention. Fractal geometry or "holography," however, is much more extensive and powerful theoretically than the visually dazzling images the swirls within swirls of the Mandelbrot set (1982). Arguably also, fractal patterning has been an important part of social anthropological theorizing long before it was recognized as such with the emergence of chaos theory.

The term "fractal" refers to phenomena of "self-similarity," or the tendency of patterns or structures to recur on multiple levels or scales. By now, several examples of fractal geometry have become rather standard. The leaf of a fern typically consists of a central stem with a perpendicular double series of separate leaflets decreasing in size from base to tip. Each leaflet is then composed of smaller leaflets of similar triangular shape, and each of those leaflets is similarly constituted of even tinier leaflets. From a high altitude above the earth, say, any given coastline could be described in terms of interconnected bays, peninsulas, islands, inlets, and so on. Seen from a lower elevation, though, any one of those features would also consist of bays, peninsulas, islands, and inlets but at magnification. At ground level, the visual line tracing any stretch of shoreline would follow a similar irregular pattern of jagged elements, and so on. The village of Bourton-on-the-Water boasts as a tourist attraction an architectural model of all its houses, streets, and other physical features. But this model of the village also contains in the pertinent location a scale model of itself (Stewart 1989: 164). Finally, consider the body of the humble flea which hosts its own parasitic "fleas," the body of each of which is also host to its own "fleas," etc.

Fractal self-similarity is significant in chaos theory inasmuch as it appears to be an inherent characteristic or consequence of nonlinearity (Gleick 1987: 114; Stewart 1989: 221-222). To the extent that the processes of nature take place in accordance with predominantly nonlinear relationships, fractal self-similarity seems to be a built-in aspect or feature of the order that otherwise appears as randomness or disorder. Above, when discussing the nonlinear logistic difference equation, it was noted how at various specific increments in the value of r above 3, recursive iterations of the formula eventually produced a cascading series of bifurcations (attractors), each series of which contained bifurcations that were self-similar (Figures 1.2, 1.3, and 1.4 above). Moreover, an additional similarity of form at differing scales is perceivable in the relations between the different cascades. The period doubling of 1, 2, 4, 8, 16, etc., in one series of bifurcations is a fractal of the period doubling of the series 3, 6, 12, 24, etc. The cascades of bifurcations are self-similar as are the separate bifurcations composing the same cascade.

This kind of structural order had been recognized in a number of areas of natural science before the interest in complexity, nonlinearity, or the development of chaos theory, but it was chiefly appreciated to be of little more than chance or random significance, more in the realm of disorder than order. In the natural sciences and mathematics currently, however, a great many of those complex phenomena have been shown to exhibit self-similar ordering in accordance with relatively simple nonlinear formulae. Also, many fractal phenomena which on close inspection seemed unrelated have been shown to be manifestations of the same chaotic processes, as discussed at greater length below under the heading, "universality." To the best of my knowledge, these sorts of connections have not yet been posited between analogous anthropological theories. For anthropology and other social sciences, the implication is, when relations of fractal self-similarity can be identified, even if at first it is only intuitively, there is reason to suspect the presence of dynamic nonlinearity.

As it happens, numerous influential social anthropological theories and analyses from the nineteenth century to the present have exhibited properties of self-similarity. One part of the problem is, there has been no quantitative means of systematically measuring or comparing these different manifestations of fractal organization so as to establish relations between them that appear to be anything more than coincidental, superficial, or subjective. Also, most instances of fractal organization in social anthropology have emphasized their structural rather than their processual implications. Thus, except for a few structuralists, cultural evolutionists, and others, most social anthropologists have regarded any particular manifestation of fractal self-similarity as well as any crosscultural resemblance of structural forms to be products of chance, historical accident, and diffusion. From chaos theory, however, there is the strong implication that such cases of fractal self-similarity are not symptomatic of disorder or randomness but manifest instead a distinctive type of order that is immanent in apparent disorder.

Perhaps the most familiar example of self-similarity in social anthropology is not so much a case of fractal geometry as fractal biology: the much-maligned notion of "organic analogy" by which the functions of organs in relation to an individual person's bodily system replicate the functions of persons in relation to a social system. Some of the most influential classical theories in social anthropology have been premised on versions of this particular dimension of anthropomorphic self-similarity (e.g., Spencer 1873; Durkheim 1893; Radcliffe-Brown 1952; Mauss 1936; Douglas 1966; 1970; V. Turner 1966). Critics of all varieties of functionalism, of course, have widely dismissed the organic analogy as "mere analogy rather than homology." But in light of chaos theory, fractal analogies are not "just analogies," and the significance of the analogy/homology distinction itself becomes questionable. Consistent with this, I suggest, much of the recent anthropological interest in the body, body techniques, left/right asymmetry, processes of embodiment, practice, gender distinctions, the social construction of personhood, and so on, can be seen as further explorations of the fractal relations of bodies, persons, relations, and societies in many of the world's cultures (e.g., Mauss 1936; Hertz 1960 [1909]; J. Needham 1970; Bourdieu 1977; Foucault 1975; A. Strathern and M. Strathern 1971; M. Strathern 1979; 1988; 1991a; 1991b; 1992a; Wagner 1986b; 1991; Martin 1987; Gell 1993; Mosko 1983; 1985; 1995; 1997b; 2002a).

The organic analogy is only one anthropological instance among many of basic epistemological tropes exhibiting forms of fractal scaling. A major share of the classic analyses and interpretations of myth, ritual, social structure, political organization, and economic exchange is based on the notions of metaphor and analogy, for example, of specifically fractal proportions. Durkheim and Mauss's *Primitive Classification* (1963), which outlines the recurrent patterning of spatial form at various levels of societal organization—the clan, the village, the tribe, the cosmos, etc.—among numerous tribal societies and early civilizations, is a straightforward illustration of fractal self-similarity. And it is precisely on this aspect of that pioneering work that much of the theorizing of Durkheim's disciples and later structuralist practitioners over the next century was based. For instance, the several examples of nonlinearity in Durkheimian theory, which have already been cited at length, entail fractal relations of self-similarity: in the relation of the specific powers of every totemic species to the totemic collectivity that they represent (Durkheim 1915); in Mauss and Hubert's notion of sacrificial substitution (Hubert and Mauss 1964); Mauss's (1967 [1925]) understanding of specific practices in relation to total social phenomena and reciprocity; and in Hertz's (1960[1909]) analyses of parallel mortuary transitions of the body, soul, and survivors of the deceased and in his treatment of right/left asymmetry.

A particularly dramatic example from the generally Durkheimian tradition would be Evans-Pritchard's (1940) model of segmentary opposition in Nuer territorial and descent organization at a variety of societal scales. At every spatial and societal level, a given territorial or descent group is counterpoised by a group of corresponding size or scale, and at the next higher level of organization the two groups which were juxtaposed at the lower level become fused in opposition to a similarly amalgamated collectivity. Similarly, Evans-Pritchard's analysis of the Nuer religious conceptualization describes how notions of "spirit" (*kwoth*) are analogously constituted among themselves and fractally self-similar as well to the patterning of relations among Nuer territorial and kinship groupings.

Many of Lévi-Strauss's classic structuralist analyses of both kinship and myth entail fractal self-similarity. His discussion of art as symbolic "miniaturization" across and within semantic domains in *The Savage Mind* (1966), for example, deals essentially with fractal relations. As I understand Edmund Leach's notion of "ritual condensation," there is again a fractal relation between supposed realities and the manipulation of their symbolic indexes (1976).

Dumont's classic theory of hierarchy for the caste system of India, which has already been noted for its nonlinearity, incorporates an almost literal definition of fractal scaling. By means of hierarchical encompassment, the superior element or part of a complementary binary pair takes on the attributes of the totality which contains both it and other contained parts (Dumont 1980; cf. Mosko 1994b). Sahlins's recent exercises in extending Dumontian hierarchy to Polynesian social organization and heroic history consist basically in a fractal relation between a self-similar part of the whole—the divine hero—whose actions encompass or embody the actions of all members of the collectivity (Sahlins 1985; 1991). It is perhaps no exaggeration to say that much of the structuralist description and analysis that dominated social anthropology well into the 1980s was premised on the replication of structures and patterns at different scales. Just for the sake of illustration, my own analyses of various dimensions of North Mekeo and Trobriand (Papua New Guinea) culture and society are replete with examples of fractal scaling (Mosko 1983; 1985; 1989; 1991a; 1992; 1995; 2000). It would not be difficult to list dozens of additional instances.

Fractal relationship is not restricted to the Durkheimian or structuralist tradition of social anthropology, however. In Marx's conceptualization of commodity fetishism, things take on the mystified attributes of the interpersonal relations of the persons engaged in the laboring process. Similarly, in Marx's theory of alienation, persons take on the characteristics of the things that they have produced (Marx 1976; Sahlins 1976: 166-204). Hence from this point of view the key relations of persons and things (or subjects and objects) in capitalist symbolism are inherently fractal.

A correspondingly fractal conception of persons and relations in terms of gender and gift exchange at a variety of scales lies behind Marilyn Strathern's recent theorizing of Melanesian sociality (1988; 1991a; 1992b; 1999; 2000). Roy Wagner's (1986b; 1991) analyses of Melanesian political leadership and the dynamics of big men and great men similarly relies on a fractal notion of person. Appadurai (1990; see also Giddens 1990: 64; Cheater 1995) also postulates fractal relations between local and global levels of interconnectedness and flow to account for ongoing transformations in the developing world economy.

Reflecting on long-standing anthropological concepts at even higher levels of abstraction, the very notions of "symbol" and "sign," "representation," "metonym," and "metaphor" on which numerous theories of meaning and culture have been based may be seen to consist significantly in fractal self-similarity. Consequently, a large share of the totality of social anthropological thinking about culture, meaning, history, and society suggests a fractal relationship between the discipline and its subject matter. This would apply even to the various contestations of hegemonic representation as constituted in the "crisis of representation" of the 1980s and early 1990s (Marcus and Fischer 1986; see also Said 1979; Fabian 1983; Clifford and Marcus 1986; Clifford 1988; Obeyesekere 1992).

These possibilities inevitably give rise to at least one other: if fractal relationships have for so long been central to social anthropologists' theorizing, then social anthropological theory may perhaps be usefully understood as a self-similar part of a larger body of theory where fractal relations are similarly prominent, that is, of chaos theory. But this predicament is not altogether new either. Since the discipline's founding, social anthropologists have viewed their craft as partly a science, partly a humanity, or both; but in either respect most practitioners would concede, I suspect, that social anthropology is itself a part of Western culture. Thus not only does social anthropology embody many of the substantive elements of the wider culture—conceptual, epistemological, and ontological—it does so in fractal relation to it. In particular, social anthropology had incorporated many of the elements of chaos theory before the latter had emerged as such among the natural sciences just as the chaos sciences have emerged as a fractal part of the development of postmodern society (Hayles 1990; 1991a; 1991b).

If social anthropology is indeed linked to the new science of chaos in this way, then another of the discipline's long-standing scientific concerns—universality—is likely to receive new impetus.

Universality

One of the more dramatic developments in the science of complex dynamical systems has been the discovery that systems which are considered to be different and unrelated exhibit certain behavioral features that are identical. This aspect of chaos theory, known as "universality," was implicit in the discussions above regarding processes of nonlinearity, period doubling, bifurcation, fractal scaling, and so on. Additional research in the 1970s and afterwards, most closely associated with the work of physicist Mitchell Feigenbaum, have lead to much greater precision in the nature of chaotic universality with the discovery of certain numerical constants that are apparently involved in all nonlinear dynamic processes. Regardless of whether it is fluid dynamics, weather patterns, biorhythms, or population changes, complex dynamical systems all behave in accordance with certain previously unknown quantitative constants. These constants have subsequently been touted by numerous authorities as equivalent in significance to other scientific constants such as π, the speed of light, the conservation of energy and matter, or the second law of thermodynamics (or entropy; see below).

Social anthropology, of course, has a long history of debate over a wide range of potential crosscultural universals, from the nature and prevalence of the incest taboo and the patterning of human cognition and symbolism to the uniformities of history and cultural evolution. Thus any suggestion from chaos theory that complex dynamical systems in other realms of reality might contain previously hidden uniformities could have enormous implications for many anthropological issues where questions of universality have been central.

The first and most celebrated of these newly discovered uniformities is Feigenbaum's constant, 4.6692016090 ... (decimals repeated indefinitely after that). It is interesting that Feigenbaum came upon this numerical constant while employing the logistic mapping equation (see above) to comprehend the dynamics of phase transitions in fluid turbulence—transitions that are highly nonlinear. As he calculated the rate at which, above parameter $r = 3.0$, the successive bifurcations arose in approaching randomness, he observed among the smallest branches of the graph's bifurcating tree that successive splittings appeared to be about four times as big as subsequent ones. The closer to randomness he looked (i.e., the closer to the twiglets of the branching tree of bifurcations; see Figures 1.2—1.4 above), the closer the ratio of scaling approached 4.669 (Stewart 1989: 198). The fractal relation between larger and smaller scales was not merely a matter of qualitative self-similarity or patterning, it was a quantitative one. Later when other natural phenomena were modeled employing the logistic difference and other nonlinear equations, numerous cascades of period doubling were found to occur at the identical scaling ratio of 4.669 (Gleick 1987: 171-180; Stewart 1989: 193, 196-207). There seemed to be no empirical reason why phenomena as diverse as electronics, optics, biology, and convection should all obey the same numerical constant. But apparently they do.

Subsequently, Feigenbaum's constant has been subjected to mathematical proofs and wide empirical verification. The mathematical term for this quantitative consistency of ratio between smaller and larger scales is "renormalization" (Stewart 1989: 200-204; Gleick 1987: 172, 179-180). Additional discoveries by Feigenbaum and others have shown there to be a number of different classes of nonlinear formulae and mappings correlated with different phenomena, with each class defined in terms of a different numerical constant or "Feigenvalue." Phenomena and formulae belonging to different mathematical classes, in other words, obey different constants. It is as though the phenomena of nature are classified according to the numerically distinct types of nonlinearity (Stewart 1989: 206-208).

Although at the present time numerical values for renormalization may be difficult for anthropologists to establish with analogous social processes and cultural phenomena, the general implication should be appreciated: fractal patterning which investigators for decades have already incorporated into many of their qualitative models and theories seems to be consistent with new mathematical proofs of the universality of such processes among many natural phenomena.

Clearly, any possible anthropological analogues to the kinds of universality identified in the chaos sciences will be radically different from many of the more conventional correlations among crosscultural practices over which anthropologists have debated in the past: whether, for example, a given practice or institution—say, the incest taboo—is universally present or not. Anthropological analogues to universal chaos processes are more likely to be found in contexts where relations are complex and dynamic. A number of models of social process which have already been discussed in earlier sections—Van Gennep's (1960) formulation of rites of passage; Lévi-Strauss's (1963c) formula for myth; Sahlins's (1981, 1985) modeling of structural historical processes—are obvious candidates for reexaminations as to whether their seeming crosscultural universality might be a function of their heretofore unappreciated convergence with one another and with nonlinear processes of the natural world.

Van-Gennep's (1960) fourfold model of rites of passage has proven to be as robust a crosscultural processual universal as any other that has been proposed by social anthropologists. It concerns dynamic social processes rather than states of systems; those processes characteristically involve nonlinear inversions or reversals; and as regards its tendency toward "pivoting" (see above), it is fractal. Most suggestive of all, some of the more recent applications of Van Gennep's formula involve historically recursive transitions of whole groups of people (e.g., millenarian movements, revitalization movements), sometimes entire societies, in a wide range of unrelated cultures (e.g., Leach 1961b; 1976; Wallace 1956; Burridge 1969; V. Turner 1969).

As another example of possibly universal nonlinear scaling, Schwimmer (2001) and Lévi-Strauss (1995) have recently argued that the canonic formula for myth can be usefully employed in comprehending historical processes. Lévi-Strauss (1963c) originally devised the formula to describe the syntagmatic and paradigmatic transformations of mythical thought. As noted above, the formula exhibits many of the key properties of chaos: recursiveness, nonlinearity, and bifurcating categories. Paralleling the discovery of numerous Feigenvalues, Maranda and Maranda (1971), Mosko (1991a), and Maranda (2001) subsequently argued that a variety of formally defined classes of both narrative and nonnarrative behaviors can be determined comparatively, each defined by slight formal modification of the original formula but preserving the qualities of nonlinearity, recursion, and bifurcation. Moreover, while Lévi-Strauss could only presume that the systematic variation among Amerindian myths reflected in the formula was a product of prior historical transformations, Schwimmer's employment of the formula suggests ways in which diverse historical transformations can be understood as universal products of the formula.

As argued by several contributors to this volume (Damon, Taylor, Mosko), temporal patterns of social reproduction and historical transformation exhibit dynamically recursive processes of nonlinearity and fractal scaling. In my other contribution to this volume, for example, I discuss ways in which some aspects of Sahlins's recent structural treatments of historical transformation might entail similarly universal propensities for aperiodic but deterministic nonlinear historical processes analogous to those in the natural sciences.

Self-Organization, Dissipative Structures, and Complexity Theory

Over the 1970s and 1980s and into the 1990s, certain facets of chaos theory as already described, in combination with new views of complex dynamical systems, have been elaborated in terms of "self-organization": the capacity of chaotic dynamical systems to generate structures of greater complexity. The writings of physicist Ilya Prigogine, on what he terms "dissipative structures," and the body of work that has emerged under the label "complexity theory" are the most salient and coherent examples. The ideas of both Prigogine and the complexity theorists, however, have become rather controversial in scientific circles, achieving somewhat less scientific consensus than the other aspects of chaos theory summarized above. Nonetheless, in the present context Prigogine and complexity theory are important for two reasons: on the one hand, both by now have become important components of the wider paradigm of chaos theory, despite the controversy surrounding their ideas; and on the other the notion of self-generation at higher levels of complexity resonates with much classical and contemporary anthropological theorizing and analysis.

Prigogine

The 1977 Novel Prize winning physicist, Ilya Prigogine, is perhaps the most prominent chaos theorist to have written specifically on self-organization in complex systems. Prigogine's writings (Prigogine 1980; Prigogine and Stengers 1984; Nicolis and Prigogine 1989) and those of his associates and followers (e.g., Allen and Schieve 1982; Scott 1991) emerged over the past few decades somewhat independently of the work being conducted simultaneously by other chaos scientists, summarized above. In the wider field of chaos science, Prigogine's perspective on the dynamics of complex systems has been controversial as it is somewhat idiosyncratic (Briggs and Peat 1989: 134-152; Hayles 1990: 91-114; Porush 1991), not the least because from the start Prigogine has been quite explicit about potential implications of his perspective for social as well as natural systems. Not coincidentally, prior to being trained as a physicist, Prigogine's education was focused on history and archaeology (Prigogine and Stengers 1984: 10; Briggs and Peat 1989: 135).

Prigogine's definitive work on chaos theory is the book *Order Out of Chaos: Man's New Dialogue with Nature* (1984), coauthored with philosopher and chemist Isabelle Stengers. The book's novel contribution to chaos theory is its focus upon the notion of time. Like other commentators, Prigogine begins his appraisal of contemporary science with a discussion of the limitations of classic Newtonian mechanics. In addition to its linearity, however, Prigogine emphasizes that classical Newtonian dynamics involves a notion of *reversible* time; that is, given a complete knowledge of the laws of motion and of the current state of a dynamic system, it should be possible to describe the system's past and future states, back and forward in time. Chronological or *irreversible* time had no place in the Newtonian world view.

With the development of the science of thermodynamics in the nineteenth century, however, and especially with the formulation of the second law of thermodynamics or entropy, irreversible time, or "time with an arrow," was introduced into physics, eventually at both macroscopic and microscopic levels. In the context of a gradually cooling entropic universe, or where the universe's general direction is toward anarchy, disorder, randomness, and a lack of order or structure, there is instead the frequent emergence of pockets of order, or higher and higher levels of structure and organization. Basically, Prigogine's work on self-organization is an attempt at explaining how higher and higher levels of structure in nature *of necessity* arise in an entropic universe. And it is in higher levels of order and structure in the sphere of human affairs as well as in the rest of the natural world that he is explicitly interested.

Irreversible time, or history, enters the entropic universe for Prigogine in situations he refers to as "far from equilibrium" systems. When a given system is at equilibrium or "near to equilibrium" as in the case of Newtonian motion, it is effectively a closed system. Negative feedback controls keep the system operating close to some average state. In this circumstance, time is reversible, and external environmental factors have no effect upon the system's steady state. When elements of the system affect one another far from equilibrium through positive feedback, however, the system's components interact so as to reinforce or amplify their mutual influences and produce dramatic fluctuations which are irreversible and unpredictable. In this far from equilibrium state, moreover, the system becomes particularly vulnerable to the influences arising from the system's external environment. Prigogine refers to such open systems as dissipative structures to emphasize the degree of communication as well as energy loss between a given system and its environments in these circumstances. While all structures of the physical universe obey the law of entropy, they overwhelmingly consist of phenomena in far from equilibrium states where entropy is particularly high. What Prigogine emphasizes is how in such highly entropic, far from equilibrium conditions higher levels of structure emerge. With reference to numerous examples from physics, chemistry, and biology, Prigogine argues that as systems move farther and farther from equilibrium—becoming more and more open, with greater and greater exchanges of matter and energy between system and environment—they first tend to approximate increasing disorder expressed as seemingly random fluctuations from one state of the system to another and another. Then at points extremely far from equilibrium, these seemingly disordered states reach particular points of "bifurcation"—points at which systems can move in more than a single direction. A given system will appear to totter on going one way or another, but once it veers off in one of the possible directions, other possibilities are eliminated for that system at that time in its history. And it is at such bifurcating junctures that the higher levels of structure and organization emerge.

In many regards, Prigogine's theorizing parallels the findings elsewhere in chaos sciences regarding nonlinearity, logistic mapping, bifurcations, and so on, as described above. The novelty in Prigogine's treatment of dissipative structures is that, paradoxically, it is from the irreversible trajectory of the entropic universe that higher levels of structure emerge. Prigogine thus provides a solution to one of the most perplexing dilemmas of post-Newtonian physics: how in a universe moving toward greater entropy and greater disorder, structures of increasing complexity and order arise.

There are several important additional points in Prigogine's perspective on self-organization that are particularly relevant to social anthropology and other social scientists but also distinctive in comparison with the views of other chaos scientists. First, Prigogine extends his analysis of dissipative structures and far from equilibrium states in the natural universe to include social and cultural systems. In this regard he departs significantly from most chaos practitioners in the natural sciences, who tend to view such applications as merely analogical or metaphorical. Second, in Prigogine's view irreversible directional time is an inherent part of the natural universe regardless of what different observers of varying cultural background make of it. Even so, third, scientists' concepts and visions are themselves only partly functions of the physical world but also of the social and cultural context of scientists since, for Prigogine, culture and society are as much a part of the natural universe as galaxies and subatomic particles.

In these ways, Prigogine's template for the temporal life of dissipative structures converges in numerous respects with many of the orthodox approaches to culture and society that have been developed by social anthropologists and others. The history and evolution of social and cultural forms unfolds in irreversible time according to natural laws of self-organization. Perhaps the most obvious counterpart to one of Prigogine's bifurcations in the realm of human cultural affairs would be when a particular society is in a state far from equilibrium and, hence, engaged in robust exchanges with factors in its social and natural environment, leading to increasingly random activities and fluctuations, followed eventually by the imposition or emergence of an entirely new structure for the system. Obviously, Marx's model of the transformation of precapitalist to capitalist society provides one example, as would any number of theories or studies involving radical historical, structural change.

For Prigogine, there is no scientific basis for the more conventional view of a profound separation of the world of nature and the world of humankind. But perhaps indicative of Prigogine's early training in history and archaeology, it is not the human world which is being understood from the premises of the natural world, but interestingly the natural world which is being understood from the perspective of human experience. This is consistent with this Introduction's argument in other contexts that social anthropologists have long been familiar with elements of chaos theory before it was known as such.

Complexity Theory

Complexity theory is most closely associated with ongoing discussions since the mid-1980s of an interdisciplinary network of scientists based at the Santa Fe Institute for the Study of Complex Systems (Lewin 1993; Merry 1995; Stewart 1997). Because many of its core ideas are still undergoing development and refinement, it has so far enjoyed limited acceptance by the more established scientific community (Sokol and Bricmont 1998: 135). Because of its reliance on some of the basic ideas of chaos theory, however, the two have sometimes been confused. Waldrop (1992), Cohen and Stewart (1994), and Stewart (1997) have provided probably the best and most accessible accounts of complexity theory and its relation to the main features of chaos theory. In this brief synopsis, I shall be following their discussions.

Modeled on Newtonian mechanics, conventional science is "reductionist," that is, the *complexities* of nature are assumed to be explainable in terms of relatively *simple* linear rules and formulations which leave out much of the nonlinear complexity of the universe. Through recourse to nonlinear but still relatively simple equations, however, chaos theory has enabled scientists to account for much of this complexity. To that extent, chaos theory is also "reductionist" in that the complex phenomena of the universe are still reduced to deeper, lower-level simplicities (Cohen and Stewart 1994: 178-180).

Complexity theory is in some respects the complement or inverse of chaos theory (Waldrop 1992: 329; Stewart 1997: 367); that is, complex dynamical systems may occasionally have simple effects as relatively simple higher-level behaviors or patterns emerge from complex lower-level interactions. By "simple effects," complexity theorists mean the synergistic "self-organization" or "emergent simplicity" of a system which, at some level of description, does not involve correspondingly simple interactions among its components. Examples in the realm of nature would include galaxies exhibiting a spiral structure which is not reducible to the interactions of its component stars; the bilateral and radial symmetries of living organisms irreducible to those organisms' physiology; the structure of DNA in relation to component nucleic acids; or the experience of mind and consciousness arising from the interactions of the human brain's neurons. In the human realm, the most commonly cited instance of complexity of this order would be market systems where simple numerical prices are, according to economists, the outcomes of innumerable individual actors' complex interactions and decisions.

According to Stewart, "The philosophical core of complexity theory is the concept of *emergence*, in which a system may transcend its components, so that "the whole is greater than the sum of its parts" (1997: 367, original emphasis). Of course, this has been stock-in-trade for social anthropologists and many other students of systems of interactive behavior for many decades (Cohen and Stewart 1994: 182): the notion of the "superorganic" explicit in Spencer, Kroeber, and White and implicit in Marx; Durkheim's formulations of "collective conscious," "social fact," and "social solidarity"; Mauss's concept of "total social fact"; Benedict's configurationalism; the structure-functionalism of Radcliffe-Brown; Gluckman's conflict theory of social cohesion; Saussure's *langue*; a large share of all structuralist and symbolic anthropology; and indeed the very notions on which the discipline has long been based: "culture," "cultural pattern," "society," "social role," "structure," "social structure," "social integration," "social process," etc. Among more influential contemporary instances of self-organization in recent anthropological theorizing would be Sahlins's structural-historical dialectic of instantiation and reproduction (1981; 1985; 1991), Bourdieu's theory of practice (1977), and Appadurai's discussion of globalization processes (1990).

It is worth noting in this context that in the recent development of complexity theory from chaos theory there has been a distinct shift from quantitative models of chaotic processes to the qualitative or subjective characterization of pattern, metaphor and analogy—terms already intimately familiar to contemporary social anthropologists. For example:

> The contextual philosophy [i.e., complexity theory] focuses attention not on the fine details of particular systems, so beloved of reductionists, but upon large-scale patterns, rules, meta-rules - analogies, metaphors (Cohen and Stewart 1994: 391).

Instead of relying on the Newtonian metaphor of clockwork predictability, complexity seems to be based on metaphors more closely akin to the growth of a plant from a tiny seed, or the unfolding of a computer program from a few lines of code, or perhaps even the organic, self-organized flocking of simple-minded birds (Waldrop 1992: 329).

The heart of the discussion is not so much about what the universe really is, as how human beings can understand it. It is about explanations, not essences (Stewart 1997: 370).

As the chapters to this volume attest, social anthropologists' deep and sophisticated experience in the qualitative analysis of complex systems of meaning with notions of pattern, metaphor, and analogy have potentially a great deal to offer to the future development of chaos/complexity theory.

Scientific Analogies

The question inevitably arises, to what extent are the various similarities between chaos theory and social anthropological theory to which I pointed in the foregoing sections the result of truly related processes or mere coincidence? This is the central epistemological issue lying behind the debates over chaos theory as "postmodern science" in the Science Wars. While no definitive answer can here be provided, a number of points can be advanced which should encourage anthropologists to keep an open mind and to take seriously the implications of the new science in the future conduct of their research and analyses. First, while some would argue that the similarities between the complex phenomena of nature and human sociocultural systems are superficial and based on "mere" metaphor or analogy rather than homology, anthropologists should be reminded that the discovery of identical patterning among realms of nature that heretofore were presumed to be separate and independent has effectively rendered as moot the analogy/homology distinction.

Second, many of the critical advances that distinguish chaos theory's development have been posited initially as intuitive perceptions of qualitative patterns or similarities across disparate realms of reality (e.g., Gleick 1987: 5, 26, 31, 66-69, 77-80, 114, 116, 127-128, 152, 160-161, 166, 168, 171, 194) which later research has shown to involve inherent features of nature (see Universality section above); quantitative or other empirical verifications of such connections have typically come later (see Morava, this volume). Therefore, to dismiss out of hand the numerous apparent parallels between sociocultural systems and complex systems of nature as superficial or intuitive is methodologically unwarranted, especially at early stages of investigation. And even in the relative absence of quantification, the history of chaos theory teaches us that analogies, metaphors, and similarities can be very useful in guiding investigators to fruitful connections and ideas; indeed, according to Kuhn (1970), they are critical steps in scientific advance.

Third, consistent with anthropology's long-standing experience with the notion of cultural relativism, many humanist participants in the Science Wars have stressed that scientific canons of logic and quantification are themselves social facts, that is, cultural models of nature which Westerners have imposed on the phenomena they perceive in the world which, in the process, they have mistakenly taken to be inherent in the world itself (see Wagner, this volume). While this would imply that the quantitative aspects of chaos theory such as universalism are attributes of scientists' mode of thinking rather than the world they are meant to explain and describe, at least then anthropological and other social scientific theorizing can be usefully aligned with the important current thinking in science.

Fourth, the recognition of similarities, metaphors, and analogies across semantic domains has for long been standard practice in much social anthropological analysis and comparison. To this extent, social anthropologists are already well-versed in the analytical procedures that have been implicated in the development of many of chaos theory's key insights: nonlinearity relationships, self-similarity, self-organization, sensitivity to initial conditions, and so on.

Fifth, Hayles (1990; 1991a; 1991b) and others have argued that, as chaos theory and postmodernist thought share the same cultural background, it is no coincidence that they have emerged at the same juncture in contemporary history as parallel manifestations of identical social forces. While not discounting this, I would add that much of modernist social anthropology and social science consists in a long prior history of engagement with elements of what have eventually become chaos theory in the natural sciences. In this respect, there are grounds for arguing that chaos theory has emerged in the natural sciences from forces not only implicit in the wider culture but long explicit in the social sciences.

Contributions to this Volume

It is not enough, however, for social anthropologists to congratulate themselves on discovering that many notions commonplace to them have recently emerged on the cutting edge of today's science—any more than it is sufficient to reject the theoretical possibilities offered by chaos theory merely because in the postmodern era what is being taken for "science" has fallen out of fashion. The following chapters of this volume thus take up the challenge posed in this Introduction to explore from a variety of analytical and ethnographic perspectives the advantages to social anthropology of an awareness of chaos theory and, reciprocally, the enhancement of chaos theory from a recognition of contemporary social anthropological practice.

Since a few of the contributors to this volume take Lévi-Strauss's treatments of myth as their point of departure for exploring the conjuncture of anthropology and chaos theory, the following chapter is devoted to a careful examination of Lévi-Strauss's canonical formula in light of chaos theory as it is understood in the natural sciences. Its author, Jack Morava, is a mathematician well-versed in social anthropological theory. His essay, "From Lévi-Strauss to Chaos and Complexity," compares the formal mathematical properties of the canonical formula of myth with the non-linearity of chaos theory. The first part of Morava's paper consists in a careful and insightful interpretation of the formula's meaning and logic, and locates them in the classic theory of proportions developed by Eudoxus of Cnidos Scholastic (cf. Gregory 2001). Morava's handling of the canonical formula in and of itself, therefore, is an enormously valuable contribution to one of twentieth-century anthropology's most intractable problems. When he turns to the relation of the formula to the mathematics of chaos theory later in the chapter, however, Morava points out the radical distinction between formal analogy and numerative quantities—what anthropologists would likely appreciate in terms of qualitative versus quantitative, or mechanical versus statistical models, respectively. Interestingly, Morava's novel and refreshingly clear interpretation of the formula concludes not only that it possesses a certain logical consistency, but that that logical consistency can be studied without being numerically quantifiable. Chaos theory as it has been developed in the natural sciences, Morava cautions, has been connected with numerically valued observables, placing it and types of abstract algebra such as Lévi-Strauss's formula at "opposite ends of the universe of mathematical discourse." Nonetheless, Morava points out that chaos theory has been particularly useful in the sciences precisely because it has enabled the crossing of certain gulfs between the qualitative and the quantitative. Referring to Leach's (1954) treatment of Highland Burma political dynamics, Morava holds up to social anthropologists the challenge of developing numerical measures of relations between conceptual entities. Importantly also, he wisely cautions anthropologists of the costs which could be incurred when making unrealistic or exaggerated claims as regards the potential applicability of chaos theory. Despite this reserve, Morava concedes that many of the most important crossdisciplinary breakthroughs that have so fully shaped the recent history of chaos theory (Gleick 1987; Briggs and Peat 1989; Stewart 1989; Nicolis and Prigogine 1989) began with qualitative insights at the level of analogies across widely disparate phenomena. Quoting Lewis Thomas (1983), Morava notes, "The task of converting observations into numbers is the last task rather than the first thing to be done, and it can be done only when you have learned, beforehand, a great deal about the observations themselves. You can, to be sure, achieve a very deep understanding of nature by quantitative measurement, but you must know what you are talking about before you can begin applying the numbers for making predictions." Thus the quantification of qualitative phenomena may well prove to be the critical hurdle in social anthropology's rapprochement with chaos theory.

In the five subsequent chapters, experienced anthropological practitioners examine various components of chaos theory in relation to detailed bodies of ethnographic and historical materials, two from Africa, two from Melanesia, and one from Amazonia. These chapters are presented in a strategic sequence which, it is hoped, will assist anthropological readers in developing progressively their competence in chaos theory—basically a movement from chaotic phenomena discernible within domains of a single cultural system, next in contexts of crosscultural and regional comparison, and then as regards processes of historical transformation. It should be emphasized, however, how each of these treatments focuses on quite distinct connections between different facets of both social anthropological and chaos theories and no one demonstration is intended to be utterly comprehensive. Charles Piot's chapter 3, "Fractal Figurations: Homologies and Hierarchies in Kabre Culture," perhaps comes closest to this, however, as he explores the symbolic replications of gender and hierarchical encompassment across a wide range of Kabre (Togo, Africa) cultural contexts and regional variations—house structures, cosmology and myth, subsistence practices, reproductive theory, community organization, and ritual performance. Through these materials, Piot demonstrates that numerous seemingly disparate elements of orthodox structuralist analytical procedure he has employed in previous analyses—Lévi-Strauss on analogy and myth, Wagner on obviation, Dumont on hierarchy—conform to the iterative logic of fractal scaling and nonlinearity. By extending these insights derived from chaos theory processually into the history of the wider Volta Basin, however, Piot is able to further comprehend the slaving and migration of the seventeenth and nineteenth centuries as instances of the recursive logic of chaotic patterning. The pervasive dualisms which cycle through the history of the region produce a series of self-similar nonlinear symbolic orders, from Dogon to Mossi, to Gourmantché, to Batammaliba, and to Kabre. In the course of tracing these transformations, Piot develops a new critique of the classic segmentary descent theory of Evans-Pritchard, Fortes, Goody, and Tait. And in response to Morava's call for quantification, Piot touches on some interesting numerical implications from the recursive combination and encompassment of Kabre gender categories ("doubly male," "doubly female," "triply male," etc.).

Fred Damon's chapter 4, 'Pity' and 'Ecstasy': The Problem of Order and Differentiated Difference across *Kula* Societies," similarly deals with the problem of variation and comparison across space among the Melanesian island cultures in the Kula Ring of the Massim region. Two components of chaos theory featured in this Introduction are central in his analysis. On the one hand, Damon shows how similar patterns of classification in Muyuw, Gawa, and the Trobriands—lineages, gardens, nets, directions, winds, etc.—can be found on different fractal scales across several domains within any given area. On the other he attempts to deal with the structured synchronic variation in this regional system; thus from small initial differences great differences emerge. In this example, Damon offers a particularly important commentary on fractal scaling: although there is a similarity or repetition of patterns within a given part, between any given contiguous social units there are minor differences which, across a significant number of steps, show evidence of phase changes and transformation. Damon adapts those elements of Lévi-Strauss's canonic myth formula which are compatible with the nonlinearity of chaos dynamics to deal with these transformations. The chapter attempts to define a significant problem for furthering the dialogue among the various disciplines that are now attempting to use chaos theory. Returning to the issues of quantification posed by Morava, Damon asks, what is the relationship between the manipulation of the properties of qualities, the standard procedure in modeling in social anthropology, and the manipulation of the properties of numbers, the standard procedure in modeling in many other sciences?

José Antonio Kelly's chapter 5: "Fractality and the Exchange of Perspectives" explores as well the idea of fractality along one of its properties, scaled self-similarity, with reference to Amazonian personhood and sociality. Like Piot and Damon, Kelly employs a strategy of detailed regional comparison examining in his case transformations across Araweté, Wari', Tupinamba, and Achuar groups. Following Wagner, M. Strathern, and Vievieros de Castro, he develops a notion of "fractal personhood" for thinking about Amerindian sociality which embodies many elements of recent treatments of Melanesian personhood. Kelly explains that in many areas of Amazonia, whole relationally-dual persons are viewed as contained or embedded in parts of themselves as well as in the replication of relations between selves and alters at different relational scales (intrapersonal, interpersonal, and intergroup). His ingenious analysis dwells on bodily modifications, the exchange of body parts, and the substitutability of places or positions with reference to various dichotomies of the order of self/other, human/nonhuman, predator/prey, life/death, male/female, and consubstantial/affine. He thus experimentally combines theoretical propositions on Melanesian exchange and Amerindian perspectivism in order to demonstrate the analytical utility of fractal personhood.

Fractal analogies as well as nonlinear bifurcations and self-organization characteristic of many chaotic phenomena reported from the natural sciences are similarly identified by Christopher Taylor in a second African ethnographic example, chapter 6, "Fluids and Fractals in Rwanda: Order and Chaos." As Taylor demonstrates, the classical structuralist opposition of "open" versus "closed" may do violence to the description of cultural phenomena that cannot be so neatly subsumed within such a static order, for beneath this apparent order lurks the apparent disorder of contingency. The channelling of potency in central Africa is characterized by a certain orderliness to be sure, but one which resides at the level of dynamic processes. For Taylor, the most fundamental of these involve the human body's physiological states of "openness" or "closure." The flows and blockages of bodily processes are analogically reproduced across a wide range of Rwandan practices and institutions in accordance with pervasive dualism—the production process, exchange, popular medicine, spirituality, cosmology, and most notably in the rituals of divine kingship. Like contributors Piot and Mosko, however, he extends this nonlinear dynamism and implicit self-organizing tendency into historical perspective, demonstrating how the unstable relations between Rwandan Tutsi kings and autochthonous Hutu clans, alternating between hyper-endogamy and hyper-exogamy, are analogous to nonlinear phase transitions in fluid dynamics. He concludes from this analysis that cultures, subjected to outside influences, are not infinitely malleable. In the latter part of his chapter, Taylor elaborates on the unsettling fractal transpositions of the imagery of fluids, flows, and blockages in the reports of atrocities in the wars of genocide which have marked Rwandan politics in the contemporary era. He thereby provides at least a partial understanding of what, to most contemporary observers, has appeared to be complete disorder in central Africa.

My chapter 7, "Peace, War, Sex and Sorcery: Nonlinear Analogical Transformation in the Early Escalation of North Mekeo Sorcery and Chiefly Practice," examines the applicability of several elements of chaos theory to a case of detailed historical change in a Melanesian chiefdom of Papua New Guinea. Sahlins's structural history program (1981; 1985; 1991) is of particular interest here as, I argue, it effectively incorporates several key features of chaos theory: "extreme sensitivity to initial conditions" (i.e., the effects of individual actors' discrepant attributions of meaning to the same happenings), "fractal self-similarity" (i.e., hierarchical/heroic organization, where prototypically the Polynesian king embodies in his actions the actions of society at large), "complex dynamical relations among variables" (i.e., structures of the conjuncture); and "irreversible time," "dissipative structures," or "systems far from equilibrium" (i.e., diachronic structures, structural change). In his dismissal of classic Saussurean semiological and structuralist reasoning, however, Sahlins has effectively rejected one of the other central features of chaos theory from his scheme: "nonlinearity," at least in the form of nonlinear analogy. Focusing on the precolonial and early historical transformations among key values and relations comprising North Mekeo chiefly offices, I suggest that the pronounced escalation of chiefs' and official sorcerers' authoritative powers, while appearing superficially to arise from contingent and/or conjunctural circumstances, can be further appreciated as chaotic nonlinear analogical transformations (i.e., bifurcations and inversions) of prior symbolic and relational structures. Through this application of one part of chaos theory, I seek to extend or enhance the potentiality of Sahlins's structural history program beyond the limits he initially envisioned.

The volume's final contribution consists in an authoritative, philosophical, and provocative Afterword on the attractions and the limitations of chaos theory for the further development of social anthropological theory. Roy Wagner is probably the first social anthropologist to have employed notions derived explicitly from chaos theory in ethnographic and theoretical treatments of anthropological materials. Thus Wagner has had the greatest opportunity to reflect on the convergences and divergences between chaos theory and anthropology as well as their ultimate significance. Several of his key works to date—namely, *Symbols that Stand for Themselves* (1986c), *The Invention of Culture* (1981), and *Anthropology of the Subject* (2001)—have relied on some of the central elements of chaos theory, fractal holography particularly, to provide a unique view of the anthropological theorizing about the cultures that such theorizing is intended to represent. Here in "Order is What Happens When Chaos Loses Its Temper," Wagner similarly deploys the chaotic notions of fractal iteration and self-scaling to discern the relation of anthropological theorizing and anthropology's representations of its own scientific practice—including those adumbrated throughout the previous chapters of this book. Wagner's style of erudition offers on the face of it a critical appraisal of the possibilities of chaos theory, or indeed of any theorizing, "scientific" or otherwise, to grasp reality, social or otherwise. Building on the nominalist views of Heidegger and Wittgenstein and extending Lévi-Strauss's treatments of "savage thought," he argues with extreme sensitivity that the models of chaos theory, like the models of all the sciences including anthropology, are in the first instance creations of human understandings about the world, subsequently imposed upon the world but mistakenly taken to be about the world itself as it is. Our scientific attempts to know reality, he argues, consist in overdetermining the facticity of the world while underdetermining our own agency in designing models of that world. By a kind of figure-ground reversal, echoing the inversions of Lévi-Strauss's canonical formula, our recognition of patterns in the world which conform to our theories are typically taken ex post facto to confirm falsely the models' "validity." In this regard, scientific theorizing is not dissimilar to the inventiveness of all cultural systems as Wagner sees it. Hence all scientific thinking and model building, including implicitly that contained throughout this volume, is essentially tautologous—symbols standing for themselves—but also, significantly, iterative and fractal. This is the ultimate paradox that apparently motivates Wagner—while cautioning against scientific pretensions to "objectivity" (including those of chaos theory), he must rely on insights gained from chaos theory itself to make this point.

This can be illustrated most clearly, perhaps, where Wagner comments on the numerical quantification that has accompanied the development of chaos theory in the natural sciences (see Morava, this volume). Wagner's basic point is that scientists' conventional imposition of their quantified models upon the world is itself an instance of iterative holography or fractal self-similarity—seemingly confirming the potential value of chaos theory to social anthropology in at least this one instance. However, his view of the resulting correspondences between patterns in the world and observers' models and theories is that they confirm falsely the validity of those models and the "truth" of their quantification. For Wagner, the very facility of quantification is an iterative fractal *quality*:

> The "sense" or meaning of number is established by a ratio called "counting," in which the various numerical values are set in correspondence with an appropriate collection of countables, and so with one another. But mathematics as such can only be said to come into its own when this validating function is mapped ("modeled") back upon itself, so that number counts number, as in the standard operations of "number-theory." The *equation*, so to speak, sets the standard of the human scale, a magical point of balance or equilibrium, like those small bones within the ear, or like our upright posture, so that we can "go straight."

Elsewhere, Wagner (personal communication) notes, "the image of the imager in the act of imaging things—is a human *device*, a virtual holography superimposed upon the action of *sensing* it. Closing upon itself rather than the object of depiction, the device *rotates* into a perspectual conundrum, becomes, as in the prints of M.C. Escher, a self-portrait of the inability to really know it." The important point here is that even scientific quantification is a cultural construction of reality, distinguishable from the reality it purports to measure but fractally related to it. Not only does Wagner, therefore, temper Morava's call for refinements in quantification; in many details of his exposition readers will detect that his estimation of the limits and utilities of chaos science for social anthropology relies faithfully (iteratively?) on the qualitative components of chaos theory itself for analyzing social anthropological theory and conceptualization: "Chaos theory does not show us what the world is like, or what thought or even representation may be like; it only shows us *how* they are like themselves."

So what is to be made of Wagner's ultimate reliance upon key tenets of chaos theory to justify his concerns over chaos theory's possible value to anthropology? It is instructive, I think, that several times in his Afterword Wagner invokes the Epimenides' paradox. For instance, "There are no single solutions to paradoxes of the Epimenides type ("All Cretans are liars, and I tell you this in all honesty, for I myself am a Cretan")" (Wagner, this volume). Notwithstanding the absence of single solutions, or even easy ones, it cannot be doubted that Wagner treats the reader to an utterly breathtaking kaleidoscope of illustrations, from Navaho and Tolai understandings of agency and Lévi-Strauss's canonical formula of myth to the fates of Captains Bligh and Cook, jokes, natural selection, the "missing lynx," Borge's imaginary planet Tlon, the number "zero," Freud's theory of neurosis, Hamlet, Sibelius's Fifth Symphony, and Mr. Data, the android of Star Trek.

Conclusion

Throughout this Introduction, I have tried to implicate numerous elements of both classical and contemporary social anthropological theorizing in the recent emergence of chaos theory, thus representing an alternative response to the current "crisis of representation" otherwise dominated by the humanities. This crisis is, of course, not the first such experienced by social anthropologists or other social scientists. Practitioners will recall, for example, that the discipline had reached a juncture similar to the current one in the years shortly after World War II. At that time, probabilistic formulations were being rapidly developed in sociology, economics, geography, and political science while structuralism in a variety of guises including Marxism was revolutionizing linguistics, anthropology, history, and cognitive psychology. A profound bifurcation, if you will, had emerged in the discourses of social science. Unlike the debates of recent years, which have focused on the relative values of scientific and humanistic approaches, the explicit questions which fostered the preponderance of debate back then had to do with what was "scientific" and "unscientific" in the first place. Merely as an indication of the degree to which things have changed in the intervening period, during the earlier crisis structuralism was condemned by the positivists and empiricists as being too humanistic and hence "unscientific." Nowadays, of course, structuralism is rejected by its humanist critics chiefly for its modernist scientific pretensions.

I compare the earlier crisis to the current one, however, neither because of the similarity of terms which define them nor to illustrate the subtle elisions that have occurred between them. I compare them because the solution to the earlier crisis points to a solution in the current impasse. At the time of the earlier debates, it could be said that Lévi-Strauss had resolved the plight many had experienced by formulating the distinction of "mechanical" and "statistical models." The expansion and elaboration of probabilistic methods, of course, had produced highly quantified statistical models of aggregate social phenomena, which Lévi-Strauss characterized in terms of differences of scale (1963a). The adaptation to social anthropology of structuralist methods of description, analysis, and comparison initially developed in anthropology and linguistics by Durkheim and de Saussure, of course, produced mechanical models of social phenomena, distinguished by elements on the same scale as the phenomena they purport to describe (Lévi-Strauss 1963c: 275-276). In statistical models, correspondingly, the elements are on a different scale. With this differentiation among scientific models, it was necessary to concede the value of different kinds of scientific formulation, productive of fundamentally different types of understanding about social and cultural phenomena. I take this to be the essential point in Morava's chapter (this volume; see also Stewart 1989: 39-40, 54-55) about the wide gulf between qualitative and quantitative methods.

Besides their many differences, however, statistical and mechanical models share one feature which was definitive of the prechaos science of the day: their separate formulations were typically linear rather than nonlinear. Or if they were nonlinear, they were either not comprehended as such or the significance of their nonlinearity was not appreciated. Discussions of the development of chaos theory by its most notable interpreters (Stewart 1989; Gleick 1987; Briggs and Peat 1989; Nicolis and Prigogine 1989) reiterate basically the same set of distinctions among types of models in the natural sciences. The two-body Newtonian model of celestial mechanics was established as the prototype of science generally at a certain stage. Its mechanistic linear formulations could not account, however, for certain phenomenal orders of mass scale; eventually, statistical methods were developed which could (Stewart 1989: 39-40). In the place of mechanical determinacy, however, statistical models could only produce statements of probability. So the two kinds of linear scientific formulation coexisted, each applicable to different sorts of phenomena—phenomena it now seems which comprise a relatively small portion of reality.

Social anthropology now stands poised on the verge of recognizing a third fundamental type of scientific model: *chaos models* of social and cultural processes. Chaos models, or critical elements of them as I and other contributors to this volume have tried to show, have long been implicit in a wide variety of social anthropological conceptualizations, but they have remained unrecognized as such. And yet chaos models are as different from Lévi-Strauss's characterization of mechanical and statistical models as those two types of models are different from one another. Considerations of scale are critical in differentiating all three. Where mechanical and statistical models reflect the phenomena they purport to describe on the same and different scales, respectively, chaos models, due to their distinctive nonlinearity, reflect similarities of form across a variety of scales, or, in other words, previously unperceived patterns of deterministic order among seemingly random events.

Such is the state of science in the postmodern era here at the opening of the twenty-first century. And it is this new science—not the statistical or the mechanical types of formulation that predate the discovery of chaos—which ought to be figured in assessing social anthropology's current predicament. The models that buoyed social anthropology up until recently in the minds of some practitioners have been floundering, but so also is much of the current humanist critique and rejection of science, as noted above. Many social anthropologists will undoubtedly be suspicious, recognizing in the new vision of chaos another inapt appropriation by social scientists of the tenets of natural science. I have tried to demonstrate in this Introduction, however, that counterparts to chaos theory and its conceptual elements have long been at the center of the very best of social anthropological theorizing, long before the rise of chaos theory elsewhere. As I and others have implied, chaos theory in the natural sciences has developed from the recognition of complexities in the natural world which are commonplace in the sphere of human affairs. Indeed, lack of interest evinced by social anthropologists and other social scientists in chaos theory may be due paradoxically to their long intuitive familiarity with its several maxims.

Beyond this, however, chaos theory does offer something new and valuable to contemporary social anthropology, viz. a conceptual framework wherein the numerous diverse theoretical insights of the discipline, until now conceived and evaluated as independent or even in opposition to one another, can be coherently linked and integrated. So just as social anthropology has recently taken a postmodern turn, a reflexivist turn, a relativist turn, an interpretive turn, or a historical turn, the time may have come for a turn to chaos.

2

FROM LÉVI-STRAUSS TO CHAOS AND COMPLEXITY

Jack Morava

"I often say that when you can measure what you are speaking about, and express it in numbers, you know something about it; but when you cannot measure it, when you cannot express it in numbers, your knowledge is of a meagre and unsatisfactory kind."

William Thomson [Lord Kelvin],
Lecture to the Institution of Civil Engineers, 3 May 1883

I. Some background, and some acknowledgments

This essay has grown through many hours of conversation with Fred Damon, who has worked very patiently to understand the ways of my community, the mathematicians, and who has encouraged me to write this account of some of our myths which have become of interest to anthropologists. I have tried to focus in particular on how my field deals with the relation between the discrete and the continuous, and how that subject relates to chaos theory and the canonical formula of Lévi-Strauss (1963c).

I am writing as a "working mathematician," which has a special meaning, rather like the "native speaker" of linguistics; in particular, it allows intuition extra weight. I am familiar to some extent with chaos theory, but I am not an expert in that field, and perhaps in this context that will not be a burden: communication between anthropologists and mathematicians attempts to span great conceptual distances, and I worry that misunderstandings and misconceptions about fundamentals, rather than questions

---

Notes for this section can be found on page 63.

about delicate technical issues, are the most prominent obstacle facing us. I will therefore try to avoid technicalities, and I will approach mathematics historically, beginning with its emergence from the Pythagorean protoscience of numerology.

My original involvement in this project grew out of an interest in the formal mathematical significance of Lévi-Strauss's canonical formula for myths. That interest continues,[1] but the topic is probably of more concern to workers in my own field than anthropologists, and here the subject has been somewhat backgrounded; but it nevertheless provides a skeleton for the essay, which begins with some remarks about the classical Greek theory of proportions as a kind of calculus of analogies. The point is that Lévi-Strauss's use of these methods is an example of a kind of mathematical thinking which can be rigorous without being quantitative (in contrast to Kelvin's narrow-minded claim, in the epigraph). The following section then approaches chaos theory, also to some degree historically, through its relation to René Thom's idea of structural stability of forms (1975). A digression on the canonical formula follows, after which chaos theory returns, in the context of the quantitative models promoted by Kelvin, and the essay ends with a plea for anthropologists to take seriously social models which are quantitative but not deterministic.

This project began in a period of some cultural tension between social and mathematical sciences, and I hope it will not be out of place if I end this introduction by trying to place myself with respect to my community and my ancestors. I work in topology, on matters growing out of early work of Thom, though not from that part concerned with the study of catastrophes and chaos; in practice I am probably more familiar with the kind of techniques used by the number theorist André Weil, who contributed an appendix to Lévi-Strauss's book on kinship (1969[1949]); indeed it was that appendix which kindled my own interest in Lévi-Strauss's later work. I owe what understanding I have of the way social scientists think to a lifetime's conversations with the linguist Ellen Contini-Morava, from whom I learned (among much else) the term "spanned opposition"; in this note I am attempting something like that, with respect to a restricted body of ideas from anthropology and mathematics, subjects which do not normally engage in much dialogue.

Finally, I want to thank Fred Damon and Mark Mosko for their interest, patience, and long-term encouragement. Without their continued support, this kind attempt at crosscultural communication would have died in infancy.

II. Analogies and Proportions

Lévi-Strauss has described his formula as a way of talking about analogies between analogies, so the status of analogies as formal objects seems a good place to begin. The foundation of geometry as an abstract discipline was the beginning of quantitative science, and the theory of proportions developed by Eudoxus of Cnidos was a key technical breakthrough in that scientific revolution. Lévi-Strauss's use of similar language to discuss analogies would have been immediately familiar to Eudoxus and his school, as a descendant of their methods. [Chris Gregory (2001) places Lévi-Strauss's work in the scholastic tradition, but I'm concerned here with finding a place for it as well in the tradition of mathematics and the "hard" sciences.]

The history of science can be framed as a long dialogue between the quantitative and the qualitative, starting in prehistory with counting and the calendar (e.g., Needham 1970: 152). In Greek geometry this theme is manifested in a tension between Pythagorean number mysticism about integral (whole) numbers [exhibited, for example, in their theory of musical harmony] and the irrational numbers (not representable as ratios of whole integers) which they knew to be important in geometry. The need to reconcile these structures led to a careful analysis of the theory of ratios and proportions. Greek geometry therefore precedes, and was formulated without, the modern notion of real number (whose history begins in the Renaissance).

Today we can speak of two towns, say fifty miles apart, one occupying an area of two square miles and the other three square miles; and while this would have been understandable to the Greeks as a figure of speech, for them the formal relation between a mile of distance and a square mile of area was extremely problematical. In their intellectual system areas and lengths were thought, like our apples and oranges, not to be directly comparable. It is, of course, useful to make such comparisons, and Eudoxus devised a rigorous way to accomplish this. We learn in grade school that the area of a circle A of radius a is πa^2; but in the classical framework one says that (the area of) circle A is to (the area of) circle B *as* the square on the radius of circle A is to the square on the radius of circle B; where by "the square" is meant not some abstract numerical quantity multiplied by itself, but an honest geometrical figure constructed by ruler and compass. The relation, or ratio, between two objects of the same sort (circles) is thus equated to the relation between two objects of a different but similar sort (squares), and the classical geometers developed rules for the manipulation of such analogies which form the background to later developments in algebra.

In modern parlance one abbreviates the assertion that "P is to Q as R is to S" by a formula such as

$$P : Q = R : S \,,$$

and the relation between the areas of these geometric objects can be summarized symbolically by the assertion

$$\text{circle } A : \text{circle } B = \text{square } A : \text{square } B \,;$$

we usually take the further step of identifying the area of square A with the numerical square a^2 of the length of its side, and if we imagine some ideal circle B of radius one and call its area π then we can write this formula as

$$\text{circle } A : \pi = a^2 : 1^2 .$$

By this stage our original statement of an analogy between geometric objects has been replaced by a numerical equation, which can be written

$$\text{circle } A / \pi = a^2 / 1 ,$$

and it is now natural to invoke the cross-multiplication rule of arithmetic, which says that

$$a / b = c / d$$

if and only if $a \times d = b \times c$, for example, $2 / 5 = 6 / 15$ since $2 \times 15 = 5 \times 6$; the result is the familiar formula

$$\text{(Area of) circle } A = \pi\, a^2$$

I have gone through this argument in some detail to emphasize that a formal analogy between geometric objects is conceptually distinct from (and more general than) the assertion of the equality of some numerical attribute of those objects; it is equivalent to the latter only if one is willing to believe that a geometrical object can be replaced by some numerical attribute. To Eudoxus our equation for the area of a circle is objectionable because areas are geometrical entities, while numbers are, well, numbers; as a hard-headed rationalist of his time, he could justifiably have rejected the identification of the area of the unit circle with a number π as a kind of mysticism.

By the Renaissance much of the logic of this classical system had been lost; but Galileo, Kepler, and others, driven by their own concerns, had great success applying "quick and dirty" numerical techniques to the fields of mechanics and astronomy. Newton's law $F = Ma$ is a prototypical example: it asserts that the force on a body equals the numerical product of the mass of the body and its acceleration. Here acceleration means the rate of change of velocity, or in other words the ratio of the change (sometimes denoted Δv) in velocity to the (small) amount Δt of time during which this change of velocity takes place. Using the cross-multiplication rule backwards, this can be restated as a proportion

$$F : M = \Delta v : \Delta t$$

in classical Eudoxian form. What's new about Newton's law from this point of view is thus not its form, but rather the fact that its terms (force, mass, velocity) are not immediately intuitive concepts, but are rather terms of art, conceived from the beginning as intrinsically numerical abstractions from the underlying physical system. The fundamental conceptual problem of this new mechanics was to identify quantifiable aspects of physical systems and to hypothesize relatively simple but testable relations between these (often unintuitive) quantities. With the success of Newtonian mechanics and its descendants, the distinction between formal analogies and numerical equations was pushed so far into the background that to many, formalization in numerical terms became synonymous with scientific thought; Kelvin's epigraph exemplifies this position. He was on the cutting edge of the intellectual developments of his day, but to think that science is coterminous with the quantifiable now seems as rhetorically excessive as the recently popular notion that markets can reliably value all things. Lewis Thomas (1983: 227) seems more balanced:

> The task of converting observations into numbers is the hardest of all, the last task rather than the first thing to be done, and it can be done only when you have learned, beforehand, a great deal about the observations themselves. You can, to be sure, achieve a very deep understanding of nature by quantitative measurement, but you must know what you are talking about before you can begin applying the numbers for making predictions.

In Lévi-Strauss's work the formalism of proportions is used with great sophistication, to extend some of the methods of quantitative science to areas thought accessible only qualitatively; but his equations were never intended to be interpreted numerically.

III. Thom's Structurally Stable Forms

But how, after all, does one come to "know what one is talking about"? I will argue in this section that it is at this point that chaos theory, or more precisely the study of attractors, becomes relevant. From the historical point of view, or in terms of the sociology of mathematics, chaos theory is a descendant of the theory of structural stability developed by René Thom in the late sixties (Thom 1975); indeed the situation calls to mind the nineteenth-century Russian writer Belyi's remark that "We're all lice who crawled out of Gogol's 'Overcoat.'" Smale, for example (discussed by Gleick 1988: e.g., 45-52), who invented the horseshoe attractor, was quite conscious of the place of his work in the framework provided by Thom's paradigm. One of Thom's central ideas is a coherent mathematical theory of "forms," which (if you wish) can be taken to be formalizations of those of Plato: he was concerned with pinning down just exactly how such ideal things can be handled. Thom starts from the observation that all data contains errors; consequently, for *anything* to be recognizable, it must be *stable*, in the sense that a small perturbation or perceptual error will not drastically alter its structure. A penny is thought to be a circular disk; but what one sees in one's hand is almost always not a circle but a tilted ellipse. This is a distortion, but a recognizable one, of a circle, and after infancy most of us learn to deal automatically with such phenomena. A reflection in water is a more complicated example: if the water moves slowly the image may be distorted, rippled, yet remain recognizable; but when the water is really disturbed, we can no longer reconstruct the original from its image. Indeed, the term "image" is not even strictly applicable in that situation. Thom's notion is that recognizable forms are thus by necessity what he calls "structurally stable": they are *not* changed by small alterations in initial conditions. This may seem an obvious truism, but the fact is that some things are stable in this sense, while others are not; the requirement of structural stability is subtle and highly nontrivial. I am to some extent putting words in his mouth, but roughly speaking, Thom's idea of a (complicated) form, for example, that of a cat, is a kind of atlas of properties of cats: smooth fur, whiskers, purring ... each of which remains recognizable under small distortions. This is an elaboration of Wittgenstein's notion of family resemblances, of a rope as a structure in which no strand needs to extend the whole length, but which nevertheless retains its integrity and recognizability. Faced with a problematic example, say a cheetah or raccoon, we compare its stable features with those in our pile of exemplary cats we have known, and since the features in that inventory have been chosen to be stable, we have a reasonable hope of coming to a conclusion through some kind of relatively conscious algorithmic computation. If the features weren't stable, then the attempt would be pointless from the beginning.

I bring this up because attractors *are* structurally stable almost by definition. Thom and his school worked out an elaborate theory of structure for dynamical systems (which is to say: things which change with time, in comprehensible ways); in this theory, complicated things are built up out of simpler components. This is a kind of anatomy of such dynamical systems, in which the stiffer bits, like the skeleton of an animal, lie at the bottom of the hierarchy; softer things like organs are hung on that framework, while even more evanescent items like blood, breath, or perhaps the id or the soul, lie, as the technical jargon says, at higher filtration. I don't want to push this metaphor too far, but for a discussion like this, such an image of the theory of dynamical systems is probably more useful than a slew of technical definitions. In any case, attractors, in this hierarchy, are the *most* concrete objects: an attractor is more or less by definition an object at the bottom of the hierarchy. Again pursuing the analogy with Greek thought, attractors are analogous to atoms, the basic irreducible constituents of structures. The possible strangeness of an attractor, by the way, seems to me something of a side issue; strangeness is an impressive technical term, but to decide whether an attractor is strange or not is really a question that requires spelling out very precisely the details of one's model. Perhaps it's safest to think of "attractor" as a cover term for stable, basic form: it's much like the undefined terms that a logical system takes for granted, for example, the points and lines of geometry, or mother, father, sibling in a kinship system. Like pornography, an attractor is something you recognize when you see it; in fact it's pretty much by definition something which is *possible* to recognize. In my limited understanding, it appears that one of an ethnographer's basic tasks is to go into the field and play "name that attractor." This seems to capture what Thomas means when he says that one must know what one is talking about: one must understand enough about a culture's basic forms to recognize them, even in the presence of moderate distortion. In linguistics, this is formalized as the difference between phonetic and phonemic differences in sound; the concept has been generalized in anthropology, to the distinction between "emic" and "etic."

IV. The Terms of the Canonical Formula

Lévi-Strauss's formula is an analogy

$$F_x(a) : F_y(b) \quad F_x(b) : F_{a-1}(y)$$

among terms of the form $F_x(a)$, in which the items labeled a and b tend to be more concrete than the terms labeled x and y; but many such questions about the rules for the interpretation of this equation, which are quite important from the mathematical point of view, are not discussed very explicitly in his work. This is a bit like receiving an enigmatic foreign appliance in the mail, with some crucial pages of the instruction booklet missing.

The symbol $F_x(a)$ represents the role, or function, played in some myth by the individual a in the context of the attribute x. In some South American data (Lévi-Strauss 1988) for example, a and b signify "Goatsucker" and "Woman," respectively, while x and y stand for "jealousy" and "potter"; symbols from the beginning of the alphabet appear to be reserved for individuals, while those from the end seem to be of a higher order of abstraction, more like properties or attributes.

The formula displays important symmetries which deserve further comment; perhaps an example will help. The theorem of Pythagoras says that the (areas of the) squares on the two sides of a right triangle sum to the area of the square on the hypotenuse:

$$a^2 + b^2 = c^2.$$

Thus in a right triangle with sides $a = 3$ and $b = 4$ the hypotenuse must have length $c = 5$. In this statement of the theorem, the two sides a,b of the triangle adjacent to its right angle play a symmetric role, whereas the side c opposite the right angle (the hypotenuse) plays a distinguished role: if we interchange a and b the equation remains valid, but if we interchange a and c or b and c its assertion will generally be false. Thus the variables a and b play a role quite different from the variable c. Similarly, the variables in Lévi-Strauss's formula have asymmetrical roles: he does not assert that his formula holds for *any* collection {a,b,x,y} of individuals and attributes taken at random from a family of myths, but rather that this relation holds for *certain* individuals in *certain* myths; such pivotal entities serve to link together myths in different cycles, and it is the role of the analyst to bring them to light.

This is connected with the interpretation of the symbol a-1: in the example cited above, a is Goatsucker and a-1 is Ovenbird, a figure from a structurally related cycle of North American myths. In another example (Christopher Gregory n.d.), a is the frog, b is the bee, x is water, y is honey, and a-1 is the jaguar. In this case the variables x and y are not attributes in as clear a sense as in the previous examples, but the variables a and b are more concrete in that they are (in English, at least) animate count nouns, while the variables x and y are both (inanimate) mass nouns. The first thing one notices is that the operation which sends a to a-1 links a system involving bees and frogs to the system involving jaguars; in a similar case (Lévi-Strauss 1973[I Sec. 2]) wasp and skunk are related, as well as bee and opossum, and tobacco and pimento; later, we have water = fire^{-1}. This surprising "knight-move" feature of the equation enables Lévi-Strauss to conclude that parallel (but perhaps not obviously related) families of myths are in fact related in formalizable ways. His notation suggests that the individuals a and a-1 are related in some reciprocal way, but no such parallel individual is required to exist for b (though such a b-1 could of course exist as a link to a separate system of myths). This is reminiscent of polarity relations of linguistics, which are frequently encountered as a classifying principle in many semantic domains: hot vs. cold, hands (or heads) vs. feet, male vs. female, animal vs. mineral (cf. Lyons 1977: 270 et seq.), and it seems reasonable to see such basic cognitive principles at work in myths. What is more surprising, from the mathematical point of view, is another reversal that occurs in the final term of the canonical formula. The variables labeled x,y seem to refer to entities of a higher level of abstraction than the entities labeled a,b, and Lévi-Strauss's symbol $F_x(a)$ refers to the role played by the "individual" a in the context of the "property" x. However, in the final term of his formula, the slot usually filled by a higher-order abstraction is filled by the individual labeled a-1, while the slot which has previously been occupied by the more specific entity is filled by the higher-order abstraction y. This suggests that the separation of entities by level of abstraction is not entirely straightforward, and that entities can sometimes be abstracted to become attributes, and conversely that attributes may be personified as entities. This again seems to reflect the linguistic situation: most languages possess well-defined mechanisms which associate noun-like substantives to adjectives, and correspondingly allow the construction of adjectival forms from nouns (Lambek 1958).*

Discussions of such formal properties of equations are technically quite important to mathematicians, and one can push this line of thought further. An important background issue in the interpretation of mathematical formulas is the role of what are called quantifiers, which tell us whether (for example) the formula is intended to hold for *every* object in an appropriate class, or perhaps only that *some* object exists, for which the relation holds. I believe it is largely because such background issues are left undiscussed in Lévi-Strauss's work, that the canonical formula has been controversial in some quarters (cf. Hage and Harary 1983). I believe, on the contrary, that the canonic formula has a coherent formal interpretation in terms of a mathematical construct called the quaternion group of order eight; this generalizes (with a twist) the Klein group of order four, which has appeared elsewhere in Lévi-Strauss's work. The arguments in favor of this interpretation are pretty technical, and are probably of interest mostly to mathematicians, but I have summarized them below. Petitot (2001) has suggested another interpretation, more directly in terms of Thom's work. I hope these two attempts at a mathematical interpretation of the CF (canonic formula) will eventually be seen as compatible, but at the moment they are formulated in incommensurable terms.

V. An Algebraic Digression

Gregory (2001) has discussed Lévi-Strauss's work in terms of Ramusian logic, but that point of view is in fact quite compatible with the framework provided by modern mathematical logic (Carnap 1958; Hughes and Cresswell 1977) and category theory (Makkai and Reyes 1977). Classical logic was concerned with assigning "truth-values" (yes or no, true or false) to propositions, but much contemporary work on the subject has been concerned with extending the possible "value-groups" for logic; a theory which assigns probabilities to assertions, rather than strict yes-no judgments, is one natural example of this sort of generalization. I believe Lévi-Strauss is describing a logical system in which truth-values lie in an algebraic system called a noncommutative group. To my knowledge such constructions have not played much role outside pure mathematics, and this may explain, to some extent, the difficulties many have had, in finding a formal interpretation of Lévi-Strauss's ideas; but it seems clear to me that such an interpretation does exist, and that as far as I can see, it fits integrally with Lévi-Strauss's earlier work on the subject.

Category theory is a framework for mathematical thought which emphasizes relations between objects more than the objects themselves; it

---

*In subscripts the sumbol a^{-1} tends to be typeset as a-1. I have respected that convention here.

is particularly concerned with similarities between objects, and it fore-grounds the notion that objects can be similar in more than one way. Thus two triangles in plane geometry can be *similar* (in the sense that corre-sponding angles are equal), without being congruent (which requires that the corresponding sides also be equal). I believe that in mathematical terms Lévi-Strauss is saying that the left and right sides of the canonical formula are related in a quite specific way; but perhaps it overstates the case a little, to say that they are equal. In the Maranda (2001) volume sev-eral authors suggest, in one way or another, an interpretation of the canonical formula in which the right-hand side is a *transformation* of the left. This might be written

$$F_x(a) : F_y(b) \to F_x(b) : F_{a-1}(y) .$$

The existence of such a transformation, turning the left side into the right, does not preclude that transformation from being an equivalence, but it focuses our attention on similarity between the left and right sides, and challenges us to examine the precise nature of that similarity. The para-phrase below is an attempt to frame the canonical formula in formal lan-guage, specifying missing quantifiers:

• In a sufficiently large and coherent body of myths we can identify characters *a,b* and functions *x,y,* such that the mythical system defines a transformation which sends *a* to *b*, *y* to *a-1*, and *b* to *y*, while leaving *x* invariant. This transformation will therefore send the ratio, or formal analogy, $F_x(a) : F_y(b)$ into the ratio $F_x(b) : F_{a-1}(y)$.

I don't think this is very controversial: Côté (2001), Racine (2001), and Schwimmer (2001) all make similar remarks. But it enables us to make the formal point (probably of interest only to mathematicians) that if we can treat the right-hand side of the canonical formula on an equal footing with the left-hand side, we would then be able to apply the canonical formula *again*; but with *b* now playing the role of a new *a*, with *y* as the new *b*, and *a-1* as the new *y*, defining a chain

$$F_x(a) : F_y(b) \to F_x(b) : F_{a-1}(y) \to F_x(y) : F_{b-1}(a^{-1})$$

consistent with the interpretation of $F_x(a)$ as kind of ratio x/a of x to a! The left and right-hand sides of the chain above then become the valid rule

$$(x/a)/(y/b) = (x/y)/(b^{-1}/a^{-1})$$

for the manipulation of grammar-school fractions. Mosko's variant

$$F_x(a) : F_y(b) = F_x(b) : F_y(a)$$

of Lévi-Strauss's formula also has such an interpretation, when the alge-braic values assigned to the variables lie in a commutative group in which every element has order two, neutralizing the opposition between *a* and *a-1*. This presents Mosko's equation as a version of the CF valid in particularly symmetrical situations.

I've spelled this argument out because it suggests that interpreting the canonical formula as expressing the existence of a transformation relating its two sides is a useful idea, which is pursued below. Maybe I should say here that a *group*, in mathematical terminology, is a system of "elements" (real numbers, for example), together with a system of rules for their combination, which abstract the usual rules for manipulation of numbers: for example, if we combine *a* and *b* to get the product *a* · *b*, and then combine that with *c* to get *(a · b) · c*, then the result is the same as if we had combined a with the product *(b · c)*, that is,

$$(a \cdot b) \cdot c = a \cdot (b \cdot c) \,.$$

There are lots of these critters, and some of them are not *commutative*, in the sense that the order in which we combine the elements may be significant. In the case of real numbers, order is not important (and hence it's conceivable one's checkbook might balance); but rotations in three-dimensional space (cf. Rubik's cube) form another example of a group, in which the order of operations *is* important. The quaternion group of order eight (there are other quaternion groups, cf. Conway and Smith 2003: 56) is the set

$$Q = \{ 1, -1, i, - i, j, - j, k, -k \}$$

with a noncommutative law of multiplication, in which the product of the elements *i* and *j* (in that order) is *k*, but the product in the opposite order is - *k*; in other words,

$$i \cdot j = k = - j \cdot i \,, j \cdot k = i = - k \cdot j \,, k \cdot i = j = - i \cdot k \,.$$

To complete the "multiplication table" for this group, we have to add the relations

$$i \cdot i = j \cdot j = k \cdot k = - 1$$

as well (last but not least) as the relation $(-1)^2 = +1$. The Klein group *K* , which has appeared previously in Lévi-Strauss's work, can be similarly described, as a commutative version of the group *Q*; in other words, the multiplication table is as before, except that we don't bother with the plus and minus signs:

$$K = \{1, i, j, k\} \,,$$

given the simpler multiplication table

$$i \cdot j = k, j \cdot k = i, k \cdot i = j,$$

together with the relations

$$i \cdot i = j \cdot j = k \cdot k = 1$$

(and of course relations like $1 \cdot i = i = i \cdot 1$, etc.). Two groups are *isomorphic* if their elements correspond in a way which preserves the multiplication laws: thus in Lévi-Strauss's writings the Klein group is described as the set of transformations which send a symbol x to the possible values x, $-x$, $1/x$, $-1/x$; the first such transformation [i.e., $x \to x$] corresponds to the "identity" element 1 in the presentation of K given above, while the second, that is, $x \to -x$, corresponds to the element i; similarly $x \to 1/x$ corresponds to j, etc. It is straightforward to check that the multiplication tables of these two structures correspond, for example, the composition of the transformations $x \to -x$ (corresponding to i) with the composition $x \to 1/x$ (corresponding to j) is the transformation $x \to 1/(-x) = -1/x$ corresponding to k, and so forth. Similarly, an *anti*-isomorphism of groups is an invertible transformation which *reverses* multiplication: it is a map which sends the product of any two elements g,h (in that order) to the product of the image elements, in the reverse order. In the case of commutative groups, this is a distinction without a difference, but in the case of a noncommutative group such as Q, it can be significant. For example: the transformation λ: $Q \to Q$ which sends i to k, j to $i^{-1} = -i$, and k to j is a nontrivial example of such an antiautomorphism: in particular,

$$\lambda (i \cdot j) = \lambda (k) = j = (-i) \cdot k = \lambda (j) \cdot \lambda (i) ,$$

while

$$\lambda (j \cdot k) = \lambda (i) = k = j \cdot (-i) = \lambda (k) \cdot \lambda (j) ,$$

and so forth. Once this is established, it is easy to check that the assignment

$$x \to 1, a \to i, y \to j, b \to k$$

sends the antiautomorphism λ to the transformation

$$x \to x, a \to b, y \to a^{-1}, b \to y$$

defining the canonical formula.

Quod, as we say in the trade, *erat demonstrandum*: this presents an example of a consistent mathematical system, satisfying a version of Lévi-Strauss's formula: it is a principle of mathematical logic, that the consistency of a system of axioms can be verified by giving just *one* example of an interpretation in which those axioms hold true. In this case, though, there may be more to the story. Logicians are concerned with questions of logical truth, which can be formulated in terms of the commutative group {+1, -1} [which can alternately be described in terms of two-valued "yes-no" judgments, or in terms of the even-odd distinction among integers]. The Klein group is an interesting kind of "double" of this group, with four elements rather than two, and the quaternion group takes this doubling process yet one step further. Something similar seems to occur in the study of kinship structures (Weil 1969[1949]), but the groups encountered in that field remain necessarily commutative. I believe the interpretation proposed here is also helpful in understanding another aspect of the canonical-formula problem, which other commentators have also found confusing: Lévi-Strauss (1988: 156) invokes the formula

$$F_x(a){:}F_y(b) = F_y(x){:}F_{a-1}(b).$$

This differs from the previous version: now x on the left of the equation becomes y on the right, while a on the left becomes x on the right, y is transformed into *a-1*, and finally b remains invariant. In the framework above, the assignment

$$x \rightarrow i, y \rightarrow j, a \rightarrow k, b \rightarrow 1$$

expresses this transformation as another antiautomorphism of Q, defined now by

$$\sigma\,(i) = j, \sigma\,(j) = k^{-1} = -\,k, \sigma\,(k) = i\,.$$

The two transformations differ by the cyclic transformation

$$\lambda : i \rightarrow j \rightarrow k \rightarrow i$$

which group-theorists call an outer automorphism, of order three, of the quaternion group Q: in these terms, $\lambda = \tau \cdot \sigma$ The point is that the symmetries (cf. Weyl 1952) of Q form a larger group; if we include antiautomorphisms among them, we get a very interesting group with twenty-four elements, in which both transformations λ and σ can be understood as playing a distinguished role.

VI. On Connections with Chaos Theory

One new ideological concern of twentieth-century physics was the technical notion of observable quantity. This metaphysical notion became theoretically prominent when the motion of the hypothetical luminiferous ether turned out not to be measurable by any reasonable physical experiment, and it gained importance in quantum mechanics, where two meaningful attributes of a system need not be simultaneously measurable. In the discussion above I opposed the observable quantities of Newtonian mechanics, which are real numbers, with the terms of Lévi-Strauss's formula, and I tried to emphasize that the latter, which are more like qualities, can be studied rigorously without being numerically quantifiable.

Chaos theory, however, is a direct intellectual descendent of Newtonian mechanics, and as such is fundamentally concerned with precisely such numerically-valued observables. To someone outside mathematics one formula may look much like another, but inside the field chaos theory is considered a part of the subject called analysis (from the nineteenth-century "analysis of continuous variation"), while the kind of discussion sketched in the preceding section belongs to abstract algebra. These subjects lie at opposite ends of the universe of mathematical discourse: algebra is the proper tool for the study of discrete systems, while analysis is concerned with the continuous. Calculus is concerned with infinitesimal changes of entities: in Newton's law, $F = M a$, acceleration is defined as the ratio between change in velocity and change in time, in the limit as the change Δt in time approaches zero. In some sense the real numbers were constructed precisely in order to give this phrase a rigorous meaning. Chaos theory is interesting to mathematicians because it is a theory of the qualitative behavior of quantitative systems: the old yang contains in it the germ of the new yin. Chaos theory attempts to span the opposition between the continuous and the discrete, and it is natural for anthropologists to hope that it might provide a useful bridge between the qualitative and the quantitative.

The basic problem is familiar to linguists, who are forced to deal with "the gooey continuity of the phenomena." The human vocal tract produces a continuum of sounds, but we learn somehow to parcel those sounds into a discrete system of meaningful (i.e., phonemic) units. Optical pattern recognition provides similarly immediate examples. Thom's ideas characterize chaotic systems by a kind of failure of structural stability: this is an instance of "sensitive dependence upon initial conditions." This suggests the hope of a principled way to partition the continuity of possible states of a dynamical system into a discrete set of identifiable (i.e., structurally stable) forms; this is the kind of problem faced, for example, by someone trying to identify the vowels in a sound spectogram. In fact a coherent system can display various islands of structurally stable behavior separated by more chaotic regions, and "catastrophe theory" is used to describe the study of transitions between such stable regions. The boiling of a liquid, that is, the transition between the liquid phase and the gaseous phase of a substance without any accompanying change in composition, is an example of a phenomenon which can profitably be studied by its techniques.

In principle, chaos theory can provide a justification for the identification of fundamental, *atomic* units of social structure, as basic attractors. Thus out of the blooming, buzzing confusion and continuity of the real world, socially and cognitively recognizable forms emerge. The canonical formula suggests a calculus of rules for the way these atoms combine, similar in some ways to the valence theory of chemistry; it provides a discrete, algebraic set of rules for the manipulation of the inventory of significant attractors. Consider the analogy provided by chess: the pieces—king, queen, bishop, pawn—are abstractions of social roles: let's call them attractors of a sort. But the game of chess involves rules for combining these basic items: pieces capture one another, kings have limited mobility, bishops move diagonally, and so forth. The rules of chess are conventions, which do not follow in any natural way from the existence of the pieces themselves, and it does not seem clear to me that the canonical formula is implied, in any natural way, by the existence of attractors. It seems more plausible to suggest that it may represent some characteristic aspect of human thinking (Percy 1975: 159). Thus in the example cited in section three, one might hypothesize a system of ideas relating the stable forms femininity, pottery-making, jealousy, and one particular bird; the systems of myth cited by Lévi-Strauss presumably encode the observation that another bird participates in a similar circle of forms derived from the same underlying structure as the first group, but separated from it by an intermediate chaotic regime. The Ovenbird and the Goatsucker would then be much like two distinct circles which happen to have the same area: similar in some ways, but different in others.

The great accomplishment of chaos theory is an analysis of the qualitative behavior of (some) mathematical systems defined in quantitative terms; but if chaos theory is to be more than a rhetorical device in anthropology, it must be applied to some quantitative model of the underlying social situation. The theorems of chaos theory may say that certain details of the underlying system of numerically-valued equations are relatively irrelevant, but if chaos theory is to provide a scientific model rather than a literary metaphor, the social hypotheses lying behind these equations need to be discussed. If chaos theory is to be anything more than an extended figure of speech in anthropology we have to suppose the existence of an underlying system of *numerical* relations between entities which will eventually be partitioned into the conceptual parcels we call pottery-making, jealousy, and various birds. This is a pretty substantial IOU, but the work of Leach on social systems of the Burmese highlands (1954) is quite explicitly concerned with stable patterns of behavior in neighboring regions, and the relatively chaotic transitions between them; here the outlines of an implicit system of numerical relations are easier to imagine. Leach seems to me admirably clear about this:

> I am asserting that at the present time certain "forces" operate which are likely to lead to the modification of the organization of particular Kachin communities ... My aim in this chapter is therefore two-fold—firstly, I want to explain what are the "forces" which lead to the instability of "gumsa" and "gumlao" systems as constituted at any given moment. (1954: 228)

Force is of course a term from Newtonian mechanics, and Leach's use of the term in quotes shows that while invoking this mechanical metaphor, he feels a need to distance himself from it. I maintain that if chaos theory really has something to say in this context, then this mechanical metaphor needs to be taken seriously and made as explicit as, for example, Lorenz's model equations for weather prediction. Of course Lorenz didn't try to use his equations to actually predict the weather; he was concerned with showing that his system predicted behavior which was qualitatively like the behavior of the weather, and his success lends plausibility to the suggestion that the bifurcation of our usual weather pattern into the el Nino / la Nina pattern is a chaos-theoretic effect. But if chaos theory is to be taken seriously in Leach's context, then someone needs to write down an old-fashioned nineteenth-century numerical, mechanical model for something like the kind of social "forces" (ecological, political, and psychological) Leach discusses, and show that they lead to results which are qualitatively like those observed by ethnographers. Work on social questions in quantifiable terms has a distinguished tradition which continues today (Axtell and Epstein 1997; Montroll 1987), but it may be taken more seriously by "hard" scientists than by anthropologists.

This may not be what many anthropologists want to hear, and I want to suggest that if so, they may not be hearing what I am really trying to say. To a certain extent chaos theory frees us from worrying about details of particular mechanistic models, but those mechanistic models are nevertheless implicitly present in any invocation of chaos theory, and they should not be locked in the attic but rather honestly acknowledged. What chaos theory really has to offer is the freedom to speculate in principled ways about mechanistic models for social phenomena, without chaining those models to notions of determinism. The hostility to determinism in the humanistic sciences is so strong that it naturally leads to the repudiation of mechanistic models in general. Chaos theory offers *mechanistic* but not *deterministic* models to social scientists. Using these tools effectively may require the reexamination of a whole series of attitudes toward the opposition between quantitative and qualitative. I hope anthropologists and ethnographers will be willing to grip such nettles firmly in their hands.

Notes

1. J. Morava, *On the Canonical Formula of C. Lévi-Strauss,* available as math.CT/0306174 at http://arXiv.org.

3

FRACTAL FIGURATIONS
Homologies and Hierarchies in Kabre Culture

Charles Piot

The Kabre of northern Togo (West Africa) have the following myth of origin. The first human being, Kumberito (an androgyne), descended from the (male) sky to the (female) earth, landing in the plain between the two small mountain ranges where the Kabre currently live. After living in caves and wandering aimlessly in the plain for several years, Kumberito became frightened by the hooting of owls at night, which he mistook for men coming to kill him, and fled to the mountains of the northern massif where he decided to settle (in the present-day community of Farang). There, tired of having to evacuate his cave because of the smoke from his fires, he built and lived in a house above ground and began to produce the children who founded the massif's other communities. At death, Kumberito and his descendants returned to the earth, for they were buried in caves in the ground—caves which are located on the massif's highest ridges and outcroppings.

A structuralist reading of this myth would focus on the oppositional and mediational logic which informs its narrative structure. Thus, the myth opens with an opposition between male sky and female earth, unsuccessfully mediated by the wandering, plains-dwelling Kumberito. It is only when Kumberito climbs the mountains, located between sky and earth, that successful mediation occurs—that is, that he lives in peace and begins to generate the life that Kabre know today, a life which cycles between above-ground houses and subterranean caves where the dead are buried. (Significantly, the Kabre term for ancestor, *ateto*, literally means

Notes for this section can be found on page 78.

"underground person.") It is important to add here, however, that Kabre houses in the mountains are rarely located in the highest reaches where the tombs (and many Kabre fields) are found. When I asked why, Kabre said that it is dangerous to live near the tombs, for the wandering spirits of the dead might afflict their families. Instead, they choose to live at lower elevations—on the hillsides leading down from the high places and in the valleys which separate the ridges of the massif.

In symbolic terms, since low is associated by Kabre with females and high with males, living down low (female) though above the ground (male), as one does during life, represents a recursive mediation of the original opposition between sky and earth (high/low). And, living up high (male) though in the ground (female), as at death, represents a similar, though inverted, recursiveness.[1] Thus, the narrative's original opposition (sky/earth) is displaced onto, and resolved in, a new opposition which inversely incorporates or bisects the terms of the old one: M:F::F(m):M(f). In other words, the failed mediation represented by plains- and cave-dwelling is more successfully resolved by the choice of the mountains as a place to live and, further, by the choice of living above ground—though down low—while alive, before returning to the ground—though up high—at death.

A similar recursive logic may be found organizing other (nonmythical) domains of Kabre social life, including the organization of houses, of communities and of the larger regional system of which Kabre communities are a part. In what follows, I want to sketch in the logic of these various domains, and, employing some of the insights of chaos/complexity theorists (Gleick 1987; Nicolis and Prigogine 1989; Stewart 1989), to reflect on the nature of this iterative, fractal patterning. A significant feature of Kabre fractals is that they are hierarchically-linked or embedded. Moreover, such embeddedness transforms the logic and meaning of the symbolic mediations—the recursive symbolizations—that occur at hierarchically-lower levels. Such revaluation, I shall suggest, must be thought not only in formal terms—through the logic of recursiveness and of the fractal—but also in terms of Kabre history. Here, then, is an opportunity to explore not only the structural implications of fractal iteration but also the interaction between figuration and historical process.

Kabre and their history

The Kabre are linguistically and culturally related to the broad band of Voltaic societies which spans the middle zone of the West African savanna—those societies located in the north of the coastal countries of Cote d'Ivoire, Ghana, Togo, and Benin and in the south of the interior countries of Mali and Burkina Faso. With the exception of the pastoral (and non-Voltaic-speaking) Fulani, agriculture provides the major means of subsistence for most of the inhabitants of this area. Cereals (sorghum, millet, corn) dominate, though various tubers (primarily yams and cassava) also play an important role in subsistence farming. Still today, there is very little cash-cropping.[2] A gendered division of labor typically organizes productive activities, whereby men do the farming and women the food processing—both for domestic consumption and for sale in the markets. Marketing itself is largely carried out by women.

For many of the anthropologists who have studied Voltaic societies—for example, Fortes (1945; 1949), Goody (1956), and Tait (1961)—kinship has been the major focus of study. Indeed, this area was in many ways the cradle of descent theory and the anthropology of its peoples has become almost inextricably identified with the study of kinship. While much of the writing of descent theorists such as Fortes, Goody, and Tait involved simply describing the internal dynamics of the kinship systems they studied—their works are virtually interminable compendia of the complexities of Tallensi/Lowiili/Konkomba kinship—their project (and, indeed, the structural-functional project in general) was theoretically framed by a larger interest in how African political systems worked, and especially in how kinship was put to political ends.

Moreover, the Volta basin seemed to provide a laboratory for the study of African political systems for it was a microcosm of what Fortes and Evans-Pritchard (1940) argued was characteristic of Africa more generally: that there existed two great political forms—highly centralized societies, on the one hand, and noncentralized or "acephalous" ones, on the other. While both types were found in the Volta basin side by side, it was especially the latter that captured the imagination and interest of descent theorists. They wanted to understand how kinship informed and constituted political relations in such societies, and how, in the absence of the state, such polities created social order.

Their approach, however, led to a sort of sterile typologizing, to "butterfly collecting" as Leach (1961a) sardonically called it. The types seemed to multiply endlessly—each system had its own twist—thereby making the comparativist goal of arriving at generalized laws of social and political behavior virtually impossible. Furthermore, as many have pointed out, by searching for the functional mechanisms which held such societies together the whole enterprise had a thoroughly ahistorical cast to it. Indeed, this sort of typological exercise would appear to require that history be ignored, for if there were history—if social systems were seen as the products of history and of the historical relations between societies—there could be no pure types to compare. And, yet, as I indicate below, these are societies that have extremely complicated histories.

A distinctive feature of many of these societies which I focus on in the present essay, though a feature rarely analyzed by descent theorists, is their highly elaborated system of dual organization. Thus, for example, the Tallensi have two clans—the Namoos and Talis—into which all Tallensi lineages are grouped (Fortes 1936; 1945). These two clans divide the ritual responsibilities for reproducing the social and cosmological order and embody a whole series of oppositional cultural categories.[3] Or, to take another example, Batammaliba houses, which are the site of most productive and ritual activity, are divided into dual complementary spaces and activities. These complementarities order major aspects of Batammaliba social life (Blier 1987). Or, in yet another register, sky/earth and male/female oppositions like those in the Kabre origin myth also frame the myths of the Dogon (Griaule 1965; Griaule and Dieterlen 1965), the Mossi (Izard 1985), and the Batammaliba (Blier 1987).

Such dualisms, I will suggest, need to be theorized in terms of the histories of these societies and of the area more generally. Only by so theorizing them, can we avoid falling back into the ahistorical typologizing of the structural-functional project, or indeed of the structuralist project. For as far back as scholars can reconstruct, the area's history has been characterized by constant flux and change, by massive dislocations and movements of people into and out of various polities. Many of these movements resulted from slaving practices in the area during the time of the Atlantic slave trade in the seventeenth, eighteenth, and nineteenth centuries. Indeed, perhaps as many as one million slaves sent across the Atlantic came from this area. There were many different modes of slave acquisition—raiding, purchase, pawning—but raiding was the dominant form and played itself out across the divide between centralized and noncentralized societies. More centralized groups such as the Dagomba, Mamprusi, Mossi, and Bariba, for instance, continually raided noncentralized polities such as the Tallensi, LoDagaa, Batammaliba, and Kabre (Cornevin 1962; 1981; Goody 1978; Law 1989; Lombard 1965; Manning 1979; 1990; Wilks 1976). Many from these raided groups, in turn, fled the domination of the kingdoms, often ending up in more easily-defensible places like the massifs and outcroppings where the Dogon, Tallensi, and Kabre live today, or along the banks of rivers where the Konkomba and LoDagaa are located (Goody 1978).[4]

But it is not just the slave trade—an intervention from the outside—that permits a characterization of these societies as having history and undergoing often dramatic change. All of the evidence indicates an active, appropriative dynamic at the very center of what sociality was all about. People, products, and ceremonies were constantly moving between households and societies: children were fostered and pawned—both between households and between different ethnic groups (Fortes 1949; Piot 1996; Tait 1961); products circulated across vast stretches through the ubiquitous small markets of the area, markets that were also fed at various points by products from the trans-Saharan trade (de Barros 1985; Levtzion 1968; 1978); rituals migrated from community to community and group to group, establishing and articulating highly complex regional and interregional relationships (Griaule 1965; Izard 1985; Piot 1992; Wilks 1976).

Herein, I examine the dualisms that are so characteristic of the societies of this area in terms of this history and in terms of the politics that such a history both relied on and engendered. But I do not so much wish to see dualism as the functional product of this history—for example, providing a stable island of fixed categories amidst the flux of otherwise constant change—as I want to understand the way in which history gets cycled through these dualisms and, in the Kabre case, refracted into a series of self-similar, nonlinear symbolic orders. I want to suggest both that history made them and, also, that it was made by them. Further, I want to think the symbolic orders of these societies through their connections to one another—and, thus, through the migration not only of people but also of ceremonies. "Locality" in the Volta basin is very much the product of ceremony—namely, of those migratory ceremonial complexes for which this area is known—and thus needs to be seen as itself the product of the larger trans-local context (cf. Appadurai 1996: chapter 8). Thus, the extraordinary built landscapes—of rock terraces and pathways and shrines that characterize the mountain enclaves of Dogon, Tallensi, and Kabre—and the ceremonial technologies that are complexly indexed to and render meaningful (and "local") these landscapes, need to be thought in terms that are trans-regional—and part of a continuum of societies in search of (ritual) distinctiveness—as much as local. Before developing these points further, however, I need to flesh out the symbolic logic of the dualisms that are so central to Kabre culture.

Houses

I suggested above that the recursive logic which frames the Kabre origin myth is also found in various nonmythical domains. This is true especially of the domains of the household, the community, and the region. I begin, then, by discussing the way in which Kabre households are recursively constituted.

Kabre households, or "houses" (*desi*), are seen as composed of complementary male and female persons, labors, spaces, and so on. When asked why they marry—marriage being the act which establishes a new household—Kabre men and women not only mention the need to produce offspring but also, and especially, they invoke the complementarities which inform their division of labor, through which men cultivate and women cook and do the marketing. Thus, the men respond that they marry in order to have someone (a woman) to cook the food which they produce as cultivators, while the women say that they need someone (a man) to cultivate food for them to cook.

These gendered productive activities (men as cultivators, women as cooks) are further associated with other oppositions—raw/finished, and contained/containers. For instance, in cultivating, men produce raw products (crops) which women transform, or finish, into food consumed at the homestead. Further, this transforming activity of women always takes place in pots on cooking fires, containers that transform the raw products of men's labor. In reproduction, the same set of symbolic contrasts holds. Kabre say that a husband's blood or sperm is "cooked" inside his wife's womb—a container Kabre explicitly associate with cooking and water pots in various contexts to produce children. They say, for instance, of a woman who has miscarried that she is like someone who has spilled her pot of water on the way back from the spring and that she must return to "refill it."

The house is gendered not only in terms of the labors and activities of its members, but in other ways as well. Spatially, for example, the inside of the house is female and the outside is male. These associations follow from the fact that the inside of the house is where women do much of their work preparing and cooking food and giving birth to children; the outside, on the other hand, is where men work—farming the fields, sacrificing in sacred groves to the spirits which govern the seasons and the community's welfare, and conducting the politics of the community such as resolving disputes. (This latter takes place under the shade trees that stand outside homesteads.) Because of these spatial associations, during the dry season, the male season, the beer of ceremonies and work groups is served outside the homestead, while during the wet season, which is female, it is served inside.

The Kabre house or homestead is thus the site of the realization and conjunction of a productive order figured through a series of gendered oppositions: male/female, raw/processed, contained/container, and outside/inside (as well as others—east/west, left/right, stasis/motion, superior/inferior—which I will not elaborate on here). But this oppositional logic has an even more complicated twist, for each gender and space also incorporates (and contains) its opposite. For example, a man's blood, that which allows him to cultivate and to produce children (the Kabre terms for blood and sperm are the same) comes largely, Kabre say, from the consumption of sorghum beer, and beer is the prototypical female product. Conversely, a woman's strength and her womb—which allow her to work and to produce children—come from the consumption of porridge, which is produced from the prototypical male product (field crops).

This reciprocal incorporation is most clearly represented in the exchanges between spouses which initiate a marriage (exchanges which model the ongoing relations between husband and wife). Just before she goes to live with her husband, a young woman makes sorghum beer and invites her future husband to come to drink it at her house, an invitation which is repeated several times. For his part, the man works the fields of his father-in-law and makes a series of harvest prestations to his mother-in-law at the time of the four major harvests (of corn, male yams, sorghum, and female yams). Kabre say that these labor and harvest gifts are for "feeding" the man's future wife—to make her strong and to give her a big stomach (womb), so that she will be able to bear many children. Symbolically, then, wives produce their husbands' blood and husbands their wives' wombs; males contain, or incorporate, females and vice versa. This oppositional logic is developed further, as well, for Kabre also say that what each gender produces—in cultivating and giving birth—belongs to the other. Thus, the food that husbands produce is said to be "owned" by their wives and the children a woman produces are "owned" by her husband.

The incorporation of opposites in the homestead is spatial as well. A man's granary (that which most typifies his productivity and identity) is located at the very heart of the homestead's female space—the center of the courtyard; and, conversely, a woman's grinding hut (grinding being that activity by which a woman transforms [male] raw products into [female] food and, therefore, being an activity which typifies her work and identity), is located in that most male of spaces—the area immediately outside the homestead.

It is important to note here that the recursive logic that constitutes what men and women are emerges from an unambiguous single-sex state and is processually constituted. A man and a woman come to marriage fresh from their initiations, which aim (among other things) to transform androgynous children into, respectively, single-sex men and single-sex women. It is from this stark contrast of male and female, then, like that of sky and earth in the origin myth, that a new mediating set of terms emerges: a man who is part female and a woman who is part male.

Community

Opposites incorporate, or mutually constitute, one another at the level of the community as well. Kabre communities are organized into two clans, one "male" and the other "female," consisting of all the houses of the community. The purpose of these clans is largely ritual: each clan is responsible for the calendrical and age-grade ceremonies which occur during its season—the male clan during the dry, "male," season, and the female clan during the wet, "female," season. However, consistent with the pattern of opposite-sex incorporation established in the homestead, even though most of the tree spirits owned by each clan (and to which it must sacrifice during calendrical ceremonies) are of the same sex as the clan itself, each clan also possesses an opposite-sex spirit.

Opposite-sex clan incorporation also occurs in another area. At one moment during each season, the season is ritually turned inside out, as it were. For instance, when a certain age-grade initiation, *kojunduku*, takes place during the wet (female) season, the male clan performs a condensed version of *doronto*, the most male of all dry season ceremonies. This per-formance "dries" out the wet season, temporarily turning the wet into the dry, and inserting a male ceremony into the cycle of wet season female ceremonies. Conversely, during the dry male season, a female fertility ceremony is performed by the female clan, the sole such ceremony performed during an otherwise consistently male ceremonial sequence.

Finally, the two clans occasionally shuffle member houses back and forth. Thus, there are houses in the male clan that used to be female (and retain their identity as such) and houses in the female clan that used to be male. I interpret these shufflings as part of the reciprocal incorporation of opposites of which Kabre appear so fond.

I should add here that all of these phenomena—female houses in the male clan and vice versa, male ceremonies during the female season and vice versa, female spirits in the male clan and vice versa—were, for me, for the longest time, totally anomalous. They seemed not to fit the otherwise tidy oppositional categories into which much of Kabre life was ordered (and, indeed, seemed to call into question those categories themselves). It was only—and the point here is similar to that argued by Mosko (1991a) in his critique of Lévi-Strauss's canonic formula for myth (Lévi-Strauss 1963c; 1988)—in terms of a more encompassing recursive logic that they began to make sense and that their anomalous nature disappeared.

Region

Finally, at the level of the larger regional system of communities, the same type of reciprocal incorporation occurs. The larger region consists of two zones—those communities founded by Kumberito's children which are located in the mountains, and those communities, offshoots of the mountain communities, located in the plain or bush immediately surrounding the mountains (as well as, and since the early colonial period, in the south of Togo). The former are symbolically "male" and the latter "female"— identities which are manifest in many domains. For instance, the male mountain is associated with the best agriculture (a male activity) and the female bush with the best commerce (a female activity). The mountain communities, like men, perform rituals, while bush communities, like women, do not.

But these sharp, gendered contrasts between the two zones are complicated during various annual rituals. In several of these ceremonies, paired communities from the two zones undertake food exchanges which, once again, follow the pattern of reciprocal incorporation already described. For instance, during one of these ceremonies, whose aim is to ensure a good harvest of yams, yams are exchanged between the mountain community responsible for performing the ceremony and its bush community. Significantly, the mountain community receives *four* yams (which are planted in a ceremonial mound) and the bush community receives *five* yams (which are planted in the fields of its important clan members). Four is a female number and five a male one. Thus, the male mountain is given a female number of yams while the female bush is given a male number: each internalizes or incorporates the other.

Beyond homologies: encompassment and the multiplication of identities

I have attempted to show that the domains of the house, the community and the region each possess a similar underlying symbolic logic. Beginning with a sharply-drawn contrast between opposed terms, mediation is sought and achieved through a recursive recombination of those terms. But before we leap too quickly to the view that the Kabre system is some sort of irrepressible fractal machine, endlessly reproducing the same homologous oppositions, and oppositions within oppositions, I need to muddy the waters some. For each of the domains I have discussed is hierarchically encompassed by another and such encompassment transforms the terms of the lower-level opposition.

Thus, a man or a woman in the "house" is also a member of a male or female clan, and of a male or female region, and these more encompassing identities transform his or her lower-level identity. Consider, for instance, the identity of a man who comes from a house in the female clan as opposed to a man from the male clan. The former, the man in a house from the female clan, becomes "female" in various contexts. Thus, when participating in calendrical ceremonies in the sacred groves, he sits on the west (female) side of the forest, and is associated with the right (female) hand and with white (a female color). He also eats female portions of sacrificed meat and is associated with the wet season and wetness generally. And, since the male clan is superior (as men are in the homestead), he must follow rather than lead during various ritual activities. This man's female identity is one that he carries with him not just at the time of calendrical ceremonies, but also when he is initiated and at death. At these crucial junctures in his life, he is associated with all of the symbols of femaleness and becomes "female."

Conversely, this man's wife may undergo the opposite transformation. If she is a member of the male clan (often, though not always, the case), she eats male portions of sacrificed animals, is associated in various contexts with the symbols of maleness (the color red, the east, the left, dryness), and will be buried in a tomb of the male clan at death. Whereas her husband is "female," she is "male."

At the level of the region, a similar transformation occurs, for here a person's identity is also governed by their membership in a particular gendered zone of the larger region. For example, for a man of the female clan in the male zone of the mountains, his male identity is reasserted when interacting with the members of the bush. And, while all members of the female zone of the bush are inferior to their mountain counterparts, the bush's identity as female serves to transform the relations between bush clans, resulting in a different system than that which operates in the mountains. In the bush, the female clan is superior to the male clan, because of the bush's location in the regional system's female zone. Thus, houses of the female clan have ritual priority, and men in the male clan are inferior. A man in the male clan in the bush, therefore, is ranked below all other men throughout the entire system.

Reconsider, then, the original set of apparently homologous domains. Each domain, taken alone, is governed by the recursive logic of male and female as set out earlier. However, since the house and the community are hierarchically encompassed by larger units, the terms within each are, in certain contexts, transformed. Thus, a man has multiple identities—a male in one context, he is a female in another and a male again in yet another. A woman, too, has multiple identities—as a woman, as a man, and so on. It is only the male identities of men in the male clan in mountain communities that remain untransformed. However, for such men, there is an intensification of what it means to be male, for they are triply male, as it were—an intensification which has its own obviational logic.

Needless to say, these identity switches are not trivial. A person's clan and regional identities are every bit as important as his or her household identity. While household identities govern the everyday, clan and regional identities govern the two most important moments in a person's life—initiation and death. So, too, do clan and regional affiliations define a person's role in the eight calendrical ceremonies which govern the annual cycle.

Fractal (re)figurations

But how to understand, first, the self-similar fractal patterning which defines the diverse domains of Kabre mythical and social life, and, second, the set of transformations that occur as they become embedded within one another? I would like to suggest that the two—recursive self-similarity and symbolic revaluation—are linked, and to provide two answers as to why. The first is purely formal, the second more contingent and leads back to the question of history.

In formal terms, recursive self-similarity—the folding in of opposition upon opposition—would seem by the logic of recursiveness itself to demand extension into and obviation (Wagner 1978; 1986c) in a new and transformed set of terms. Thus, as each opposition provides the condition upon which its doubling occurs, each new bifurcation in turn becomes the (initiating) moment for the creation of a new, crosscut set of terms; and so on. So, too, with discrete levels or domains. As one, say a hierarchically-superior domain, comes to encompass another, a lower-ranked domain, it will lead, by the logic of recursiveness itself, to a reversal of the terms of the opposition. Put otherwise, if the logic of the tropic relation is recursive/bisecting, then fractal iteration ipso facto leads to a reversal and obviation of the original set of terms. One would expect, then, on purely logical grounds, an almost interminable fractal doubling and redoubling—and this is what occurs in the Kabre case.

While this formal explanation can account for the reversals that take place in different domains, and thus the switches in identity that accompany persons as they move from context to context, it does not account for the specific linkages—the hierarchy—that exists between domains. Here, I suggest, we need to resort to history. Indeed, symbolic operations like these always occur within history, a history that inevitably shapes, just as it is shaped by, them. For present purposes, I can merely suggest some of the ways in which I think this was the case for Kabre.

As mentioned above, slaving and the waves of migration it triggered were a central feature of the history of the Volta basin in the seventeenth, eighteenth and nineteenth centuries. Kabre—and other acephalous groups like the Tallensi, Dogon and LoDagaa—figured in this history as refuge areas, where migrants could find some protection. Thus, during this period, Kabre absorbed thousands, probably tens of thousands, of outsiders into their polity. They were absorbed, however, according to a very specific cultural logic. As outsiders, they were always assimilated to the category of "female"—either into the female zone at the base of the mountains, or into the female clan in mountain communities. This process still operates today. When outsiders enter the system, they become members of the female clan (for example, when people move from one community to the next; ten of the fifty-six households in the community of Kuwdé where I conducted research were from outside, often neighboring, communities). (If the male clan needs to recruit new members, it does so from the female clan of its own community, rather than recruiting members from an outside community.)

The practice of putting outsiders into the female clan or into female communities has a certain cultural logic to it, for women are the prototypical outsiders in the homesteads into which they marry, and in the communities they visit when they go to market. Indeed, one of the terms for a married woman—*ayado*—is derived from the verb *yapo*, "to buy," because, I was told, she comes into the homestead from the outside like a product one has bought in the market.

But the practice of putting newcomers into the female clan or region has a political logic as well, for the female clan/region is subordinate to the male. Thus, for example, the highest form of prestige which the system has to offer—performing the rituals that bring the rains, that make the crops grow, and that renew the relationship between Kabre and their spirits—is reserved for communities from the male mountain. And, within mountain communities, all of the most important of these ceremonies are organized by members of the male clan. Thus, assimilating outsiders to the status of "female" represented an act of encompassment and submission. Such, then, was the way in which Kabre culture, to appropriate a phrase from Sahlins (1981; 1985), structured historical practice.

But what about the other side of the coin? What was the effect on such a culture/structure of adding tens of thousands of outsiders into the system? I do not have the historical data to speak to this point with any certainty. Nevertheless, I want to speculate on, to imagine, what that effect might have been—given what we know about the system today.

As mentioned above, those outsiders who were added to the polity were added into its peripheral zone, into those plains communities identified as female and/or into the female clans of mountain communities. These are precisely the loci of greatest population concentration in the system today.[5]

Further, it is almost certainly because of such a high concentration of population in plains communities (combined with the fact that soils there are poorer and rainfall less) that members of these communities have developed various nonagricultural pursuits—especially marketing—and, thus, that the zone they inhabit is the most prosperous in the region. I risk tautology here, but it strikes me as reasonable to suggest that the symbolic categories and associations, the dualisms, at the heart of the Kabre system—male mountain/female bush, agriculture/marketing, ritual/wealth—are rooted in these historical practices and, thus, ultimately in the history of migrations which slave raiding engendered in the Volta basin. At the very least, these symbolic categories would have been recharged, and perhaps given new valences, by the historical changes of the slaving era.

There is another way, too, in which this history may have influenced Kabre culture. The increasing wealth of the periphery may have been responsible for the creation, and/or elaboration, of the regional ritual system in place today whereby mountain communities symbolically convert the wealth of plains communities into mountain community prestige. Such conversions annually reinscribe the hierarchies which govern the relationships between communities. Such hierarchy-assertion, and the elaborate ritual system to which it is tied, no doubt became all the more important to those in the mountains as the wealth of the periphery began to grow.

Finally, I would suggest that the multiple identities which members of this system possess may also be linked to this history. In so far as such identities are tied to various hierarchies (between male and female clans, and between male and female zones of the region), and in so far as these hierarchies emerge from (or at least are revalued by) this history, any attempt to account for the existence and importance of Kabre multiple identities must locate itself within this history, and in terms of those forces which promoted a Kabre preoccupation with the politics of identity.

It is through a political history of Kabre, then, that we are enabled to see the way in which the relations of clans trump those of the house, and of regions those of clans and houses—and, thus, the way in which politics and history account for the hierarchical embeddedness of domains and influence the particular nature and value of Kabre fractals.

Fractured figuration?

Now reconsider this symbolic order in terms of some of the insights of chaos/complexity theory. The latter insists that we pay attention not only to fractal patterning in (social) systems but also to those moments when such patterns break down—and chaotic nonlinear outcomes appear. In the Kabre case, such breakdown occurs at the edges of those vertical and horizontal—temporal and spatial—orders described above. Thus, those men and communities at the very top (and center) of Kabre hierarchical and regional orders—those who are "triply male"—are culturally anomalous in striking ways. The highest-ranking ritual figure (*cawcaw*) in the top-ranked Kabre community (*Farang*)—he who inaugurates the annual ritual cycle and brings the rain—is a strangely isolated, symbolically-ambiguous figure. Despite being a "man" in the most extreme (categorical) sense, he is forbidden from cultivating—like a female—and confined to the homestead for long periods. During some of the most important annual ceremonies, he is replaced by a young child who serves as master of ceremonies (and whom he must "respect"). Moreover, he has an uncommonly close tie to the lowest-ranked (bush) community in the entire system (Asiri). Thus, several myths describe his dependence on this (reputedly disrespectful and recalcitrant) "child," and account for why the highest-ranking community must wait for the lowest-ranking before inaugurating key moments in the mountain community ritual cycle.

Now one might see this closing of the circle—this codependent relationship between top and bottom (first and last, male and female, parent and child)—as little more than a further instantiation of the recursive logic described above. Thus, in a system organized around the value of gendered differences, and the work that such differences perform, it might appear logical that the most male of communities is paired with the most female. Is this not, perhaps, a model of the Kabre system writ large? But I don't think this is what's going on here. The dependence of this high-ranking ritual leader on the lowest-ranking Kabre community is less a wedding of opposites—of gendered complements—than the uniting of anomalies. Not only is the *cawcaw* a symbolically blurred figure but also Asiri, unlike other communities from the bush, is figuratively overdetermined. This lowest of the low not only *begins* ceremonies—a prerogative shared only with the highest of the high (*Farang*)—but also permits, and indeed encourages, women to dance in a ceremony (*doronto*)—the dance of death—that is everywhere else the exclusive prerogative of men. Were any but postmenopausal women to dance in any of the other communities, it is said, they would either give birth to monstrous children or become infertile.

And yet in Asiri, what is taboo elsewhere is openly encouraged. I wish to suggest here that the system's blurring of high and low (mountain and bush, male and female) represents something like the exhaustion or break-down of categories, and indeed of the Kabre system of fractals as such.

Moreover, it is also through this low-ranking "bush" community that the Kabre system intersects with that of its eastern neighbors—the Likpa of Benin (who in turn connect with groups farther to the east). Thus, the (eight) calendrical ceremonies (Piot 1999: 136-143) that cycle around the mountain communities descend to the plains community of Asiri, before being "thrown" to the Likpa (who then launch their own ceremonial cycle). I know little about the Likpa ceremonial complex, except what Kabre say—that it is related to theirs but different, an echo that both is and is not recognizable. Asiri, then, might be thought of as a type of symbolic operator or switch that not only marks but also enables the transformation of Kabre into Likpa.

Again, I do not have the data to show with any certainty that the entire region might be thought in such terms—with, for example, Dogon turning into Mossi, Mossi into Gourmantché, Gourmantché into Batammaliba, Batammaliba into Kabre, Kabre into Likpa. But there are myths through-out this area that suggest strong genealogical and cultural connections between these groups,[6] and there is everywhere an intimate connection between fractal figuration and the area's fraught history. It should not be surprising, then, to find a version of Kabre throughout—though also transformed in—the region beyond.

Conclusion

Chaos theory, by training a powerful light on specific domains of cultural life, helps resolve certain anomalies in the Kabre socio-symbolic material. To wit, it enables us to identify and come to terms with symbolic orders that more conventional symbolic/structuralist paradigms are ill-equipped to handle. It also forces us to explore and attempt to theorize (in a way that other paradigms have not) issues of scale—for instance, the existence of diverse domains of self-similar fractals that are central not only to Kabre but also to many other sociocultural worlds *and* their breakdown (into nonlinearity).

But the Kabre material forces us in the opposite direction as well—to a further questioning and refinement of key components of chaos theory itself. Namely, by enabling us to begin to theorize the *linkages* between nonlinear logics and fractal self-similarity, it pushes us to explore features of complexity theory that are often seen as distinct. Moreover, the Kabre material moves us beyond the rarefied air of the merely symbolic and log-ical into the contingent realm of politics and history. As symbolic systems realize themselves in specific histories, they may attempt to shape contingency according to their own logic—and no doubt often succeed. But just as often they will be called on to compromise and made to conform to history's often-quixotic and always-political mandates and processes.

Notes

1. I follow both Wagner (1991) and Mosko (1991a) in their use of the term "recursive."
2. The Kabre, and other peoples of northern Togo, are drawn into the wider political economy in other ways, primarily as migrants to areas of southern Togo where they engage in cash-cropping, and, increasingly during the post-Cold War period, through their interaction with those horizontally-linked global institutions—the new NGOs, the human rights organizations, global Pentecostalism—that characterize the landscape of the new world order (Hardt and Negri 2000).
3. See also Rattray (1932), Goody (1956), and Blier (1987) for other examples of Voltaic dual clan systems.
4. Contemporary Kabre remember this moment with uncommon specificity. Elders, for instance, are able to point to houses in the community where "sister's children" were sold as slaves, to homesteads in "bush" communities where mountain slaves were gathered, and to markets where these children were sold to middlemen who funneled them into the Atlantic slave system. As well, Kabre oral tradition is replete with references to slave raids by Samasi, a kingdom in northern Benin, and the ceremonial complex is thick with figurative allusion to the time of slaving (Piot 1999: 89, 143-145).
5. The population of plains communities is much higher than that of mountain communities, despite the fact that the mountains were where the first people settled. So, too, the numbers of people in the female clans of mountain communities are significantly higher than those in the male clans (often 2-3 times higher).
6. For one such example, see Fiske (1991: 346-347).

4

"PITY" AND "ECSTASY"
The Problem of Order and Differentiated Difference Across Kula Societies

Frederick H. Damon

'System of exchange' sounds like something out of a car gear-box manual. At stake, however, are the greatest human passions, the very nature of being a person, and the strange intimacies that giving establishes between things and personhood (Taussig 1993: 92).

I have noticed that Anglo-Saxon writers sometimes misunderstand the writings of Claude Lévi-Strauss for precisely this reason. They say he emphasizes too much the intellect and ignores the 'feelings.' The truth is that he assumes the heart has precise algorithms.... These algorithms of the heart ... are, however, coded and organized in a manner totally different from the algorithms of language (Bateson 1972: 139).

Introduction

The Problem

Although Goodenough Island culture does not now participate in the Kula, Michael Young's magisterial *Magicians of Manumanua: Living Myth in Kalauna* supplies us with a great moment of Kula Ring ethnography. The location of his study, Kalauna, is a peculiarly prominent village perched on Goodenough's mountainside (see Figure 4.1). Young is setting up his discussion of biographical myths of eminent elders of the leading clan with respect to the culture's paramount form of action, *unuwewe*, glossed as "victimage," "the basis of an indigenous theory of social action" (Young 1983b: 40). In Young's understanding, *unuwewe* is "self castigation [that] becomes an indulgence adrift from the moral ends of redress and restoration. It connotes intransigent and willful destructiveness—the destruction of others by means of self destruction" (ibid.: 73). According to Young, *unuwewe* is "institutionalized in two principal modes; a projective system of vengeance, homicide, and sorcery, and an introjective system of self-castigation. Although these types of victimage may sometimes appear in pure form as vicarious sacrifice and self-sacrifice respectively, they are often found in combination. The mythology is replete with heroic victims, and Kalauna people seem to read their own history in terms of the complex interplay of these themes of victimage" (ibid.: 29). Shortly after these words Young writes:

> Whether the relatively closed sphere of Kalauna thought could articulate conceptions of tragedy is a moot point (I know of no term for it), but I would claim that the affective dispositions are incontestably present. I observed, for example, that Kalauna men sometimes wept "for pity" (*nuavita*), not when they narrated myths, but when I played back their tape-recorded narrations for them to hear. They apprehended tragedy in the mirrored form of the playback. Such, in essence, is theater (ibid.: 32).

"Apprehended tragedy in mirrored playback," these are the words that reverberated through my mind when I first considered Young's account. For they were oddly like one of my first vivid experiences in fieldwork among Muyuw people, who anchor the northeast corner of the Kula Ring some 250 km northeast of Goodenough. Involving one of my best instructors, Aisi, it was in 1973 or early 1974 after I knew the Muyuw language well enough to follow Kula talk. Shortly after what appeared to be an intense, heated debate and then a classically angry "throwing" of a valuable, we started walking back to Aisi's village. We passed down a beach, the sun setting off in the west, his young daughter skipping in tow. I was keeping up with both of them, but Aisi was really somewhere else. He spoke of giving away the valuable to his partner, Gideon, and how in the coming days it would be off—literally, by airplane!—to the Trobriands, to Gideon's elder brother, God. God would then give it to Vanoi, the paramount chief in Omarakana.[1] In his mind he followed the valuable along this agreed upon path. It wasn't long before Aisi was not so much walking as dancing. As he rehearsed the movement of the armshell he became "ecstatic." *Mwan won*[2] is the Muyuw word for this "emotion." It is an expression I've only heard in the context of the Kula, and usually is used to describe one's self after one has "thrown" a Kula valuable to a partner. Kula exchanges are sacrifices. One throws down a valuable and with it one's name "falls," although one's partner's name rises. This is sacrificial because, first, what one wants is a high name, and the 'first' act of the Kula diminishes it. Kula action depletes one physically, the fact represented in the fast aging of very successful Kula actors. However, when the first recipient next throws the valuable, his name falls, his partner's rises, and with the rise of the third person's name the first person's goes up. As I have noted elsewhere (1983b; 2002), success in the Kula is understood by one being "seen," "known" on distant islands. Visualizing the movement of valuables, which serious Kula participants do fanatically, is tantamount to watching one's resurrection. And the image of Aisi's name climbing along that list of names that evening made him soar.

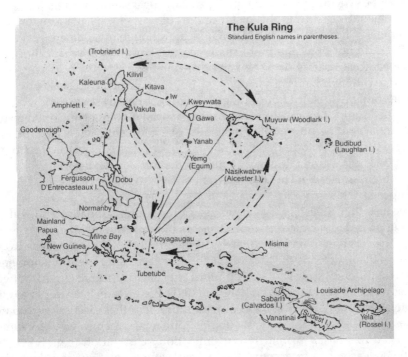

Figure 4.1: The Kula Ring

These data are indigenous models for social action, the one reposing pitiful tears in the apprehended tragedies of its results, the other, practically contiguous if juxtaposed to the first, much the opposite. Goodenough is peripheral to the Kula, the institution festering in Young's description of the culture (e.g., 1971; 1983a; 1983c). For Muyuw, of course, the Kula is central. And the inverse of Goodenough "self pity" is, in Muyuw, the "ecstasy," the near unutterable joy, its participants experience. Both Goodenough self pity and Muyuw ecstasy involve self-sacrifice. In the former, through a virtual negation of reciprocity, one destroys one's self to destroy others in one's own society, while in the latter one builds up another by destroying an aspect of a self by means of relations with and through others. Understanding these *forms*, what they are, not their origin is, of course, a multifaceted project. And there is no substitute for one of those facets being the close description of what Young understands to be "a small ... self-sufficient, and relatively isolated community like Kalauna," (ibid. p. 32). I suggest, however, that a larger and different frame of reference must complement that approach, because we do not understand all of the heart's reasons, nor exactly where they are located in the consciences that constitute social existence.

This chapter is an experiment. I suggest that ideas drawn from chaos theory and Lévi-Strauss's canonic formula for the study of myth can help describe synchronic variation in the zigzagging systems of order that exist in regional systems, in this instance the cultures of the Kula Ring area in Milne Bay Province, Papua New Guinea. Although my data are very specific, I do not think the problems I face are. Variation in what otherwise appear to be orderly data sets can be seen in many of the world's regions, and in different kinds of phenomena, both social and ecological/physical (e.g., Shugart 1998). Anthropologists have customarily done their work in single locations to transcend the limits of social models bequeathed us by the nineteenth century. Yet at this dawn of a new century it is past time to reconfigure how to understand the macro-collective orders in which all social action figures. It is very unlikely that any of our informants' lives were circumscribed by the spatial confines our fieldwork traditions imposed. This is not just because many of them move around. It is also because their lives are and have been drawn by regional relations that long preceded the modern world system of European making.

The essay unfolds in two parts. In the first I draw on two ideas from chaos theory. One is the idea of fractals, that across different phenomena and at different scales the same pattern appears to repeat itself.[3] Although this concept, beginning with Wagner (1991), has already been deployed in Melanesian anthropology, I deal with a problem that discussion to date has not faced: that the patterns do not quite repeat themselves. Modeling procedures based primarily on replication or imitation (e.g., Sornette 2003) clearly cannot account for the part/whole relations in which the social lives we examine exist.[4] This brings me to the second issue, the idea that from little differences big changes may result—known in the chaos sciences as "extreme sensitivity to initial conditions"—the essence of nonlinearity. I shall note how this fact may lead to the question of "phase changes," an apparent randomness that appears during the transformation of one state to another. The idea of little changes turning into major differences brings me to the issue of "strange attractors," and Lévi-Strauss's canonic formula for the study of myth, and my second part. I present Lévi-Strauss's formula as a way of operationalizing chaos theory for the kinds of data best suited to the traditions of social anthropology. For the special "twist" to the formulae gives it the likeness of a nonlinear relation (See Mosko Introduction, this volume; Maranda 2001).

For present purposes, a short biography of my thinking might be most useful for introducing what kinds of issues and data I think are most important for us to analyze, what I am doing with this material, and how this work may be extended in the future. A central question here is "what is a 'strange attractor'?" And what might this idea add to received ideas about culture, structure, and pattern?[5]

I finished my book, *From Muyuw To The Trobriands: Transformations along the Northern Side of the Kula Ring* (1990) just as Gleick's discussion of chaos theory was popularizing its essential ideas (Gleick 1987). I attempted to show that the differences across the northern side of the Kula Ring could be described in terms of a synchronic transformation between diametric and concentric forms. "Diametric" and "concentric" are concepts I took from Lévi-Strauss's article "Do Dual Organizations Exist?" (1963a). Such ideas are abstractions for indigenous spatial constructions that some-times—and do in the cases with which I am concerned—consciously model social action. For Lévi-Strauss a "diametric" form encased an ideal of equivalence among the social units represented in a spatial form. In the conventional understanding, virtually all concentric forms model hierarchy of one kind or another. This implies an asymmetrical relationship.

For Lévi-Strauss these ideas were used to talk about relationships among different aspects of the same societies. In the conventional sense of society, I used them to talk about differential dominance among contiguous soci-eties. Diametric forms—in houses, villages, and gardens laid out along east to west axes, symmetrical exchange relations located among clans defined by egalitarian relationships—were clearly dominant in Muyuw, although I could show there was an undercurrent of concentricity. Drawing on the existing Trobriand ethnography, I argued that the opposite holds there: dia-metric relations are undercurrents to a dominant concentricity. In the Tro-briands center/periphery models govern the relationship between villages and gardens, and an overt and extremely visible hierarchy governs the vast majority of Trobriand relations (Damon 1990: chapters 5 and 6).

Although I was, and remain, confident that the general lines of my argu-ment are correct, two issues were of immediate concern, and these are what brought me to the issues of this essay. First, these two areas are very similar. The languages are near 80 percent cognate. They share almost identical kinship terms. Clan and subclan terms are identical, though not relationships between these units, and there is a peculiar doubling of clans, from four to eight, in the passage from the Trobriands to Muyuw. In spite of these overt similarities, the basic forms of Muyuw culture are very dif-ferent than those in the Trobriands. However, and this was the issue, fur-ther reading and my own subsequent travels across the northern side of the Massim demonstrated that there is a continuous series of changes from eastern Muyuw to the Trobriands. This is evident not just to the analyst; it is also a matter of common experience among many of the people on these islands. An accurate description of this social system must show continu-ous transformation, ordered variation. Second, while it eventually became relatively easy for me to see how a Muyuw practice could be logically transformed into a different Trobriand reality, I could not devise a way of figuring how either the Trobriand or Muyuw cases could be transformed into the patterns that typified the cultural constellations of the southern Kula Ring. It would not suffice to say that since the two sides represent different branches of the Austronesian language family the cultural discontinuities are as easily explained by historical discontinuity as the similarities in the north are explained by historical continuity. This argument cannot work because just as there is continuous interaction along the northern side of the Kula Ring, so there is continuous interaction between the north and south. Without in the least denying the historicity of this area, regional differences were, and are, being produced and reproduced: arguably they are a systemic property, not an external history. This is a common feature of Melanesian societies, if not all regional systems. The question then is not so much are they related—they are— but how do we manipulate our own analytical models to devise ways of ferreting out the nature of the relationships? What constellation of features generates difference?

For me the first step out of this apparent impasse came from considering Mark Mosko's essay on the canonic formula (Mosko 1991a). Although I find the infamous "twist" precisely what I need to generate variation, Mosko's argument and handling of various kinds of Mekeo data made the formula relevant to something other than the analysis of myth. And it promised a more rigorous way of moving among contiguous domains. With it I hoped I could dispense with, or transcend, the intuitive grasping for relations that governed the analysis in my book. Of Lévi-Strauss's formulae, Hage and Harary write "lacking precise definition, it remains a tool of rhetoric, not of analysis" (1983: 131). Mosko's article made it a tool, for me at least.

The next critical steps for me entailed interacting with Dr. Jack Morava, Professor of algebraic topology and mathematical physics at Johns Hopkins University and Dr. H. Hank Shugart, a forest ecologist at the University of Virginia who specializes in modeling procedures. Both of these scholars practice a kind of rigor, if with very different data, that is quite foreign to much of social anthropology. Yet it seems to me a dialogue with others is precisely how our discipline is organized, and what we need. Moreover, the facts of my case suggest this is not a matter of anthropology trying to be like mathematics or thinking that by virtue of being able to run a computer program that provides some (usually aesthetically distasteful) simulacrum we have explained something. The point rather derives from the overwhelming ethnographic experience I have had in the Kula area that suggests that people there have very well formed totalizing models, that these models change regularly from place to place, and that these changes are known as well as created. In short, while this paper is trying to use new ideas, some new theories about the order in complex phenomena, it is driven by a gap between my ethnographic experience and the ideas contemporary anthropology has to account for that experience.

Although our relationship is the youngest, I note my interaction with Shugart first. During the first of our shared seminars I spent one evening trying to convince an extremely skeptical audience of undergraduate anthropology majors that I could use my versions of Lévi-Strauss's canonical formula to transform the logical relations of one place into those of another. To a particular rendering of Lévi-Strauss's combination of "terms" and "relations," for example $F_x(a)$ in the formula $F_x(a) : F_y(b)$ $F_x(b) : F_{a-1}(y)$, Shugart said the expression was a "strange attractor." Although "strange attractor" is not the easiest thing to find defined in the literature, by most definitions Shugart was correct.[6] The sense I give to this concept for my present ethnographic concerns should be evident below. For my purposes here, Shugart's statement means that Lévi-Strauss's formula is a hypothesis about relationships between strange attractors.

The critical encounter with Morava began one afternoon as we both went over Mosko's article and Lévi-Strauss's formula. Morava deals in knot theory—a world of twenty-plus dimensions—yet is literate in ethnography. He does not think anthropology needs mathematics to deal with its descriptive problems, and he readily tosses scathing humor at the social sciences that mimic their idea of the more mathematical sciences.

Morava *then* stated that the formula did not make sense from a mathematical point of view. Nevertheless, he allowed that it could still be useful. As a mathematician, Morava continued, he was used to dealing with nonsensical formulas from brilliant people that, eventually, lead to real insight.[7] So he turned the formula into a proportion, we started plugging in ideas that I thought were useful abstractions from my book, and by the end of the afternoon I thought I had finally figured out how I could pass from the northern to the southern side of the Kula Ring. The "twist"— $F_{a-1}(y)$,—in the formula's right-hand side doubles the pattern of differentiation the left-hand side juxtaposes. This seemed like a suggestive beginning. Formal relationships in nearby cultures that did not seem related to each other now seemed relatable—because the canonic formula transformed my limits on ideas about "relation" and "order." And this is what we need from theory.

I. The limits of Self-Similarity

"Fractal" characterizes a process that somehow produces the same pattern through different levels of reality, "on finer and finer scales" (Gleick 1987: 100). I sketch two perturbing examples here.

The first case concerns Muyuw views of exchange spheres, described in greater detail elsewhere (Damon 1983b: see especially Figure 1 [p. 311]). There are two complementary sets of these, descending from the Kula exchange on the one hand, and the one that concerns us here, containing what I call Muyuw kinship. These are formal models, part of a conscious order, the kinship form effectively part of the aforementioned diametric order. In Dumont's usage (1985), the construction is the culture's encompassing value.

The prototype and most encompassing of the ranked set of exchange spheres entails the exchange of women (and men) among four clans. An intersection of east-west and north-south garden paths provides Muyuw with their formal model of the device. Muyuw people see this model every time they walk into their gardens; I have had people write it in the sand for me when I asked what clans are or what "marriage" is. The form shapes actual practice in subtle ways.

People say the exchange of pigs at mortuary ceremonies follows the same logic. In fact, the form of these mortuary rites—*anagin tavalam*—is perceived to be embedded in the shape the garden model defines (see Damon 1989 and 1990: chapter 4 for details). A pig of a certain size and sex that people of the "east" clan (Malas) give to people of the "west" clan (Kubay) must later be returned, size and sex remaining constant, in very specific contexts. There are several exchange spheres scaled below this one, and informants say all replicate the relations defined as fundamental in the highest sphere. For "this," "that" must be returned. The scales of these lower spheres are different. The bottom sphere concerns betel nut and betel pepper, and everybody knows exchanges of women on the one hand and pigs on the other are vastly more significant than the exchange of betel nut. So the same pattern is perceived to hold through different scales.

In Young's terms these ideas constitute an indigenous theory of social action. They specify *relations* between formally prescribed social units. Provisionally at least, they are the relations in the relation/term coupling of one of the functions in Lévi-Strauss's canonic formula. It was this pattern, which I assimilated to one of Lévi-Strauss's term/relations combinations, to which Shugart said, "that is a strange attractor." And there is no question that this model governs a great deal of Muyuw culture. For example, after many attempts, in the late 1970s my best informant in southeastern Muyuw succeeded in marrying a child, his son Dibolel, to a woman from Mwadau village in far western Muyuw. The man, Dibolel, is of the Kubay clan, the woman from Sinawiy. Some time in the late 1980s or early 1990s a young man and woman themselves arranged a return on this marriage, a Sinawiy woman from the southeast going to the west to marry a Kubay man. Elders denied they enforced the marriage, although they approved it. Rather, the couple figured they were making a return. The makeup of every village on the island derives from a very complex working out of the operations of this form. It may begin from what would appear to be random decision[8]—a man forges a unique marriage—yet results in the application of what is effectively a determinant structure— the symmetrical exchange of persons among clans. Yet while the rule, the model of marriage, remains constant across the island, every village takes a different shape in terms of its constituent marriages.

In any case, the perceived redundancy is true only from one point of view. The top two spheres separate genders—of persons and pigs—so like exchanges for like. The next lower sphere preserves gender separation.[9] However, male items are exchanged for female items, and vice versa. It might be said that the "north" clan gives male objects and receives female ones; the south clan gives female and receives male values. Rather than exchange preserving gender separation, gendered entities take each other's place (and facilitate determined activities). One instance of this exchange sphere serves to define a married couple as actually married, and at their concrete level they are not really thought to be exchanged at all. Rather, they combine their gender identities and labors (after having been separated from their opposite-sexed siblings). Neither a brother nor a father would allow that he exchanged his sister or daughter. Moreover, the marriage of persons follows from the lowest exchange sphere, one concerned with betel nut and betel pepper. In this one too the modality of the transaction shifts: in the top spheres like takes the place of like; in the middle ones unlikes (by gender designation) replace each other; in the lowest sphere differences are combined (in the mouth). Consequently, inside the model of encased similarity is a set of substantive differences, in a sense the encompassed contrary of Dumont's terminology (ibid.). With some degree of coherency, principles—for example, genders separated versus trading places versus combined—shift as one changes positions in a system of positions. Although one view of the system is that principles of the top are reflected throughout a series of lower-level relationships, established differences rather than self-similarity organize the set of relations as a totality.

We can see the same phenomenon, only at a more encompassing scale, shifting to another set of ordering principles. These are in fact the culture's most comprehensive "design for living," to use a phrase from Benedict. They are the *terms* by which Muyuw define themselves.

Although I am repeating descriptions produced in earlier publications, I am adding materials I learned from returns between 1991 and 2002.

Let me begin with a Muyuw net. These products are, first of all, extremely complicated creations classed and used in a number of different ways all related to their obvious function as means of production. They are likened to bodies (female ones in particular) with a "throat" (*kayon*), "navel"(*pwason*), and "feet/legs"(*kakein*). Left and right sides are distinguished (*simugwey* and *sinoyem* respectively). The central half of the net, formally the whole *daban* ("forehead") area, divided by the "navel," is considered the "basis" (*wowun*) of the net, a distinction to which I return. The net's identity as feminine makes it explicitly part of a ramified order in which what is at issue is the proper combination needed to make things productive. So prototypically Muyuw distinguish two kinds of yams, *kuv*, which are male, and *parawog*, which are female. In order to grow best they should be planted next to one another so their differential properties—

merely growing up, to the right and fast versus growing many, to the left and slow respectively—are combined. Nets follow this model, being feminine, slow, but very productive when they are combined with the moving male energy of human males and their boats. The combinatory properties of both yams and nets are understood to be miniature replicas of the ways men and women should combine their productive capacities. So far as Muyuw are concerned, the productive order of things follows that of the encompassing productive order of persons.

There is another way in which Muyuw encompass nets in larger understandings. After it is used the net must be hung up to dry before it can be stashed away in the corner of a house. Stakes are set out in a row; the net is folded in half, and staked up so the weights are at the bottom, the floats at the top. If done correctly the "basis" of the net should be to the east, the ends to the west. I did not know this when I published my diagram and description of the Muyuw net (Damon 1990: Appendix 5). However, in 1996 looking through my book several eastern Muyuw friends told me that this orientation was normative, and—I knew and they told me—that order replicated the ideal order of a village layout. It is to this form I now turn.

Although not every village conforms to the pattern and although some say that there are two patterns, basically one formed and the other haphazard, many Muyuw people say that villages should be organized in two east to west rows of houses. This means that the front and back of each house should face north or south. People figure this order with respect to sunrise and sunset. The rows should replicate the direction of the movement of the sun over the day, the sun jumping over the north/south ridgetop of each house. The eastern end of the village is formally called the *kalatatan*, the western end the *kalamatan*. *Tatan* is the word used for what we would call the stalk of a taro plant. Thus, the word refers to something like "trunk," or "support." And a village's *kalatatan* is considered the "basis" (*wowun*) of the structure, because the sun rises first in the east. *Matan* has a range of meanings, the critical one here "point" or "end." This order is thought to be necessary for proper production. If villages are not constructed this way, or houses should be oriented otherwise, one's crops would not do well, according to the ideology. Social precedence is not attached to any village location. Although every village has some person and usually group—subclan—considered to be most important, that importance, unlike in the Trobriands, or even Goodenough, is not considered to be part of the culture's fundamental order.

Although everybody can reproduce the above description, not everyone was insistent about its relationship to productive conditions. However, everyone is—now (1995-2002) there are some exceptions among younger people—insistent that the basic garden structure, which is analogous to the village, is a condition for production. Muyuw gardens have to be laid out as squares or rectangles with at least one east to west and one north to south path. The four or more sections created by these paths are internally divided east to west, creating smaller units of the garden which figure as production and exchange divisions prototypically concerned with brother/sister relations (and the exchange sphere called *takon*). Their function as exchange units fits within the encompassing clan/marriage model, mentioned above, deduced from the intersection of the east/west and north/south paths. This structure is far and away the culture's most complicated ordering of and model for social relations. Complete descriptions of this order, and some of the variation I do not detail below, can be found elsewhere (Damon 1990: chapter 5). For here suffice it to note that the eastern end of a garden is referred to as the *wowun*, "basis," and the western side the *matan*, or point. Most gardens have two or more north to south paths, and thus a difference is created among the intersections. The eastern-most is called the *pwason*, again "navel." These are the same terms and relations found in the drying layout for nets and for villages, and people are cognizant of these correspondences. Although some people say that one formally goes to and from a village to a garden on a path that ideally corresponds to the garden's north/south path, this direction is not orienting for the garden. The garden is parallel to but separate from the village.

Most people also understand the eastern end of the island to be the island's "basis," and the western end the "point," an orientation also derived from the east-to-west passage of the sun. The only social significance of this island-wide orientation I could discover is that Muyuw New Year celebrations should begin in the east and go to the west village by village. So it is known and easily inferred that the island is laid out in a way that gardens and village replicate.

So, fishing nets, villages, gardens, and the island as a whole are all understood by virtue of the same terms formed in near identical fashion.

In 1996 I learned that another instance of this structure may exist, or have existed, between the level of the village and the island as a whole. I was talking with a member of a village I have previously pronounced and written as Unamatan. This is the western-most village along the island's southeastern shoreline. Previously I had not considered the name of any significance, but while talking that day my pronunciation was corrected. The pronunciation is Unmatan. *Un* is a noun-classifier for the noun meaning "village" (*ven*), and as is often the case the noun is dropped and just the classifier is used in speech. So you can say *Unaboug* for an "old (*boug*) village," or *unavaw* for a "new (*vaw*) village." It follows that Unmatan refers to "a village at the point or end" of a line. I then asked this informant, and later others, if this name implied a line of villages and if other village names would take their place along the line. The answer was yes to both questions. Although the eastern-most settled area along the southeastern side of the island is usually called Guasopa—the Government center, school area, and airstrip location—it is often referred to as "Obwilim," a word which means "to" or "at" the "east." One of the next old villages moving to the west is called Wayavat, which means "to the west." Thus the major village site names along this shoreline take their sense from a position on a line.[10]

Once I realized the name of this village implied an organized row I wondered if it was one of two rows, and so half of a structure like that found in an ideal village.

To understand this you must realize that the southeastern sector of the island is a miniature version of the whole. It is basically a rectangle with slightly rounded east and west sides, uplifted so that the northern side, of some fourteen kilometers, rises about thirty meters above sea level while the southern side sinks below the water (forming a lagoon bounded by several small islands). From the historical record and all of my experience on the island I had been aware of a set of villages along the northeastern sector of the rise. This is a region called Kweyakwoya (cf. Damon 1990 s.v.), and it once was prominent because it was the location of the island's traditional carvers and fiercest warriors. By 1995 I had learned, mostly because the archaeology graduate student (and now Dr.) Simon Bickler was accompanying me, that there was an old village site along this northern ridge directly north of Wabunun. This is an area people called Simgwayas, which turns out to be their name for the "mountain," ridgetop really, that runs along the whole east-to-west side of this platform. To the east of "Simgwayas" the area is known by many names, Kweyakwoya and Sinamat among many others, that are generic and specific village sites, abandoned within the last 100 years. They remain a living presence by virtue of their secondary forest growth. West of the area north of Wabunun there are no individuating names and no current recognition of villages. I had no reason to expect any to be there because I had conducted three tree surveys north of the shoreline villages and within those survey sites there was little evidence of occupation (Bickler surveyed around and within my sites, each about a hectare, and likewise found no evidence of former occupation). However, as soon as I realized Unmatan referred to a line of villages it occurred to me that it may be a *southern* line, and another one might have existed from Kweyakwoya, where I knew there were villages, to the western end of Simgwayas. Virtually the next day I went to the western end of Simgwayas, and sure enough there was evidence— potshards and clamshells—of former occupation. Such scattered evidence could be found clumped here and there east to the region Bickler had already investigated. Moreover, in the region north of Wabunun I found a small megalithic ruin vaguely reminiscent of those known in North Central Muyuw. Bickler then returned to this area and found another.[11]

Finding the old village sites confirmed the possibility of there once having been two rows of villages like there should be two rows of houses. Two interesting things then happened when I explored this possibility, and its further implications across the island, with four sets of people.

First, although this is not a structure in any current person's memory, people in southeastern and North Central Muyuw said "of course" to the idea that the arrangement of villages in various parts of the island replicated the arrangement of houses in a village. In North Central Muyuw the model gains veracity because a new set of communities (Lidau) organized along the northern uplift west of Dikwayas are found to be over ground in which evidence of old villages is common. All previous maps, including my own, have featured only two villages on the north coast, Dikwayas and Kaulay. Now it is clear there were others, at least to the west. Those villages then would parallel a series of villages that did or do lie along the southern shoreline. As is the case in the southeastern sector, nothing is known to be in the central and western middle area, and in one surveyed hectare there was no evidence of any human occupation.[12] Second, I received a different reaction when I brought up this model with two elders, and their associates, in Western Muyuw. One, the son of one of the more amazing people I have ever met on the island (See Damon 1990: 17-18), reacted angrily to my newly created model of the island. Several times he had told me—or mailed me—stories of the island like I had heard from his father and others—that before the Europeans arrived, there was only chaos and warfare. When I gave him my model he immediately recognized that it implied, given all the observable realities of his lifetime, a quite extraordinary population and formally ordered distribution of the population over the island. That so violated what he thought that he started shouting about how it could not be true.[13] The reaction of the other group, people from Mwadau village, was more measured, yet also different from those to the east. I first described Mwadau as it had been in 1975, and as I had illustrated in my book. Then I went into my new model asking if villages on Mwadau Island had been so organized. I was then told that the "Mwadau" I had produced in my book was largely a product of Government insistence that houses be ordered in a line. That, by contrast, the pattern on Mwadau Island—a part of Muyuw formally called Nayem—should be more like what is found on Gawa, Kweywata, and Iwa Islands to the west. There, my informants stated, houses tend to be scattered into smaller hamlets or clusters and are not ordered into straight lines. "Mwadau village" in fact is taking this "old" appearance now. Only a half dozen or so houses line up in the way I described them from 1975; instead clusters are forming in the nearby vicinity.

When I heard these Mwadau facts (June 1996) I had a comparative ability to explore them in detail. The previous January and February I traveled across the northern side of the Kula Ring spending up to ten days each on Kitava, Iwa, and Gawa Islands. The organization of houses, villages, and gardens on these islands, especially on Iwa and Gawa, is very different from Muyuw's. The most obvious differences were the apparently chaotic layouts of houses, the intermixing of gardens and houses, and the placement of yam houses next to or in front of peoples' houses as virtually permanent structures. I often took compass readings of alignments as well as asked people how things were supposed to be. I discussed the idea of "pattern" or "model" with the word, *kikun*, which can be translated as "follow" or "principle," in the sense of guide. There was no discoverable pattern—"*kikun*"—to the house alignments on either Iwa or Gawa, and my informants—including several people who had resided in Muyuw for some time or who had close Muyuw Kula partners—denied there was supposed to be any pattern. They were fully aware of the Muyuw arrangement, insisting that their places were different.

As it turns out, however, these are among a number of little differences.

When my Mwadau village sources said their model was not like the rest of Muyuw, but rather more like Gawa and Iwa, I inquired if, also, houses need not be oriented to the sun. Here they demurred. Although houses need not be organized in east to west rows, they should be set out so that the fronts and backs of the houses pointed north or south. Because there is an appearance—to an outsider—of a random order and no series of straight paths connecting the various hamlets that now compose the Mwadau village area, it was not obvious to me how its many houses in fact preserved this order. However, different people easily specified which way was east, which way west, and how their houses (and yam houses) fit the paradigmatic model. And as I had previously noted, yam houses were to be behind their houses, more or less in the "village" setting rather than in the garden. So Mwadau did indeed look more like Gawa and Iwa than, say, Wabunun or Kaulay, and this is an intentional look. Yet it also diverged from the former while taking on the form of the latter in ways that people from both areas could specify: Iwa and Gawa people denied that their house and yam house orientations were guided to the external directionalities that are the Muyuw order.

It would appear, then, that my two Western Muyuw informants denied the "fractality" of the model I was finding back to the east because in fact their reality is slightly different, the one informant using an image of absolute anarchy as a replacement, the other drawing on what he perceived to be as the normative order the relatively unordered Gawa. Yet these differences are, perhaps "fractally," reproduced through a number of different phenomena.

Variation is fixed in the awareness of different collective representations/activities inside the relations that compose this set of island cultures. Northeastern Kula Ring people know that different regions identify with a different kind of wood that takes precedence in their respective sets of affinal obligations. Newly married women should carry this wood to their husband's brothers, sisters, and mothers and fathers. Husbands should carry it to their wife's relatives when the latter put on a significant mortuary ritual. All of these trees are considered excellent firewood, but they describe differential properties that are understood to match attributes of the social group using them. The class constitutes ritual firewood. Unlike clan or subclan totems that just mark differences, this totemic-like system specifies the locational properties of a group as it differentiates it from others. So, much of eastern Muyuw considers itself an area that customarily gardens in early fallow gardens, a special class of forest known throughout this area as, in the Muyuw spelling, *digadag*. The tree most of these people use as ritual firewood is found in these areas.[14] Gawa's tree is one that grows along the shore and that is extremely dense and heavy. It marks the difficulty of a people whose lives are tied to the sea—by canoe production—yet who live some 150 meters above the sea on a disc-like platform reachable only after climbing up two steep cliffs: young women climb the cliffs with the heavy loads of wood balanced on their heads.[15] To repeat here, empirical properties of trees are being used to represent differentiated relations among groups. The tree types formally mark differences between units and function as models that effectively prescribe behavior.

These kinds of differences accompany gradual transformations across these islands. Mwadau Island houses have to be ordered in relations to the sun as elsewhere in Muyuw. But Mwadau gardens vary by exactly 90°. The path that goes east to west elsewhere on the island has to go north to south on Mwadau. The orientation is not to the sun, but rather to the movement of the Creator, who took a north/south detour up and down Mwadau Island during his travels (see Damon 1990: 144). However, the sun does figure in these gardens, for a morning sun and afternoon sun are supposed to bounce off the cheeks of the piles of rocks used to mark the gardens' intersection points. It is to be noted that what is becoming important here is not the sun's movement, but a time change with respect to the sun, morning and afternoon.

Gardens are not the models for social relations in Gawa that they are in Muyuw, so Munn (1986) does not provide the kind of data about Gawa gardens that are required for Muyuw. Yet she notes that it is held that

> Tudava/Gerew [the Creator, as in Muyuw] established the Gawan garden layout that requires the orientation of stones and garden plot dividers (or paths) so that the sun always travels across them diagonally rather than coinciding with the paths. Without this ancestrally fixed orientation, the garden will die because if the sun travels along the garden paths (plot dividers) its "eye" will be "closed" (Munn 1986: 83).

This description, and personal communication with Munn, led me to think that Gawan gardens were set at about a 45° angle off from the Muyuw garden. I was then surprised to be told by different Gawa people in 1995 and 1996 that Gawan gardens had small subdividers called *lapuiy*. This is the same term as found in Muyuw, and that, as in Muyuw, they were supposed to go east to west, an order set by the Creator as in Munn's description (unlike in Muyuw, in Gawa they also go north/south, thus forming small squares). Although identical to the order in eastern and central Muyuw, this is unlike that in Western Muyuw, where *lapuiy* are coordinated with the aforementioned 90° shift. However, Gawans told me that the perimeters of a garden do correspond to the directions Munn specified. They have to follow lines Gawans call *takulumwala*. These ideally crisscross northeast to southwest and southeast to northwest. Ideally one of these corresponds to a *wowun/dabwen* distinction along which is the main axis bisecting the island.[16] The impression Gawans gave me is that *takulumwala* begin from standing rocks scattered about the island's perimeter, isolated or sets of stones called *vadayi*. At least three of these sets, toward the southeastern end of the island, are megalithic ruins on the same order as those found in Muyuw, Iwa, Kitava, and the Trobriands. However, people told me these *vadayi* can be found in many places. In any case, I took compass readings of a number of garden orientations, and the garden perimeters were on the order of 40° - 220° and 130° - 310°, thus more or less corresponding to the expressed Gawan order. I did not learn of any way that these forms are supposed to be related to houses or villages, and given what I was told, there is no necessary order to village or house orientations.[17] Gawans told me their houses used to be more spread out than they have been recently, and so they would be more intermixed with their gardens. Moreover, Gawan spaces, villages and gardens, are full of breadfruit and other trees of substantial productive use.[18] I do not believe there is a major distinction between village and garden land spaces. So while it is accurate to say that Muyuw villages and gardens are in two parallel planes, the order in Gawa, and Iwa, is all mixed up.

The minor empirical incongruities evident from one place to another in this area show, across a significant number of steps, evidence of "Phase Changes" or "Phase Transitions," and significant transformation. The notion "Phase change" (cf. Gleick 1987: 131; Waldrop 1992: 229), refers to the apparent randomness displayed in numerous processes when one form is transformed into another. "Transformation" refers to such a radical change of an item's properties that it becomes effectively a new entity, A to B, a rectangle into a circle. The physical sciences customarily deal with changing stages of matter altered by temperature, pressure, etc. And it has been the virtue of chaos theory to see in this apparent randomness a new kind of order. But as the contributions of Mosko and Taylor make clear in this volume, so is social life constantly an experience of gradual and then sudden change. This is true whether these transformations are effected by life cycles, positions within differentiated regional settings, or the relatively abrupt social transformations that percolate through the historical record.[19] The relatively conflicted order found in Gawa and Iwa is, I believe, indicative of such a phase change.

The situation on Iwa intensifies this impression of a phase change. Befitting Iwa's different geological setting—it is more ovoid than the circular Gawa—its main axis is, in Western terms, roughly northeast/southwest. This contrast is understood as one between a *wowula* and a *dabwela*, along which the island and its inhabitants roughly divide themselves into two main areas called "*Obomatu*" and "*Wayovila.*" In Muyuw and Gawa *bomatu* could be unambiguously translated as "north" and the latter term as "toward the sea" [literally "at-sea-community"]. This latter expression in fact works in Iwa too, as everyone notes that there is a gradual slope down from *Obomatu* to *Wayovila*. However, hard as I tried, I failed to get a sense that anything like a simple set of north/south, east/west distinctions are pertinent for Iwa people. They never use wind directions to specify the analogues of Western cardinal directions, and for most people I received five or six different names and directions, never easily graphed by right angles.[20] *Bomatu* is a place on the Iwan landscape, not a direction external to it. Now although houses are clustered toward these two poles, they can also be found haphazardly related to this axis. People again told me that the noticeable organization along the central path was Government inspired, and that they were now getting away from it. Now and again as I was shown this and that garden we would come across a staked tree trunk marking an old *dibedeb* (see Munn ibid., s.v. *dabadeb*), village center. Drawn from an extremely hard and rot-resistant tree, these were designed to last, and they give evidence of villages having been scattered all over this tiny landscape. And as there is plenty of evidence of some old house clusters having been out in the area that looks naively like garden land, there are plenty of small fenced gardens in amongst contemporary house clusters. This appearance is hard to describe, but when I first saw it in 1995, having been socialized in Muyuw's near absolute separation between villages and gardens, I was stunned, and not so much by an appearance of chaos as by a manicured order very different from the one I knew.

Iwa gardens seem to be organized in the same way. Although I could decipher no order to Iwa gardens—they have varying shapes, and compass readings I would take in one place would rarely conform to any other place—people say they are laid out, as in Gawa, to follow *takulumwala*, and if one neglects these the crops will not grow. However, unlike in Gawa, *takulumwala* are not conceived to be of any fixed direction. I recorded several to be along a 40° bearing, one at 330°, and another still that was close to north/south. Several old men said they crisscross the island in a very random pattern. Once I scribbled an ovoid shape on a sheet of paper and then randomly drew lines, some going the island's diameter, some not, some crisscrossing the others. I asked if this was how *takulumwala* ran, and was told yes. In cleared garden areas they are easily observed as lines of coral rock, but they are not easily followed for any distance. People do not think of them necessarily, for example, going from one end of the island to another, as is the case at some ideal level in Gawa. Gardens are keyed to them, and I saw several rectangular shaped gardens two of whose sides were formed by *takulumwala*. However, I saw other gardens which people told me were aligned to these lines but I could not see how. In one case the line of rocks, *takulumwala*, went more or less north/south seemingly forming a triangular shaped tip to a garden somewhat oriented like a rectangle with its longer sides east to west. Yet it had seven distinguishable sides. There was nothing conceived to be wrong with the shape of this garden—in fact it was the owner's prize yam garden for that season. In Muyuw its shape would have demonstrated appalling ignorance or disregard.

Takulumwala are conceived to distinguish different garden areas, *kwab*, and it may be that if one stayed on Iwa long enough to plot each such unit some overall pattern would emerge. However, I did not receive an impression that these divisions were rigidly followed. I was told that if a person found that they needed to put a particular garden over two plots, all one needed to do was ask the person who claimed ownership rights to it and they would consent. Clearly this is not a hard and fast system of order.[21]

Takulumwala, however, are understood to derive from an order, an order the ancestors laid down in a past time. Although not fixed in space analogous to the Muyuw or Gawan cases, the *Takulumwala*-derived order divides spaces by means of a temporal reckoning.

And this is, I believe, the case in the Trobriands. There are single references to this term, *takulumwala*, in Malinowski's two-volume set *Coral Gardens* (1966, Vol. I: 133; Vol. II: 83), in each case nothing indicated other than that the term constitutes a "boundary" for the subdivision of a "field" (*kwabila*) into smaller units called *baleko* that form specific gardens. However, this is a term that needs serious ethnographic inquiry. I had no reason to ask about the term when one was casually shown to me when I walked through gardens near Okaibom in 1995. Yet it is clear in retrospect that my companion was showing me something important. When in Mwadau in June of 1996 and by then realizing the term was critical, I asked the Trobriand wife of a Trobriand schoolteacher what the term connoted. She said they were land dividers, distinguishing one group's land from another, that they set an order that had to be followed, and that the ancestors laid them down long ago when "warfare ended." As is the case in Iwa, there was no sense from this person that the order related to anything like the solar directions found in Muyuw, nor Gawa's the crisscrossing directions. Rather, this is a matter of past times and the ancestors. Not unimportantly, I think that some are organized to radiate out from villages. For the sense of disorderliness I encountered in Iwa was very different from what was conveyed to me by Linus Digim'Rina and his brothers one evening in Okaibom in 1995. They produced the map shown here (Figure 4.2). The circle toward the top left is a village. Note the lines, and subsequent named garden sections emanating from it.

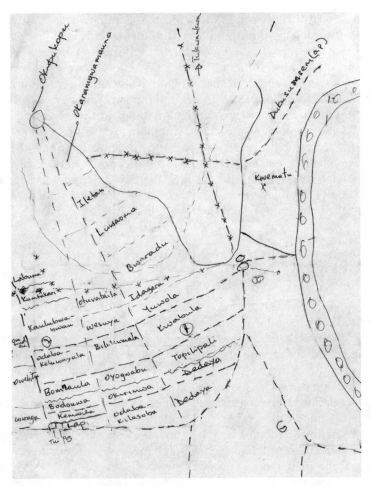

Figure 4.2: *Takulumwala* lines in C. Trobriands

As has been evident for years by the various reanalyzes of the Trobriand corpus, time is a major organizing feature of the social system. A
more complete exposition of the transformations here would require an
extensive discussion of the calendrical systems that did and do span the
islands from Muyuw to Iwa, Kitava, and the Trobriands. I have written
about this issue elsewhere (1982; 1990: chapter 1). However, subsequent
work (e.g., Gell 1992) and my own new findings call for major reanalysis
because Iwa, just where "space" no longer takes a preeminent role, is
where the "Trobriand" calendar is supposed to begin its movement from
one island to the next, at least according to Iwa and Kitavan people. This,
however, is another chore.

My point here is to demonstrate a set of continuing minor variations on
an epitomizing set of ideas, not exhaust their description. What I have

tried to do in this section is illustrate how similar ideas are reflected, apparently fractally, through different domains and on different scales. But in each case these leading ideas go through subtle changes. This is true from the top to the bottom of Muyuw's ranked exchange spheres as well as the spatial configurations that provide the terminology for social relations, as one goes along a series of contiguous places from east to west, from Muyuw to the Trobriands. Although these examples are specific, I do not think the phenomena are. Transformation, even within the synchronic analytical terms of this presentation, is the fundamental order we have to analyze. What remains missing from our theoretical tool kit is an analytical language that forces us to grasp these orders as differentiating. In the next section I use the cryptic algebra of Lévi-Strauss's canonic formula as a first approximation of what such a language might consist.

II. Lévi-Strauss's Canonic Formula

A Device for Ordering Transformations?

The previous section considered two aspects of Muyuw society that appear to show evidence of fractality. However, when one pays attention to little differences, it becomes clear that those differences become important, that relations are not just repeated across scales, and that, at least in the case of the changes in the organization of space, something akin to a phase change occurs between Muyuw and the Trobriands. If the assemblage of relations I have partially described for Muyuw is a strange attractor, the analogous attractor in the Trobriands is different.

It was not by accident that in the previous description I allowed myself to refer to the description of exchange spheres as a set of relations or functions and the spatial forms as a set of terms. The exchange model specifies relations between units or transforms the behavior of categories brought into relation by the spheres. The terms demarcate forms of action across spatial zones. Lévi-Strauss used the relation(function)/term set in his discussion of the canonic formula, and giving it an operational meaning has been one of my difficulties. For perhaps like for many anthropologists, this formula was gibberish until I could convince myself that it could be made to relate to very concrete ethnographic details I knew well and until it cast those details into an interpretative framework that added insight to our apprehension of those materials.

It is the purpose of this section to suggest that indeed the formula may be useful for generating such insights, at least the logical if not generative relationships among components of cultural orders, in this specific case orders arrayed across a regional system.

In the original presentation the formula looked like this, what I shall call FORM I :

FORM I $\qquad$ $F_x(a) : F_y(b) :: F_x(b) : F_{a-1}(y)$

with its conditions:

(1). one term be replaced by its opposite, "a-1" for "a."

(2). an inversion be made between the function (also "relations")
   value and the term value of two elements, y and a.

In *The Jealous Potter* (1988), Lévi-Strauss added a variant formula, my
FORM II:

FORM II $\qquad$ $F_x(a) : F_y(b) :: F_y(x) : F_{a-1}(b)$

Mosko (1991a) effectively surveyed the literature to create another. Côté
(2001) has sought to generate the limits of possible variants. Such work
could extend the analyses proffered here, but remains a different task.

Let me first deal with these peculiar "conditions."

(1). one term be replaced by its opposite, "a-1" for "a."

In his discussion of Trobriand territorial categories and rank, Jerry Leach
writes that there is a formal distinction between "high people" (*Kulakaiwa*)
and "low people" (*Kulitilawa [kulatanawa]*). "The distinction between
[high people] Kulakaiwa and [low people] Kulatanawa seems to connote
'highness' or 'lowness' on three dimensions: (1) chiefly customs relating
to height such as in raised houses, raised sitting platforms, high yam
houses and head height, (2) the growth of long yams, and (3) participation in the kula." (Leach, J.W. 1983: 138-139) These high people were the
Trobriand *guyaw*. All of this, of course, made the Trobriand high people
the most *visible*.

In Muyuw the North Central part of the island considers itself and is
considered by others to be the island's *guyaws*, thus roughly like the
Kulakaiwa of the Trobriands. And they were primarily agriculturalists,
having the island's most if not the best soil. Yet if in memory this area once
had the villages with the highest population concentrations (see Damon
1990: 70-83), the "highness" of its representation is inverted. First, leveled
rank is part of Muyuw culture's self-definition. Many people throughout
Muyuw claim that once their "subclan" or others' subclans, had *guyaw*
status. Their ancestors, however, ate the "forbidden foods" and so "fell
down." Trobriand rank is *negated* when it comes to Muyuw. But, in con-
tradistinction to the visible form of Trobriand hierarchy, concentric spatial
patterns ultimately realized in the central highness of Tabalu chiefs and
manners, Muyuw *guyaw* status was primarily represented by a funeral
custom that is not seen: central Muyuw people, Wamwan, were, and are,
buried in the ground sitting in an upright position, called *siguyaw*, and
this connoted their high status. Trobriand highness is visible; the identical
Muyuw highness becomes invisible in the negated rank that defines
Muyuw existence.

What of the same functions and the second condition?

(2). an inversion be made between the function (also "relations") value and the term value of two elements, y and a.

That what is below, rather than what is higher up, supports Muyuw culture follows from another set of representations. The epitomizing structures of Muyuw culture flow from the ideas represented in spatial forms, gardens first and most importantly, and then village structures. Muyuw origin mythology presents these ideas in the form of a single character refracted into two crosscousins who then define conditions for Muyuw productive success. In describing this mythology and its relation to Muyuw culture elsewhere (Damon 1990: 45-53; Appendix 1, pp. 228-229), I have suggested that it begins with a centralized image of efficacy, in a sense invoking Trobriand cosmological forms, and then separates Muyuw from that imagery.

When Muyuw tell the origin myth they recount the initial character, Geliw, then switch to Geliw's refractions, Tudav' and Malit'. Tudav' and Malit' go through one or another of two episodes from which contemporary socioecological and productive orders result. When these scenes are over, the account returns, usually only with a sentence or two, to Geliw, who goes traveling. Muyuw assert that when Geliw's travels are finished he/she returns to the island, goes beneath it, and carries the island on his/her head. Thus the creator supports the island exactly like —the same verb, -geb is used—women carry their loads. The creator now and again turns causing earthquakes. There is more. In 1991 I was told that Geliw's movement, which causes the island to shake, often marks the ends of droughts or prolonged rainy periods.

Thus, Muyuw's spatial patterns and very position in space facilitate or hinder productivity, just like Trobriand chiefs whose positions, I would argue, locate and located by their place in time, whether that time is the temporal orders created by "the Tabalu chiefs [who] were, and still are, accredited with power over both life and death, movement of the heavenly bodies, onset of seasons, droughts, etc." (Lawton: 1980: 131), or their emplacement along a landscape which seems to depict movement in time (see Baldwin 1946: 236; A. Weiner 1977: 40).

The *functions* remain the same but their *terms* are switched from time in the one case to space in the other.

When I could see these kinds of facts in this fashion, I felt it would then become legitimate to try to work out the whole formula to see what it generated. I had wanted to produce ways for thinking about some of the relationships I have just described. After a moment of disbelief, I think I produced ways for thinking about how to move from the northern Massim to some of the cultural configurations in the south. This occurred each time I selected a different set of apparently ethnographically significant values. Here I shall just illustrate the procedure using the following for relations/functions and terms:

Equivalence (Fx) and hierarchy (F_y) for the two relations and diametric(a) and concentric(b) for the two terms.
FORM 1: Equivalence in diametric form : hierarchy in concentric form :: equivalence in concentric form : inverted or negated diametricism in hierarchy
FORM 2: Equivalence in diametric form : hierarchy in concentric form :: hierarchy in equivalence : negated or inverted diametricism in concentricity.

I did not have to be convinced of the reality of these ratios before it became clear that in various ways these formulations capture some relationships that organize similarities and differences between various Massim societies.

So, for example, FORM 1, Equivalence in diametric form : hierarchy in concentric form :: equivalence in concentric form : inverted or negated diametricism in hierarchy, arguably sets these groups in order:

MUYUW : TROBRIANDS:: TUBETUBE-DOBU [22] : GOODENOUGH

"Equivalence in concentric form" is suggestive for the Tubetube-Dobu region because the mortuary rituals in these societies work in terms of the symmetrical exchange of pig and vegetable food located in villages whose overt form is concentric (see Macintyre 1989; Thune 1989). One has to work a bit harder to see how "inverted or negated diametricism in hierarchy" corresponds to Goodenough realities. However, this comes close to the pattern evident in the set of competitive exchanges Michael Young describes as *abutu* and vis-à-vis *nibai* relationships. These are mostly symmetrical relationships designed to shame opponents.[23] Why are these negative? Because "The rationale for *nibai* formation is usually as follows: an ancestor of *unuma* A1 of clan A was killed, and generally eaten, by the ancestors of *unuma* B1 of clan B. Whether there was vengeance killing (*miwa*) or not, the descendents of these two *unuma* A1 and B1, regarded each other as *nibai*, perpetual antagonists" (Young 1971: 71). In what sense is hierarchy entailed in these relationships? Because their form, at least as they occur in the context of Goodenough's moiety structure, is conceived to devolve out of the differentiated and hierarchical structure embedded in Goodenough clan concepts (see Young, 1971: 61*ff.*).

FORM 2: Equivalence in diametric form : hierarchy in concentric form :: hierarchy in equivalence : negated or inverted diametricism in concentricity sets the same group of cultures in the order:

MUYUW : TROBRIANDS:: GOODENOUGH [24] : TUBETUBE-DOBU

Here I ignore the notion of Goodenough as "hierarchy in equivalence" (see note 22). Instead I attempt to suggest what the depiction of the Tubetube-Dobu areas as "negated or inverted diametricism in concentricity" captures.

This relationship is manifested in the stress on *susu*, the matrilineage. Of this entity Macintyre writes, in terms which more or less fit Lobada and probably Dobu as well, "mortuary ceremonies ... reflect an ideology of the inviolability of the *susu* and the ephemeral nature of all social relationships other than those consanguineal matrilineal bonds with the *susu*" (Macintyre 1989: 133). Although the mortuary ceremonies in this south central sector of the Massim entail reciprocal forms by no means uncommon elsewhere, their stress is on clearing away everything but the matrilineal essence of the person. In Lobada and Dobu the essentials of this susu stress is/was finalized with corpses' bodies placed in the center of a concentric village. In discussing the symbolism of Tubetube manipulations of the corpse, Macintyre writes:

> This regenerative process was formerly symbolically represented in the treatment of the corpse as it changed from something black and stinking into a bundle of pure white bones. This process was a concrete expression of the lineage's triumph over death. The cave of whitened bones testified to the lineage's control over its own regeneration and continuity, for the bones were believed to have been formed by *susu* breast milk (fn omitted). The flesh and blood, now vanished, were produced by foods and "paternal substance," their disintegration proclaiming the ephemeral nature of the affinal relationship (ibid.: 138).

Although aspects of this interpretation would fit less important facets of northern Massim practices, the overriding forms to the north reproduce matrilineal interdependencies. These are either the hierarchical forms of the Trobriands, or the interclan relations ultimately expressed in the ideal model of *clan* marriage exchanges in Muyuw. In the north affinal relations are central rather than ephemeral. This realization could generate another set of contrasts employing clan and subclan notions in this area. Based on a critical new addition to the Trobriand ethnographic corpus from Debbora Battaglia (1992) and using Dumont's ideas about encompassed contraries one run from FORM 2 generated the following: Encompassing clans : encompassed subclans :: encompassed encompasser : negative clan in form of subclan. This first struck me as patently absurd. Yet if it works on the order of MUYUW : TROBRIANDS TUBETUBE-DOBU :GOODENOUGH it forces an imaginative insight. "Negative clan in form of subclan" calls to mind Goodenough's anomalous patrilineal ideology in a social field dominated by matrilineal notions.[25] "In the form of a subclan" is suggestive too. The kind of differentiation that across the northern Massim is defined by *dala*, subclans—they come out of the ground with different ranks, customs, etc.—rather than *kumila/kum*, clans—which are usually understood without respect to rank—is set up, in Goodenough, in the idea of clan (Young 1971: 61*ff*). Goodenough clans effect the kind of differentiation usually found among subclans in the north.

Conclusion

The Taussig and Bateson quotes inscribed at the beginning of this essay suggest that thinking that social life is systematic is incorrect on the one hand and, on the other, that the algorithms of consciousness may be complex, but they are not linguistic. In both cases, therefore, the oppositional logic of Lévi-Strauss's structuralism would be inappropriate. The first quote begs the question of "what kind of system." The argument of this essay, and the volume, is that a new idea about system is available to us. There is a logic between and among Goodenough's sacrifice-induced "pity" and Muyuw's "ecstasy." Intrinsic to Bateson's assertion is the problem of where are the orders that govern social life. If the deep psychology of Freud has governed the answers to this question for most of the twentieth century, it is perhaps time to relocate the problem. The analysis that derives from this material suggests they lie among, or between, and not within, the human actors in these relationships. And that an understanding of how these people feel and act will necessarily derive from the structures of ideas they have assembled to construct their worlds.

In the original version of this paper I conceived of Lévi-Strauss's formula as a way of operationalizing chaos theory for the kinds of data best suited to the traditions of social anthropology. The main difficulty with this idea is that the mathematics of chaos theory deal with quantities whereas the canonic formula, and much anthropological practice, analyzes and describes discontinuous relations. In a way this essay forces the issue of this problem. If its second part is correct, it suggests that relationships of difference and then doubled differences, which the canonic formula either reveals or generates, govern social discontinuity across the island cultures directly and indirectly participating in the Kula. Yet the first part shows that the discrete entities that become the featured attractors in the formula become distinct by the selective attention to continuous variation. But this is a continuous variation of kinds and not quantities. Or is it? If the mathematics of chaos theory are seen to describe realities that govern the entities we examine, is there necessarily a missing equation in our understanding of these regional relations? This is a problem partly forced by my stressing the continuous variation across these cultural units. That selective attention certainly belongs to me as an analyst. But not just me, for the participants in this regional system are not ignorant of its variation. And they are the ones who, for example, select *different kinds* of wood to stand for the same kinds of affinal obligations. Their ritual life is organized to display the properties of the collective distinctiveness of particular places. Are these *attractors* their equivalent of our numbers?

In this essay I claim to have been able to describe some of the zigs and zags that constitute social life, and the experience of social life, in these contiguous cultures. The analysis of this essay suggests that the differences between self-destructing victimage of Young's Kalauna people and the productive sacrifices of the Kula are on the same order as the various contrasts revealed by the application of the canonic formula. The question this analysis creates, but does not answer, is this: Does the method of analysis typified by Lévi-Strauss's formula merely reveal the patterns it helps draw? And so the generative source of those relationships is elsewhere? Or, is it at least part of the process that generates the swirls of social life that make some people full of pity while others soar with ecstasy? Like my empirical problems, this issue is not just a question for social anthropology.

Acknowledgments

The ethnography in this paper derives from nearly forty months of interaction with the people of the Kula Ring, and especially those on Muyuw, between 1973 and 2002. Their lives have led me to this synthesis, and for their time and patience I have the greatest respect. I also thank Mark Mosko, Claude Lévi-Strauss, and Jack Morava for reading and commenting on drafts of this essay, not one of whom would express themselves in quite the way I have here. All errors of fact and interpretation are mine.

Notes

1. In my naiveté things could not have been more significant than this string of names might imply, but this exchange and its relationships were small change by Aisi's standards. Which made the "feeling" no less significant.
2. "Husband's" (*mwan*) body (*won*) would be the literal translation of this expression.
3. While I believe our discussion of "chaos theory" may add new possibilities to our discipline and facilitate dialogue across disciplinary boundaries, I do not think what the phenomenon "fractals" denotes is new to anthropology. Phrasing this issue slightly differently than Mosko does in his Introduction, describing regularities in social fields has been, and remains, the primary purpose of social anthropology. We know regularities as and from patterns. Patterns, structures, are primarily understood by redundancy. Redundancy becomes the proof of connection. This stress on pattern, on redundancy, has been common to both the American tradition derived from Benedict (e.g., *The Chrysanthemum and The Sword*), and the modern extension of Durkheim and Mauss's work on classification, the various structuralisms that have been coming in and out of fashion for more than forty years. To Benedict should be added Schneider (1980;

1969). I fail to see that Mandelbrot's discovery of regularities in cotton prices, as discussed by Gleick (ibid. pp. 83-86), is any more dramatic than, say, Needham's analysis of the Purum (1962: chapter 4). Given Lévi-Strauss's inspirational nods to D'Arcy Thompson, one is inclined to wink when Kauffman (1993: 643-644) locates his work along a trail earlier defined by Thompson.

4. Sornette's fascinating study bears a formal resemblance in its models to those employed by Lansing in a series of important analyses of Bali's irrigation system (e.g., Lansing, J. Stephen and James N. Kremer 1993; and Lansing, J. Stephen, James N. Kremer, and Barbara B. Smuts 1998). However appropriate imitation models may be for many Western societies whose encompassing sociological models are based on notions of equality, in much of the Indo-Pacific region the analogous perspectives presuppose the organization of differences, not similarities.

5. Goertzel (1995a and b) and Abraham (1995) invoke ideas about pattern and structure with respect to the idea of strange attractors, and their invocation of the likes of Gregory Bateson puts their work into concepts well-worn in anthropology. Yet it is not clear to me that their vocabulary gives us any more ideas than we have already had or that, for example, are well illustrated in work by, among others, Bloch (1992).

6. One of the earlier anthropological uses of this term is James Fox's in his discussion of Austronesian houses (Fox 1993: 1). For Fox the idea connotes something like a featured symbol around which coherent social action is formed. For a formal mathematical definition I once found the following useful: "An attractor is a region of state space that captures the long-term behavior of the system. It is now known that structurally stable systems can possess attractors on which the systems behave in an apparently random manner. The equations that define a dynamical system are fully deterministic; that is, given initial conditions lead to uniquely specified behavior. The sense in which a deterministic model can produce random effects is a major discovery of the last few decades, giving rise to a central branch of dynamical systems theory known as chaotic dynamics. The word chaos—more accurately, deterministic chaos— refers to any instance of such behavior. The associated attractors are said to be strange or chaotic." "Analysis (in Mathematics): DIFFERENTIAL EQUATIONS: Dynamical systems on manifolds," Britannica Online. <http://www.eb.com:180/cgi-bin/g?DocF=macro/5000/17/140.html> The following is also a useful source: http://www.exploratorium.edu/complexity/CompLexicon/catastrophe.html. A recognized set of cultural practices, undoubtedly organized around a contradiction, might then reasonably be said to be a "strange attractor." Given this definition, the hierarchical rules of Trobriand culture, which its concentricity embodies, constitute a strange attractor. Muyuw's is different.

7. Morava's perspective is underlined by Alain Côté's review of the history of mathematics that prefaces his discussion of the formula (Côté 2001: 199). The acquisition of knowledge is not mechanical. My experience with this material is enhanced, also, by Turner's early (1969a), but far from outdated, discussion of other aspects of *The Structural Study of Myth*; and second by Roy Wagner's many writings about "obviation." Wagner's method diverges to some degree from Lévi-Strauss's (but note p. 221 of *The Structural Study of Myth*). Working from Wagner's approach, I also found Weiner (1988) extremely useful.

8. Random from the point of view of the model; Dibolel's marriage was designed to facilitate the acquisition of outrigger sailing craft from Kweywata Island.

9. The third sphere is called *takon*. The complex of exchanges associated with this sphere is noted in Damon 1983 and discussed throughout my book *From Mutuw to the Trobriands* (1990).

10. Wabunun, where I spend most of my time, literally translates to "At" or "In the point." The village was originally located on a rise just west of the prominent point evident on the maps. The whole shoreline from Obwilim to Unmatan is lined with villages—or clamshells and fractured pots indicating some 1,500 years of inhabitation.

11. See Damon (1979) and Ollier (1978) for early descriptions of these ruins. Bickler's dissertation (1998) provides a much fuller description and offers a temporal setting for these ruins, which can be found on every island (except possibly Kweywata) from Muyuw to the Trobriands. Skeletal material dates from approximately 1200 BP to 400 BP. At least the north central megaliths were used for burial procedures, and suggest different practices than those described by me and other Massim ethnographers—all of us describe or imply secondary interment. These findings, and others, raise astonishing historical questions that must be left unasked here. Although I am avoiding a temporal location for this paper, I am certainly aware that such a framework is needed. Highlights of Bickler's dissertation concerning megaliths are in Bickler and Ivuyo (2002).

12. The verbal reports are interesting because they are consistent with a current cognitive map of how things should be, not because they describe a past. Muyuw people do not hold stores of information about the past, whether organized by genealogical or other means. My model is merely consistent with how Muyuw would remember a past, if they did, which they do not. The archaeological evidence is consistent with the cognitive model and current sites, but remains too scattered to be anything more than a hypothesis warranting further research.

13. However, several hours earlier he had shown me evidence of old village sites along the far northeastern corner of the main island and told me of another that would roughly correspond to a place on the western end of the island that Kavatan occupies on the eastern end.

14. Not all of eastern Muyuw uses this tree. One of Unmatan's (Pometia *pinnata*) is from a very old forest area, a tree only commonly found west and north of the platform on the western end of which Unmatan is perched. For Unmatan is at the end-point of inhabited areas. See Damon (1998) for further discussion of the role of trees in modeling social relations.

15. Although she was unaware of the use of this tree, in order to gauge how this specific practice is part of a system of transformations, readers may wish to consult Munn's analysis (1977) of the symbolism of fabrication entailed in the production of Gawa's famous canoes.

16. Munn writes for what I call *wowun, wowula* (1977: 55-56 s.v.). I spoke Muyuw to Gawans and they often answered in Muyuw. The terms are the same, only reflecting a common transformation of Muyuw "n" to Gawan "l" with the addition of a final vowel, what Muyuw call the word's "wife," *nakwav*.

17. Munn reports that Gawan hamlets vary from being sort of linear to sort of circular, and are roughly positioned along a southeast to northwest path that bisects the island (Munn 1986: 21, 90).

18. This includes the Calophyllum species they use to produce their large outriggers, *anageg*. As I have shown elsewhere (Damon 1997; 1998), these trees are dependent upon human activity in order to grow beyond the seedling stage.

19. Wallerstein toys with the idea in his recent work (e.g., 1993).

20. Muyuw people specify their directions in terms of "winds," of which there are four. However, they will then say that the "east" wind is not just east, it comes from the southeast too. In short they treat their system as an abstraction and understand how concrete experience diverges from it. The same "abstractions" no longer carry any force from Iwa west.

21. The island cultures of Gawa, Kweywata, Iwa, and Kitava are, of course, spatially between Muyuw and the Trobriands. That such interstitial places are vehicles of transformation is hardly a novel ethnographic point. See Olson (1967: 34) for a description of the anomalous Nexadi, a bizarre out of order Tlingit group that is the conceived origin location for the highest Tsimshian Eagle clan. Nor is such an analysis novel theoretically. Victor Turner's *oevre* is predicated on the observation that the liminal is a facilitator. So too the structuralist analyses of Leach and Douglas whereby it is in the

interstitial/ambiguous zones where considerable power/potency lies, hence functions as a "facilitator."

22. In this formulation I assimilate the Tubetube-Dobu region as one, including in this set what I understand of Thune's descriptions of Lobada village on Normanby Island. See for example Thune (1989). While there are many commonalities among this set of cultural forms, I recognize differences. The forms and functions, for example, of many Tubetube practices closely resemble those in Muyuw although the cosmological and to some extent sociological contexts—the "terms"?—are quite different. By contrast, I see little resemblance between Muyuw and Lobada-Dobu. In short, there may be a continuum of differences between Muyuw and Dobu, via Tubetube, that is similar to the continuum of differences between Muyuw and the Trobriands, via Gawa.

23. If two units are *nibai*, they "give each other food competitively, either simultaneously or in delayed exchange, depending upon the ceremonial context" (Young 1971: 72).

24. Note what Mike Young writes of one of the subjects of his study of living myth in Kalauna: "[Iyahalina] affected to live in quotation marks, as it were, and projected himself as a synecdoche of his ancestors and his lineage. One might even fancy that he saw himself as a kind of divine king, a cosmic corporation sole (Kantorowicz 1957). But, as I argue in chapter 7, Iyahalina's sense of irony was so developed that the quotation marks he put around his actions were done with the knowing wink of one in complete self-possession. And we can infer from this, too, that Iyahalina was attempting to make *himself* exemplary for those who succeeded him" (Young 1983b: 19). Young's insight is important here, although more important when put in the context of the fact that divine kings—on the order of Southeast Asian models—is the appropriate model for Trobriand hierarchy. This too is just one of a number of inverted parallels with, e.g., Muyuw (see absence of insignias of rank, Young 1983b: 54, etc).

25. *Unuma* is the term that connotes the patrilineal descent line that takes the place of what elsewhere along most of the D'entrecasteaux is *susu*. Among Goodenough people "a man calls those kin who constitute his mother's unuma by the term *susu*" (Young 1971: 38). So the term by which others denote their descent identity is part of Goodenough culture.

5

FRACTALITY AND THE EXCHANGE OF PERSPECTIVES

José Antonio Kelly

Abstract

This essay explores the potential of the idea of fractality borrowed from chaos theory along one of its properties: scaled self-similarity. The notion of fractal personhood is proposed as a way of thinking about the Amerindian person. When speaking of fractal personhood, what is meant is the containment of whole persons in parts of persons and the replication of relations between selves and alters at different scales (intrapersonal, interpersonal, and intergroup). Three Amerindian ethnographies (Araweté, Wari', and Tupinamba) are compared and analyzed combining propositions from Melanesian exchange theory and a theory of Amerindian perspectivism in order to elicit the usefulness of "fractal personhood" as an analytical tool.

Introduction

Not long after engaging anthropological studies one is faced with an apparent paradox: anthropologists are, on the one hand, fascinated with the recurrence of social patterns, and on the other, skeptical or uneasy with elucidating these patterns in the form of a system. Anthropologists emphasize both regularity and unpredictability; the similarities of humankind and the unity of the human subject; determinism and disorder. This is why the idea of fractality borrowed from chaos theory (see

---

Notes for this section begin on page 130.

Mosko "Introduction," this volume) can be found to be so appealing: self-similar scaled patterns that can arise from stochastic systems. What other image could characterize the anthropological project better?

In this essay I will explore the potential of the idea of fractality along one of its properties: scaled self-similarity. I will propose the notion of fractal personhood as a way of thinking about the Amerindian person. When I speak of fractal personhood I will be emphasizing both the containment of whole persons in parts of persons and the replication of relations between selves and alters at different scales (intrapersonal, interpersonal, and intergroup); two sides of the same coin.[1]

My method consists in merging aspects of two anthropological theories developed in distant regions: the idea of the Melanesian dividual (Strathern 1988) and the idea of Amerindian perspectivism (Viveiros de Castro 1998), the hinge being the common thread of relationality: the relational constitution of persons and contexts.[2] This is an exercise of Melanesian-ing Amazonia, highlighting the gift exchange elements in the sustenance of a perspectivist ontology, the purpose being to open a field of interpretation to some well-known Amazonian issues. Above all this is an experiment, and as so the reader is reminded that the goal of this piece is to suggest some connections rather than present hard findings.

I will base my analysis mainly on the comparison of three groups. The Araweté is a hunting and agriculturalist Amerindian group of which only one village remains on the middle Ipixuna River, a tributary of the Xingu, in the Pará state of Brazil. Linguistically they are of the Tupi-Guarani family (Viveiros de Castro 1992: 30, 38). The renowned Tupinamba were inhabitants of the Brazilian coasts at the time of the Portuguese conquest. Finally, the Wari', another Amazonian group also known in the literature as Pakaa Nova. They are of the Chapakura linguistic family and live in the west of the Rondonia state of Brazil (Vilaça 1997: 91). Some reference is also made to the Achuar of the Jivaroan ensemble of the Ecuadorian and Peruvian Amazon. The threads I use to link these groups are the themes of warfare and human or divine cannibalism.

There are three steps to this exercise: first, I will present a succinct account of two propositions about Amerindian sociality common in the region's anthropological literature; the contextual nature of the us/them categories and the dependence of social reproduction on relations with the outside, relations with others. These two aspects allow me to introduce the analytic figure of the relationally dual person. Second, I present two alternative versions of how "others" can become "us," of how boundaries are crossed and the potential for reproduction of the outside is realized. On the one hand, the exchange of body parts that make us think relations between selves and others as mediated by exchange; on the other hand, I will outline some points of a theory of perspectivism with a specific bearing on the body. This presentation underscores the role of the body and its modifications in the sustenance of relations between the self and the other.

The last step is the core of this essay, where I examine in more detail three Amerindian examples. In showing the workings of both exchange of body parts and of body modifications as two steps of a perspectivist process, the potential of the notion of fractal personhood emerges. The order of the presentation might appear awkward but this was the way I came to the idea of fractals as a heuristic (trying to reconcile exchange and perspectivist theories). In a sense the essay tells its own story.

An exercise of seeing Amerindian personhood through an "exchange lens" constitutes a change of balance on theoretical emphasis that Maussian gift exchange has had in Amazonian anthropology. An analytical-historical framework for this piece is eloquently provided by S. Hugh-Jones (2001) in a volume precisely devoted to Melanesian and Amazonian comparison. Speaking of the respective theoretical traditions:

> These traditions [Melanesian and Amazonian writing] have common roots in exchange theory, but it has been developed in two very different directions. In part, at least, these developments reflect the concrete experience of ethnographic fieldwork that has molded each one to suit local conditions.... Building on the works of Mauss and Malinowski, the exchange theory of Melanesia has been predominantly that of gift exchange, with its emphasis on economics and interpersonal transactions. The Amazonianists' exchange theory also has Maussian roots, but, following Lévi-Strauss, this version has been largely that of marriage alliance, with its global emphasis on system, category, and classification, a version developed in tandem with a focus on mythology and cosmology.... In this scheme, economics tends to be squeezed uncomfortably between structuralism and cultural ecology, often figuring as an unhappy compromise between "symbol" and "subsistence." (246-247)

Some Amerindian Themes

It was long ago noted (Seeger et al. 1979) that Amerindian societies gave priority to identity rather than juridic or economic solidarity as the main referent of social organization. Further works reveal, in political economy (Rivière 1984), eschatology and funerary practices (Carneiro da Cunha 1978; Vilaça 1992; Viveiros de Castro 1992), social organization and naming systems (Maybury-Lewis 1979), the operating of the "symbolics of the identical and the different" in Amerindian sociality in several contextual guises:

Self : Other :: consanguines : affines
       living :   dead
       us :   enemies
       predator :   prey
       human: divine
       male: female

Insofar as these are basic oppositions they are not static. Who is Self and who is Other depends on who is being compared. The dynamics of this categorization is resumed in the Araweté usage of the term *bïde*:

The opposition *bïde/awi* is the strong form of a central opposition: *bïde*, "we," "us people," and *amite*, "other," "the others." *Amite* ["other," "nonrelative"] is not a category of person, but a position, one of alterity in relation to the unmarked pole, an "other" versus a "same" (Viveiros de Castro 1992: 64-65).

which resembles the usage of the Jivaro term *Shuar*:

> This expression refers to a multi-layered set of relations between contrastive terms: thus, according to context, the term *shuar* refers to "my bilateral kindred" as opposed to others, "my local group" as opposed to other territorial groups, "Achuar" as opposed to other Jivaroan tribal units, "Jivaro" as opposed to Whites or other Indians, and so on (Taylor 1996: 204).

Another established proposition is the symbolic dependence on the outside for social reproduction (Fausto 2000). Of this we have several examples at hand: for the Wari' the blood of a slain enemy is incorporated into the killer and transformed into semen that will "fatten" the killer's wife, "Effectively ... the killer will have a son: the soul of the dead enemy." (Vilaça 1992: 103-104). The ritual treatment of the Jivaro *tsantsa*, the head of a slain enemy, was expected to yield a child from the killer's kin in the following year (Descola 1997: 276). In the case of the Tupinamba, one could assume based on Viveiros de Castro's analysis, a similar association. Through the execution of an enemy, the symbolic incorporation of his blood and the concomitant acquisition of new names and renewed self-hood youths reached the status of full persons, who could marry and have legitimate children (Viveiros de Castro 1992: 151). Moreover, these names, based on today's data for other groups, could have been closely associated with the enemy's soul. Hence forth let us retain these propositions.[3]

The relational nature of the canonical Self/Other divide together with the passages from Other to Self that must occur due to the dependence on the outside for social reproduction allows the analytical suggestion that, in being able to take the position of Self and Other, persons are constituted as relationally dual. Hence, persons could be seen as Self/Other—or us/enemy, consanguine/affine, predator/prey, and so on—composites. A second analytical derivation, borrowing from M. Strathern, is that the person is divisible: in certain contexts, a person's integrity can be separated (albeit by forceful extraction). It is by virtue of these two conditions, then, duality and divisibility, that persons can assume or be forced into a position at either side of the canonical Self/Other divide.

Thinking from an exchange theory point of view one could propose that it is through the real or symbolic exchange of parts of the person that the canonical divide is traversed; the passage is mediated by a transaction: the enemy always gives a part of himself. So in a Strathernian sense, blood/heads become transactable parts of the person. Yet we could also think of an alternative proposition following some aspects of a theory of Amerindian perspectivism (Viveiros de Castro 1998). The positional nature of the Self/Other divide requires means of differentiation, of clear demarcation of who is who. Perspectivism as a theory sheds light on the conception of body and its relation with the dynamics of identity and alterity.

Amerindian perspectivist ontology can be seen as a "multinaturalist" one: it supposes a raw subjectivity (culture) that builds its multiple objective realities (natures). The consciousness common to many species and humans gives them a perspective of the world. Persons are thus defined as potential subjects, those with access to a point of view. Having a perspective confers animals and plants with a "humanness" by which they see themselves as humans see themselves: jaguars have wives, children, clans, and huts and feast as humans do. Yet a jaguar, as a predator, will see a human as prey (e.g., a peccary), to the same extent that a peccary, as prey, will see a human as a predator (e.g., a jaguar). The point is that jaguars, peccaries, and humans see things in the same way but what they see is different, and depends on perspective: humans can see themselves as subjects (culture), but are at the same time the object (nature) of another subjectivity and vice versa. The passage from subject to object is a change in the position of perspective. Hence the content of categories such as subject/object or nature/culture is not static but relational.

In this perspectivist world it is the body that functions as the main differentiator. Beyond the well documented Amerindian focus on the fabrication, modification, and destruction of bodies (Seeger et al. 1979), the body as locus of differentiation is also locus of perspective. What you see, the world you construct, depends on the body you have. (Viveiros de Castro 1998: 478). Bodies seem to be conceived as a clothing that can be changed (Rivière 1994) yet not in order to conceal an inner reality; new clothing, that is, modified bodies, bring new capacities. But the body must then be understood not as the material aspect of the person, the physical being, but rather as "bundles of affects," the set of capacities and behaviors typical of a being (Viveiros de Castro 1998: 478).

A perspectivist theory integrates the importance of names and material decor. It is partly names and ornaments that allow a perspectivist ontology to be maintained in the face of the fixity of human and animal skins. They become evidence of the divisibility and dual nature of persons, making the body a social object par excellence, a perfect substitute for material exchange (Turner 1995: 147).

But we seem to have run into a problem. We saw how the exchange of body parts served as a means to traverse the Self/Other divide. A perspectivist theory, nonetheless, shows how the body is the site of perspective and how its modification is what effects changes of position. Insofar as all exchange of body parts is a body modification, implying that the latter includes the former, I will argue that the exchange of body parts plays a different role in maintaining a perspectivist ontology.

A Closer Look at Fractality

Let us now suggest a way in which the idea of fractality, can bring together a theory of exchange and one of perspectivism in the examination of three cases that illuminate different aspects of this meeting point. First, let us build a framework for analysis:

(1) Persons are dual beings, their duality lying in the possibility of assuming positions at either side of the canonical Self/Other divide. In a perspectivist ontology, this is precisely what defines human and nonhuman persons: persons are those subject/object dual beings who are credited with perspective and agency (participate of culture and an immortal soul) but at the same time are objects of another subjectivity (part of someone's nature). Let us recall how many of the animals that could make humans their prey are persons. (See Vilaça 1992: 59-64 for a Wari' example.) Persons' awareness of their subject/self-object/other duality is expressed mainly in the possibility of becoming someone's prey.[4] Persons, then, are neither subjects nor objects but both; the conscious site of a Self reflexive and the Other's perspective. Context will determine whether subjectness or objectness is prevalent in a relation. Importantly, to become an Other (person), is not desubjectifying whilst it is Othering, and hence, changes your perspective on the world. Such changes require a transfer of body parts and other body modifications (this is fully detailed later). Nonetheless, there are also nonreversible positions as in the case of the Araweté gods who hold the dominant perspective of predators (Viveiros de Castro 1992: 254; 1998: 485). This defines supernature: Araweté gods are never eaten (never prey), they are pure subjects.[5] At the other end lies nature, soulless animal, plants, and things that are always prey or pure objects. (This does not mean that they are not subjected to the dynamics of perspectivism: human blood can be the jaguar's manioc beer.)

(2) From a gift/Strathernian stance, let us see persons as dividuals: here a composite duality is evinced in the possibility of detaching and attaching parts of persons in exchange relations. My usage of the idea of divisible persons is not an analytic caprice. The partible nature of the Amazonian person needs little demonstration.[6] Beyond the cases we have already mentioned, we can recall how Araweté and Achuar children have a soul which is not properly attached or fixed to the body, making them prone to illness. In general, many of the couvade restrictions common in Amazonia are premised on the fragility of the body-soul integration (see Descola 1997: 233; Viveiros de Castro 1992: 183). Illness, at any age, and killing tend to loosen the body-soul tie. Viveiros de Castro's comments on the Araweté, I think hold for many other groups:

Anyone who is not yet conscious or who has fallen unconscious is in danger: either he is not yet a complete human being or he is on his way towards ceasing to be one (1992: 194).

Let us also recall the commonality of soul loss and aspects of persons that appear in dreams and are credited with independence from the subject.

A composite person always participates in relations as a term, which I take to be a person whose subjectness is brought to the fore by the certainty of being a transactor in an exchange relationship, as opposed to a detached or incomplete person who participates as a signifier, an operator of a relation.[7] Operators, following Gell (1999) and M. Strathern (1992), are the "objectification of a relation," pure relationship value, persons whose objectness is brought to the fore by the certainty of being transacted. The mark of personhood is then the possibility to transact and be transacted. The mark of godhood is the impossibility of being transacted: you might exchange with the gods but gods are never exchanged.

In this attempt to bring together perspectivism with gift exchange we must not conflate terms: when speaking of subjects in a perspectivist theory we refer to an agented being with a view on the world. This is not the opposite of a transacted person who objectifies a relation; an operator. A captive enemy does not lose his perspective on the world. In fact, his perspective is precisely what makes him valuable to his slayer. So even when he is a transacted party, in a Strathernian sense he is also "the object of the relations" between enemies. In short, his perspective (subjectness) is the object of exchanges. An operator is a temporary object of the transacting parties. Correspondingly, terms, are temporary subjects with reference to the transacted party. After the transaction all resume their "normal" subject/object personness, and, as we hinted above, and will detail below, Others are encompassed by Selves, the enemy is encompassed by the killer.

Encompassment achieved via the exchange of a part of the person leads to the fractal quality I wish to refer to; the containment of the whole (of a person) in the part (of a person); parts of persons become whole persons. (Examples are the son of the Wari' killer; the son of the Jivaro killer; and we speculatively add the new name (soul) of the Tupinamba killer.) It must be kept in mind, then, that when I later speak of body parts being exchanged, what is exchanged is a downscaled version of the whole person.

(3) Groups and persons (human and nonhuman) can appear as one person when compared with other groups or persons. A person can refer to many individuals united by the sharing of a common position opposed to another similar group. The unitary status of a group points to the notion of body as a "bundle of affects," as the shared capabilities of a species. In this case what is shared is position. Wari' consubstantials think of themselves as one body even though there are several participating of this unity; they also attribute the gregarious behavior of peccaries to their bodies (Vilaça

1992: 52). Several other points support this idea: warriors tend to become cokillers in raids; even if only one has caused the enemy's death, all the participants are subjected to the post-killing precautions. (See Descola 1997: 304; Vilaça 1992: 103 for Achuar and Wari' examples.) In the case of the Tupinamba, villagers became coeaters of the enemy; they all ate his flesh (Viveiros de Castro 1992: 302) as if to make themselves all guilty and worthy objects of their enemies. The same can be said of the Araweté gods: they all eat the flesh of the dead upon arrival in the other world (Ibid: 211).

This is basically an expression of the contextual character of the us/them categories we referred to before and another expression of fractality: the person-as-group is an upscaled version of the person-as-individual and a twice upscaled of the person-as-part. What will become evident below is that fractal personhood implies that relations between persons, at any scale, are replicas of each other, that is, they are self-similar.

(4) The relations a detached person, as an operator, can signify are one or more of those constituted by the canonical Self/Other divide:

Relation	*Self*	*Other*
Enmity (vengeance)	Us	Enemies
Affinity	Consanguines/Consubstantials	Affines
Predation	Predator	Prey
Reproduction	Male	Female
Death	Divinities/Dead	Living

Unpacking the Fractal Person[8]

Following the path of a Tupinamba enemy, from enemy to being one with the slayer, will reveal the fractal quality of persons by revealing the relations that constitute them.

The person is constituted by all the relations above mentioned:

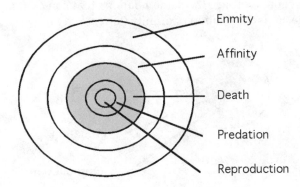

Figure 5.1: Relational constitution of the Tupinamba person[9]

Yet when the enemy is caught and brought back to the captor's village he becomes a signifier of the relations between enemies. This can be seen as the Enemy giving one of its parts, an upscaled instance of a person giving a body part. As such the captive is no longer a term but an operator; the relation of enmity, of vengeance, has been "unpacked."

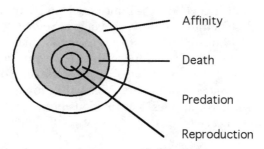

Figure 5.2: Person as operator between enemy groups

Once in the enemy village, the captive could follow two routes: (1) he was given as a gift to the affines of his captor. A newlywed was obliged to give captives to his younger affines for their initiations (to acquire names and marry). The captive was given to brothers-in-law, as counter to a previous wife received. In this context the captive is a sister's daughter to his affines but can also be seen as a counterpart for the captor himself: a sister's husband (Viveiros de Castro 1992: 295). What would be a reciprocal situation of exchange between affines in the captor group is unfolded: there are two types of affines, those who give captives and those who give women, and enemies are of the first type; (2) the captive is given to the sister or daughter of the captor. Here the enemy stands as a wife taker.

Insofar as the captive seems to be staging affinity itself, revealing all the possible positions of affinity,[10] in all these exchanges the captive has a relationship value, he is an operator (objectification) in relations of affinity within the captive group, the same relations that constituted him in his own village. So is the relation of affinity "unpacked."

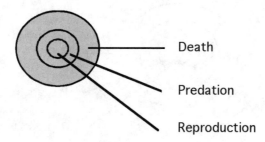

Figure 5.3: Person as operator between affines within the enemy group

There are still three relations that constitute the person of the warrior. These "inner" relations require the reconstitution of the captive; he is made again a term, a full person with value placed on his subjectness. He was prepared and decorated for the final killing festival. In an opening dialogue with the killer he revealed himself as a predator; knowing himself dead, he would end by saying that his people had already taken revenge, as if it were him that was going to kill as opposed to be killed.

> The greatest care was taken so that the entity about to be eaten was a *human being*, a being of words, promises and memories. Innumerable details of the rite ... testify to this effort of constituting the victim as a thoroughly human subject (Viveiros de Castro 1992: 292).

The captive taking a slayer's position, is a crucial moment of mutual identification: the captive represents the killer's future (to be slain by the enemy) while the killer represents the captive's past (slayer) (Ibid.: 291). They incarnate the two time-displaced facets of the person; in a Strathernian reading they are two "half" persons, together "one" person. What is at stake depends on perspective: the killer's social reproduction; the enemy's immortality; the continuity of both. The Tupinamba shifted the relation with the dead to the enemy in such a way that enemies contain each other's history and are each other's future. This is the fractal person "in the making."

In his killing, the captive is made separate once more. Could we suggest that his male/female duality is unpacked in the distribution of the parts of the body? Flesh is mainly eaten by women, and skulls (bones) are cracked by the killer in such a way that:

male:female::bones:flesh

If we retain the idea of the Tupinamba name being a divine element of the person, a manifestation of the soul, we see how his human/divine duality is unpacked in the separation of name (that goes to the killer) and substance (that goes to the rest of the village) adding to the above association:

male:female::bones:flesh::names (divine):substance (human)

His predator/prey duality was also realized: whereas he was an obvious cannibal prey he was also a not-so-obvious cannibal predator. The killer was the only one who didn't eat the captive:[11]

> [W]ithdrawing to his house after the final blow ... he wore around his wrists the lips cut from the victim, as if inverting the cannibal relation.... Fasting for days in his hammock, with a cotton thread tied around his chest (like a corpse?).... Finally the killer was scarified (so that the blood would not rot in his belly) (Viveiros de Castro 1992: 293).

So are relations unpacked: the captive's relational constitution, his multi-layered duality, is either played out (e.g., being an affine relationship value) or revealed in the constitution of his being (e.g., names [divine] and substance [human]).

Finally, a part of the captive, his blood/names, became part of his slayer. The killer resuscitated with a new name. Could we see this as a process whereby an Other has been encompassed by the Self, a change in position mediated by enemy blood? This process is as much a matter of the Other becoming a Self as the contrary. The killer is "othered" in different ways: he can now legitimately marry, the captive has affinised him; he has died and resuscitated, which makes him a somewhat divine being, and most importantly, he becomes an enemy. All the relations that were unpacked via the captive, are rebuilt in the person of the killer; the lengthy process of the captive within the killer's camp might just well be a display of all that he will become. The killer has encompassed, "eaten," his enemy, and, after all, you are what you eat. But what does the killer eat? Relations. (See Viveiros de Castro 1992: 303 for a similar argument.)

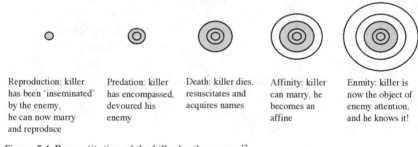

| Reproduction: killer has been 'inseminated' by the enemy, he can now marry and reproduce | Predation: killer has encompassed, devoured his enemy | Death: killer dies, resuscitates and acquires names | Affinity: killer can marry, he becomes an affine | Enmity: killer is now the object of enemy attention, and he knows it! |

Figure 5.4: Reconstitution of the killer by the enemy[12]

Incidentally, this description highlights how a person only contains relationships in which he/she has participated. You can only take a position if you contain it. This is why the killer must die; participating in a relation of death, he becomes immortal. This also gives killers, when caught (enemies), the ability to signify immortality in the unpacking and transmission of their divine element: names.

Let us now discuss an Araweté case where we can see in the death process of the person a similar unpacking of the constitution of the person. The relations the Tupinamba sustained with his enemies, the Araweté sustain with his *Maï* gods.

When an Araweté dies, his person undergoes a series of transformations. His body rots, which is understood as the cannibal consumption by two types of spirits, the *Ani* and *Iwi yari*, Grandmother earth. His *i*, vital principal that is evidenced in life both by blood pulsation and in the image of the person, divides and follows two paths: the first aspect becomes a *ta' o we*, a spectre, a double of the corpse, a kind of mechanical body deprived of subjectivity. This being lasts during the decomposition of the person, turning into "something like a dead opossum," and then into a night monkey. This aspect corresponds to the part of the *i* that in life was associated to the person's shadow. The sight of a *ta' o we* can cause death. They are feared by the living, who flee the village after the death until they suspect the *ta' o we* is no more. The other aspect of the *i*, which corresponds to the vitality of the person, rises to the sky where the *Maï* gods live. Here the dead are first painted with genipap in a pattern called "new soul." Next they are met by the *Maï* who request gifts from them. (If the dead is a woman, they want to have sex with her.) The dead never reciprocate these requests. This unethical behavior is met with death by the *Maï* (the dead are enemies in the world of the *Maï*). Killed and skinned (the *Maï* keep the skin as a kind of trophy), they are boiled; their flesh is eaten by all the *Maï*. Their bones, nonetheless, remain and are used by the god *Tiwawi* to reconstitute the body of the dead that is later bathed (or rather cooked) in effervescent water: this "'changes the skin' of the soul and revives it, making it strong young and beautiful. A male soul is painted with genipap in a pattern of fine lines; a female soul has her vulva painted" (Viveiros de Castro 1992: 211). All these transformations correspond with the decomposition of the corpse of a dead person. In the end the dead marry the *Maï*, entering into formal friendship, *apïˉhi-pihã*, relations with them. In this way the dead (as operators) affinize the *Maï* with respect to the living (Ibid.: 202-212).

This exegesis recalls the unpacking of the fractal person discussed for the Tupinamba warrior, although in this case, as Viveiros de Castro shows (1992: 211-214, 252-272), it seems to be cast in terms of a regression to nature and a passage to supernature. A person's human/nature component rots and is eaten by spirits. The human/supernature component is further divided in spectre, an enemy aspect perhaps (recall that the *ta' o we* is a deadly being; enemies of the Araweté don't enter the sky of *Maï*, in this sense they are only *ta' o we* [Ibid.: 238]) and celestial aspect, the Araweté component. The celestial aspect is then separated again: flesh (female) is eaten and bones (male) are reconstituted. If death is a female thing, both because one is eaten and one is a women given to the *Maï*, then what remains, bones (future *Maï*), must be male. (This, by the way, exposes the relative nature of gender as a metaphor of the Self/Other divide; I will come back to this later.) This final separation is also an instance of setting supernature aside from nature: "Only the bones forget" say the Araweté, meaning that the dead, once *Maï*, having been ripped from their flesh, the site of emotions and memory, forget the living.

The fractal quality of the person is here evinced in the embeddedness of persons in parts of persons as figure 5.5 depicts; it is also suggested by the use of the term *hiro* (which refers to any container) in the context of death:

> *Hiro*, like *i*, has a positional meaning. A living person is a *hiro* in opposition to a spectre [the double derived from the shadow]; a spectre is a *hiro* in opposition to an i-image [the celestial vitality *Maï*-to-be], and an image [celestial vitality]

is a *hiro* [the dead is eaten, he/she has flesh and bone] in opposition to that which is neither form or cause, that which is subjective (Viveiros de Castro 1992: 203).

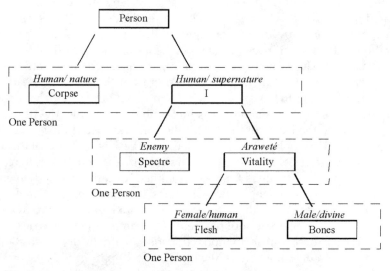

Figure 5.5: Unpacking the Fractal Araweté person[13]

Relations of death, enmity, and reproduction are revealed via the separation of the constituent aspects of the person and, as in the Tupinamba case, relations of predation and affinity are revealed "in action" by first being eaten and then marrying the *Maï*. All this is possible because the dead are operators in relations between the *Maï* and the living.

Relations with the Dead; Relations with Enemies; Issues of Scale

We have so far focused on the process of unpacking of enemies as operators in relations. This analysis conceals the fact that killers after slaying their enemies are also operators: they must seclude themselves, follow diet restrictions, avoid sexual relations, etc. In short, they are in a fragile state similar to that of the ill. The relations between the Wari' and their dead, as well as the relation between the Wari' killer and his enemy shed light on this issue. I will return to the Tupinamba and Araweté cases later.

In Wari' eschatology when a person is gravely ill, their soul travels to the world of the dead. Here he/she is offered beer by *Towira Towira*, a man with huge testicles. Acceptance, symbolically entering in a relation of affinity with *Towira Towira*, corresponds to the definite death of the person. If the person rejects the beer he/she will live (Vilaça 1992: 250). A recent dead is referred to by the term *napiri*. This term is used in two other situations that establish an important symbolic connection between recent dead, women, and killers. *Napiri* is a designation applied to young girls whose bodies are seen to be ready for marriage: "[N]*apiri* is a young woman ready to realize a marriage, an alliance; ready to receive semen." (Vilaça 1992: 104). The term has an important temporal dimension, and designates a person in a particular period: a woman at the moment of marriage exchange, in this sense it refers to a "woman given." In this context:

> It is interesting to remember that a recent dead is also called *napiri* … what appears to be related with his role of mediator between the living and the dead. If *napiri* is a "woman given" … the arriving dead affinise the dead for the Wari; transforming them into sons-in-law and brothers-in-law, turning them into prey, potential *karawa* ["food," "animal," "hunt"], which is exactly what the dead will become for the living. (Ibid.: 250).

The dead reappear on earth as peccaries which can be hunted by the Wari'. They can also reappear as foreigners, who come to dance in festivities, or as enemies. The last point worth mentioning is how in the funeral the *nari paxi*, affines and distant relatives of the deceased, eat the body of the dead as a service to the *iri'nari*, who being consubstantial with the deceased, are prohibited from eating in order to avoid autocannibalism (Vilaça 1992: 209).[14]

Wari' living-dead relations are mediated by exchange; the whole (the living) gives a part (deceased), like persons give body parts. On the one hand, there is a relation of affinity: recent dead Wari' being called *napiri* are "women given" to the dead. They are operators in this relation defining the dead as wife takers (term). Yet the recent dead finally become cognates of the dead. This passage, which corresponds with the cooking and consumption on earth of the dead person's corpse, is also mediated by the exchange with *Towira Towira* which symbolizes affinity. After this exchange the dead are bathed and reconstituted as young Wari' and they recognize the dead as their cognates. In this way the recent dead cease to be operators and become terms in relations with the living. On the other hand, there is a relation of predation: the dead reappear in the world of the living as peccaries that can be hunted by the Wari'. These peccaries are operators in this relation defining the living Wari' as predators (term). The combination of these two relations establishes a clear association between predation and copulation.[15] Figure 5.6 synthesizes the relations just described.

Let us switch now to the relations between the Wari' and their enemies. A killer holds in his belly the blood of the enemy, part of which he transforms into semen. This he does during the seclusion period that follows the killing. Like young girls who have reached sexual maturity and are ready to receive semen, during seclusion, slayers are also called *napiri*, suggesting their association with women at the moment of alliance. Moreover:

> This association [blood with semen] allows us to think of the penetration of blood of the enemy into the killer's body as symbolically associated with sexual

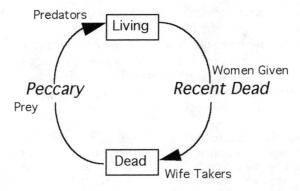

relations. Effectively, after this the killer will have a son: the soul of the dead enemy (Vilaça 1992: 103-104).

After seclusion, the killer, who has transformed part of the enemy's blood into semen, can "fatten" his wife (Ibid.: 109).

Let us note how what the dead do to the living, affinize them, is what the enemy does to his killer, he affinizes him through sexual relations (penetration of blood), thus placing enemies and the dead in the position of Others: first, the killer is a woman given (as a recent dead) and second, he becomes consubstantial with the enemy (as the recent dead recognize the dead as cognates). This is why he does not eat the substance of the enemy. But the rest of the Wari' do eat, which is precisely what the living do to the dead in their peccary form. It is also what the affines do as a service to the consubstantials in a Wari' funeral.[16] Figure 5.7 shows enemy-killer relations:

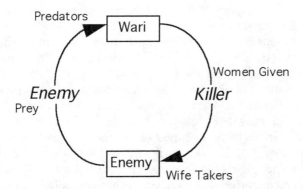

Figure 5.7: Wari'-Enemy relations (operators in italics, terms in boxes)

When focusing on the killer/captive pair we can see, as in the Tupinamba case, the encompassment of the Other by the Self. The killer might not eat the dead enemy's substance, but he symbolically eats his soul turned blood (Vilaça 1992: 112). A relationship between terms is mediated by the symbolic exchange of blood and incorporation of the enemy's soul.

When we zoom out, so to speak, and look at this from a different scale we note that both captive enemy and the killer are operators in the relations between the generic positions of Wari' and Other (terms). The enemy is an operator: his substance is prey and hence is eaten; the killer is an operator: he is consubstantial with the enemy, he is secluded, he needs to rest and digest the enemy's blood, his relation to the rest of the group is special. This identification leads to thinking of the dead enemy and the secluded killer as both detached/incomplete and the same; together one person. Here M. Strathern's notion of dividuals, as we saw for Tupinamba, is most explicitly useful: "An internal duality is externalized or elicited in the presence of a partner: what was 'half' of a person becomes 'one' of a pair" (1988: 15). The killer, in the position of a woman given, is analogous to a deceased's soul (recall how they are both called *napiri*), that is, he incarnates the "half" of a person that goes to the other world. The enemy, as prey, follows the path of a deceased's corpse, the "half" of the person that is eaten by affines.

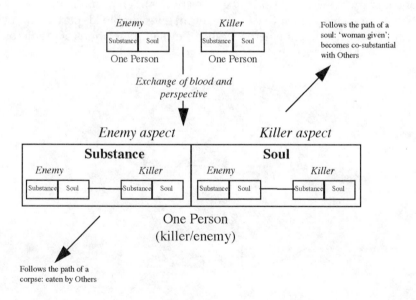

Figure 5.8: Wari' dividuality during seclusion of the killer[17]

Since the corpse of the enemy eventually disappears, it can be said that after this and prior to the lifting of seclusion (which lasts about a month) the killer is "half" a person, as we shall see later, and a process of body modifications makes him complete once more. Figure 5.9 resumes the living-dead relations and those between enemies, showing how they mirror each other.

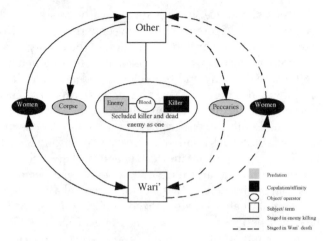

Figure 5.9: Living-dead and enemy relations

The same rationale seems to be operating in the Tupinamba case. A whole (enemy group) gives a part (captive) which signifies relations of affinity and enmity between two enemy groups (terms). A replication of this relation occurs when the captive (whole, term) gives his blood (part, operator) to his slayer, a moment where together they signify relations of predation, death, and reproduction.

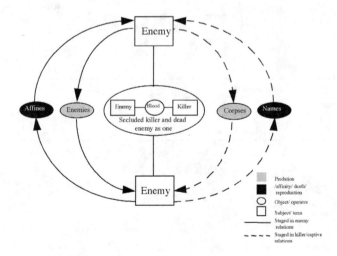

Figure 5.10: Tupinamba relations between enemies

The difference with the Tupinamba case is that there are no relations with the dead, only reciprocal exchanges between enemies. But even though enemies subsume relations that are distinct in the Wari' case, they at the same time mark the separation of two types of relations: those between the killer/captive and those between groups. This is evidenced in the resubjectification of the captive when he was going to be killed. Enemies as groups are the parallel of the Wari' dead; it is at this scale that the Tupinamba killer/captive pair are one operator between the captor's group and the enemy's group (terms).

If in the Wari' case, the dead do to the living what enemies do to the Wari', tying enemies and the dead in a common position of Others, here enemies do to each other what they do to each other, as it were. The reciprocal relation between enemies leads to a somewhat paradoxical situation of linking Others to Us, and only time serves as the displacement where the equation I = Enemy can be sustained. (Viveiros de Castro 1992: 291-292, is surely correct in highlighting the production of time in the context of the ritual killing of the captive.)

This leads us to discuss the final case of the Araweté. Here raiders usually return home with a body part of the slain enemy, a humerus or scapula which is kept as a trophy, like the *Maï* gods keep the skin of the dead. The actual killer, like his Tupinamba counterpart, withdraws and follows a series of interdictions. The killer takes the blood of his enemy within him and mirrors the enemy's death with his own. This marks the beginning of a new relation with the enemy; in life, killer and enemy's soul become *apĩ˜hi-pihã*, formal friends, and the enemy gives songs and names for the killer to transmit; in death this relation fuses in the constitution of a single *Maï* (Viveiros de Castro 1992: 239-245). As in the Wari' and Tupinamba examples, the killer/enemy pair take up the two facets of a person that are revealed explicitly at death: the killer parallels a deceased's vitality aspect of the *i*: he ritually dies and resuscitates to enter into *apĩ˜hi-pihã* relations with the enemy (like a normal Araweté dies and finally enters into *apĩ˜hi-pihã* relation with the *Maï*). The enemy follows the path of a deceased's corpse: he rots in the forest (presumably liberating a *ta' o we*, a spectre). They are one and the same; the blood/soul of the enemy has been incorporated, which makes them both Others of the Araweté.

The Araweté display another variation of the logic presented which can be seen to combine Tupinamba and Wari' features. On the one hand, like the Wari', for the Araweté we can distinguish relations with enemies from those with the *Maï* gods. On the other hand, the *Maï* gods do to the living what the Araweté do to their enemies, linking the *Maï* with the Araweté as "Us."[18] But this leads to the contradiction noted for the Tupinamba: the *Maï* eat the recent dead, they are enemies but at the same time we take their place among the living. The Araweté are the earthly equivalent of the *Maï*, the Enemy, only time (death) manages to sustain the equation I = Enemy. Another important difference is that whereas the Tupinamba and the Wari' relate to the enemies reciprocally, the Araweté relation with the *Maï* is not reciprocal, the *Maï* are destiny; final destiny.

Exchange of Perspectives

Let us now address an important issue: how do people manage to live with enemies within? If the killer becomes the enemy, how can he be "Us"? This is precisely what the exchange of perspectives implies, Others becoming Us. Let us return to the Wari'.

A killer is secluded, a detached "half" person, he is consubstantial with the Other (dead enemy). The completion of the killer's person after seclusion involves the enemy within gaining a Wari' perspective. This is done by the killer being carefully painted and bathed. After this his enemy blood fertilizes him: the enemy becomes a son of the killer, and the killer can now resume sexual relations with his wife. But this is an inversion of the enemy's point of view: the killer's son is the soul of the enemy but, through the painting and bathing of the killer (modifications of the body), he is made to see the Wari' (enemies) as "Us" (ex-enemies). This stage has its parallel in the bathing of a dead person on arrival in the other world, after which he/she recognizes the other dead as cognates. Once dead, "We" (Wari') is a position of the dead. This explains how the killer/enemy pair are temporary objects (one operator) of another subjectivity: the one is the object of the Wari' as the dead (a women given), the other is object of the Wari' as living (prey, food). Body modifications, then, complete a incomplete (detached) person. A "half" becomes a whole with an internal Self/Other duality. Insofar as a subjectness is regained, it is one that can be inverted (a killer can kill again or become prey, the dead can be hunted by the living Wari'); what is reconstituted is a person.

Here the roles of exchange and painting/bathing are crucial: first, in exchanging (blood/affinity-symbolizing taking of beer from *Towira Towira*) an enemy becomes a Wari', second, in the painting/bathing (of the killer after seclusion and the recently dead after the exchange with *Towira Towira*) enemies (Wari'/dead) are recognized as "Us" (ex-enemies).

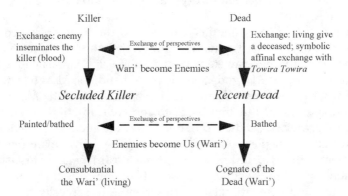

Figure 5.11: Parallels between Wari' killing and dying

This corresponds to the treatment of the corpse, which is first cooked then eaten; it also ratifies that every change of perspective is a bodily modification/transaction.[19]

A similar situation can be read into the Tupinamba treatment of the captive before the killing festival. In a sense, in identifying himself with the position of his slayer (taking his wife or daughter, speaking as a predator, being decorated, etc.) he is making the Other and his group, "We." Moreover, once caught the captive was considered a dead man in his own village, and he would not be accepted if he were to return, lest the captors imagine they could not avenge a death (Viveiros de Castro 1992: 287). So for the captive "We" was his captor's group both through his identification with the killer, his "killerness," and the nonidentification with his group, his "deadness." "We" can only be the Other of others.

The exchange/body modification pair can also be found operating for the Tupinamba, but here eschatology is found in the relations between enemy groups. First, in an exchange (captive/blood) an enemy becomes part of the captor group or the captor himself, second, with body modifications (resubjectification of the captive/new names) an enemy (captive/secluded killer) becomes "Us."

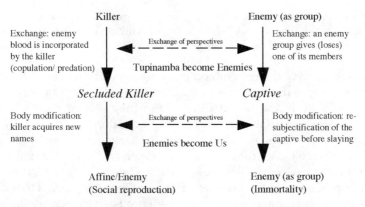

Figure 5.12: Parallels between Tupinamba killing and enemy exchanges

The case for the Araweté is more complex. Since there is no reciprocal relation with the *Maï* gods, the Araweté killer, in acquiring his divine features, never really ceases to be a *Maï*, an Other amongst his covillagers. The relation with the *Maï*, is more one of attracting than reciprocal exchange; the *Maï* are not persons (like the Wari' dead), they are gods; nobody eats the *Maï*. In becoming a *Maï* the killer never regains his personness.

The killer takes the enemy's point of view in two ways: he mirrors his victim's death, on the one hand, and he resuscitates as a *Maï* on earth, on the other. The Araweté have two kinds of Others, living enemies and the cannibal *Maï*; killers are both. A killer enters into seclusion and follows interdictions (as detached/incomplete persons do), but his body is not later modified by either painting or new names. The second step we have seen for the Wari' and the Tupinamba doesn't happen. Several facts indicate his "enemyness": (1) the Araweté killer confers names his enemy's soul gives him, but does not "wear" them himself. (2) He must not resume sexual relations with his wife until long after the killing, for it would be his enemy who would first have sex with his wife. (3) His weapons must be kept away from him in the post-killing period to avoid the enemy taking revenge on the killer's covillagers. (4) In the songs the killer sings, it is the enemy who takes the subject position. (5) Most importantly, a killer is the only person who is spared from divine anthropophagy at death; killers go straight to the reconstituting bath (body modification). Neither does the killer liberate a spectre (some say he does, but only a harmless one).

A killer has ridded himself of his *ta' o we*, his spectre, which is embodied in the rotting corpse of the enemy. This is as much a matter of the killer becoming a *Maï*, an enemy, as of the enemy being incorporated to the killer. Enemies are pure *ta' o we*,[20] and by becoming a subject with his slayer they become *i*, and *Maï* gods on earth. But since no body modifications complete the person of the killer, he remains detached (incomplete), the only individual:

> This is the paradox of the Araweté warrior: pure spirit, a man without a shadow and without flesh, he is his own enemy and the centre of a society without centre (Viveiros de Castro 1992: 251).

If the killer is a *Maï* then his subject position cannot be reversed. Evidence of this is the idea that in times past killers never died, but rather went to the skies in flesh and blood (Ibid.: 246); they cannot be made prey. Whereas Araweté nonkillers achieve the equation I = Enemy through time, by dying, passing from "We" on earth (Araweté) to "We" in the skies (*Maï*), a killer collapses time in his ritual death and hence becomes I and Enemy on earth, he embodies the ambiguous position of the *Maï*, that first eat us but then are "Us" in heaven. The point is that a process that began on earth, by killing and becoming an enemy (step 1), is only ended in heaven by changing the body in the reconstituting bath (step 2). But this asymmetry with the process undergone by all other Araweté means that the killer never ceases to be an Other, not even in the world of the *Maï*. Here he is an *Iraparadï*, a being feared by the *Maï*:

> As a designation for the status of the Araweté warrior, the concept of *Iraparadï* is revealed to be essentially a perspective. If the *Maï* are one and the same time the celestial parallel of the Araweté and a figuration of the Enemy, that is, if they contemplate us with the eyes of an enemy and we eye them as enemies, the *Iraparadï* are the Araweté actively thinking of themselves as enemies. They are something that the *Maï* fear, just as the common dead fear the *Maï* (Ibid.: 248-249).

The killer is an Other on earth by virtue of exchange with the enemy and an Other of the *Maï* by virtue of a body modification.[21] The difference from the other cases is that here the first step of the process occurs when the "We" are the living Araweté, and the second step occurs when "We" are the *Maï*. So instead of enemies (recent dead) becoming "Us" (*Maï*) it is "We" (*Maï*) that become enemies (of the *Iraparadï*).

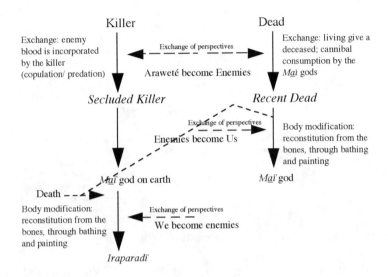

Figure 5.13: Parallels between Araweté killing and dying

Vehicles of Perspective

So far we have dwelled on how relations between groups (enemies, the dead) are replicated between individuals. In the former, persons (captives, recently dead) are the operators, in the latter, parts of persons (blood) serve as operators. But if blood can be operator it is only because it can signify relations and hence must be able to be Other at one point and Self at another. Blood is a downscaled fractal of the person.

In the Wari' case, the transformation of (enemy) blood into (killer's) semen is an instance of just this. For the Araweté it is a person's vital aspect of the *i* that becomes a *Maï* god ("Us" in the afterlife). For the Tupinamba we can suggest the association between (enemy) blood that became (killer's) names. In all cases a part of an Other becomes the Self, affinity is transformed into consubstantiality. It is because parts of persons (blood, Araweté *i*) participate in the fractality of the person that the latter are dual and can assume opposed positions, take up different perspectives. Containing transformable and transactable parts, persons are dual, transformable, and transactable themselves.

If we focus on the blood transactions we can discern the switching of positions, the reversibility of persons. The Wari' blood transaction brings to the fore the male/female duality of persons: the (male) killer is first inseminated and fertilized (female), then, after the painting and bathing, he is an (male) inseminator to his wife whom he "fattens":

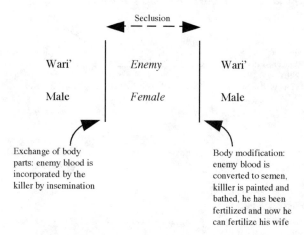

Figure 5.14: Wari' killer's positions in ritual killing

We can see for the Tupinamba a similar process: (1) enemy blood enters the killer, (2) the killer's body is modified by new names and ornaments (transformed blood), after which he can marry and have children:

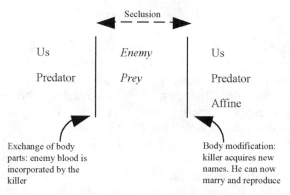

Figure 5.15: Tupinamba killer's positions in ritual killing (the example is that of a youth's initiation)

For the Araweté we find the living when they die are first consumed (female) and then marry the Maï.

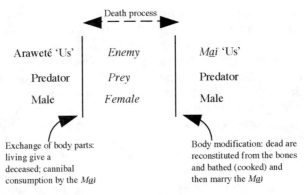

Figure 5.16: Araweté positions in the process of death

Conclusion

The fractality of the person is revealed through the unpacking of the relations that constitute persons. This process reveals scaled self-similarity. The encompassment of the Other in the Self is the end of this trajectory, enemies become Us, living become the dead. This process involves transactions of body parts and body modifications: with the former, Others (enemies) become Selves (killers); with the latter, Others are redefined as Us. The first is an exchange of places within a framework—you become me and vice versa—the second is a switching of the framework—you will see the world as I did before the exchange. The first implies multinaturalism, the second implies the humanity of the reflexive subject position. These two steps form the essence of perspectivism: (1) encompassment (predation/sexual intercourse) via transactions makes Others versions of Us, (2) the body, as the site of perspective, is modified making Others see the world as Us, that is, as ex-Others. "We" always have the upper hand, the point being to carry subjectness with myself. If the body is the site of perspective, then its parts, really or imaginarily transacted, are the vehicles of perspective. Perspectivism is literally an Exchange of Perspectives, sometimes mediated by exchanging body parts, that is, parts of the site-of-perspective. These parts contain whole persons: blood is to the person as persons are to groups, all are "a fractal person."

The analysis of how relations with the dead and relations with enemies are articulated, coupled with the idea of the fractal person appears as a useful heuristic for comparison. It has shown the crucial roles of exchange and body modifications as well as the differences between reciprocal relationships (Wari') and nonreciprocal or attractor relationships (particularly evident in the Araweté example, although also the case for the Tupinamba).[22] The latter, in their turn, highlight that even though there are only two positions possible in relations based on identity, on opposing the Self to the Other, the basis of this system is a triad: transactor A, transacted, and transactor B. On the one plane, transactors are differentiated from the transacted (see M. Strathern 1988: 177), on the other, A (wife-giver/living/enemy) is differentiated from B (wife-taker/dead/us) as history is to destiny. Here time and death play the differentiating role.

As for theories, this essay hints at a theoretical proximity between Melanesian and Amazonian anthropology, underscoring the importance of certain transactions for the sustenance of a perspectivist ontology,[23] an aspect perhaps downplayed in a theory of perspectivism but the bread and butter of Melanesian anthropology.[24] This is not to say that the Melanesian and Amazonian situations are identical; they are not. This is not the place for a fully fledged comparison. It is enough to say that the parallels with Melanesian gift exchange seem to be more to do with "exchange" than "gift." At least one important difference lies in that predatory exchanges culminate with a fusion of distinct identities; the Other is encompassed by the Self, whereas gift exchange maintains partners' distinct identities even when one may be seen as a metaphor of the other.[25] However, some ideas in the direction of an "exchange view" of the person possibly constitute a theoretical opening that can serve as a link to analyze groups that are characterized more by trade than warfare.

Acknowledgements

I would like thank Eduardo Viveiros de Castro for revising previous drafts and offering his encouraging comments, Aparecida Vilaça for her general comments and revision of the Wari' material, and Stephen Hugh-Jones, who led me to these themes and revised several drafts of the essay. I am also grateful to Marilyn Strathern and Fred Damon for their insightful and encouraging comments.

Notes

1. There is of course more to fractals than scaled self-similarity. What I am borrowing from the mathematical field is the image of figures that present the same form at different scales. Other important mathematical aspects of fractals are their noninteger dimensionality and the fact that they can appear as attractors in chaotic systems. For an example of the use of the noninteger dimensionality aspect of fractals, see Wagner (1991).
2. The intellectual debt owed to Eduardo Viveiros de Castro and Marilyn Strathern cannot be overstressed. I must also emphasize Alfred Gell's "Strathernograms" (1999); this work has been most valuable as an aid in comprehending both these anthropologists' theoretical contributions. The mark of all three is very explicit in my text. For reasons of space I cannot reference all the theoretical notions taken from these authors. M. Strathern (1988; 1992b) and Viveiros de Castro (1992; 1998) constitute the two main the-

oretical sources of this essay. I would further like to emphasize that I make no claims to fully comprehend the complex theories deployed by these authors; this work is based on my understanding, which is partial at its best.

3. The contextual nature of the "us" category together with the reproductive value of the outside can be seen as an analytical distillation of an interplay of the values of consanguinity and affinity within Lévi-Strauss's original scheme of diametric and concentric dualism. Viveiros de Castro's synthesis of Amerindian kinship (1993; 2002) draws upon Lévi-Strauss's (1963b) distinction proposing a general model where a diametrical opposition between consanguinity and affinity runs through social, genealogical, and spatial relationship distance. Their relative weight is, however, importantly shifted by a concentric component: in the close relationship distance - community level - the value of consanguinity is predominant over that of affinity and encompasses it. This weight is balanced in the mid range and is inverted in the extreme distance. Here it is a value of unrealized potential affinity – referring to exchanges with enemies, the dead, divinities, spirits - that encompasses consanguinity and kinship in general.

4. Vilaça is, in a way, suggesting just this: "it is necessary to remember that Wari' and *karawa* ['food,' 'prey'] are *reversible positions* and that this reversibility is produced precisely in the act of cannibal devouring, that simultaneously constitutes them as different categories. *The position of prey is contained in that of predator, and vice-versa*, this certainly is related to the fact that Wari' classify their preferred prey as potential predators" (1992: 291, emphasis added).

5. This is not exactly so, it would be more correct to say that gods are *almost* pure subjects. The case of the Araweté gods (discussed later) shows how their subject position can be "challenged" even though they are never eaten or transacted.

6. This is not to say that a "part of the person" in the Melanesian context is equivalent to the Amerindian soul or other aspects of the Amerindian person. The equivalence I wish to establish is not *what* can be attached or detached, but precisely *the possibility* of separating aspects of the person. It is the commonality of *divisibility* I am hinting at. Moreover, it is only in certain contexts that aspects of the person that would otherwise be fused or indistinguishable become distinguishable, disintegrated from the whole person and hence separable from it (in the examples below we can see how death disintegrates the person in parts or aspects that in life are either inseparable or indistinguishable).

7. My usage of the terms Operator and Term, which I find simplifying, comes from Gell (1999). The notions of being detached and incomplete come directly from M. Strathern: "To be rendered incomplete, the social person may despatch a part of him or herself, or be detached from a nexus of relationships." (1992b: 180).

8. This technique of "unpacking" relationships, which I find most enlightening, is taken from, and outlined in Gell (1999) where he calls this "the detotalization of the fractal personhood." I prefer "unpacking" just for the sake of economy of words.

9. The color grey is to indicate that at this stage in the unpacking process the captive enemy is made a subject once more, his blood becoming an operator in the relation between himself and the killer.

10. Except father-in-law. I can propose three reasons for this. (1) The position of father-in-law wields too much power to be even symbolically given to a captive. (2) Following Viveiros de Castro, the object of the "affinal game" seems to have been a mockery of the position of youths in their villages. If youths are "prisoners" of their affines, living uxorilocally, and subjected to their father-in-law's whim, the captive enemy is an extreme case of a youth being subjected to his affines (Viveiros de Castro 1992: 298). If this is so, the captive will never take the position of father-in-law. (3) The positions played out are all related to reproduction rather than production. If the whole exercise has this prime focus, the position of father-in-law is irrelevant.

11. Neither does the Wari' killer: the killer is consubstantial with the dead enemy. Quite explicitly the Wari' say "if we eat ourselves we die" (Vilaça 1992: 103).

12. First we must recall this example is assuming the case of an initiation. Second, although exchanges between the Tupinamba and their enemies, it seems, were couched more in terms of acquisition of names than in terms of reproduction, some stages in the final ritual apparently associated killing with the reproductive function of women. Carlos Fausto also notes that even though there was a relation between killing and the capacity for reproduction, this was not a condition for it (personal communication). I leave it to the Tupi specialist to judge the degree of speculation in this instance of my argument.

13. This depiction and my description are in truth only telling half of the eschatological story of the decomposition of the person. The parts "left behind," so to speak, also have decompositions of themselves: for example, it is the rotting body's *i* that is cannibalized by the spirits whilst its substance is "eaten" by the earth. For the sake of simplicity I have left this to one side; it in no way invalidates the argument.

14. The Wari' sharing of substance is couched in terms of the mixing of blood and commensality, on having one body which unites offspring with parents and spouses (Vilaça 1992: 34, 52-53).

15. Consider Viveiros de Castro: "if there is no exchange of persons in marriage, then this shall be done via cannibal reciprocity. In the absence of marriage or a unidirectional flow of persons (women) a cannibal credit is open, reciprocal or unidirectional (in the inverse direction)" (Viveiros de Castro in Vilaça 1992: 293-294).

16. Note that these two events that involve eating are staging the relations dead = affines = enemies. For it is the affines who eat the Wari' dead in the same way that all the Wari' of a village eat the enemy. The same rationale is operating: consubstantials (spouse and children in the first case, and killer in the second) cannot eat, this would amount to autocannibalism.

17. The format of this diagram follows from Gell (1999).

18. Referring to the violent reception of the dead by the *Maï*, quite explicitly the Araweté "would compare this aggressive reception of the gods to what they themselves used to do when they came across white hunters in the forest before contact" (Viveiros de Castro 1992: 211).

19. In general all the processes to which the dead (as aspects of the person) are submitted have a corresponding body equivalent: cooking, consumption of flesh, of bones, rotting or transformation into animals (see Vilaça 1992: 247; Viveiros de Castro 1992, chapter 7; Descola 1997: 367).

20. "The souls of enemies, upon arriving in the *Maï* village, are hurled back down to earth, where they perish for good. In this sense, enemies only have, or are, *ta' o we*: being deadly, they die ... enemies, not properly human, have no celestial soul, the principle of the person" (Viveiros de Castro 1992: 238).

21. Let us recall that being an Other is not to be an object. The *Maï* might fear the *Iraparadï* but they are not objects of exchange or consumption. In this sense we could see their subject position challenged but not reversed.

22. This idea I take from Viveiros de Castro (1992): for the Tupinamba one of the objectives of ritual warfare was to invert the uxorilocal and dominated position of married men. Important warriors did not live uxorilocally, it was an honor to give them women; they led a band of warriors. Virilocal, wife-takers and leaders, they incarnate all of what a youth is not and hopes to be. This inversion (othering) is the same that characterizes the Araweté *Maï* gods, the celestial wife-takers who don't reciprocate. These two positions, Tupinamba leader and *Maï* god, are thus final conditions to which all are "attracted."

23. M. Strathern herself has written recently on the parallels between Viveiros de Castro's perspectivism and her views of Melanesian gift exchange (M. Strathern 1999: 249-256). If I understand correctly, she has focused on how the Melanesian gift is in a sense equivalent into Amazonian vision as the means of effecting exchanges of perspectives "Gifts in the hands could almost be like Amazonian eyes." (ibid.: 254). I have however focused more on the parallels *via* the concept of dividuality.

24. Viveiros de Castro's (1998) lucid presentation of the theory of perspectivism shows little on the theme of real or imaginary exchange of body parts or other objects. In some parts of Melanesia the exchange of women seems to be based on the same rationale of gift exchange (M. Strathern, 1988, 1992b). Viveiros de Castro, in tying up cannibalism with women exchange (see ff. 31), has left the terrain open to pursue the exchange of body parts further.

25. I want to thank Eduardo Viveiros de Castro for bringing this crucial point to my attention.

6

FLUIDS AND FRACTALS IN RWANDA
Order and Chaos

Christopher C. Taylor

Background

In April 1994 the last of this century's genocides began in Rwanda shortly after the country's president, Juvenal Habyarimana, was assassinated under mysterious circumstances. At the time I was living in the capital city of Kigali and working as a behavioral research specialist for an AIDS prevention project directed by Family Health International and The US Agency for International Development (USAID). This was my third extended period of residence in Rwanda, having done fieldwork there in the period 1983 to 1985, and again in the summer of 1987. In sharp contrast to the 1990s, my earlier periods of fieldwork transpired in a country that was peaceful and relatively prosperous. Even then, however, Rwanda had not yet resolved the ethnic divisions of its bloody past. Minority Tutsi, the dominant group in precolonial and colonial times, had been overthrown in the violent revolution between 1959 and 1962 and were now living either as second-class citizens in what had abruptly become a Hutu ethnocratic state or as refugees outside the country.

Tutsi still resident in Rwanda could not serve in the army and almost none participated in politics until after slight democratization of the Rwandan political system in 1991 (Prunier 1995: 124-125).[1] During the 1980s expatriate Tutsi negotiated with the Government of Rwanda (GOR) to obtain the right to return, but were continually rebuffed. President Habyarimana justified his policy against refugee repatriation on the grounds that the country was already overpopulated. Frustrated, Rwanda's expatriates threatened force, but this too fell on deaf ears. Finally in October 1990, the most prominent of the refugee groups, the Rwandan Patriotic Front (RPF), a group which also included some disgruntled Hutu, mounted an armed invasion of Rwanda from neighboring Uganda where many of them had been serving in the Ugandan army. After three years of fighting, the RPF held the advantage on the battlefield, but French military and economic support of the Habyarimana regime prevented the RPF from achieving full victory.

I arrived in Rwanda in October 1993 about two months after the signing of peace accords between the RPF and the GOR in Arusha, Tanzania. At that time most of my Rwandan acquaintances expressed optimism that the peace would hold and that a coalition government consisting of the RPF and all the other principal Rwandan political parties would be in place before the end of 1993. Many continued to be optimistic in early December, even though Hutu extremists from the president's party, Mouvement Revolutionnaire National pour le Développement et la Démocratie or MRND, and the Coalition pour la Defense de la Republique (CDR) opposed the accords as tantamount to capitulation to the rebel RPF. Extremists feared that peace with the RPF would undermine the state of Hutu supremacy that had prevailed in Rwanda since the Revolution between 1959 and 1962 and that it would permit a return to the Tutsi monarchy that had characterized Rwanda before 1959.

When several attempts to install the new government failed in late 1993 and then again in early 1994, and when violent incidents grew more daring and frequent in early 1994, it became clear to everyone except the United Nations Security Council, that keeping the peace in Rwanda would not be as easy as the international community had hoped (Prunier 1995). Rwandan friends and coworkers began to express doubts that peace would endure. When President Habyarimana's most popular political rival, Felicien Gatabazi of the Parti Social Démocrate (PSD), was assassinated in late February,[2] many of my Rwandan acquaintances concluded that the GOR had not been sincere when it signed the Arusha accords and that it had no intention of sharing power either with the RPF, or with the internal opposition parties of largely southern Hutu composition. In early 1994 the GOR, encouraged by France, was treating the Arusha accords as "just a scrap of paper."

In the final months before the genocide, many Rwandans had grown anxious and fearful for their lives. Some asked me to procure arms for them, others, to help them flee the country. Obviously, I could do neither. My wife's parents on the other hand, Tutsi who had supported Habyarimana during most of his reign, asked something of me that I could do. They asked me to return in a few days and pick up a trunk that they were packing with important objects and papers. There were things they wanted to save, even though they probably knew at the time they would not be able to save themselves. Little did I know then, 3 April 1994, that I would be unable to fulfill my promise to them and that this evening would be the last time I would see them alive. They seemed anxious as indeed tension in Kigali had risen during the last several weeks, but made no mention of fear for their lives. I noticed, though, that for the first time in the ten years that I had known them, they no longer had the president's portrait displayed on their living room wall. A dark rectangular stain bore witness to the location where the picture had hung for two decades. My wife's father had known Habyarimana personally, and after Habyarimana stopped the violence against Tutsi during the ethnic disturbances of 1973 and helped find him a job, felt personally indebted to him. I was struck by the absence of the portrait. It was as if they were committing their first and last act of defiance against a regime that would willingly sacrifice them for the sake of an ethnically pure, all Hutu Rwanda. Yet by removing his image they were also abandoning all hope of Habyarimana's symbolic protection.

Three days later on 6 April 1994, the president's plane was shot down by a missile as it approached Kigali airport, killing everyone aboard. Later, at around 3:00 a.m., we heard the sound of hell breaking loose when Rwandan Government Forces (RGF) attacked the RPF garrison in Kigali and the genocide began in earnest.[3] The following morning Rwandan radio advised everyone to stay at home as Kigali's neighborhoods turned into killing fields. For the next fifty hours, we remained ensconced in our house and at times when the explosions seemed frighteningly near, sheltered in the innermost corridor with mattresses on either side. Occasionally when there was a lull in the fighting, I ventured out onto our front porch to have a look. From there I could see just above the courtyard wall and into the street as every now and then a loaded car or pickup truck raced by. At other times I could make out the bobbing heads of looters carrying booty on their heads, as people in the neighborhood were killed and their houses pillaged. It was genocide for some, opportunity for others.

Then on the afternoon of Saturday 9 April, a USAID employee banged loudly on the outdoor gate and yelled, "Chris, get your stuff. You've got five minutes. We're being evacuated." By land convoy we traveled first to Bujumbura, and a few days later took a plane to Nairobi. Once there and settled, I began to visit Rwandan refugees housed at the Shauri-Moyo YMCA. From them I learned about a diviner named Magayane, who two years earlier had predicted the genocide, the president's death, and a number of other occurrences. These predictions had been printed in one of Rwanda's numerous cheap political magazines. One of Magayane's predictions, that Habyarimana would be the last of Rwanda's Hutu kings, particularly intrigued me. Although during the time of the monarchy all Rwanda's kings had been Tutsi, here Rwanda's foremost Hutu, Juvenal Habyarimana, was being spoken about as if he too were a king. At the time I wondered how significant this identification was between former kings and Habyarimana.

Figure 6.1: "Habyarimana will die in March, 1994"

The presentiment that Habyarimana would not live beyond March 1994 was stated more than once in the popular political literature of the time, and not just by the diviner, Magayane. Here in *Kangura*, one of the more infamous and widely read Hutu extremists' organs (Chrétien 1995), Habyarimana's death is predicted four months in advance (Figure 6.1). He is also depicted as doing the bidding of RPF leader Paul Kagame. I was first shown this cartoon by a Hutu friend in January 1994. His comment at the time was that there was more than a bit of truth to the idea that Habyarimana had become Kagame's beast of burden. For many extremist foes of the Arusha accords, Habyarimana by early 1994 was no longer to be trusted as the champion of Hutu ethnonationalism. Indeed, Habyarimana by that time was a leader alone. Deserted by increasing numbers of extremists, he had long since been abandoned by Hutu moderates, although obviously the two camps differed on why they deemed him a bad ruler. When I asked a Rwandan friend late in 1993 why it was that Habyarimana never appeared in public anymore, I was told that if he did, he would be subject to verbal and possibly physical assault by the population.

The Problem

Scholarly and journalistic analyses of the 1994 genocide in Rwanda are by now quite numerous. The more perspicacious of these analyses, going beyond the "ancient tribal hatreds" explanation that characterized early journalistic accounts, concentrate on the political dimensions of the genocide. Many show clearly that the genocide was planned and organized in advance by MRND party officials and other Hutu extremists close to the reins of power and then was executed at the local level by burgomasters, police, military, and party members opposed to the RPF. These studies also show the organizers' use of a variety of means ranging from intimidation to the promise of material gain to induce the local population to exterminate their Tutsi neighbors. While many of these analyses have been illuminating and have clarified the strategies and motives of groups and individuals during the genocide, they have tended to neglect its sociocultural and symbolic dimensions.

In this essay I intend to focus attention more on the sociocultural and symbolic aspects of the genocide by using concepts borrowed from chaos theory, notions such as: nonlinearity, onset of turbulence, and fractality. By using chaos models to analyze Rwandan symbolic forms, I hope to shed light on the war of meaning that took place in the pregenocidal popular Rwandan political literature and that was most evident in its use of cartoons and illustrations. I also hope to chart an intermediate course between the overly rigid and static models of Rwandan society and culture that have characterized classic scholarship, and the "anything goes" epistemological relativism of postmodern anthropology. I argue that chaos theory sensitizes us to all that lies between rigid structure and formless anarchy in what was surely Rwanda's most disorderly historical moment.

I will pay particular attention to the symbols of historical Rwandan sacred kingship and will attempt to show that during the days that preceded the "onset of turbulence," Rwandan journalists used comparable symbolic forms and structures to represent the Rwandan president, Juvenal Habyarimana, and his followers. In another work I try to show that embodied notions of Rwandan cosmology influenced some of the forms of violence that perpetrators inflicted upon Tutsi victims in 1994 (cf. Taylor 2002). Here my intention is similar. Journalistic use of the symbols of Rwandan sacred kingship helped prepare the terrain for Habyarimana's assassination and for general violence, rendering it do-able by first of all rendering it thinkable at a profound and not always directly apprehensible level. Sometimes journalists used these symbols as part of conscious political strategies; at other times I am convinced that they could not have been fully aware of the deeper ontological levels that they managed to touch (cf. Kapferer 1988). Nevertheless, the symbolic structures of Rwandan sacred kingship were not reproduced in a mechanical or ahistoric fashion. Integrated in an almost seamless way with symbols that predate the colonial era, we find symbols whose origin is more recent, reflecting Rwanda's experience with colonialism and modernity. The sources of these symbols include: Christianity, the commodity economy, and Western democracy.

Between Determinism and Disorder

Classic analyses of Rwanda and other Central African societies have often been characterized by a certain rigidity. Sometimes this rigidity is sociopolitical in nature, as in J. Maquet's *Le systéme des relations sociales dans le Ruanda ancien* (1954), where the inequality that characterized relations between central Rwandan Tutsi patrons and Hutu clients during the colonial era was presumed to have been dependent upon a functionally necessary complicity between the dominant and the dominated. In other cases symbolic structures have been described as relatively static and immune to the fortuitous tides of accident and history, as in L. de Heusch's *Le Rwanda et la civilisation interlacustre* (1966). More recently the revisionist pendulum has swung in the opposite direction. Anthropologists, justifiably concerned with the ahistoricity of many structural-functionalist and structuralist analyses, have emphasized the contingent, transactional, and protean nature of the social, symbolic, and political formations that are found in the world (Appadurai 1996) and in Africa (Vansina 1983; Comaroff and Comaroff 1992).

In both cases the classical and the revisionist views may neglect an important middle ground: that which lies between rigid structure and random contingency. Classical ethnology betrays an a priori commitment to the condition of order in its depiction of social and cultural systems. Homeostasis, dear to structural-functionalist analysis and implicit in many structuralist models as well, resembles the model of a clockwork universe in Newtonian mechanics, where heavenly bodies were thought to move in relation to one another in precise orbits predictable according to the straightforward application of the inverse square law of gravitation. Problems with the Newtonian model included: it could not be applied to objects moving at velocities approaching the speed of light and it could only be applied to two bodies at a time. Once fast-moving objects or three or more formed part of the system, a situation which conforms more closely to nature, the universe came to look a bit more like an ocean and a little less like a clock. In like fashion in classic ethnology, whether the homeostatic structures being described are sociopolitical in nature or symbolic, they appear as if sheltered from history and human volition.

On the other hand, the apparent corrective to ahistorical depictions of structure, antistructural descriptions of agency and process, may also have gone too far. To some who advocate the latter, the claim that there exist patterns or regularities of any sort, structural or otherwise, is perceived as overly totalizing. In their haste to overthrow the procrustean models of classic ethnology, they end up throwing out the baby with the bath-water, placing too much emphasis on individual choice and political strategization. This can ultimately lead us to a subjectivist impasse where all epistemology becomes reduced to the political and where hypotheses come to be judged solely on who they empower, who they disempower, and whether or not subaltern voices are being heard (cf. Ortner 1995).

The middle ground between pure structure and pure contingency can be reclaimed by drawing inspiration from "chaos theory" (Gleick 1987) and its insight that order and disorder are in many, if not most natural systems, but two faces of a single coin. I would extend this insight to include cultural systems, not in opposition to natural systems, but as a subset within them. As Paul Friedrich points out in his review of Gleick's book (Friedrich 1988), the lessons of chaos theory could be applied to the study of sociocultural phenomena. Is it merely the antecedent prejudices of ethnographers that cause some to see order in culture and others to see only disorder? Or is it rather that culture embodies both, that beneath the appearance of order lurks an "eerie chaos," while beneath the appearance of chaos, lies an "eerier order" (ibid.)?

Arjun Appadurai echoes this sentiment in reference to ethnic disorders, a subject to which I will return below:

> Why do ethnic riots occur when and where they do? Why do states wither at greater rates in some places and times than in others?... Why do key events occur at a certain point in a certain place rather than in others? These are, of course, the great traditional questions of causality, contingency, and prediction in the human sciences, but in a world of disjunctive global flows, it is perhaps important to start asking them in a way that relies on images of flow and uncertainty, hence chaos, rather than on older images of order, stability, and systematicness. (Appadurai 1996: 46-47)

Chaos theory does indeed posit the futility of trying to predict exactly how a congeries of diverse forces will interact and what result this interaction will produce. Despite this, it also demonstrates that not just anything goes. Chaotic events have been shown to manifest pattern, even if one cannot predict final outcomes (Gleick 1987). Where I would differ from Appadurai's interpretation of "chaos theory" then, is that as Gleick points out and Friedrich notes, a kind of "order" lurks beneath the appearance of disorder that characterizes chaotic phenomena. Chaos theory does not extirpate notions of system, quite the contrary (ibid.). It is rather that the systematicness in question is not of the ordinary, input—output, single cause—single effect, linear variety.

Chaos theory is also the source of inspiration for Roy Wagner's notion of the "fractal person" (Wagner 1986b). Fractality in its strict sense refers to "a dimensionality that cannot be expressed in whole numbers" (ibid.). In this instance, the "fractal person" refers to a relational entity, one who is never complete, neither singular nor plural, and never a discrete monad (Strathern 1988). Use of notions such as "fractality" or "fractal person" does not mean that the activities of human social actors can be reduced to mathematical functions, but it does imply that the social system composed of such persons is never in equilibrium, although never completely random in its dynamic movement. Although the activities of social actors under ordinary circumstances, such as that which prevailed in Rwanda during the 1980s, may appear to conform to preexisting norms, structures, and rules, indeterminacy, disorder, and fortuitousness are likely to creep into the social system as the unintended consequences of human action. On the other hand, even in a situation like that of pregenocidal Rwanda (between 1990 and 1994) where the norms of ordinary social life began to be radically transgressed, patterns emerged. A preexisting sociality did not completely disappear, nor did the mythic and symbolic structures which subtend this sociality.

It is here that another key insight of chaos theory applies: the "onset of turbulence." In the physical systems studied in chaos theory such as fluid dynamics and weather, the systems behave linearly under ordinary conditions—any additional input such as heat or mechanical motion changes the output by an expected amount. After a certain point has been reached (cf. Mosko, Introduction: the "point of bifurcation"), additional input does not result in the predictable change in output. The system begins to behave erratically or nonlinearly. This erratic behavior, or turbulence, a condition which before chaos theory defied analysis, has now been shown to be patterned. Beneath the apparent disorder lies an "eerier order" (Friedrich 1988).

When we integrate the notion of scale, corollary to that of fractals, we find fractal patterns reproduced at progressively more encompassing levels. In the specific case of Rwanda, this includes: the body, notions of the moral person, representations of the land and its rivers, and notions of the polity as a whole. While the contours of these fractal patterns differ in many ways, they show relatedness of form, not unlike a "Mandelbrot set" in that a small number of logical operators, in this case metaphoric and metonymic in nature, generate a large number of different yet similar forms (Gleick 1987: 221-232). While many of the characteristics of the "Mandelbrot set" bear close resemblance to the Lévi-Straussian notion of homology and transformation (Lévi-Strauss 1958; 1962; 1976), "chaos theory" differs from classic structuralism in admitting a dynamic principle, the "onset of turbulence," that the latter appears to exclude. In this instance I take the "onset of turbulence" to refer to the human capacity for radical innovation, be this creative or destructive. In a sense social systems are always in a state of flux, but there are moments when this is more pronounced. Exercising their volition, social actors constantly refashion their world, but they do so under the constraint of institutions and patterns of thought that they have inherited from previous generations and of which they may be only dimly aware (Bourdieu 1977; 1990). At other times contradictions accumulate as different forms of sociality confront one another, such as that of the gift and that of the commodity (vid. Strathern 1988), a process which has characterized Rwanda's postcolonial era (Taylor 1992). However, even in an extraordinary moment of turbulence such as that which prevailed in Rwanda during between 1990 and 1994, the constraint of previous patterns of thought retain some organizing influence in the manner of what chaos theory terms "strange attractors."

Rwandan notions of the person

At the least encompassing level of scale and underlying the fractal nature of Rwandan symbolism is the construct of the person. The Rwandan person is fractal, less than one, perennially incomplete. He or she is ever involved in the process of being added to, built upon, and produced by the gifts of others. Through his or her own gifts such a person is habitually adding to and producing others. Rwandans relate to one another through various aspects of themselves and not as integrated bounded unities. Nevertheless, even in the part, there are aspects of the whole. Let us start with the body. According to anthropologist Edward Vincke writing about Rwandan practices of sorcery:

> The person is conceived according to a fractal model, implicated as a conceptual entirety in all of its parts: finger nails, hair, dandruff, excreta, speech, gaze, dreams, shadow, and footprints. The means by which harm enters the person can be by fortuitous contact (a pregnant woman crosses paths with someone who is ill) or by malevolent actions taken against one of the person's bodily extensions, including his or her bodily fluids (Vincke 1991: 180).

The fractal nature of Rwandan symbolism can also be discerned by the manner in which concrete things are manipulated in social life that both sustain and signify human existence at corporeal, social, and spiritual levels. In the Rwandan case, these are liquids: bodily fluids such as breast milk, semen, and blood; liquid aliments such as milk, honey, and beer; the fluids of earth and firmament, rivers and rain; and even the metaphysical fluid, *imaana* (for extended discussion and examples, see Taylor, 1992). Liquids are employed symbolically as metonyms, parts of persons standing for and embodying the whole—bodily fluids, for example, or as metaphors mediating between separate semantic domains, both uniting and differentiating them.

That there is a degree of systematicity in the Rwandan use of liquids as symbols became apparent to me for the first time when I studied Rwandan popular medicine. For eighteen months during 1983 to 1985, I interacted with healers and patients during a time when Rwanda was at peace and the economy was doing well. Indeed at the time, the Rwandan franc was the region's most stable currency and ethnic tensions were probably at their lowest ebb in the last half-century of Rwanda's troubled past. I interviewed a number of healers who employed various theories and techniques of healing and visited many of their patients.

Fluids are emphasized in popular medicine. Perceived disruptions in the flow of bodily humors, for example, are indicative of illness and frequently, of ensorcellment. Symptoms include: instances where fluids are lacking or blocked within the body, as with dry mouth, constipation, impotence, inadequate vaginal secretion during intercourse, amenorrhea, insufficient lactation, and invisible loss of blood. In other instances fluids leave the body in an uncontrollable manner, as in the symptoms of diarrhea, vomiting, the vomiting of blood, the urination of blood, leukorrhea, and hemorrhagic menstruation. "Flow/blockage" symbolism suffused the narratives of patients whom I interviewed in the 1980s and 1990s.[4] This symbolic patterning focused on the body, but I subsequently found that it extended to local notions of production and exchange, fertility in general, and the well-being of the polity as a whole (Taylor 1992).

Earlier symbolic forms, Rwandan sacred kingship and its symbolism

The fractal patterning which characterizes the person can be discerned at more encompassing levels of scale. For example, imagery of the sort discussed above once also characterized earlier ritual and mythic forms and in particular, those associated with the institution of sacred kingship.

Let us begin with the Rwandan concept of *imaana*. Before Christian evangelization (early twentieth century), the term *imaana* referred to the notion of a supreme being both as a specific though unfathomable personality and as a more generalized "diffuse, fecundating fluid" of celestial origin whose activity upon livestock, land, and people brought fertility and abundance (d'Hertefelt and Coupez 1964). Elaborate state rituals called *inzira* or "paths," which often took months to complete, aimed at channeling the fertility effects of *imaana* to the entirety of the Rwandan polity. The Rwandan king (*umwami*) and his coterie of ritual specialists (*abiiru*) were charged with the responsibility of enacting these rituals, and their credibility and tenure were dependent upon tangible success.

In 1931, the Belgian Colonial Residency and Rwanda's Catholic missionaries weakened the institution of kingship when they deposed the non-Christian Tutsi king and replaced him with his mission-educated son. Already waning in importance during the 1920s due to colonial and missionary influence, the rituals of kingship after 1931 were either not performed at all or only performed in a perfunctory way. Politically this period witnessed the expansion of Tutsi supremacy, a kind of indirect rule promoted by Belgian colonialism, over the entirety of Rwanda (Louis 1963). As Christian evangelization progressed, Catholic missionaries substituted the idea of the Judeo-Christian God for the Rwandan idea of "diffuse fecundating fluid," while retaining the term, *Imaana*, in Bibles translated into Kinyarwanda (Linden, 1977). Then in 1959 to 1962, the agricultural Hutu majority, aided by a shift in the sentiments of Belgian colonial masters and support from the Rwandan Catholic Church, overthrew Tutsi dominance and the Tutsi kingship institution formally came to an end (ibid.).

Rwandan sacred kingship can be considered the earliest historical example in which we find evidence of flow / blockage symbolism. It therefore behooves us to examine some aspects of the rituals in detail. Rwanda is unique among the former kingdoms of sub-Saharan Africa in having preserved texts of almost all the rituals practiced by the Rwandan *umwami* and his coterie of ritual specialists. Collected from those royal ritualists who were still alive during the 1940s by Alexis Kagame and others (cf. Kagame 1947), the rituals provide us with a glimpse into late-nineteenth century Rwandan symbolic thought and its emphasis on fluids. In the seventeen royal rituals assembled, annotated, and translated into French in *La royauté sacrée de l'ancien Rwanda* by Marcel d'Hertefelt and André Coupez (1964) the importance of liquid aliments is striking. There are dozens of references to milk, honey, mead, and beer, while there is only a single reference to a solid food. Obviously the rituals bear the ideological imprint of the Tutsi elite who performed them in pre- and early colonial times as members of this elite prided themselves on a highly liquid diet (de Heusch 1985). Yet most of the rituals were similar in fundamental ways to those practiced by Hutu kings (*abami*) either in adjacent areas or in times anterior to that of the Tutsi-led kingdom (d'Hertefelt and Coupez 1964; Smith 1970).

Assuring the fertility of land, cattle, and people was the ultimate aim of the royal rituals. Six of them expressed this concern through their direct focus on liquids. Two rituals, "The Path of Dust" and "The Path of Inundation," concerned rainfall. Then, as now, the Rwandan year consisted of two rainy seasons and two dry seasons, but these tended to be irregular. Rwandan agriculture was perennially at the mercy of occasional drought, flooding, and rains which arrived at the wrong time. The *umwami* was the land's most important rainmaker and it was also incumbent upon him to stop the rains when they fell in excess. Other "fluid rituals" concerned the production of milk and honey, and the health and productivity of cattle and bees. Perhaps the most important fluid ritual, however, was "The Path of the Watering" which was performed by the first king of each dynastic cycle. In the "Watering" ritual, officiants conducted the royal cattle herds to the Nyabugogo River where they were given water, an action which signified the rejuvenation of the entire magico-religious order of Rwandan kingship.

Ritual functions of Rwandan kings were divided. Only kings named either Mutara or Cyirima, that is, "cowherd kings," performed "The Path of the Watering." A "cowherd king" inaugurated each dynastic cycle of four kings. He was followed by two warrior kings or "kings of the belt," while the fourth king was said to be a "fire king." It was the latter's responsibility to renew the perpetually burning sacred fire at the end of the dynastic cycle during the ritual called "The Path of Fire."

The political functions of Rwandan kings were also divided. "Cowherd kings" and "fire kings" were said to be peaceful kings and were forbidden to engage in wars of conquest. They were confined within the two sacred portions of the Rwandan kingdom. "Kings of the Belt," however, Kigeri and Mibambwe, were not confined, but were encouraged to cross boundaries and to conquer new territory. Ideally then, two of the four kings within each dynastic cycle had the responsibility of conquest, while the other two had the responsibility of consolidation and renewal. In reality, so-called "peaceful" kings might also engage in wars through their surrogates, but they were not to leave the sacred half of the kingdom in which they resided.

Both the Nyabarongo and the Nyabugogo Rivers defined the movements of cattle and people during the enactment of "The Path of the Watering." As an imaginary cosmological incarnation, the Nyabarongo ritualized space by serving as a ritual and political boundary defining the movement of Rwandan kings; the Nyabugogo River ritualized time by serving as the conduit which conjoined the *imaana* of dead kings with that of living kings. Deceased cowherd kings eventually found their way to a place called Rutare, where they were finally buried. It should be emphasized that the Nyabugogo River is fed by streams from the land near Rutare where these royal tombs are located. Thus the waters from the Nyabugogo ingested by the royal cattle during the "Watering" ritual were waters that had filtered over the bodies of the buried kings. By coursing over their bodies, these waters captured their *imaana*. These waters sustained the royal herds during the "Watering" ritual and served to revivify dynastic time. Death, in precolonial Rwanda, thus flowed into life, just as life inevitably flowed into death.

In several instances during the "Watering" ritual, a group of eight cows along with one bull was presented to the king, either to be given water or to be milked. This group of eight cows and one bull was referred to in the ritual as "a flow" or *isibo* in Kinyarwanda. In other contexts *isibo* referred to a multitude of living beings in movement, such as cows rushing toward a water source, or soldiers streaming onto the battlefield. But the verb from which *isibo* is derived, *gusiba*, means: (1) to plug, to fill up, to obstruct, to fill a hollow or empty space; (2) to decimate, to eliminate, to make something disappear; (3) to reduce an adversary to silence by an irrefutable argument; (4) (when speaking of mammary glands) to be obstructed; (5) (when speaking of a path) to become covered over with plants. Other usages include: *gusiba inkaru*—to do grave harm to someone; and *gusiba inzira*—(lit.: "to block a path"), to have one's daughter die before marriage (Jacob 1984: 167). The noun *isibo* and the verb *gusiba* encompass two apparently oppositional fields of meaning. One field of meaning focuses on the image of living beings in movement. Another set of meanings crystallizes around the image of blockage and loss. A single verbal concept in Kinyarwanda thus incorporates the notion of "flow" and its contrary, the idea of "blockage."

In this second instance, the notion of "blockage" is related to the idea of doing harm to someone as in, *gusiba inkaru*, as well as to the idea of losing an unmarried daughter, as in *gusiba inzira*. With regard to *gusiba inzira*, an analogy is drawn between "blocking a path" and "losing a daughter before she marries." In effect, when one loses a daughter, death blocks the "path" between one's own family and that of another family. In other words, the alliance relation which might have resulted from the gift of one's daughter to another family has been preemptively extinguished. Similar to the imagery reported by Chris Gregory for New Guinea (1982), paths are often thought of as exchange conduits in Rwanda. We see this in a prohibition related to matrimony discussed by Pierre Smith. During the entire period that matrimonial negotiations are underway, the concerned girl must not walk on paths used by cattle. This is because the exchange destinies of women and cattle are opposed (Smith 1979: 28); stated another way, women flow in one direction and cattle flow in the opposite direction.

Connotations of the terms, *isibo* and *gusiba*, capture much of the internal dialectics of early Rwandan social life. Just as exchange relations could proceed normally along their accepted pathways or be obstructed, just as the sky could yield its fertilizing liquid in the right measure and at the right time, so could the body's humors flow properly in health and fertility, or improperly in infertility and illness. These terms also embody the recognition that one could not have "flow" along a pathway without encountering obstruction or "blockage."

In effect, the king's legitimacy in precolonial Rwanda arose from his capacity to control the flows of substances along hierarchically defined trajectories. But, one could only control these by occasionally interdicting them, even though total obstruction entailed drought, infertility, and death. The power to control flows resided in the institution of kingship and in the person of the king as an embodiment of *imaana*. The Rwandan king had his hands on the celestial udder. This is why in some instances, although ordinarily called *umwami*, he was referred to by the term *umukama*, which means "the milker." The king could enrich his subjects with his gifts of cattle and fertility or he could impoverish them, either by withholding these gifts or by being an unworthy repository of *imaana*. In this latter instance, the king himself might be killed.

The king, as *Imaana's* earthly representative, channeled fertility to the rest of humanity. The king's body could be compared to a conduit through which celestial beneficence passed. But, this passage was neither immediate nor direct. The royal body retarded the process of flow. By temporarily serving as the obstructing agent, he acted as a condensation of the flow/blockage process. It was only by taking the risk of completely "blocking" the system, that the king's role in perpetuating "flow" became tangible and visible. In one legend that I heard in 1987, for example, fertility power passed through the king's alimentary canal according to this delayed rhythm:

> Ruganzu Ndori was living in exile in the kingdom of Ndorwa, a neighboring kingdom to the north of Rwanda. There he had taken refuge with his FZ (*nyirasenge*) who was married to a man from the region. In the meantime, because the Rwandan throne was occupied by an illegitimate usurper, Rwanda was experiencing numerous calamities. The crops were dying, the cows were not giving milk, and the women were becoming sterile. Ruganzu's paternal aunt encouraged him to return to Rwanda to retake the throne and save his people from catastrophe. Ruganzu agreed. But before setting forth on his voyage to Rwanda, she gave him the seeds (*imbuto*) of several cultivated plants (sorghum, gourd, and others) to restart Rwandan cultures. While en route to Rwanda, Ruganzu Ndori came under attack. Fearing that the imbuto would be captured, he swallowed the seeds with a long draught of milk. Once he regained the Rwandan throne, he defecated the milk and seed mixture upon the ground and the land became productive once again. Since that time all Rwandan kings are said to be born clutching the seeds of the original imbuto in their hand.

The king's body was both a synecdoche of the cosmological system and a metaphor of it in human form; he was a part of the whole, but he was also the part that resembled the whole. Since he was the conduit between sky and earth, his body had to be kept open and this was imprinted upon his physiological processes (Taylor 1992). In essence by attuning the king's body to the collective symbolic order and then metaphorically extending this to the cosmos as a whole, it was hoped that the inherent randomness of weather, pestilence, and human social life might be kept in abeyance, if not stymied once and for all. Precolonial Rwandans were more than likely aware of the illusory nature of such a desire despite the assertions of the king's ritualists to the contrary. Yet they might entertain this illusion—just as we in the United States tend to believe that the president is responsible for the economy—as long as a certain degree of prosperity prevailed within the kingdom and some semblance of predictability was maintained to human social life. This was of course tempered by the realization that states of predictability and order were relative and ephemeral and that the default state of the universe was entropic. Everyone was aware, for example, that keeping chaos and calamity at bay came at a price. This demanded sacrificial victims and in some instances, the victim might be the king. In instances of natural disaster (e.g., drought, epidemic, epizootic, flooding, or crop failure) or humanly caused disasters (e.g., military defeat, invasion by a neighboring kingdom), the king might be seen as an inadequate embodiment of *imaana*, and thus the ultimate human obstructor. In such a case he himself could be sacrificed. Later, his death would be depicted in dynastic legends as an *umutabazi* sacrifice, that is, as if the king had heroically given his life for the survival of Rwanda (d'Hertefelt and Coupez 1964). Vansina claims that *umutabazi* sacrifices were in reality attempts to disguise Rwandan military defeats (1967).

President Juvenal Habyarimana and the "Onset of Turbulence"

The precipitating event which set off the Rwandan genocide was the killing of President Juvenal Habyarimana when his private plane was shot down near Kigali airport by a shoulder-held surface to air missile. Although Habyarimana's government had been at war for almost four years with the Rwandan Patriotic Front, this event transformed the dynamics of hostilities from tit-for-tat, attack-reprisal violence into a genocide. In chaos theory terms this could be considered the war's "phase shift" or its "point of bifurcation," where a linear and symmetric schismogenic process (Bateson 1958 [1936]), became nonlinear and asymmetric. In effect, the heretofore linear dynamic underlying the violence: "We will get you back," became overnight a nonlinear one: "We will eliminate all of you." Preceding this phase shift and catalyzing it was the symbolism of kingship and *umutabazi* sacrifice.

No one has ever claimed responsibility for killing the president, but the two most credible hypotheses place the responsibility either on Hutu extremist members among Habyarimana's own followers or on members of the rebel group at the time, the Rwandan Patriotic Front (RPF). Felip Reyntjens, for example, once an adherent to the Hutu extremist thesis, has more recently given credence to the RPF thesis (Reyntjens 1999). Although there is certainly merit to the RPF thesis, I lean more strongly in favor of the Hutu extremist explanation and recent research supports this (vid. Martin 2002: 17-30). The death of President Habyarimana could have served the interests of the RPF, just as it could have served the political interests of the extremists. As for the RPF, they saw the president as an obstructionist who was delaying full implementation of the Arusha Accords and thus preventing their participation in a coalition government. Among the extremists, however, many were convinced that Habyarimana had become "soft" on Tutsi and that he needed to be replaced by someone more unequivocally "genocidaire" and that is certainly one of the messages of the first cartoon in this chapter.

Looking at the event in hindsight and in terms of its psychosocial and symbolic efficacy, one would have to say that Habyarimana's death did more to rally moderate Hutu (those unwilling to engage in whole scale massacres against Tutsi civilians) to the extremist cause, than it did to rally Tutsi and moderate Hutu to the RPF cause. If the RPF or certain officers within the RPF were responsible for killing Habyarimana, they grossly underestimated the effect that this was to have on the Rwandan Presidential Guard, the Rwandan Army, the *Interahamwe* militias,[5] and even many among the Hutu population in general. Were they not aware that the assassination of Habyarimana might serve as the flashpoint the extremists were waiting for? Did they not realize that his death could very well have been the extremists' preordained signal to begin the genocide in earnest? Or, was the RPF willing to risk igniting the fires of genocide and having many of their friends and relatives killed, just to have Habyarimana out of the way? (There are of course many who would argue this.)

In the two years preceding Habyarimana's death, the path was being prepared in Rwanda's print media for "king" sacrifice. At first we see hints of this in the opposition press and its portrayal of the president as a tyrannical or incompetent ruler that the country would do well to be rid of. Later, even Hutu extremists deserted him (see cartoon above). Rwandan journalists attacked the president in ways that constituted a radical departure from the timidity that had prevailed during the 1980s. This was due in part to democratization, supported by France and other Western powers, that occurred during the 1990s and to which Habyarimana and the MRND were forced to acquiesce. The press became free and open, but the sudden easing of restraints did not coincide with a corresponding rise in concern for journalistic standards. Innuendo, calumny, and veiled and not so veiled calls for assassination characterized the printed and spoken media of the time (vid. Chrétien 1995). More often than not, followers of the president, who occupied many of the key positions in the national media including control of the infamous "hate radio" station, Radio Television Libre de Mille Collines (RTLMC), used the weapons of fabrication and exaggeration against the president's perceived critics and rivals. The president's critics, however, were not above the occasional smear campaign, the use of obscenity, and the liberal use of disinformation (ibid.).

Comparing Habyarimana in the popular political literature to a traditional sacred king was not without irony, for the president was Hutu (all former kings had been Tutsi) and much of the avowed ideology of his party, the Mouvement Revolutionnaire National pour le Dévelopement et la Démocratie (MRND), was antimonarchist and superficially at least, egalitarian. In addition to the predictions of Magayane, there were many examples of President Habyarimana and other leading political figures in the political literature (between 1990 and 1994), that show the influence of the kingship institution.

In hindsight it is not difficult to perceive some equivalence between the Rwandan presidency and the country's former monarchy. When I began my first period of fieldwork in Rwanda in 1983, I quickly became aware of the "cult of personality" surrounding President Habyarimana. At the time Habyarimana was running for reelection and MRND party faithful were very busy campaigning. There was little chance of his losing the election, however, as he was running unopposed and the MRND was the country's only authorized political party. Shortly after he overthrew the country's first Hutu President, Gregoire Kayibanda, in 1973, Juvenal Habyarimana assumed the presidency on an emergency basis. Later he established the Mouvement Revolutionnaire National pour le Développement (MRND),[6] a party whose most enthusiastic support derived from his natal region of northwestern Rwanda. In the 1983 elections, Habyarimana asked for and was reported to have won, an incredible 99 percent of the vote. For many years afterward, it seemed as if he would hold power forever.

Rwanda was a closely controlled military dictatorship at the time, with very few people daring to raise a dissenting voice. Rarely did one hear a critical word being muttered against Habyarimana and the army's tight control of the Rwandan state. In the capital of Kigali, the presence of army and gendarmerie was pervasive. Commitment to the government was obligatory. Every Saturday morning people everywhere in Rwanda, especially employees of the state, but many others as well, would meet to participate in *umuganda*, community service. They would come with their shovels and hoes and fill in the ruts of dirt roads deeply gouged out by the rain; they would repair municipal buildings; they would plant trees. There was very little complaining. Even most Rwandan Tutsi during the 1980s supported Habyarimana recalling the violence of 1973 when Habyarimana and the army stepped in, stopped the violence against Tutsi, and then took power from then-President Kayibanda and his central and southern Hutu supporters. Of course along with the paternalism of the Habyarimana regime, came the army's close surveillance of the population and the threat of force. On weekend nights, soldiers would enter bars shortly before midnight and make sure all patrons left to go home. Sometimes soldiers patrolling city streets after midnight would challenge people still out after that hour. Once I was stopped myself when I returned to my hotel from a friend's house just a little after midnight. Two soldiers berated me for several minutes about my lack of morals for staying out so late. "Don't you know you should go to bed early, so you can work tomorrow?" It didn't seem to matter to them that the tomorrow in question was a Saturday and that as a foreigner, I was not expected to participate in *umuganda*.

At the time adulation of Habyarimana was de rigeur for Rwandans; it was a key element in the enactment of their *civitas*. Virtually everyone had a portrait of the president hanging on a wall at home and many wore the MRND party button on their shirt or blouse. On Wednesday afternoons groups met to practice chants and skits in celebration of the Rwandan state, its overthrow of the Tutsi monarchy, and its rejection of the *ubuhake* cattle contract signifying Hutu servitude to Tutsi, and most of all to honor the country's president, Juvenal Habyarimana. Termed *animation*, it didn't seem to bother anyone that these Wednesday afternoon get-togethers took people away from their jobs and did nothing to augment the country's gross domestic product. Even songs on the radio seemed to equate Rwanda, its beauty, and relative prosperity with the person of its president.

Of course much of this adulation was self-interested, as the state, with Habyarimana at its head, was the country's primary source of patronage, and the country's prime guarantor of inequality.

For example, although the land holdings of the average Rwandan peasant family (before the genocide) amounted to a little over two acres, close to 17 percent of Rwandan farms were larger than two acres. These comprised about 43 percent of Rwanda's total area of arable land, and 60 percent of the total in Kigali Prefecture (Chrétien 1997: 77). Many of the owners of these larger farms were military officers and/or MRND party notables with commercial interests, prompting some scholars to speak of Rwanda's elite as a "military-merchant" class. Although some Rwandan entrepreneurs earned their position in this elite by providing needed products and services to the Rwandan economy, most became that way due to their proximity to Habyarimana and to the organs of state power. The group of Habyarimana's most privileged clients was termed the *akazu* ("little house"); they were the ones who dominated economic and political life in pregenocidal Rwanda.

> More than competence, connections to the regime have given rise to a new form of pseudo-technocratic bourgeoisie and conferred prosperity upon it. Following the ups and downs of political favor, we see a rapid turnover in these *bourgeois gentlemen*. In three years one such high personality exercised four different functions: administrator of the pyrethrin factory in Ruhengeri, general director of the Social Fund of Rwanda, Prefect of Kibungo, and finally, Minister of Education. What pleasant diversity, what guaranty of effectiveness!
>
> Without over-generalizing, the claim is justified that a portion of the Rwandan bourgeoisie is simply parasitic and prebendal. One must also admit that a fraction of it does reinvest some of its earnings. Many industrial ventures started out as commercial operations.
>
> (F. Bezy 1990: 51 cited from Chrétien 1997: 78, my translation)

Nevertheless, although opposition political parties would later accuse the Habyarimana regime of regional favoritism, nepotism, and corruption (see below), during the regime's golden years of the 1980s, few people called attention to the country's deepening class divisions. Even in contexts where there was nothing obvious to be gained, many people expressed their admiration of the country's president. Some people made comments about the appropriateness of Habyarimana's name, from the verb *kubyara* (to engender) and *imaana*, which together could be translated as: "It is God who gives life." Nothing could have been more appropriate in a Catholic, antiabortion, and basically pronatalist culture, yet very few names could have at the same time resonated so well with the more "traditional" themes of fertility, prosperity, and good luck, manifestations of the "diffuse fecundating fluid." Yet it seemed at the time to hold true. During most of the 1980s Rwanda was doing well economically (in comparison to neighboring states) and many Rwandans attributed this to the good stewardship of its president. The orchestrated affection for Habyarimana was part theater, certainly, but there were many who were sincere.

Closely associating the country's fertility and prosperity with the person of the president was not the only way in which we see the lingering influence of the representations of sacred kingship. In other instances we see this influence in references to the country's rivers, the body, and violence. At increasingly encompassing levels of scale then, we find the fractal pattern repeated. Sometimes the assimilation of Habyarimana to a Rwandan sacred king was explicit; at other times it was more implicit, bordering on the unwitting. In many cases the association was intended to be flattering, in other instances, it was intended to be critical. Let us look at some examples.

Rivers

One reference to Rwanda's rivers with an explicit association to sacred kingship appeared in the popular political magazine *Zirikana*, in an article written by Bonaparte Ndekezi entitled, "Habyarimana hagati ya Mukungwa na Nyabarongo" (Zirikana, 30 January 1993: 4-6). This magazine, *Zirikana*, supported the viewpoint of the party known as the Coalition pour la Défense de la République, the infamous CDR, a party formed from extreme right-wing elements of the MRND and known for its anti-RPF stance and racist views against Tutsi (Chrétien 1995: 386). Ndekezi as well was known for his extremism. The title of the article translates as: "Habyarimana between the Mukungwa and the Nyabarongo" and refers to a river in northern Rwanda, the Mukungwa, and of course, to central Rwanda's main river, the Nyabarongo which in earlier times divided the Rwandan kingdom into two sacred halves (see discussion above). The article can be interpreted in several ways. At one level, and this is the theme most strongly advanced in the article, is that Habyarimana in 1993 now finds himself in trouble and with little room to maneuver politically. The article goes on to describe Habyarimana as a good leader, but if anything, a little soft on his opponents, particularly the Tutsi-dominated RPF and the internal Hutu opposition. In other words, Habyarimana is in trouble because of his magnanimity in the face of his adversaries' treachery.

At another, less explicit level one could interpret Habyarimana's finding himself between the Mukungwa and the Nyabarongo as his being confined within the most sacred portion of his "kingdom"—the north, his natural constituency, that portion of Rwanda enclosed within the confines of the Mukungwa in the north and the Nyabarongo in the center. Is the article subtly exhorting Habyarimana to be less of a peaceful, consolidating "king" and more, a "king of the belt," that is, a warrior king? The article may carry a subtle warning to Habyarimana: "Leave the confines of your sacred kingdom, proceed southward, cross the Nyabarongo and wage war! Otherwise you will lose everything." The assertion that the author was thinking about earlier Rwanda, the days of sacred kingship, and about Habyarimana as a sacred king is clear from one of the author's sentences: "At the level of authority, there is no difference between him [Habyarimana] and the former kings of traditional Rwanda, only the fact that he was not born clutching the imbuto (magic seeds of fertility) in his hand" (ibid.: 4).

The allusion here to traditional Rwandan sacred kingship is interesting because it was intended to flatter Habyarimana. This is ironic, even paradoxical given its source, the Hutu extremist, Coalition pour la Défense de la République (CDR). After all, it was Rwandan Hutu who overthrew the monarchy in 1961. This apparent contradiction is diminished somewhat when we realize that the CDR was not really opposed to autocrats, dictators, or even monarchs as much as it was opposed to Tutsi and to the RPF. What the author appears to be saying is: "Habyarimana, a Hutu king, is every bit as worthy a king as his Tutsi forebears. His only flaw is his reluctance to use the iron fist."

In another popular political journal, *Umurangi*, closely associated with the party known as the Mouvement Démocrate Républicain (MDR) and opposed to the MRND and CDR, Habyarimana is pictured in proximity to the Mukungwa and about to attack southern Rwanda with his army and militia (Figure 6.2). *Umurangi's* indirect allusion to the boundaries of the sacred kingdom and to Habyarimana is not intended to flatter. In this cartoon we see the three major democratic opposition parties, the Mouvement Démocrate Républicain (MDR), the Parti Social Démocrate (PSD), and the Parti Liberal (PL) poised close to the Nyabarongo and preparing to fend off Habyarimana's descent into what was once the most sacred territory of the Rwandan kingdom. To the northeast we see the RPF delighted that southern Hutu (MDR, PSD, and PL) and northern Hutu (MRND and CDR) are divided among themselves. At another level the cartoon seems to be saying that Habyarimana is an illegitimate pretender to the throne, a northerner, an outsider, and one responsible for terrorist killings in the south and center.

Figure 6.2: Front cover of *Umurangi*, No. 13, 27 November 1992. Translation: Headline beneath the cartoon: "In 1980 when things could have been arranged, we told Habyarimana, but he wouldn't listen. When things flew out of control, all he could say was: I am Ikinani (the invincible)."

Habyarimana (upper left): "We are well dressed (i.e., in military uniforms). We are descending to the Nyabarongo to conduct the campaign. Try to spare a few so that they will tell the story of Ikinani's victory. But once we have crossed (i.e., the Nyabarongo), my children, what I haven't told you, figure out for yourself."

RPF (upper right): "What are they thinking in Rwanda!? Is it true that he wants the votes of cadavers!?"

The Body and its Violation, Adorning the Royal Drum, Castration

The use of other symbols associated with the institution of sacred king-ship is also indicative of fragments of pattern amidst the turbulence, or as Friedrich would state it, evidence of an "eerie order" lurking beneath the anarchy of impending genocide. For example, the mystical power of the early monarchy was said to reside in the royal drums, particularly the one named Karinga. Loss of the drum signified the king's defeat and Rwanda's takeover by an enemy. Even though the drums of Rwandan kingship have long since been relegated to the museum, the term *ingoma* continues to be used to refer to a specific group or individual's political hold over a region or a group of people. In "Habyarimana hagati ya

Mukungwa na Nyabarongo," the author sometimes refers to Habyari-mana as the one who possesses *"ingoma Nshiru,"* in other words, power over the region of Nshiru in northern Rwanda.

Rarely does one find ideological consistency among the various uses of kingship symbols before Habyarimana's assassination. Indicative of the impending "onset of turbulence," about eighty popular journals each with a different point of view arose in the period between 1990 and 1994, quite extraordinary for a country with a population of about seven million. Some, but not all of these journals employed symbols of kingship, but it was more often the case that Hutu extremist journalists explicitly accused the Rwandan Patriotic Front of wanting to restore the monarchy, its trappings, and its rituals. Routinely, Hutu extremist journalists referred to RPF members as "feudo-monarchists." Several of their cartoons recall the former custom of emasculating slain enemies and then using these body parts to adorn the royal drum. For example:

Figure 6.3: Ndadaye's crucifixion and impalement. Translation: A civilian RPF supporter: "Kill this stupid Hutu and after you cut off his genitals, hang them on our drum." Ndadaye: "Kill me, but you won't exterminate all the Ndadayes in Burundi." Kagame (formerly RPF general, now President of Rwanda) [right side of cartoon]: "Kill him quickly. Don't you know that in Byumba and Ruhengeri we did a lot of work? With women, we pulled the babies out of their wombs; with men, we dashed out their eyes." The drum: "Karinga of Burundi."

In the above cartoon from an extremist Hutu magazine, *La Medaille-Nyi-ramacibiri*, RPF soldiers are depicted crucifying, impaling, and castrating Melchior Ndadaye, neighboring Burundi's first democratically elected

Hutu President. Elected in October of 1993, he was subsequently killed by Burundian Tutsi army officers in an abortive coup attempt.[7]

In the annals of Rwandan Hutu extremism, very few images encapsulate as much symbolic violence and in so many ways as this one. At one level we see a clear iteration of the oft repeated charge by Hutu extremists that the RPF were "feudo-monarchists" intent upon restoring kingship, the royal rituals, and the monarchy's principal emblem—the drum named Karinga. Another claim is advanced by depicting Hutu victims of the RPF as Christlike martyrs, for Ndadaye is crucified. Beneath these claims, however, a subtler message is being conveyed. By impaling Ndadaye the RPF torturers are turning his body into an obstructed conduit and as such they are transforming his person into an inadequate, unworthy embodiment of *imaana*. In former times, Rwandans killed cattle thieves in this way (cf. Taylor 1999: 136–140). At another level a complex synthesis has been forged. Specifically Rwandan symbols with deep historical and ontological roots have merged with those that are the more recent product of Christian evangelization.

The imagery of castration occurs repeatedly in the popular press of the time. In the following cartoon from *Umurangi* (Figure 6.4), there is also an interesting synthesis of Christian and earlier Rwandan imagery. Here members of the MRND and CDR parties (two women and three men who correspond to real personalities from these parties) are seen accepting the severed scrotum of a defeated enemy. Two snakes, one wearing an MRND cap bearing the party insignia of a hoe crossed over a curved knife and the other wearing a hat from the CDR, are coiling up the "tree of knowledge" in the "Garden of Eden," which is labeled: the Interahamwe Club. In fact, Rose and Matthieu Ngirumpatse (formerly secretary general of the MRND and now accused of war crimes before the International War Crimes Tribunal in Arusha, Tanzania) were proprietors of a popular Kigali restaurant and night spot called "Eden Garden," a noted hangout for MRND, CDR, and Interahamwe militia members. The snake says: "I castrated him, and he wasn't the only one." Accepting the snake's gift, a woman of course, is likely, Rose Ngirumpatse. The bearded man at the right says: "How can they ever defeat us!? Let's go do our rituals. You'll see."

Figure 6.4: "Eden" cartoon from *Umurangi*, No. 9, 22 June 1992

In another cartoon also from *Umurangi* (Figure 6.5), CDR and MRND members are depicted enjoying a cannibalistic feast seated around their version of Karinga, in this case a drum named *Karaso* (blood), adorned with the testicles of slain enemies. The headline reads: "Among the greedy, you can never get enough." The woman with her finger pointed in the air says: "Bring me the guts of Byabagamba." The other woman says: "I won't be satisfied until I get Nsengiremye's flesh to eat." The man seated next to her replies, "I'll do anything to make you happy, dear. You shall have him."

Figure 6.5: "Karaso" cartoon from *Umurangi*, No. 12, 9 November 1992

Yet another use of the castration image appears in *Umurangi* (Figure 6.6). Here a woman named Habimana, a close associate of Habyarimana's and head of the Rwandan Office Nationale de la Population, instructs a doctor with scissors to castrate each man standing in line. Mme. Habimana commands: "Castrate them in the name of the *umwami w'akazu* (i.e., king of the "akazu"— "little house," the small clique of people who were Habyarimana's closest supporters and most favored clients). He has his aim in mind. Don't ask questions."

Figure 6.6: "Castration" cartoon from *Umurangi*, No. 11, 7 October 1992

Many of the explicit references to the former kingship institution are ideologically motivated and this accounts for the differences seen among the various Rwandan political factions in their depiction of Habyarimana and others. Other linkages cannot be explained solely as ideological, for they appeal to a deeper, more ontological level (Kapferer 1988). Indeed, the various Rwandan factions were contesting who would control the power of the state, but the contest was being waged through the mediation of a common body of symbols. For example, imagery of the body as conduit is where ideological motivation gives way to a realm of thought having to do with a specifically Rwandan way of imagining the body as a being in time and space, a being that acts as the focal point of processes, physiological and social, redolent with cosmological import—a being through which *imaana* should pass in its descent from sky to earth. Although the following cartoon (Figure 6.7) manifests the symbolic pattern of "body as conduit," it adds to the instantiation of the pattern, its negation. Here Hutu opponents of Habyarimana portray his body as a "flowing" but corrupt conduit, one which turns all flows back upon itself.

MURI MRND BAKOMEJE KWITUMA KU MBEHE BAKIRIRAMO NO MU MAZI BAKIVOMA.

Politiki y'abashimusi b'inka idukozeho.

Figure 6.7: "Eat shit" cartoon from *Umurangi*, No. 14, 10 December 1992. The headline reads: "In the MRND they continue to excrete on the plate from which they eat and into the water from which they drink." At the left an MRND youth holds up a severed leg and says: "Let's kill them, let's get rid of them, let's eat them." Habyarimana replies: "Yes, let's descend on them all right." To his right, one CDR man and another who is MRND exclaim sarcastically: "In the Rwanda of peace, there sure is a lot of delicious food." Beneath the cartoon are the words: "The politics of the cattle thieves causes problems."

Much is condensed in this illustration. At an ideological level, Habyarimana and his MRND and CDR followers are being compared to cattle thieves. It is also quite obvious that the president, according to his detractors, is a man who eats shit. But there are other elements that are not directly ideological or even logical in an ordinary sense. What serves as Habyarimana's latrine in the picture is Rwanda and its hapless population. The spoon that we see him moving from beneath his anus and about to place in his mouth is labeled, "taxes." The Rwandan people's taxes are swallowed by Habyarimana, shat out by Habyarimana, only to be swallowed by him again. Only if you are a follower of his are you likely to get anything to eat as with these CDR and MRND party members who manage to grab the occasional severed limb, the occasional errant turd. Habyarimana reverses the flow of beneficence. Instead of it descending downward from the sky, passing through his body, and then to the earth and people, it moves from down to up, from people to ruler. Once there, most of it is continually recycled in a sterile "closed circuit flow" within his body. What little passes through him gets gobbled up by his lackeys.

At an ontological level, a more profound message is being communicated: Habyarimana is an inadequate conduit of *imaana* and thus not a worthy king. He is an inversion of Ruganzu Ndori. A king like Ruganzu Ndori would never have allowed his bowels to selfishly retain the mystical powers of the original *imbuto*. Ruganzu Ndori's body was a moral "conduit," one through which *imaana* could pass from sky to earth, a body capable of performing "open circuit flow," a potentially good alliance partner, a giver and not simply a receiver of gifts, an adequate embodiment of *imaana* on earth. King Habyarimana is the antithesis of Ruganzu Ndori and the embodiment of *ishyano* (ritual impurity). These cartoons seem to be saying and at a level beneath, yet more powerful than the ideological: "Habyarimana must be sacrificed."

Conclusion

Chaos theory provides insight into Rwanda's pregenocidal period, especially its final two years, by allowing us to see it as a time of "bifurcation" in which a linear dynamic of war turned into a nonlinear dynamic. This period culminated in the "onset of turbulence" precipitated by the sacrifice of "King Habyarimana" and ultimately in the genocide of 1994. It also constituted the historical moment when several different and conflicting social logics collided: (1) gift sociality and commodity sociality, (2) hierarchical holism (autocracy) and egalitarian individualism (democracy), (3) essentialist and nonessentialist notions of ethnicity. Leading up to this time a synthesis occurred of Rwandan symbolic thought with symbols of Christian and Euro-American origin. This is why we see evidence of both in the discourse and iconography of Rwandan popular political literature. Remarkable in this synthesis, however, was the degree to which Rwandan journalists resurrected the symbols of sacred kingship in an attempt to make sense of the changes leading the polity to chaos.

Before the genocide Hutu extremists resorted to a wide array of demonizing symbolizations of Tutsi. But both in representation and in the actual violence meted out against the bodies of their victims, there was method in the madness, as it often followed symbolically conditioned forms—severing of Achilles tendons, anal impalement, etc. (vid. Taylor 2002). The same holds true of representations of President Habyarimana as a sacred king by his Hutu supporters and opponents. Whether one saw him as a dupe to the RPF, a tyrant, or a king who reversed the flow of *imaana* becoming the embodiment of ritual impurity (*ishyano*), Habyarimana had to be sacrificed. Yet lurking beneath the rampant disorder of a social system run amuck, the imagery of "closed circuit flow" and the "body as conduit" acted as a "strange attractor" around which representations of malevolence could crystallize.

There have been many changes in Rwandan symbols over the years, but the system itself has exerted some constraint on the direction of change. Stated in terms of chaos theory, turbulence and historical transformation have not completely erased an original generative schema. History has not completely worn away the discernible contours of Rwandan symbolic thought about the body, the nature of malevolence, and the relation of both of these to the body politic. As we see in the final cartoon, the introduction of money into the Rwandan economy has not expunged the imagery of "flow/blockage," even though it is also acknowledged that money and commodities in following their own logic can instigate chaotic "disjunctive flows" which cannot always be easily channeled and contained. The fertility of money can be positive in its limitless potential and yet subversive of human relationships when it is hoarded among a small ruling clique and ceases to flow from top to bottom—hence a sovereign who eats and excretes on the fount of beneficence—Rwanda and its people. Although the capitalist system possesses its logic, its own "laws of motion" (Marx 1976), money is not *imaana* and it is unlike the cattle transferred between families in socially significant transactions. It does not embody social memory and in most instances, effaces it. Moreover, it can cross social boundaries with singular and at times subversive rapidity. Yet in an ideal world as imagined by many Rwandans and that we can infer from the cartoons above, its flows should be as subject to social control as the descent of *imaana*.

Colonialism, Christianity, and multiparty democracy altered the perception of evil. Many of the earlier forms of real and symbolic violence became syncretized to Christian, Euro-American, and transnational forms. This is apparent in the cartoon depicting the Garden of Eden and in other juxtapositions of transnational images and those of local vintage. Clearly the violent imaginary looks for inspiration to all possible sources, supporting Appadurai's assertion that we need to look to "global disjunctive flows." Nevertheless, the newly integrated elements do not efface the specifically Rwandan character to the imagery employed in popular political journalism and to the subsequent real violence. This specifically Rwandan element continues to operate as something of a patterning armature or in chaos theory terms, a "strange attractor" (Gleick 1987).

Chaos theory serves as a useful heuristic device for understanding these complex interactions of structure, process, and agency in Rwanda, because it implies that dynamic systems, although responsive to internal and external changes and sometimes productive of them, are not infinitely malleable. Even as new symbols, meanings, and values become part of Rwandan social experience, something of a familiar pattern persists. A process of creative synthesis and invention has always characterized Rwandan symbolic thought, but the products of this are not completely novel in form or pattern. Instead, the resultant symbols are predicated upon the forms and patterns which preceded them. Beneath the apparent randomness of historical forces impinging on Rwandan cultural forms, lurks an "eerie order." Using Rwanda's mountainous topography as a comparison and despite "the hideous complication of such shapes," an organizing structure lies within the fractal curve (Gleick 1987: 114). Rwandans do not remake the world anew with each gesture of the body nor with each choice of the will; neither do they march in lockstep formation to the beat of an invisible drummer. There is method and madness, anomie and order, to their history and to their cosmology.

Notes

1. The democratization wave pushed by Western powers during the late 1980s and 1990s also touched Rwanda. Feeling that it would have to open its political system in order to continue receiving aid from Western donors, Rwanda allowed other political parties besides the MRND to come into existence, although most power continued to rest with the President. Many different political parties quickly saw the light of day, but the principal ones besides the MRND were: the Mouvement Démocrate Républicain (MDR), the Parti Liberal (PL), and the Parti Social Démocrate (PSD). In an effort to scramble the situation the MRND also created other parties that were in effect clones of itself, such as the Parti Ecologiste. The CDR party, Coalition pour la Défense de la République, was an MRND splinter party that was more openly anti-Tutsi and anti-RPF than the MRND. Later in the 1990s, President Habyarimana and other Hutu extremists managed to split off anti-RPF factions from the MDR and the PL parties that became known as "*Hutu Powa*" (Hutu power) factions. Many later supporters of the genocide were recruited from the "Hutu Powa" groups.

2. According to Rwandans who spoke with me in the days which followed this assassination, it had been carried out by soldiers in Habyarimana's crack army unit, la Garde Presidentielle. This seems plausible. I was home at the time of the assassination and because I lived in the same neighborhood as Gatabazi, heard the bursts of machine gun fire that killed him. Such arms would not have been available to ordinary Interahamwe militia members. Felcien Gatabazi's party, the Parti Social Democrate (PSD), was arguably the most anti-ethnicist among Rwanda's opposition parties. Possessing both Tutsi and Hutu members, the PSD had resisted all attempts on the part of Habyarimana and his followers to split the party into "Powa" and non "Powa" factions. This was not the case for the Mouvement Democrate Republicain (MDR) nor for the Parti Liberal (PL), both of which had been split. Many members of "Powa" factions joined forces with the "genocidaires" after Habyarimana's assassination. PSD members were targeted during the genocide, whether they were Hutu or Tutsi.

3. As part of the Arusha accords, the RPF was allowed to station one battalion of its troops in Kigali in order to protect its political representatives. Although the first violent incidents that followed the President's assassination were against prominent Hutu opponents of the genocide and some individual Tutsi, the RPF garrison was attacked early on 7 April 1994. It then asked and received permission from the United Nations Mission to Rwanda (UNAMIR) to leave the confines of its garrison in order to defend itself.

4. This opposition is certainly not the only one which characterizes Rwandan popular medicine; there are others such as: purity vs. pollution, hot vs. cold, and wet vs. dry. However, the flow/blockage opposition appears to be the dominant one in much of Rwandan popular healing and may be prominent in other domains of Rwandan symbolic thought as well. Its analysis has nevertheless been neglected in the earlier ethnographic writing on Rwanda. It should also be noted that Rwandan medicine is pluralistic. Many Rwandans consult biomedical and other practitioners whose theoretical and intellectual bases differ from that which I will describe in this paper. I do not

claim that all Rwandan symbolic thought about the body conforms to the described model. Nonetheless, I believe that the thought of a sufficient number Rwandans is indeed characterized by these patterns and that we need to understand them.

5. Interahamwe means "those who attack together." Most Rwandan political parties had youth wings and for the MRND party (the party in power at the time of the genocide), theirs was the Interahamwe. Recruited largely from among un- or underemployed young males who had drifted into Rwandan cities, the Interahamwe received political and arms training from MRND party officials, Rwandan Government soldiers, and possibly also from French military advisors. Practically every urban neighborhood possessed at least one Interahamwe member and in the rural areas, every hillside. They aided the pregenocidal apparatus in keeping regularly updated lists of all Rwandan opposition party members and all Tutsis. Before the outbreak of whole scale massacres, the Interahamwe intimidated people on their lists with actual or threatened violence and extorted "protection" money from some of them. Even before the genocide Interahamwe were occasionally given authorization to set up roadblocks and to rob, beat, and sometimes kill the people they had trapped, or to steal or damage their vehicles. On two occasions I narrowly avoided being trapped in such a roadblock and on one of these occasions, bricks hit my vehicle just beneath the windshield. On another occasion at a small barrier, consisting merely of a motorbike straddling a Kigali back street, a Tutsi friend of mine and I were caught and hassled for twenty minutes or so by a group of Interahamwe and in the presence of two Rwandan police officers. After lengthy negotiations with the police officers, who were probably nonplussed by the presence of a foreigner, the Interahamwe released my friend although not before they had cut him slightly near the eye. During the genocide Interahamwe weapons of choice were the machete, the nail-studded wooden club, and the grenade.

6. The Mouvement Revolutionnaire pour le Développement or MRND changed its name in 1991 to Mouvement Revolutionnaire pour le Développement et la Démocratie after multiparty democracy was authorized in Rwanda. It retained the acronym, MRND.

7. Melchior Ndadaye was Burundi's first democratically elected President and first Hutu President. Elected in June of 1993, Ndadaye was taken prisoner in late October and then executed (not by impalement) by Burundian Tutsi army officers in a coup attempt. Almost universally condemned by other nations, the coup eventually failed, but not before it had provoked reprisal killings in which thousands of Tutsi civilians died and counter-reprisal violence in which thousands of Hutu were killed. The coup and Ndadaye's death served the cause of Hutu extremism in Rwanda quite well and extremists lost no time in exploiting it. Unfortunately the extremists' point that the Tutsi could never be trusted as partners in a democracy gained enormous credibility in Rwanda in the wake of Ndadaye's tragic death.

7

PEACE, WAR, SEX, AND SORCERY

Nonlinear Analogical Transformation in the Early Escalation
of North Mekeo Sorcery and Chiefly Practice

Mark S. Mosko

For many good reasons, Sahlins's (1981; 1985; 1991) "structural history" has
been widely celebrated as successfully tackling many of social anthropology's long-standing theoretical problems having to do with cultural continuity and change. In the present context Sahlins's program is of particular
interest as it conceivably incorporates several of the key features of chaos
theory (Gleick 1987; Stewart 1989; Prigogine and Stengers 1984; Briggs and
Peat 1989): "extreme sensitivity to initial conditions" (i.e., the effects of individual actors' discrepant attributions of meaning to the same happenings);
"fractal self-similarity" (i.e., hierarchical/heroic organization, where prototypically the Polynesian king embodies in his actions the actions of society at
large); "complex dynamical relations among variables" (i.e., structures of
the conjuncture); and "irreversible time," "dissipative structures," or "systems far from equilibrium" (i.e., diachronic structures, structural change).[1]

In his programmatic formulation of the structural history approach at
the opening of *Islands of History* (1985; see also pp. 102-103), however,
Sahlins effectively turns away from one of the other core elements of
chaos theory: nonlinearity. From an anthropological viewpoint, this issue
is perhaps best appreciated as the source or location of categorical ambiguity and contradiction in cultural systems. Instead of a "strict Saussurean synchrony" (1985: xvi) which he sees as characteristic of most
structuralism in social anthropology, Sahlins pursues a more temporally
oriented diachronic notion of structure, focused on the interaction

between the culture as constituted, on the one hand, and the culture as differentially lived and experienced by various actors over a series of chronological events on the other. In some respects this conceptual shift from the nonlinearity of chaos theory is a positive one as it recapitulates Prigogine's perspective on irreversible time, systems far from equilibrium, and perhaps even self-organization. However, this same shift implicitly elides, or at the very least equivocates over the possibility of ambiguity and contradiction—likely indices of nonlinearity (see below)—as inhering in the structure as constituted.

The problem, as Sahlins views it, derives from the atemporality and, therefore, seemingly random reversibility of cultural categories in most anthropological appropriations of Saussurean structuralism. At issue are the

> famous "logical instabilities" of the cultural categories. The Fijian king appears both as male and female; his ritual and political nature is dual, or contextually one or the other. Taken as a synchronic and empirical description, there is little more to make of this: it seems a "permanent ambiguity" or "inherent contradiction" of the system (Sahlins 1985: xvi; see also 1985: 102-103).

Sahlins refers here to the "extended lists of paired contraries or Saussurean proportions" of much orthodox structuralist presentation: "I mean the tables that read: male is to female, as king is to people, culture is to nature, life to death, and so forth—yin-yang structuralism, without a Book of Changes. These proportions too are logically unstable and contradictable. From another vantage, the king is female rather than male, and nature (ferocious outside) rather than culture" (Sahlins 1985: xvi). As he sees it,

> The alternatives come down to this. We can try to develop the structure from (or as) the indefinite set of contextual permutations—in certain specifiable contexts, the king is male, in other female; not only an inelegant solution, but probably hopeless. Or, in contrast to this aporetic endeavor, we can conceive the structure the way it is in abstract cosmic schemes (Sahlins 1985: xvi).

And thus, Sahlins continues, one can "account for the genesis of the contradictions precisely as partial or situational views on the global order" (1985: xvi). Alternations and ambiguities emanate from the "interested selection of social agents among the numerous logical possibilities—including contradictory possibilities—that are presented in any cultural order. In the case of events surrounding the death of Captain Cook, the two Hawaiian parties, out of their own self-conceptions, conceived different (proportional) relations in the same event, whence their own conflict in the structure of the conjuncture whose outcome was Cook's death" (Sahlins 1985: xvii).

In sum, it would appear that Sahlins's general conception of cultural structure, purportedly "the way it is in abstract cosmic schemes," is free of ambiguity and contradiction.

And it is here that the notion of nonlinearity becomes relevant. From the vantage of chaos theory, reality, whether natural or social, consists predominantly in complex, overwhelmingly nonlinear interactions among variables. If it can be safely presumed that human sociocultural systems of the order of Sahlins's structural history are complex phenomena, then the key dynamical processes of such systems would expectably be nonlinear as well. In chaos theory, nonlinearity refers to relations which are not proportional. Mathematically, for example, two equations are linear if they can be added up to produce a single solution; two equations are nonlinear when they cannot be added up to produce a single unambiguous solution (see my "Introduction," this volume). By contrast to Sahlins's model, in the view of complex systems and chaos theory, the presence of ambiguity and contradiction is not merely a function of the partial or situational viewpoints of differently interested actors but essential nonlinear components of the global cultural order itself.

In this chapter I seek to illustrate these ideas through an historical analysis of a cultural structure (or rather, a major part of a cultural structure) which is inherently nonlinear in the above-defined sense. This happens to be a cultural structure rife with contradiction and ambiguity, which in numerous writings on the North Mekeo of Papua New Guinea I have characterized in terms of systemically "bisected dualities" (Mosko 1985; 1989; 1991a; 1992; 1994a). Where in the earlier treatments I attempted to lay out synchronically the parallel inconsistencies across diverse cultural and social contexts, in this context I shall show how nonlinear analogical relations among the four categories of North Mekeo chiefly clan officials were played out in the early history of encounters with Europeans as something more than the combined viewpoints of diversely situated interested actors. Without denying the analytical validity of the latter, I shall argue that the ambiguities and contradictions manifest in the sequence of historical events which implicated North Mekeo chiefs and official sorcerers are themselves indicative of the categorical ambiguities and contradictions inherent in the nonlinear constitution of the cultural structure itself. This chapter, then, seeks to employ the notion of chaotic nonlinearity as a vehicle for carrying structural historical studies into new analytical directions.[2]

The remaining sections of this essay are presented in the following order: first, I shall delineate the specific form of nonlinear analogical thought and practice with which I am concerned; second, I shall illustrate the precolonial ethnographic relevance of this analogical form to the relations and distinctions among the several categories of North Mekeo chiefly clan officials; third, I shall illustrate the dynamic potentialities of nonlinear analogical reasoning and practice as they are revealed in the historical transformations of a North Mekeo chiefdom in the decades just prior to and following colonial encounters with the West; and fourth, in the course of this exercise I shall venture to explain a number of long-standing ethnographic and historical anomalies particular to the Mekeo case: a pronounced emphasis upon sorcery and associated ritual forms including organized love or courting magic; a certain frequency of illicit marriage; and a decided cultural "conservatism" despite more than a century of contact and interaction with exogenous forces. In this final regard I shall argue that the apparent anomalies of the supposed "traditional" system are not traditional at all but represent rapid and dramatic transformations of the precolonial system—transformations profoundly shaped by the nonlinear analogical implications of the overall system. The kinds of instability and dynamism exhibited in Mekeo early contact history, in other words, appear to have been strongly programmatic.

Nonlinear Analogy

The specific formulation of nonlinear analogy I examine in this chapter is a modified version of Lévi-Strauss's (1963c) canonic formula for myth: $F_x(a):F_y(b) \cong F_x(b):F_{a-1}(y)$:

> Here, with two terms, *a* and *b*, being given as well as two functions, *x* and *y*, of these terms, it is assumed that a relation of equivalence exists between two situations defined respectively by an inversion of *terms* and *relations*, under two conditions: (1) that one term be replaced by its opposite (in the above formula, *a* and *a-1*); (2) that an inversion be made between the *function value* and the *term value* of two elements (above, *y* and *a*) (Lévi-Strauss 1963c: 225).

As in the above discussion of nonlinearity and structural history, contradiction (if not also ambiguity) is central in Lévi-Strauss's view of the very structure of myth. For Lévi-Strauss the function of myth is first to articulate or express and then overcome (ultimately irresolvable) contradictions. The corresponding purpose of the canonic formula is to capture formally the logic by which mythical contradictions are first posed, then tentatively resolved. As for Sahlins's perception of the contingency of historical events, Lévi-Strauss (1963c: 204) asks, while the content of myths might appear to be similarly contingent, how is it that comparatively myths are so similar? The situation confronting Lévi-Strauss on myth is closely analogous to that confronting Sahlins on history (see Lévi-Strauss 1995).

In the present context it must be stressed that Lévi-Strauss's original rendition of the canonic formula was directed to the analysis of myths drawn across a wide range of different cultures, eventually spanning all cultures of North and South America (Lévi-Strauss 1969[1949], 1973; 1978; 1981; 1988). An earlier revised version of the formula (Mosko 1985; 1991a; see Morava this volume), which reads, $F_x(a):F_y(b)::F_x(b):F_y(2)$ (or X':Y"::Y':X"; see below), however, was expressly adapted to analyses of a wide variety of cultural materials, nonmythical as well as mythical, drawn from a *single* sociocultural system (political organization, economic exchange, kin classification, ritual operations, and so on). The chief difference between Lévi-Strauss's and my versions of the formula involves the role of the puzzling "second twist" contained in the final element, $f_{a-1}(y)$ which, I argued from Lévi-Strauss's numerous demonstrations, consistently arose at the juncture of crosscultural comparison, that is, moving from the internal dynamics of a myth in one cultural system to what he treated as "the same myth" in another cultural system. My simpler version of the formula which lacked the second "twist," in other words, was justified to the extent that I was not employing it for purposes of comparison across different and possibly unrelated cultural systems. In this chapter, I again explore the analytical potentialities of the same revised formula, limited still to contexts of a single sociocultural system but in their historical or diachronic extension.[3]

Since Aristotle, a relationship of *analogy* has been taken to obtain "whenever there are four terms such that the relation between the second and the first is similar to that between the fourth and the third" (quoted in P. Maranda 1971: 117; cf. Siemens 1991). Conventional analogy, such as A:B::C:D, is essentially simple and linear; that is, if A:B::C:D, then it can be deduced that A:C::B:D, but not, for example, A:B::D:C. The latter possibility is excluded in as much as the reversal or inversion of the relation between C and D (i.e., as D:C) constitutes a contradiction of the relation C:D. According to the rules of formal logic, two propositions cannot both be true if they contradict one another, as in this instance. However, it is a commonplace ethnographic observation that such contradictions are not merely tolerated in many if not most of the world's cultures but they are central aspects of much cultural or symbolic reasoning and the hallmark of their internal complexity. It is contradictory logic of this sort, after all which was the raison d'etre of Lévi-Strauss's whole treatment of Amerindian and other myths, and it is the explicit source of Sahlins's frustration over Polynesian kings being both female and male: "It becomes clear that any given proportion (A:B:C:D) is a partial and interested statement of the structure. It assumes some determinate spectator or subject in a determinate relation to the cultural totality" (Sahlins 1985: xvi). In terms derivative of chaos theory, I shall suggest instead that an analogy on the order of A:B::C:D is *linear* to the extent that it allows deductions of only one other solution, A:C::B:D, while excluding other possible *nonlinear* permutations which, on the basis of inversion or reversal of terms, would contradict it (e.g., A:B::D:C, A:D::B:C, or A:D::C:B) (cf. Siemens 1991: 238-240, 245-246, 248). The reasoning embedded in human mythical and nonmythical cultural systems seems not only to allow the possibility of such complex nonlinear analogical relations but, again as Lévi-Strauss has argued, positively centers upon it.

Now one important aspect of this formulation is that nonlinear relations, which from the viewpoint of linear analogy would contradict and mutually exclude one another, possess a mutual implication or at least partial identity. For example, acceptance or tolerance of both A:B::C:D and A:B::D:C implies that in some respects C and D are similar to or partial surrogates of one another, and by further extension so would be A and B (for example, if the relation of A to B resembles that of both C to D and D to C, then A and B must share in a similarity analogous to that of C and D). As these internal relations among the four members of classic linear statements are either outlawed or deemed irrelevant, there is no necessity that they be marked; hence the conventional notation of A, B, C and D is adequate. But with non-linear analogy, it is precisely these internal relations which provide for the extra dynamical relations among the terms or members of the analogy. This is why each of Lévi-Strauss's four members in the original canonic formula consists of basically two kinds of components, a "term" and a "function" (e.g., in $f_a(x)$ there is a "term" x and a "function" a) that reappear in other members of the formula either through recursion or inversion. For this reason I earlier suggested, given the materials I was dealing with, that there were neither four distinct terms nor two terms plus two functions but rather a single binary contrast which was recursively crosscut by its own reversal or inversion; hence the nonlinearity. In the alternative notation (X, Y, ' and ") that I developed to account for these complex internal relations, each of the two initially opposed categories, X and Y, was bisected by its own respective inversion, resulting in a total of four composite members: X'::Y"::Y':X". Each member of the analogy thus contains explicitly within itself indices of similarity and difference to the remaining three members.

And it is through these internal nonlinear relations that all other systemic permutations of the formula are possible: X':Y"::X":Y', X':Y'::X":Y", X':Y'::Y":X", etc. In synchronic comparisons across diverse contexts of a single culture, any given analogical formulation can thus be contradicted by inverting or reversing any of the implicit internal relations. In the earlier work, I labeled this specific quadripartite structure as consisting in systematically "bisected dualities" (Mosko 1985; 1991a).[4]

In diachronic perspective within a single cultural context or domain, I here propose that temporal expression of these dynamic potentialities can be anticipated as successive transformations. In this regard, contrary to Sahlins (1985: xvi), the system *is* contradictory. The Polynesian king is "now male, then female" not merely through partial and interested perspectives of different actors; the contradictions inhere in the very character of the culture's cosmic scheme. These same alternatives or permutations can thus be manifested processually, now in one formulation and then in another. While, as Sahlins argues, events of this order undoubtedly reflect different actors' interested and constestable perspectives, they are also indicators of the potentialities inherent to the system, of the "culture as constituted" as he phrases it.[5]

I can now turn to an analysis of the nonlinear constitution of the system of chiefly officialdom among North Mekeo at the time of European contact before proceeding to outline how that system was transformed in accordance with those relations in the context of the subsequent imposition of colonial domination.

The Structure of Mekeo Politico-Ritual Officialdom

The ethnographer Epeli Hau'ofa records that the Central (Biofa) Mekeo peoples of Papua New Guinea possess a "marked tendency towards dualistic thinking about themselves, their social groupings, and their environment ... [and] their cosmology" (1981: 290). Hau'ofa notes just as forcefully, however, a "deep-seated ambivalence [lying] at the heart of the culture" (1981: 5). He sees this "ambivalence," moreover, as "sustain[ing] and in turn receiv[ing] its sustenance from, the system" (1981: 289). It is this systemic coupling of dualism and ambivalence which I earlier formalized in terms of "quadripartite structures" or "bisected dualities" across a wide range of categories and contexts in the culture of the neighboring and closely related North (Amoamo) Mekeo peoples (Mosko 1985; 1991a; 1994a; cf. Bergendorff 1996 en passim).

The earliest ethnographic account of Mekeo culture and social organization is contained in C.G. Seligmann's classic, The Melanesians of British New Guinea (1910: Chapters 24, 29, 30), on the basis of his observations on the 1898 Cambridge Expedition to the Torres Strait and 1904 Cook-Daniels Expedition to British New Guinea. Mekeo were living then as they do now in consolidated villages on the alluvial plain just inland from the southeast Papuan coast. Until they were "pacified" by Government forces in 1890 and administered as a unit, they never constituted a single politically integrated entity but were grouped into several named politically autonomous "tribes" (Biofa, Ve'e, Amoamo, Kuipa). Although linguistic and cultural differences from tribe to tribe have been noted, these differences appear to have been generally minor throughout the historical era (A. Jones 1998). In terms of social organization specifically, the several tribes have exhibited only slight variations according to the same schema (Hau'ofa 1981; Mosko 1985; 1989; 1991a; 1994a; Bergendorff 1996; cf. Stephen 1974; 1995).

Seligmann (1910: 311-312) and subsequent ethnographers (Hau'ofa 1971; 1981: 290-291; Stephen 1974: xix-xx; Monsell-Davis 1981; Bergendorff 1996) have taken the specific configuration of hereditary chiefly and sorcery offices among Mekeo as the principal nonlinguistic criterion for distinguishing them as a people from contiguous Austronesian-speaking populations—the Roro, Kabadi, Lapeka, Nara, Kuni, and so on.[6] For Mekeo, official political and ritual power and authority have been distributed among personages known as au akaisa, or "Akaisa Men."[7] Akaisa (also known in some myths as Oa Rove or Walope) is the name of the culture hero or deity for all of the Mekeo peoples and many of their closely related neighbors, such as Roro. It was Akaisa in mythical times who bequeathed to the people all of the practices and institutions which they consider "customary" or "traditional" (kangakanga) including chiefly Akaisa Men titles and capacities (Mosko 1985: chapter 8; 1991c; 2002b; Seligmann 1910: 304-309; Hau'ofa 1981: 77-83, 186, 229; Stephen 1974: 12-

15; 1979b: 156). The ability to perpetuate the social and cultural order that Akaisa ordained was left initially to his ritual heirs, the original Akaisa Men, and over subsequent generations their ritually installed successors.

The most distinctive aspect of Mekeo politico-ritual authority is the fourfold differentiation among the official types of Akaisa Men: "peace chief" (*lopia*), "war chief" (*iso*), "peace sorcerer" (*ungaunga*), and "war sorcerers" (*faika*). Each of these positions presumed specialized spheres of legitimate "authority" or "law" (*oa*), "power" or "heat" (*tsiapu*), and "strength" (*kabula*), which were based upon officeholders' monopoly on the spiritual agency of Akaisa and the spirits of the dead (*tsiange*). As implied in the English glosses I have chosen (i.e., "peace," "war," "chief," "sorcerer"), there is a distinct pattern of conceptual and functional complementarity among the four Akaisa Man positions (Seligmann 1910: 342-348; Mosko 1985: chapters 6, 7, and 8; 1991b; 1992; 2001a; Hau'ofa 1971: 155; 1981: chapters 7-8; Bergendorff 1996: 45, 51-52, 93, 129; cf. Stephen 1974: 5-10, 18-36, 54-56; 1979b: 149-152).[8] The domain of peace (*paisa*) involved the social relations among members of the same politically autonomous tribe. In precolonial times the tribe was a named, ideally endogamous collectivity, so peace involved relations within and among its exogamous agnatic units (moieties, clans, subclans, lineages). Then as now, relations of peace involved principally two connected contexts of legitimate interaction, exchange and agency—intermarriage, through which cognatic kin relations were extended among agnatically unrelated tribespeople; and mortuary feasting, wherein those ties of cognation were abrogated ("de-conceived") so that erstwhile kin, becoming classificatory nonrelatives, could marry, and members of patrilineal clan units could lay claim to long-term agnatic purity (Mosko 1983; 1985: chapters 6-7; 1989).

These two dimensions of intratribal peaceful agency were the joint concerns of clan peace chiefs and peace sorcerers. The power and strength of peace chiefs consisted in the capacity to officiate at mortuary feasts, the proper performance of which relied upon clanspeople's observance of the chiefly rules of orderly intermarriage. Peace sorcerers' official capacities of causing death through snakebite or illness were used to ensure that ordinary villagers obeyed the marriage and funerary laws of the peace chiefs. They did this by manipulating ancestral or other spirits (*tsiange*) such as Akaisa to make sick or kill those (or their close relations) who shamed or angered peace chiefs by disregarding their laws. Interfering with or obstructing a peace chief in the conduct of his official duties, indeed, was a capital offense; and in the absence of any cultural theory of illness or death from "natural causes," all nonviolent deaths were considered the result of peace sorcerers' secret ritual attacks at the behest of peace chiefs. Also, it was usually peace sorcerers who were qualified to cure repentant villagers of peace sorcery attack. Similarly, peace sorcerers were expected to employ their special ties to spiritual beings for detecting when sorcerers of other groups were illicitly attacking members of their own clans so that the latter could be warned and protected. In all these regards, as Hau'ofa (1971: 162; 1981: 48) has aptly phrased it, peace sorcerers were the "custodians of Mekeo traditions."

In the complementary domain of "war" (*uani* or *aoao*) prior to pacification by colonial forces, there was an analogous division of legitimate political and ritual agency between the war chiefs and the war sorcerers of a tribe (Mosko 1985: 114-123; 1992; 1994a; Seligmann 1910: 218, 295-298, 342-348; Hau'ofa 1971: 155-156; 1981: chapter 7; Stephen 1974: 54-57; 1987b: 268). It was the prerogative of war chiefs to lead the warriors of their respective clans in battle, whether in offensive surprise attacks against their enemies of other tribes or in defense when their own villages were raided. Similar to their counterparts in the domain of peace, the war sorcerers of the clans composing a tribe were entrusted with the secret ritual responsibilities of ensuring the collective success of the war chiefs' endeavors in battle. Before a raid they solicited the aid of ancestral and other spirits to protect and strengthen their clans' war parties and to weaken and make vulnerable their enemies. And in the event that men in their clans emerged as successful homicides, war sorcerers performed the rituals that protected them while they remained in isolation so that eventually they could rejoin the community safely.

Summarizing the distinctive features by which the four categories of Akaisa Men are differentiated:

peace	:	peace	::	war	:	war
chief		sorcerer		chief		sorcerer

internal	:	internal	::	external	:	external
public		secret		public	:	secret
agency		agency		agency		agency

On these criteria, the relations of the two peace officials parallel the functions of the two war officials. The relations of the four Akaisa Men thus far correspond with linear analogical relations of the order of:

$$X' \quad : \quad X'' \quad :: \quad Y' \quad : \quad Y''$$

However, as regards the critical criteria of whether they participated in homicide or mortuary exchange, the relation of the two peace officials are reversed in the context of the homicide and mortuary functions of the war officials:

mortuary	:	homicide	::	homicide	:	mortuary
exchange		exchange		exchange		exchange

These relations also parallel the distinctions of officials' single or collective agency (i.e., whether the chief or sorcerer performed his specialized homicide or mortuary ritual on single persons or collectivities):

collective	:	single	::	single	:	collective
death		death		death		death

The analogical relations among the four officials can thus be expressed just as easily with the third and fourth terms inverted, that is, nonlinearly:

$$X' \quad : \quad X'' \quad :: \quad Y'' \quad : \quad Y'$$

Closer examination of two additional dimensions of significance involved in the classification of Akaisa Men—transactions of gender-marked bloods, and calculations of genealogical seniority—provide additional indications that the division of politico-ritual specialization is more comprehensively understood in terms of nonlinear analogical relations. First, the ritual capacities of all four officials, despite their differences otherwise, focus uniformly upon "death" (*mae*) vis-à-vis exchanges of gender-marked "blood" or "bloods" (*ifa*). In villagers' classifications of kin and clan relations internal to the endogamous tribe, "male blood" shared among persons by virtue of purely agnatic connections is differentiated from "female blood" reckoned on the basis of affinal and/or matrilateral ties (Mosko 1983; 1985: chapters 6-8). In the course of overseeing exogamous intermarriage internal to the tribe, peace chiefs and peace sorcerers effectively regulate reciprocal transactions and interclan mixings of female blood. Complementarily, war chiefs and war sorcerers are responsible for the reciprocity and mixing of intertribal male blood through violence and killing. However, peace chiefs in mortuary feasting and war sorcerers in warfare ceremonial have the parallel responsibility of removing or unmixing female and male bloods, respectively, from the skins of their fellow clanspeople; and in actively causing death peace sorcerers and war chiefs correspondingly mix intratribal (i.e., interclan) female and intertribal male bloods, respectively, on victims' and homicides' skins. Simply put, in these particular contexts, the chief and sorcerer of peace respectively remove (unmix) and deposit (mix) bloods where the chief and sorcerer of war rather deposit (mix) and remove (unmix) them.

In these fuller terms of gender marked blood mixing and unmixing, relations among the four categories of Akaisa Men exhibit the same type of "permanent ambiguity" and "inherent contradiction" noted by Sahlins, except that in these instances it is not simply a function of partial or situational views of different subjects but a systematic function of the total politico-ritual authority system. Expressed analogically, these finer distinctions of gender marked blood suggest an inversion and further specification of the terms composing the two right-hand columns of the linear analogical formulation above. Official ritual specializations of Mekeo chiefs and sorcerers can be expressed nonlinearly as:

peace chief	:	peace sorcerer	::	war chief	:	war sorcerer
internal public agency	:	internal secret agency	::	external public agency	:	external secret agency
mortuary female-blood unmixing	:	homicide female-blood mixing	::	homicide male-blood mixing	:	mortuary male-blood unmixing

In some of these contexts, as above, the relation of the peace chief to the peace sorcerer is parallel to that of the war chief and war sorcerer, or $X':X''::Y':Y''$, but in other contexts the relation of the war officials to each other is the reverse of that between the chief and sorcerer of peace, or $X':X''::Y'':Y'$.

The nonlinearity of these relations is not the consequence merely of the possible ambiguities or inconsistencies inherent in the context of gender distinctions, for the analogous complications are evident as well in the indigenous classification of the same set of authority positions in terms of genealogical seniority. Elsewhere (Mosko 1991a; 1992; 1994b; 2001a), I have traced the systemic contradictions of "senior"/"junior" calculation among the four categories of Akaisa Men. Villagers frequently portray the idealized relations between the peace chief, peace sorcerer, war chief, and war sorcerer of their patriclan in classificatory sibling terms according to the prevailing "Hawaiian" generational nomenclature system. Same-sex siblings are either genealogically *fakaniau* "senior" or *eke* "junior" in reference or address (hence, *itsi au* "my senior sibling" or *itsi atsiu* "my junior sibling"). A man's "brother" or a woman's "sister" is thus unambiguously either senior or junior; there is no same-sex sibling term without this asymmetry.

Nonetheless, these calculations inevitably give rise to certain contradictions. The most obvious example involves a polygynous man's offspring by his first and second wives (or a woman's offspring by different husbands). The last-born child of the first wife, even if he/she is many years junior by age to his/her half siblings, is genealogically senior (*fakaniau*). Similarly, among two sets of first cousins the firstborn senior member of the junior parent is, according to this logic, genealogically junior (*eke*) to all of the members of the genealogically senior sibling set, even its subsequent-born junior members. But these contradictions are not limited simply to a conflict between relative age and seniority. Typically as well as by rule, a peace chief's younger brother will be classified as genealogically senior (i.e., "elder brother") to all of his same-sex, same-generation siblings within the clan; yet he would rank as a "poor" or "ordinary man" (*ulalu*) in contrast to those of his junior clan brothers who, as the clan's installed war chief, peace sorcerer, or war sorcerer, will be acclaimed Akaisa Men.

This predicament is symptomatic of the relations among the different types of Akaisa Men, the lineage units they head, and all same-sex, same-generation clanspeople who belong to the different lineages. The four offices are stereotypically distinguished in terms of relative seniority (*faka-niau*) and juniority (*eke*). However, there is no clear or unbroken linear rank ordering from most senior to most junior. Although villagers frequently discuss the four kinds of Akaisa Man as a total set, never once, even in response to my direct questions and encouragement, has anyone, in private or in public, ventured a linear series of "first, second, third, fourth." Although it is consistently maintained that within a clan the offices and lineages of the peace sorcerer, war chief, and war sorcerer are all ideally junior to the clan peace chief, establishing unambiguous relations of seniority among the three junior positions (or among members of the different lineages they represent) usually proves problematic and historically has often been the source of contestation. There does seem to be a strong consensus that a peace sorcerer and war chief of the same clan (along with commoner members of their respective lineages) are junior in common to their peace chief. But from my observations among North Mekeo, villagers never similarly attribute a categorical seniority to the relation between a peace sorcerer and a war chief (or, correspondingly, their lineages). Also, there does seem to be clear priority accorded to the war sorcerer in relation to both the peace sorcerer and war chief, and particularly the latter.

My early frustrations at making sense of these ambiguities were overcome during my second period of fieldwork in 1990. I was sitting with a group of both old and young men in my own clan's clubhouse as afternoon rains began to fall. In response to my pressing inquiries, one man, Auabala, eventually laid four areca nut skins before me on the floor of the clan clubhouse in a broken or bent line (Figure 7.1).[9] Pointing to the uppermost peel, Auabala said, "This is the peace chief. Of them all, this one, the peace chief, is senior (*fakaniau*)." The single rind off to one side (left, facing), he said, "is the peace sorcerer who helps and watches after the peace chief, and he is junior (*eke*)." The two rinds descending on the opposite (right, facing) side of the peace chief, he explained, "are, first, the war sorcerer, then the war chief." To my questioning, the other men indicated their agreement with Auabala's account and explained further that, just as the peace chief was senior to the peace sorcerer, the war sorcerer was senior to the war chief; but the most senior of them all was the peace chief, they noted, and after him came the war sorcerer. When I then asked who came next, the war chief or the peace sorcerer, I was told, "No, it does not work that way." I had to think instead of each "side" or "half." "On this side," Auabala said as he grabbed the two peace rinds, "the peace chief is senior; on this other side," gesturing with the other two peels, "the war sorcerer is senior." [10]

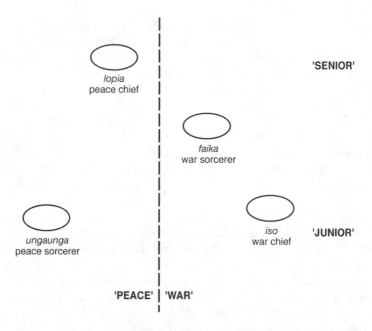

Figure 7.1: Senior/junior ranking of chiefs and sorcerers

This discussion illustrates precisely the inconsistency of reckoning genealogical seniority linearly among Akaisa Men categories. In the context of peace it is the chief and his lineage who are senior and the sorcerer and sorcery lineage junior. But in the context of war, it is the other way around; the sorcerer and his lineage are senior to the chief and his lineage. In terms of analogy, the relations of chief to sorcerer in the context of peace are reversed in the context of war.

peace chief	:	peace sorcerer	::	war chief	:	war sorcerer
senior peace	:	junior peace	::	junior war	:	senior war

Moreover, the ambiguity and contradiction in assigning genealogical seniority to peace sorcerers and war chiefs and their respective lineages within a clan parallels the ambiguity and contradiction noted above in classification of Akaisa men in terms of their respective agencies regarding gendered bloods, reaffirming that the dynamics of these relations are structural or systemic. And because of that, the frequently reported cases across Mekeo of junior men or officials contesting the seniority of Akaisa Men positions are not strictly a matter of historical contingency or individual actors' instrumentality (see Hau'ofa 1981: 77-109, 184-288; Bergendorff 1996: 234ff.; Mosko 1985: chapter 5; 1994a; 2001a).

Not coincidentally, it has long been recognized by other investigators that complications of this sort are characteristic of "Hawaiian" type sibling terminologies, especially for Polynesia (see, for example, Firth 1970: 273-274, 278-279; Sahlins 1958: 140-148; Goldman 1957: 387, 1970: 446-473; Murdock 1965[1949]: 228-231, 1967; Ortner 1981: 403n; Marshall 1983; Thomas 1986b: 29-31; 1986a: 79; Salmond 1991; Mosko 1994a; 2001a; Sagir 2003). In many cases, though, the possible theoretical significance of these complications has not been fully developed.

In sum, calculations of genealogical seniority among the four categories of hereditary clan official generate the same structure of systematically bisected dualities elaborated earlier in terms of nonlinear analogy.

Cultural Anomalies in Wider Context

I mentioned above that my treatment of nonlinear analogical thought and practice would illuminate a number of long-standing anomalies in the ethnographic and historical literature on Mekeo: a pronounced preoccupation throughout the postcontact era with ritual "sorcery" of various forms, including a distinctive type of collective ceremonial courting and love magic termed *bakai*; a persistent statistical pattern of illicit marriage; a pronounced "conservatism" as regards cultural traditions generally; and the persistence into contemporary times of considerable power and authority in the hands of clan peace chiefs. These, as well as a number of other contextual factors, are implicated in North Mekeo understandings of the reciprocities of peace and war regulated by Akaisa Men, as described above. Also, most investigators have presumed until now that the practices and anomalies observed in the postcontact era more or less consist in preexisting "traditional" arrangements extended into the present.[11] I shall argue, however, that in many respects the observed anomalies represent systemic nonlinear analogical transformations of preexisting patterns in response to specific identifiable factors of early European contact and intrusion. In order to demonstrate this, it will be necessary to describe each of these factors more fully.

Marriage Regulation

In the precontact era, it seems, marriage and mortuary exchanges were articulated according to a set of precise rules.[12] Each person was expected to marry within the tribe but outside his/her own patriclan and patrimoiety and into a clan of the opposite moiety. Villagers were also prohibited from marrying anyone of their mothers' clans, so one's own spouse and mother had to come from different clans of the opposite moiety. Typically, this left one of a tribe's four clans for every person to find a mate. Since on average half of the people of that fourth clan could be expected to have mothers who came from one's own clan, villagers were effectively left to select a legitimate spouse from on average one-half of that fourth clan (i.e., assuming different clans reproduced their members in roughly equal proportions). Thus, the "traditional" Mekeo marriage system consisted of a type of second cross-cousin marriage whereby only one-eighth or so of the population in each generation was eligible for legitimate marriage, much like an eight subsection Aranda system (Mosko 1985: 125-142; Keesing 1975: 83). This one-eighth ratio will be of considerable significance when I discuss the frequency of postcontact illicit marriage and depopulation.

Peace Sorcery

Many observers have remarked upon what they interpret to be a Mekeo "obsession" with "sorcery," particularly peace sorcery (*ungaunga*) which they have taken to be an extension of precontact patterns (Seligmann 1910: 278; Haddon 1901: 262; Stephen 1974; 1977: 4; 1979b: 149; 1987a: 42-43; 1995; 1996; Bergendorff 1996). It can be assumed that the threat of peace sorcerers' official retribution for illicit marriage and adultery in defense of peace chief's "law" during precontact times was enough to achieve a fair degree of adherence to the rules of marriage and feasting, all else aside (and particularly with the constant threat of enemy war raids; see below). But also in the event of illicit unions, villagers nowadays argue, peace sorcerers would not always attack just the guilty party or parties. Sometimes they would attack close relatives of the bride or groom instead. In order to avoid such occurrences, precontact marriages were ideally prearranged by parents and other kin. Elopements (*kepiau*, "they run away") arising from men's use of love or courting magic upon women of the preferred marriage category were tolerated in certain circumstances but strongly discouraged, and probably, according to villagers' contemporary accounts, they were infrequent (Mosko 1985: 127-129, 132-133; Stephen 1974: 41, 48; cf. Bergendorff 1996: 30).

Courting and Love Magic

Throughout the course of postcontact history, the Mekeo, and especially the young men, have developed a reputation as "dandies." They have earned this renown in part because bachelors (*koae kongo*) live together in dormitories, are expected to do no work (indeed, according to indigenous notions of labor exertion and bodily sustenance, are incapable of doing work; see Mosko 1985: chapter 3), and spend the greater portion of their

time and energies in daily ritual courting behavior, including elaborate
body decorating, directed toward women. The term for the full complex
of these courting practices, *bakai*, is the same term that is applied specifically to the secret ritual spells and charms involved in courting magic.
During precolonial times when the threat of war dominated much of daily
life, infrequent mortuary feasts provided the only occasions when collective *bakai* performances were staged.[13]

Warfare

In the precolonial era, Mekeo warfare (*uani, aoao*) consisted in early morning raids on single villages of enemy tribes, the overt aim being to kill as
many inhabitants as possible. Typically the attacking force would have a
considerable numerical advantage, with the warriors from several villages
in one tribe raiding a single village of an enemy tribe. Attackers also had
the element of surprise to their advantage. Since only members of different tribes ever fought in this way, war chiefs' and war sorcerers' responsibilities were coterminous with authority over the external intertribal
relations, as distinct from the internal or intratribal relations of the peace
officials. Nevertheless, as the senior officials of their subclans and clans,
peace chiefs retained a nominal authority to override the plans of their
own war chiefs and war sorcerers and forbid the participation of their
groups in any proposed raids.[14]

Death by Peace and War Sorcery

Although death figured significantly in both spheres of peace and war, the
scale of death involved in each was different. The ritual techniques of
peace sorcery involved the killing of single villagers. The ritual powers of
war chiefs and war sorcerers, however, involved the potential deaths of
many persons in a single action. For this reason, the officials of war, and
especially war sorcerers, were regarded as possessing considerably
greater powers over death than were peace sorcerers (Mosko 1994a;
Hau'ofa 1981: 46; Stephen 1979b: 219n).

The Incompatibility of Peace and War Activity

Finally, it must be emphasized that the two modes of blood reciprocity
distinguishing peace and war were mutually incompatible. According to
indigenous tenets, sexual intercourse, or for that matter peaceful intercourse of any kind with women and children, was strictly inimical to the
ability to wage war, and vice versa. Men could engage in only one of the
two activities at once. Before colonial "pacification", all men, in order to
achieve combat readiness, had to protect themselves with war sorcery,
which required that they effectively "close" their bodily orifices so no

sorcery entered, even their own. They did this by observing a complex set of rules of fasting and sexual abstinence (*ngope*). Briefly, fasting and abstaining are understood to close or tighten the body ("nothing goes in, nothing goes out"), so that enemies' aggressive war sorcery remains outside. Also, by closing his body, a man becomes "light" and better able to run swiftly and dodge enemy projectiles. According to the rules of ritual closing, it takes some six months of rigorous fasting, abstinence, and other restrictions for a man to reach a state of war readiness. Moreover, it is understood to take some six months for a man to reverse the process in safety (i.e., to "open" his body) so that traces of his own deadly war sorcery clinging to his skin have time to dissipate before they might pass to the inside. It is only after he has put aside his charms and other war paraphernalia and continued his closing ritual for an additional half year, in other words, that a man is able to open his body by eating a more regular diet, drinking fluids, and engaging in sex (Mosko 1985: 87-90; 1997a; cf. Hau'ofa 1981: 234-243; Stephen 1987a; cf. Stephen 1974: 107-111; 1998).

In the era of aboriginal wars, therefore, husbands and wives had to schedule their sexual interactions cyclically. They began with a phase of great sexual frequency and intensity—according to indigenous views, of bodily openness, for a minimum of three months—until the woman was recognized as pregnant. From that moment they would suspend sexual relations while the husband started to close himself. And he would continue to keep his body closed following the birth of this child until the time it was weaned at roughly the age of one-and-a-half or two. During this time he was able to devote himself completely to war. But the husband would put aside his war sorcery as the time of weaning approached so that afterwards he and his wife could safely approach each other and reopen their bodies to conceive their next child. If they did happen to open their bodies sexually while he still had traces of war sorcery on his skin, it would enter both of their bodies and kill them.[15]

The obvious implication is, with the constant threat of war in the days before European domination, most men of a village devoted their energies most of the time to warfare and war preparations. Also, not all men of a clan or village fighting unit could engage in sexual relations with their wives simultaneously. They had to take turns. At any one time, only a few men would be actively conceiving children with their wives so as to replenish the society's population from within while the rest were occupied with protecting it from enemies without.

So this, briefly, is the situation prevailing just before contact with Europeans in the latter half of the nineteenth century: chronic war as an obligatory reciprocal exchange of male blood between different tribes; orderly exchange of female blood between clans and moieties of the same tribe through peaceful intermarriage and mortuary feasting; regulation of intertribal hostilities and large-scale killing by war chiefs and war sorcerers; and the use of peace sorcery against individuals intratribally by peace sorcerers under the legitimate control of clan peace chiefs.

Contact and Transformation

From what little is known, sporadic contacts of European explorers with peoples living on the southeast coast of what is now Papua New Guinea may have begun as early as the seventeenth century. The first sustained encounters in the Mekeo region did not occur until 1875 with the several months' visit to Yule Island of the Italian naturalist D'Albertis. He was followed shortly thereafter for a brief period by two English naturalists, James and Thorngren, and in 1880 the LMS missionary James Chalmers may have patrolled through a few of the inland Mekeo villages (D'Albertis 1881; Stephen 1974: 66; Monsell-Davis 1981: 40-50; Bergendorff 1996: 105-109; Mosko n.d.a). The first consequential missionary contacts did not occur until the Catholic missionaries (Order of the Sacred Heart) arrived in 1885 (Dupeyrat 1935; Stephen 1974: 67-68; Monsell-Davis 1981: 54-61). Still, it was not until 1890, five years later, that government forces entered the heart of the Mekeo area for the first time.

"Pacification"

This first Government penetration was under the personal authority of the Government Administrator of British New Guinea, William MacGregor, himself (British New Guinea Annual Report (BNGAR) 1890a: 80; 1890b: 89-90). The stated ambitions of the British in this instance were solely to establish peaceful relations among the warring tribes so that they could henceforth be administered. On this occasion, peace was temporarily achieved between three of the recently warring tribes. After a few short-lived outbreaks of subsequent violence in ensuing weeks, the Government responded with force and quickly established an unstable peace in the region (Stephen 1974: 72-76; Monsell-Davis 1981: 62-64; but see Mosko n.d.). It is noteworthy that in these initial encounters, MacGregor and other Government agents dealt with villagers principally through the titled war chiefs, who seemed to be in control of then-current affairs, rather than peace chiefs (Stephen 1974: 88-90, 92, 96).

From what I outlined above regarding precolonial peace and war practices, some of the immediate consequences of forced pacification should be easily predictable. As it became clear that the British were there to stay and possessed the firepower to suppress resistance, for example, the need for men to fast and abstain the majority of time for the sake of war readiness was removed, enabling them to focus their energies on other pursuits. And this was what Government and the Catholic Mission wanted: a cheap source of wage labor and cash crops.

But things did not go entirely as expected, or that simply.

Recall that the aboriginal wars operated according to a direct, obligatory, and balanced exchange of homicides or male blood. If the warriors of one tribe killed five people of another, surviving kin in the latter tribe were obligated to reciprocate the same number of homicides. Also, it seems that at any one time the tallies between any two sides were such that each tended to regard themselves behind in the tally of deaths they were required to pay back. So when peace was eventually imposed by the colonial forces, each tribe was left with what it figured were blood debts outstanding.

As these homicide obligations were regarded by villagers as nontrivial, the colonial presence meant that war chiefs and war sorcerers were prevented from eliminating them. Since war chiefs had been the active public agents of violent death of large scale, their responsibility in perpetrating violence was virtually impossible to conceal from the authorities. And without actual battles lead by war chiefs, war sorcerers' secret preparatory rituals could have little effect. Peace sorcerers' killings through sickness and snakebite, however, while involving lone victims, could be done effectively in secret and were thus much easier to conceal from colonial authorities. So peace sorcerers were quickly recruited to avenge outstanding debts of male blood between enemy tribes.

This was a role peace sorcerers had never possessed previously. They were now performing in secret the public functions of war chiefs, that is, of causing the deaths of members of other tribes—at least, this seems to have been the prevailing view amongst villagers initially (see below). And to the extent that peace sorcerers were regarded as doing the legitimate bidding of peace chiefs, the two officials of intratribal peace were seen together as assuming the legitimate intertribal functions of war chiefs and war sorcerers.

Actions by Government and Mission agents seem to have augmented villagers' perception of the peace officials' enhanced public powers. By the mid 1890s, the Government Agent at Mekeo Station and the missionaries had begun to deal routinely with peace chiefs rather than war chiefs whenever they visited the villages, and native delegations were typically led by peace chiefs (BNGAR 1900: 70; Stephen 1974: 95). Becoming the effective agents for enforcing pacification and suppressing intertribal hostilities when they subsequently emerged, peace chiefs were in principle performing the preexisting mortuary function of war sorcerers, that is, of removing male blood.

Pacification quickly resulted, therefore, in unprecedented opportunities for the two categories of peace officials to enhance their "hot" power and strength in intertribal affairs. It must be emphasized that more than quantum increases in power were involved. For in the unprecedented historical appropriation of the official capacities of war chiefs and war sorcerers by peace sorcerers and peace chiefs, respectively, new analogical relations among the underlying categories, previously latent in the cultural scheme, became manifest. These new potentialities reflecting nonlinear categorical shifts and realignments accordingly produced novel ambiguities and contradictions in the distribution of underlying cultural categories focused critically on the two peace officials while, for the time being at least, war chiefs and war sorcerers had been rendered obsolete. Rather than as before pacification,

peace chief	:	peace sorcerer	::	war chief	:	war sorcerer
internal public relations	:	internal secret relations	::	external public relations	:	external secret relations
mortuary female-blood unmixing	:	homicide female-blood mixing	::	homicide male-blood mixing	:	mortuary male-blood unmixing

after pacification, the peace officials had appropriated in parallel the capacities of the war officials:

peace chief	:	peace sorcerer	::	war chief	:	war sorcerer
external public relations	:	external secret relations	::	[obsolete]	:	[obsolete]
mortuary male-blood unmixing	:	homicide male-blood mixing	::	[obsolete]		[obsolete]

These changes consisted in more than analogical reshuffling of agencies and functions among the four officials, however. While peace chiefs and peace sorcerers and strength were perceived as having gotten "stronger" and more "hot" in the early contact period, the war officials were seen to "weaken" and "cool" (cf. Stephen 1974: 54). Responding to this loss of power and renown in the new circumstances, as I shall describe below, many knowledgeable war chiefs and war sorcerers applied their ritual capacities to practice what is now commonly regarded as peace sorcery.

In wider comparative perspective, these initial North Mekeo responses appear to have been unusual. For much of the rest of Papua New Guinea the typical consequence of pacification and the imposition of colonial rule has been a decrease in the powers of secular leaders such as "chiefs" and "big men" and an increase in the capacities attributed to sorcerers, witches, and other ritual agents of death (A. Strathern 1966; 1982; Zelenietz and Lindenbaum 1981). As discussed below, this is a particularly apt indication of the extent to which the system of North Mekeo leadership classification, and particularly its inherent nonlinear propensities for ambiguity and contradiction, contributed early on to possibly distinctive historical effects.

Disease and Epidemics

Villagers' early experiences of disease and depopulation seem to have been at least as significant as pacification in facilitating the transformation of the system of chiefs and official sorcerers in new nonlinear directions. While rendered effectively obsolete in the performance of their precontact official duties, war chiefs and war sorcerers continued to be active in new ways having to do with villagers' accommodation to the arrival of foreign diseases.

Like most Melanesians, Mekeo lacked a natural resistance or immunity to a wide spectrum of introduced European diseases. There is considerable evidence that the result was catastrophic. From what I have been able to reconstruct from historical sources, genealogies, and oral traditions, wave after wave of "virgin soil" epidemics (Crosby 1976) swept through this part of the coast and subcoast during the first decades of contact before as well as after pacification. Possibly as early as 1852 and definitely by the 1870s onward, Government reports and other sources record for the region outbreaks of smallpox, chicken pox, pneumonia, influenza, pleurisy, measles, dysentery, tuberculosis, bronchitis, scarlet fever, typhoid fever, yaws, whooping cough, and so on (Table 7.1) (Mosko 1973: 66; Oram 1977: 92; Scragg 1977; Monsell-Davis 1981: 42-45; cf. Stephen 1974: 45-46, 112).[16] In some cases, these diseases swept through the area a number of times. Typically, the outbreaks occurred in the aftermath of droughts and famines that periodically hit the area, that is, when the population's resistance was already lowered so that their effects were magnified. Some regions, it appears, even became uninhabited entirely (Oram 1977: 92). In the early decades following the imposition of colonial domination, the situation led to much generalized alarm among expatriates at what appeared to be the imminent extinction of the Melanesians (e.g., Rivers 1922; Roberts 1927; Pitt-Rivers 1927; Hogbin 1930; McArthur 1967; McArthur and Yaxley 1968). Subsequently, there has been considerable debate over the extent to which epidemics in Melanesia and other parts of the Pacific and beyond resulted in actual declines in population (Denoon et al. 2000: 72-79). Some investigators have presumed that Mekeo population figures in the postcontact era held relatively steady (e.g., Stephen 1974: 112) until dedicated health reforms were introduced by Government and Mission shortly after World War II. Scragg (1977), who analyzed the epidemiological history of Mekeo on the basis of the Sacred Heart Mission's records of births and deaths, identified numerous periods of large-scale illness and dying but could find no evidence of a massive fall in population numbers; the records on which he relied, however, began only in 1900, well after many virulent epidemics in the region had been documented by numerous firsthand observers (see Mosko 1973; n.d.).

Table 7.1: Disease epidemics in the Mekeo Region, 1850-1950

Year	Epidemic	Source
1865-70 (1852?)	Smallpox (chicken pox?)	Chalmers 1887: 318; Seligmann 1910: 35; Murray 1912; Oram 1977: 92
1874-75	pneumonia, bronchitis, fever, measles	D'Albertis 1881: 28, 265, 286; Dupeyrat 1935: 118; Oram 1977: 91; Seligmann 1910: 196
1886-87	pneumonia	Romilly 1889: 78; Bevan 1890: 140; Murray 1912
1889-90	tuberculosis, leprosy, yaws	BNGAR 1890a: 77; 1890b: 88
1891-94	scarlet fever, influenza, "sickness"	BNGAR 1893: 91; 1894a: 15-16, 17; 1896: xv; 9
1896-98	typhoid fever, dysentery, pneumonia	Monckton 1921: 124-126; British New Guinea Colonial Report (BNGCR) 1898: 26-27; 1899a: 59-60; 1899b: 39-40; 1900: 22; BNGAR 1898a: xxiii; 1898b: 52-53; 1898c: 86, 90; 1898d: xxxiv-xxxv; Papua 1912b: 156
1899-1901	whooping cough, dysentery, pleurisy	BNGAR 1901a: xxiv; 1901b: 111; 1902: xlvii; 1904b: 16; BNGCR 1901: 40
1902-03	measles (rubeola)	BNGAR 1904a: 41; 1904b: 16; Scragg 1977: 104; Papua 1919: 57; 1927: 78
1906	pneumonia, pleurisy	BNGAR 1907: 27
1908-10	dysentery, whooping cough	Scragg 1977: 104, 105; West 1968: 133-134; Papua 1909: 16-17; 1911b: 32; 1911a: 33; 1911c: 65; 1918: 45; 1919: 56; Murray 1912
1912-14	dysentery	Papua 1912a: 164; 1912b: 156
1916	Measles (rubeola), influenza	Papua 1917: 35; 1927: 78
1917-19	whooping cough, pneumonia	Scragg 1977: 104; Papua 1919: 56
1921-22	influenza, pneumonia	Papua 1923: 55; Scragg 1977: 104
1925-27	influenza, measles (morbilli)	Papua New Guinea (PNG) 1929; Papua 1927: 78-79; 1928: 78-79
1931-33	influenza	PNG 1932a; 1932b; 1932c; 1932d; Papua 1933: 4; 1933b: 21; 1934: 11; Stephen 1974: 190-191; Scragg 1977: 104-105
1939-41	influenza	PNG 1941b; Hau'ofa 1981: 255; Stephen 1974: 159, 190-191; Scragg 1977: 104-105
1947-48	influenza	PNG 1948; Scragg 1977: 104-105

Even so, it remains difficult to reconstruct with great confidence the actual scale of death in the proto- and initial postcontact phases, despite the frequent reports of epidemic illness and mortality. But by the time the accuracy of colonial records had improved, which was many decades after Mekeo had already experienced several waves of foreign disease, single outbreaks were still taking heavy tolls. During an eruption of influenza in 1931, for example, government patrols reported the deaths of "many people" and people "dying by the 100s." One village apparently lost every adult male (PNG 1932d; 1932b; 1932c). In 1941, when reliable figures for the North Mekeo become first available, 64 persons of a population of 676, or nearly 10 percent, died from a single outbreak of influenza over a span of nine months. One village fell from 122 to 108 persons, another from 139 to 128, and another 170 to 141 (PNG 1941a; see also Hau'ofa 1981: 255; Stephen 1977: 2). For this period, Belshaw (1951: 22) recorded a mortality figure at one village for children, who are particularly vulnerable to epidemics of this nature (Crosby 1976: 294), of 36 percent. Between 1941 and 1949, the Amoamo North Mekeo tribal population dropped from 346 to 310—a net loss of 11 percent in just eight years (PNG 1941a; 1949; see below). On the basis of comparable histories of contact elsewhere in the world, it is possible that upwards of 80 percent or more of the Mekeo people died between the mid-nineteenth century and the beginnings of World War II (Crosby 1976: 293; Denoon et al. 2000: 72-79).

Consistent with recent expert opinion (McArthur 1967; Stannard 1989; Denoon et al. 2000) on depopulation elsewhere in the Pacific and beyond, therefore, it would appear that in the first three and four generations of European contact and colonial rule, the Mekeo lived—and died—with vastly fewer personnel than they had previously.

To a certain extent, however, it is not critical to my argument that there was an actual statistical increase in mortality during this period. As far as villagers at the time were concerned, on the basis of oral traditions and archival records, they were suffering sickness (if not also death) from attacks of peace sorcery to an extent unprecedented in the precontact era. According to the indigenous terms of the culture, there was no acknowledgment of "natural death" or death without some form of "sorcery" involving both human and spiritual agency. During the last half of the nineteenth century and the first half of the twentieth, in other words, the epidemics presented villagers with abundant empirical signs to confirm their suspicions that peace sorcerers were acting now with greater frequency and intensity. Death was all around. The only explanation the people had for all the dying was increased peace sorcery.

And as it was, there were whole new categories of peace sorcery, capable of causing death in unprecedented numbers, as well as lots of peace sorcerers, new and old.

New Categories of Peace Sorcery

The extant documentation of the earliest epidemics offer little direct evidence of their effects, other than mass sickness and death. Villagers' oral traditions, however, offer some interesting suggestions. According to North Mekeo, a new type of peace sorcery termed "all" or "everyone peace sorcery" (*okauka ungaunga*) emerged in the years when Europeans first started to become active in the region (i.e., the latter half of the nineteenth century). This new kind of peace sorcery was regarded by some as the property of certain clans of the Biofa and Ve'e (Central Mekeo), tribes who used it against their enemies in other tribes, wiping out whole clans and villages in single attacks. The mass killings have stopped in recent decades, villagers argue, only because the owners of this sorcery have buried it or otherwise hidden it away, but they could still retrieve and use it if they so wished (but see Mosko 1999).

Interestingly, there are indications in some records from the colonial era and current oral traditions that the newly arrived Europeans—both Government and Mission agents—were widely suspected of being either the sorcerers or "bush spirits" (*faifai*) who were directly responsible for particular epidemics (Monsell-Davis 1981: 42-45; Mosko 1985: 271; n.d.).

In several respects, however, the new "everyone peace sorcery" also reflected preexisting or traditional war sorcery. Like war sorcery, it was applied to many people in a single application. And because it could be performed in secret it was relatively easy to conceal. The new "everyone" sorcery resembled war sorcery also as the spiritual agents it employed supposedly flew through the air to attack its victims. My informants in the 1970s claimed that their ancestors reported hearing the new sorcery flying with the wind in the air above. But war sorcery as supposedly applied to enemies in "traditional" times does not in itself kill them; it only renders them "weak," "lazy," "slow," "heavy," and so on, making them easy prey to enemy warriors swooping through the village under the authority of war chiefs. Some people claimed also that the ancestral spirits of the new large-scale peace sorcery attacked the "souls" (*laulau*) of their victims with invisible spirit spears and spirit bows and arrows. The violent manner of spirit attack here is quite distinct from the methods supposedly used in peace sorcery of other categories (cf. Hau'ofa 1981).

There is considerable evidence as well that the chronic intertribal warfare prevailing at the time of European contact was itself directly conditioned by the early epidemics (cf. Bergendorff 1996: 31). Numerous elderly villagers I have interviewed have remarked that, according to people in their parents' and grandparents' generations who lived through the early contact period, as many of their ancestors died from the fighting as from sorcery epidemics. The meticulous genealogies recorded by the Sacred Heart missionaries (Egidi n.d.) in the early decades of contact include many lineages and subclans which suddenly end with no survivors. Oral traditions also support the hypothesis that much of the protocontact inter-tribal warfare and resulting disruption was triggered by communities that suspected they were being attacked by their enemies in possession of the new kinds of peace sorcery (cf. Swaddling et al. 1977). If the increased mortality from introduced diseases was being interpreted as arising from the emergence of new kinds of peace sorcery, villages that lacked the new techniques would have had to retaliate with the appropriate ritual capac-ities that were still available to them, that is, the ritual skills of war chiefs and war sorcerers. It is consistent with this that the earliest Europeans to arrive on the scene initially perceived war chiefs to be "village chiefs" on the evidence that they seemed to be in control of local affairs (cf. Stephen 1974: 88-92, 96).

Contrary to the typical presuppositions of European observers, the state of chronic warfare prevailing at the time of contact was not neces-sarily indicative of the remote precolonial past, but rather reflected rela-tively recent indirect contacts with Europeans in the form of new pathogens. To that extent, the epidemics of the protocontact era would very likely have inflated substantially the powers of the war officials along with those of the peace officials as described above. In sum, initial indirect European contacts contributed to the escalation of both the peace and war chiefly hierarchies. The scale and intensity of chiefly domination and sorcery obsession which many have presumed to be distinctive to indigenous Mekeo "tradition" appears to be in significant measure an ironical result of European influences.

Marriage, Sex, and the Era of Bakai

Other circumstances of the early colonial era involving the institutional-ized courting and marriage regulation contributed even further to the escalation of peace sorcery, with additional implications for the nonlinear analogical transformation of relations among Akaisa Men.

As noted above, in precolonial times villagers were expected to obey the peace chiefs' law forbidding sex or marriage with anyone of their own clan, own moiety, or mothers' clan of the opposite moiety. Such illicit unions, it was said, "spoiled mortuary feasts" and "shamed" and "angered" the peace chiefs. Since this prohibition applied to the adults, male and female, of all four clans of the tribe, each person had on average only one-eighth of the endogamous tribe's adult population in which to find a legit-imate mate. Villagers nowadays argue, however, that with the large losses of population in the early decades of contact, many young people found that when they were ready for marriage there just was not anyone of the preferred category available. For many, if they wanted to marry at all, it had to be with a relative or kinsperson who was by rule prohibited—someone of their own moiety, clan, or mother's clan, or adulterously with someone else's spouse. And as it was virtually impossible to arrange marriages formally with illicit spouses, most marriages in the postcontact era were initiated through elopement (see above).

Working with Australian Aboriginal materials, Yengoyan has argued that tribal population size puts limits on the actual operation of particular idealized marriage, section, and subsection systems (1968: 196-198; see also Yengoyan 1970; Godelier 1975). Among Australian foraging societies with marriage systems structurally similar to that of the Mekeo (specifically, with the same one-eighth proportion of the tribal population capable of supplying suitable mates for every marriageable adult), he calculated that a minimum population of 1070 was necessary for the normal operation and reproduction of the society—at minimum, for every member upon becoming marriageable to find a legitimate spouse. Below that figure, Yengoyan predicted, the frequency of marriages in deviation from the ideal rules would increase. While Yengoyan's precise figures have been subsequently challenged and disputed, his general point has been sustained, I think, and would apply to the Mekeo case. By 1949, the population of the endogamous Amoamo tribal unit had fallen to just 310 persons—less than one-third the predicted minimum population size necessary for all or most adults to marry according to the idealized marriage rules. Seligmann's observation in 1898 of a certain frequency of illicit marriages is thus consistent with a dramatic decline in tribal populations.

Mekeo depopulation is related to pacification, changes in marriage regulation, and the analogical transformation of chiefly offices in other ways as well. As it became evident to villagers that colonial domination and the policy of enforced peace were to stay, there was no urgency for war readiness on a day-to-day basis. A new regimen of daily village life emerged focused on competitive *bakai* courting (PNG 1955; Mosko 2002a; 2002b; cf. Stephen 1974: 110-111). Contemporary villagers testify that following pacification their ancestors—married and unmarried, male and female—would return from their gardens early in the afternoon fully decorated to spend the rest of the day and evening singing, dancing, drumming, and courting. Previously, displays of *bakai* courting took place only in the context of the large mortuary feasts that grieving clans sponsored only infrequently—every five or ten years, perhaps—with people from the rest of the tribe in attendance. During *bakai* performances, men employed love charms and secret love spells to make women desire them. If used successfully, *bakai* performances resulted in sexual unions and, often, in elopement or adultery (Mosko 1985: 127-132).

As noted above, legitimate marriage in precontact times involved alliances between prescribed categories of relations that were prearranged by the parents and other close relatives of the prospective bride and groom. So from the very earliest days after contact and pacification, marriage patterns were substantially affected by an increase in the number of elopements as a consequence of young men having successfully applied their love charms upon their lovers, including other men's wives, in the context of daily collective courting.

Much of the courting competition among the men seems to have been for the sake of demonstrating sexual prowess and not for marriage. Previously, clans and villages competed as units for warfare fame and renown, and single warriors did the same. This was critical. It was largely on the basis of the power and strength of its war leaders and warriors, as demonstrated in previous engagements, that a community discouraged enemies from attacking. But with the European presence, this urgency disappeared. Clan and village groups competed for renown instead in daily *bakai* courting. Rather than dissuading enemies from attacking, the objective was to stage the most splendid *bakai* performances so as to elicit the participation of the greatest number of people from other villages. And in the context of these large gatherings, men competed to seduce with their charms and spells the greatest number of women—single women and married women.

As a peace activity involving potential exchanges of female blood, *bakai* courting fell within the sphere of ritual influence of peace chiefs and sorcerers. The postcontact intensification of *bakai* thereby contributed further to the escalating power and strength of peace officials. Also, the various love charms and spells of *bakai* were classified in the culture as types of peace sorcery (*ungaunga*). To the extent that male adults, clans, and village units competed in *bakai* after pacification, they demonstrated in effect their competence in the arts of peace sorcery generally. Success in *bakai*, in other words, was, and is still today, a sign of possessing other types of peace sorcery, including those categories that involve capacities for killing others by illness. And in the same respect, the principal way villagers could dissuade peace sorcerers in other groups from attacking them in the new circumstances was to demonstrate that they were themselves in possession of hot and effective peace sorcery. This underscored further the necessity to stage publicly impressive *bakai* performances. So in the very terms of the culture, the intensification of *bakai* ritual itself constituted a dramatic heightening of peace sorcery.

Nowadays villagers claim that in the decades of intensive postcontact *bakai* there were many cases of illicit sex, illicit marriage, marriage by elopement, and adultery. Much of this qualified as offenses against peace chiefs and their laws, punishable by death through official peace sorcery. With the increases in epidemic disease and death that continued to occur during the period of *bakai* intensification, villagers had good reason to suspect tribal peace sorcerers under the authority of their own peace chiefs of attacking them. The responsibility for periodic outbreaks of large-scale peace sorcery in the postpacification era shifted back, in other words, from external to internal agents of female-blood reciprocity:

peace		peace		war		war
chief	:	sorcerer	::	chief	:	sorcerer

internal		internal				
public	:	secret	::	[obsolete]	:	[obsolete]
relations		relations				

mortuary		homicide				
female-blood	:	female-blood	::	[obsolete]		[obsolete]
unmixing		mixing				

The concentration and intensification of the ritual and other activities of peace in the early postcontact era was not limited to peace officials, however. Untitled commoners (*ulalu*) were deeply shamed when any other man, particularly a kinsman, seduced their sisters, daughters, or wives through *bakai*. The appropriate response for an offended party became either to seduce the interloper's daughter or wife or, if that proved impossible, to recruit a peace sorcerer to kill the interloper secretly. So commoner villagers not only began suspecting their own tribal peace chiefs of sending peace sorcerers to kill them in unprecedented numbers, they began to suspect each other of seeking to do it secretly without the official sanction of peace chiefs. But this amounted to commoner villagers infringing the legitimate powers of official peace chiefs, which itself qualified as a capital offense punishable by peace sorcery. Eventually, as money and commodities became more available for payments to peace sorcerers, this problem intensified even further (Mosko 2000; 2002b). The capacities of peace sorcerers, which before European intrusion had supposedly been monopolized by peace chiefs dedicated to the general welfare, could after contact be procured by all villagers. Anyone, not just peace chiefs, had new access to the powers of peace sorcery but at the risk of having peace sorcery used legitimately against him.

It is important to note the active participation of women, both married and single, in the *bakai* courting displays with the acquiescence of their parents, siblings, and spouses. From oral sources, it seems that the new ongoing threat of peace sorcery attack was one perceived in common by clan and village populations regardless of gender, marital, or kin affiliation. Women's participation in *bakai* in accordance with their culturally recognized roles, very simply, was as crucial as men's with respect to the total community's sense of urgency. Just as much as the community, for the sake of its survival and protection, needed men who could demonstrate their peace sorcery skills to the world at large, they needed persons upon whom they could work them; basically, women. In the new circumstances of depopulation and pacification, it was the responsibility of women no less than men to do all they could to help project to other groups their own community's possession of hot peace sorcery. Despite all the potential conflicts that might eventuate, this meant that women, single and married, had to join in the *bakai* displays with all their enthusiasm as well as the blessings of their relations. In my own conversations with old women who in their youths had participated in the pre-World War II courting, those were the happiest times of their lives. As Mangemange Muniapu, my clan mother, put it, women in those days devoted themselves mostly to being attractive to men, and the men were uncommonly responsive to their whims and desires. The women were allowed to do pretty much whatever they wanted. When I asked her who then did all the gardening, she responded, with so few people alive back then, little labor was required to feed them.

"New" Peace Sorcerers

Contributing further to these changes, there appears to have been in the proto- and early postcontact eras a dramatic increase in the number of men who claimed to be peace sorcerers or who possessed peace sorcery skills. In the early epidemics and associated intertribal fighting, the peace sorcery lineages of some clans were totally wiped out. Lacking skilled peace sorcerers of their own, survivors in these groups were particularly vulnerable to peace sorcery attack from outside and, according to contemporary villagers, they actively sought replacements. But also, these lacunae presented new opportunities to a number of types of would-be peace sorcerers.[17] As confirmed by mission genealogies, untitled but knowledgeable junior peace sorcery adepts were sometimes recruited to reconstitute peace sorcery lineages in the clans of their affines and/or cognatic kin (Mosko 1985:115-118). In other cases, commoner men with no hereditary claims to peace sorcery sought new recognition as peace sorcerers in a variety of ways. As already noted, the secret love charms and spells used in intratribal *bakai* courting were classified as a type of peace sorcery. With parents and relatives either unable to find legitimate mates for their children or unwilling to wed them to prohibited relatives, many young men who lacked *bakai* love magic had to apprentice themselves to practicing peace sorcerers in return for the latters' bestowal of bits of *bakai* knowledge. In these transactions, many young men gained unprecedented opportunities to acquire portions of peace sorcery ritual to which previously they were unentitled.

In the same respect, aggrieved commoner men, compelled to seek revenge either for the loss of their wives or other close relatives in the epidemics or for the shame of their wives', sisters', or daughters' seductions, apprenticed themselves to peace sorcerers in exchange for their assistance. This contributed further to the number of commoner men with new access to the secrets of peace sorcery. And as the new values associated with money and European manufactured goods became better understood, the incentives to practice peace sorcery increased for knowledgeable commoner men as well as legitimate sorcerers. These processes have continued to such an extent that by the 1970s there were men in many villages who lacked hereditary peace sorcery titles but who publicly comported themselves as peace sorcerers. These men have been labeled "new peace sorcerers" (*ungaunga mamatsi*). Oral traditions as well as ethnographic accounts suggest that many of the peace sorcery rivalries that have emerged in the postcontact escalation of peace sorcery have consisted in competitions between established and "new" peace sorcerers (Hau'ofa 1981; Stephen 1974; Bergendorff 1996).

Surviving war chiefs and war sorcerers also contributed early on to the intensification of peace sorcery's practice. Because their conventional ritual powers had been rendered obsolete under colonial pacification, the war officials initially suffered a tremendous decline in fame and renown proportional to the increase of power and importance attributed to peace chiefs and peace sorcerers. As already outlined, the early postcontact transformations of peace chiefs' and peace sorcerers' functions amounted partly to appropriations of the war officials' capacities through systemic analogical inversions in the new circumstances. Eventually, however, on the evidence of some of the Sacred Heart genealogies, many war chiefs and war sorcerers, along with members of their lineages, switched ritual specialties to become peace sorcerers themselves, adding further to the statistical numbers of ritual specialists comporting themselves as such. Here a further analogical inversion of the categories differentiating peace and war sorcery contributed to a further escalation of the powers and capacities of peace sorcery, and an effective reduction of the fourfold chiefly hierarchy to an essentially binary one:

peace chief	:	peace sorcerer	::	war chief	:	war sorcerer
internal public relations	:	internal secret relations	::	internal secret relations	:	internal secret relations
mortuary female-blood unmixing	:	homicide female-blood mixing	::	homicide female-blood mixing	:	homicide female-blood mixing

As war leaders began to comport themselves as peace sorcerers, they, like other "new sorcerers," were subjected to attack by established peace sorcerers intent upon eliminating the upstarts. For many decades in the early twentieth century, the local history of many villages across North and Central Mekeo is dominated by stories of attempts by legitimate and upstart peace sorcerers to outdo one another in perpetrating successful homicides, by taking credit for attacks either on commoner villagers or on each other. The large mortuary feasts occasioned by the rise in epidemic deaths provided opportunities for all of the peace sorcerers of a tribe to test out the relative strength of their "hot" powers (e.g., Stephen 1974: 61-62). Deaths experienced by peace sorcerers or their close relatives were routinely attributed to such rivalries. The ability to survive the attacks of one's rivals was the principal way that peace sorcerers demonstrated that they were in possession of "hot," powerful peace sorcery, eventually legitimating new sorcerers' claims to official Akaisa Man status.

Also in this process, it seems that much of the knowledge that was previously conceptualized as belonging to war chiefs and war sorcerers was transferred to the domain of peace. Many of the detailed rituals which are nowadays considered to be parts of indigenous peace sorcery very likely derived from early adaptations of war ritual to peace sorcery, adding to the intensification and expansion of the latter in the early postcontact period. Villagers' perceptions of an increase of peace sorcery attacks in the early contact era, in other words, were not merely a recognition of more peace sorcery practitioners in their midst. Many kinds of destructive ritual knowledge which previously were directed to external enemies through warfare were being applied to kin and allies within tribal groups.

The Augmentation of Peace Chiefs' Authority

By itself, the general intensification I have described for Mekeo peace sorcery is quite typical of the postcontact change reported for other parts of Melanesia. Usually, however, such transitions have accompanied a "democratization" of secular leadership (A. Strathern 1966; 1982; see also Zelenietz and Lindenbaum 1981). Not so with Mekeo, for the power and authority of their peace chiefs have simultaneously increased also. Even as late as 1970, the ethnographer of the Central Mekeo, Hau'ofa, estimated that peace chiefs "exercise[d] direct influence over their people in their daily life to a far greater extent than, for example, in a stratified Polynesian society such as Tonga, where contact between commoners and chiefs is no where as intensive as it is in Mekeo" (1981: 4). Rather than "democratization," in the proto- and postcontact eras, Mekeo have experienced an increase in peace chiefs' domination in accordance with the "continuing partnership of [peace] chiefs and sorcerers" (Hau'ofa 1981: 22).

Several observations consistent with the nonlinear analogical relationships underpinning the classification of the four categories of official Akaisa Men help explain this peculiarity of Mekeo history. First, all legitimate attacks of peace sorcery are supposedly performed only at the explicit behest of peace chiefs. Second, many of the opportunities for war chiefs, war sorcerers, or commoner men to become new peace sorcerers did not usually result in the founding of utterly new peace sorcery lineages, but in the substitution and reproduction of ones that had gone extinct in the wars and epidemics. Third, peace sorcerers in the precolonial era were unambiguously junior in genealogical terms to peace chiefs. Their relative seniority vis-à-vis war sorcerers, however, was already potentially ambiguous and contradictable. When peace sorcerers began to appropriate the intertribal prerogatives of war sorcerers, it did not flatly conflict with established genealogical precedence. Fourth, peace sorcerers' new domination of intertribal male blood homicidal reciprocity was parallel to peace chiefs' eventual monopolization of dealings with external European forces (see below). Fifth, peace chiefs' new role as external peacemakers with both European groups and other tribes was analogous to the war sorcerer's removal previously of the homicidal male blood. In this respect, peace chiefs' blood-removing function, whether of male or female blood or involving intratribal or intertribal relations, seems to have sustained its precontact categorical ascendancy over homicidal blood causation and mixing. Finally, sixth, to the extent that new peace sorcerers in the early days of contact and pacification up through the present were responding to the incentives presented by the new situation, they could only do so in terms intelligible to and consistent with prevailing cultural values and understandings. To "really make it" as a peace sorcerer—to join and advise the other sorcerers and chiefs during feasts, marriage exchanges, or other ceremonies—having mastery of the requisite ritual powers was not enough; one had to have those powers legitimated. To really make it as a peace sorcerer, one had to accede to the genealogical seniority of the peace chief of one's own clan.[18]

The postcontact escalation in the power and authority of clan peace chiefs is thus to be explained at least partly as a consequence of the nonlinear analogical relations among Akaisa Men categories.

Early Mission and Government Policies: Burial, Sorcery, and Religion

Responding to the early postcontact epidemics, Government and Mission authorities introduced a number of policies which ironically contributed to the epidemics' further severity and to the further augmentation of the peace sorcerers' and peace chiefs' control of village affairs. While the fuller history of these developments lies well beyond the scope of this analysis (see Mosko n.d.b; n.d.a), it is important to trace out how the indigenous nonlinear analogical constitution of Akaisa Men helped to produce those paradoxical effects.

Shortly after realizing their folly in selecting war chiefs to serve as "village chiefs" following the imposition of colonial peace, Government agents began to appointed peace chiefs to serve as "village chiefs" and later "village constables" and "village counselors" (Mosko 2001a; n.d.; Stephen 1974: 96; 1979a). With the Government's support, peace chiefs were in a position to draw upon a range of external political and economic resources which were unavailable to them in the precolonial era.

Concerned to limit the spread of the epidemics, the Government early on required villagers to bury their dead in cemeteries cleared away from villages in the bush. Previously, the deceased were buried either under domestic dwellings or beneath the open thoroughfare that ran the length of every village so that survivors could protect freshly buried corpses from marauding sorcerers. For the mourning kin of the deceased, this was crucial to their future security. If a peace sorcerer acquired the traces of the blood of their dead relative which, as kin, they shared with the deceased, he would then have the means to easily attack them all, one by one (see Mosko 1985: 29-30, 33, 157-158; n.d.).[19] The Government's burial regulations (BNGAR 1894a: 51; 1894b: 37, 51; 1898c: 93; 1899: 70) which were intended to restrict villagers' exposure to the germ vectors of the epidemics were thus interpreted by villages as giving peace sorcerers easy access to corpses and a new and ready means to kill them. In many instances, mourning relatives responded in ways that effectively exposed themselves further to the fatal infections by secretly exhuming the bodies and reburying them underneath houses back at the village or by taking up residence in temporary huts erected directly atop the shallow cemetery graves (cf. Stephen 1974: 93-94; Bergendorff 1996: 127-128). Rather than suppressing the epidemics, the Government's cemetery burial policy contributed to their further spread.

The Government's and Mission's official policies of condemning and punishing the practice of "sorcery" produced similarly paradoxical results. As Zelenietz (1981: 12) has argued for Melanesia generally, Government agents in the Mekeo district were caught in an irresolvable dilemma: sorcery, for the sake of its disruptive effects, had to be outlawed and its practitioners prosecuted; but since the European administrators did not themselves accept the ontological and epistemological premises of sorcerers' powers, they could not justify punishing the accused peace sorcerers to the extent of permanently removing or killing them. It was virtually inevitable, therefore, that Mekeo would interpret the regulations and actions against peace sorcerers, despite the Government's disclaimers, as tacit admissions of the ritual's efficacy. There is abundant evidence also that Government and Mission agents occasionally represented their own extraordinary powers as based on the White Man's version of "sorcery" (Mosko n.d.). The situation was complicated further in that, among Mekeo, official peace sorcerers were hardly marginal members of their communities but legitimate and respected officials (Hau'ofa 1971; 1981; cf. Zelenietz and Lindenbaum 1981). What is more, convicted sorcerers received maximum sentences of only six months. Upon release, many comported themselves much as villagers expected them to—as though seeking revenge against those people they suspected of conspiring with Government authorities against them (PNG 1931; 1935; Hau'ofa 1981: 255). The Government's policies did not just tacitly affirm belief in the powers of sorcery; in villagers' eyes they actively supported and reinforced the powers of hostile peace sorcerers and, through them, the authority of peace chiefs.

The Sacred Heart Mission's more subtle policies of combating sorcery contributed as well to the opposite result. The priests preached against the practice of all types of indigenous "magic," "sorcery," and "superstition" which, as sins in terms of Christianity, were punished by God with misfortune and death. But in order to convey their own Christian message, they could not flatly deny the efficacy of indigenous spiritual agents. Indeed, many villagers interpreted the priests' efforts to affiliate ancestral spirits and the culture-hero, Akaisa, with the Devil (Diablo) and "evil" (*abala*) in contrast to the morally "good" (*lopia, verlo*) spirits of Jesus (Jesus), Dio (God), Maria (Mary) and the saints, as an explicit admission that the customary beliefs underlying the efficacy of peace sorcery and other ritual were valid. Moreover, as Hau'ofa (1981: 22; Bergendorff 1996: 118-124, 25-26; cf. Stephen 1974: 101-102) has argued, the Mission authorities from the very beginning never condemned the official sorcerers directly, and they attempted to solicit the cooperation of the traditional leaders, particularly the peace chiefs, in implementing their various programs. But to the extent that peace chiefs depended upon peace sorcerers for the enforcement of their laws in legitimate spheres of activity, the missionaries' reliance upon the former for their own projects tended to sustain and reinforce the influence of the latter. In fact, one of the terms both villagers and priests use to refer to the generic powers of "good" is the same term for "peace chief": *lopia*. In directing their moral appeals to the principle of *lopia* or moral goodness and offering their support to the authority of the *lopia* peace chiefs, the missionaries have inadvertently reinforced what villagers regard as the moral basis for legitimate peace sorcery.

Conclusion

This reexamination of the early encounters between Mekeo peoples and Europeans leads to a number of conclusions, both substantive as regards the character and historical transformation of the system of chiefly and sorcery authority along with related beliefs and practices, and theoretical as regards the nonlinear analogical underpinning of those cultural distinctions and changes. Contrary to the views of other investigators, it has been argued here that North Mekeo leadership patterns underwent a series of profound and complex changes as a result of initial European contacts. Some of the most consequential effects of contact, such as the dramatic increase in the domination exercised by all four categories of Akaisa Men following the introduction of epidemic disease and depopulation, occurred even decades before the first European personnel physically entered Mekeo territory. In the face of the prepacification epidemics, peace chiefs and peace sorcerers greatly inflated their domination of local affairs while war chiefs and war sorcerers intensified the scale and frequency of intertribal warfare. Subsequent interactions between Mekeo and Europeans after direct physical contact in 1890 and their consequences—colonial pacification; intensified competition for *bakai* courting magic, for lovers and spouses, and for courting renown; increases in illicit sex and adultery; the introduction of money and commodities; and the enforcement of numerous policies of Government and Mission administration, and so on—resulted in a further escalation of the power and authority of the peace officials and a dramatic decline in the influence of the war officials, until many of the latter eventually changed ritual specialties to join numerous commoner men who were intent on becoming new peace sorcerers themselves. This was the greatly changed situation that Seligmann observed less than a decade after the imposition of colonial control but which, except for the cessation of the native wars, he and subsequent investigators have taken to reflect precontact or traditional Mekeo culture and social organization. Viewed in this way, Mekeo contact history also allows new substantive light to be shed on the several long-standing ethnographic anomalies mentioned above: the pronounced interest among Mekeo in magic and sorcery generally; the emphasis upon daily *bakai* courting; marriage by elopement and the frequency of illicit marriage; the unusual extent of power and authority accorded peace chiefs and peace sorcerers late into the colonial and postcolonial eras; and the stereotype of Mekeo villagers as culturally conservative.

But it is not just the scale or extent of the historical changes that has largely passed unnoticed. Their nature as defined in Mekeo cultural terms points to the theoretical relevance of nonlinear analogical reasoning for the comprehension of processes of historical transformation in complex sociocultural systems. Postcontact modifications in peace chiefs' and peace sorcerers' roles entailed systemic inversions of the preexisting categorical distinctions that also delimited war chiefs' and war sorcerers' capacities. In very general terms, by engaging with the forces of European contact, the preexisting system of Mekeo chiefly officialdom proved to be historically unstable; but the character or form of that instability as well as its eventual historical trajectory were at least partially programmatic in accordance with the complex dynamical potentialities contained within the nonlinear analogical structure of bisected dualities.

Even so, some of the details in the transformations experienced by Mekeo may well strike Western readers as peculiar, especially at first glance. But think about it. Given the empirical fact that European contact threatened them with their very extinction, Mekeo took precisely the steps necessary to increase their numbers and reproduce their relations. They adapted effectively to the changing circumstances, and they did it in terms consistent with the values and possibilities present in their view of the world at the time. From this, we can draw an additional conclusion pertinent to chaos theory: the internal directionality of change and transformation I have identified illustrates a sensitive dependence upon the specific conceptual and pragmatic conditions which initially prevailed.

But the historical account provided thus far is not the end of the story either. It seems that the preexisting quadripartite structure of four chiefly offices did not collapse into a dual hierarchy of peace chiefs and peace sorcerers and remain that way. The nonlinear analogical reasoning which facilitated that transformation early on also fostered its eventual elaboration back into a modified fourfold structure with many of the same internal contradictions and tensions. Recall that prior to the European intrusions, politico-ritual authority within clan groups was articulated in terms of the various nonlinear, crosscutting oppositions involving peace and war and chief and sorcerer to produce the fourfold classification of Akaisa Men. Peace chiefs and peace sorcerers dominated the internal relations of the tribe, and war sorcerers and war chiefs controlled external relations involving other tribes. In the aftermath of the epidemics and pacification, peace chiefs and peace sorcerers assumed power and authority in external affairs. Not long after, however, two new authority positions were introduced by colonial agents specifically to take over external relations from the indigenous peace officials but clearly reflecting the earlier generic prerogatives of war chiefs and war sorcerers. The full details of these developments would again carry me far beyond the bounds of the present discussion, but it appears that as Government and Mission authorities implemented their policies in the first two decades or so of the colonial era, they appointed two kinds of functionaries in every village to mediate between themselves and the people: "village constables" (later replaced by "village counselors" and "local government counselors") and "village catechists." Interestingly, by the late 1890s, most Government appointments of Village Constables went to men who were not titled peace chiefs (Mosko n.d.; Mair 1970; Rowley 1966; Dupeyrat 1935; Stephen 1979a: 89-90; Monsell-Davis 1981: 62-68; cf. Stephen 1974: 54; Bergendorff 1996: 129-130). The new authorities operated in spheres of influence resembling those of the precolonial war chiefs and war sorcerers. Village counselors were charged with enforcing the Government's externally imposed regulations, and their performance of these duties was distinctly public. Village constables' and counselors' responsibilities possessed strongly male-gendered connotations inasmuch as the overwhelming majority of villagers arrested over the first seven decades of colonial rule were men; only adult men have been required by Government to pay the annual head tax; and the most onerous and unpopular duty on the part of village people to the Government—carrying for official patrols—fell almost exclusively upon men. Also, the preponderance of village constables' activities on behalf of the external Government relied on brute physical force (handcuffs, jail, manual labor, firearms etc.) if not the occasional letting of blood through beatings and other abuse. Interestingly, there were even occasions in which village constables were intimately involved in attempts to organize fellow villagers in violent confrontations against exogenous Government and Mission authorities (Mosko n.d.; Stephen 1977).

The Catechists trained and appointed by the Catholic missionaries can be seen as mediating relations with external Church authorities. Compared with village constables, though, their functions have been considerably less public if not surrounded in secrecy analogous to the war sorcery of precolonial times. In a multitude of ways, village catechists endeavored to represent to communicants the Church's distinctly enigmatic messages. For villagers, the veil of secrecy concerning Church relations has been projected in numerous ways (e.g., the exclusiveness of the priesthood; the celibacy and abstinences of priests, nuns, and lay brethren; the confidentiality surrounding the confessional; the restricted access to the literal Bible; and the general focus upon spiritual beings, both Christian and indigenous) (Mosko 2001b). Also, it has not been lost on villagers that the Church's chief orientation to the removal of earthly sin is mediated through the mortuary blood of a male person (i.e., Jesus):

peace chief	:	peace sorcerer	::	village constable	:	village catechist
internal public agency	:	internal secret agency	::	external public agency	:	external secret agency
mortuary female-blood unmixing	:	homicide female-blood mixing	::	homicide male-blood mixing	:	mortuary male-blood unmixing

In the later colonial and post-National Independence history of Mekeo, then, villagers have reconstituted their local authority structures along lines that resemble the earlier fourfold structure of politico-ritual organization. There are nowadays peace chiefs and peace sorcerers, whose internal powers have been modified in the aftermath of contact, pacification, depopulation, and so on as I have described; but for long now there have also been village constables or counselors and catechists who, in supplanting war chiefs and war sorcerers, have effectively reconstituted the specialized sphere of external relations in accordance with the nonlinear analogical parameters of the earlier system.

If I began this chapter by criticizing Sahlins on the utility of analogical reasoning in anthropological studies, with this conclusion I am forced to endorse his general claim for a structural history on at least one crucial count: "different cultural orders" such as Mekeo may indeed "have their own, distinctive modes of historical production" (Sahlins 1985: x). But historical performance in this instance does not merely consist in systems lacking contradictions except in their developmental effects. The complexities I have outlined here reveal the extent to which systemic cultural contradiction in the form of nonlinear analogical transformation is inherent in the very structure of bisected dualities.

Acknowledgments

This chapter was initially drafted while I was a Research Fellow on the Comparative Austronesian Project in the Department of Anthropology at the Australian National University over the period 1989 to 1991. It has subsequently undergone numerous revisions in the course of seminar and conference presentations at Hartwick College, the University of Sydney, Macquarie University, the University of Western Australia, and the European Society for Oceanists. I am deeply indebted to the many colleagues who at various stages have offered their comments and criticisms: Eugene Ogan, Margaret Jolly, Chris Ballard, Nick Thomas, Roger Keesing, Jadran Mimica, Judith Huntsman, Ann Chowning, Penny Graham, Robert Tonkinson, Michael Allen, Jeremy Beckett, Christine Boulan-Smit, Connie Anderson, David Anthony, Richard Haan, Sugwon Kang, Frs. P. Didier and A. Boudaud, Jos Platenkamp, Michael Young, and Marshall Sahlins. Frs. Diaz and Boudaud (MSC) at the Veifa'a Catholic Mission station in Central Mekeo very kindly allowed me access to certain crucial mission documents. Fr. Seville, curator of the Archives of the Sacred Heart Mission in Rome, was very generous in providing me unhindered access to missionary records that were not otherwise accessible. Don Tuzin and Cathy Creely were very hospitable as well during a brief period of archival research that I conducted at the Melanesian Archives at the University of California at San Diego. Various organizations have generously provided the finances which have enabled me to persevere on this project over a very long interval: National Institute of General Medical Sciences, the Research School of Pacific and Asian Studies at the Australian National University, Hartwick College, the Royal Society of New Zealand, and the National Institute for the Humanities. As ever, I am chiefly indebted to the many people in North and Central Mekeo who have shared with me their understandings of their culture and history. Any and all errors and omissions naturally remain my own.

Notes

1. For numerous other examples of convergence between established anthropological theory and chaos theory, see my "Introduction" to this volume.
2. I have elsewhere conducted several studies from structuralist or structural historical perspectives, each seeking to refine a different aspect of that approach. Of particular relevance to the present argument, in a pair of earlier critiques of both Dumont's notion of hierarchy and Sahlins's incorporation of it in his model of "hierarchical organization," I examined the systemic contradictions and inversions among North Mekeo

chiefly positions from a synchronic perspective (see Mosko 1994a; 1994b). Here I seek to extrapolate the nonlinear dynamism of those same relations from their historical performance.

3. Although she has refrained from formalization to the degree attempted here, Marilyn Strathern's (1988) understandings of the core dynamic of mutual elicitation between the partible persons of Melanesian sociality appears to conform closely with this logic (see Mosko 2001b; 2002a). For another part of the Pacific, Sahlins's (1976) classic account of the recursive bisection of sea/land dichotomy in Fijian social organization is congruent with the structure of bisected dualities. Gell's (1993) more broadly comparative account of Polynesian social hierarchies and tattooing practices is similarly based on a pattern of bisected dualities. Wagner's (1986c) trope of obviation involving internal reversibility and inversion of analogical relations strongly resembles the dynamics of nonlinear analogy presented here. For additional ethnological examples in wider comparative perspective, see Bourdieu (1973), Willis (1967), and Allen (2000).

4. Needless to say, there are passages in Sahlins which seem to take a position on this point close to that articulated here. For example, "For if we put ourselves in the divine intellectual place of the transcendental subject, i.e., outside the system as commentator, we can see history working through the interested selection of social agents among the numerous logical possibilities—including contradictory possibilities—that are presented in any cultural order" (Sahlins 1985: xvii).

5. As noted above, in other studies I have myself adopted Sahlins's view of categorical instability and contradiction as reflective of the distinguishable perspectives of differently situated actors (see Mosko 1991c; 2001b).

6. For the sake of outlining the overall contours of Mekeo hereditary authority, I employ the literary device of the "ethnographic present" as referring to circumstances roughly at the time of initial encounters with Europeans. However, in most areas of social organization there has been considerable continuity as well as change, as the remainder of this chapter seeks to document, so that the "traditional" configuration of chiefly authority prevailing at the time of European encounter remains highly relevant in contemporary local and regional politics (see Mosko 1985; 2001a; n.d.).

7. Here as elsewhere in this chapter I employ the orthography for the North (Amoamo) Mekeo dialect, with which I am most familiar. In most instances, dialectical differences in the Mekeo language consist in a few simple sound changes. Thus the culture-hero Akaisa in North and West Mekeo is known as A'aisa in Central (Biofa and Ve'e) Mekeo (A. Jones 1998). Such differences across Mekeo dialects are for the most part systematic and, in my experience, present native speakers with little difficulty of interpretation or intelligibility.

8. For the sake of avoiding unnecessary complication, the account given here of chiefly titles within clans is oversimplified. Typically, a dispersed clan (ikupu) will consist of several subclans (ikupu) which ideally should consist of four distinct specialized lineages (ikupu), each possessing one of the four Akaisa Man titles. The situation is further complicated by residential patterns. Subclans of a clan often live adjacent to one another in the same village, but sometimes senior and junior subclans of the same clan live in different villages. While lineage units of the same clan should live together, it is not uncommon for them to reside in different villages (see Mosko 1985: chapters 6-7; Hau'ofa 1981: chapters 4, 7-8; Stephen 1974: chapter 1; 1995: chapter 1; Bergendorff 1996: chapters 1-5).

9. All personal and village names cited are pseudonyms.

10. Other ethnographers' accounts contain similar ambiguities. Seligmann (1910) never really commented directly on the relative ranking of peace sorcerers or war chiefs except to note that they are both junior to the senior peace chief, and that on the battlefield the authority of war chiefs is subordinate to the war sorcerers (1910: 218, 342-348). This latter observation turns out to be critical (see below). Hau'ofa emphasizes that the principle of relative seniority orders the idealized relations of the specialized hereditary

offices and lineages. But beyond the unrivaled preeminence of the senior peace ("civilian") chief, he specifies only that peace sorcerers are "of high status and political ranking second only to [peace] chiefs" (1981: 297; cf. Hau'ofa 1981: 193, 218, 297). Stephen does provide a ranking of lineages and lineage titles in order of senior peace chief, junior peace chief, and war chief, but she mentions that a clan might also contain both senior and junior war chief sections. In addition, she indicates that the remaining two titles, peace sorcerer and war sorcerer, are subordinate to the senior peace chief, but ventures no further specification of their seniority relative to each other or to the junior and war chiefs (1974: 4-7, 56; cf. Stephen 1979b: 149-150).

11. See Seligmann 1910; Hau'ofa 1971; 1981: 2-3, 40-48; Stephen 1974: xx-xxi, 62; Bergendorff 1996.

12. For fuller ethnographic accounts of this and other practices, I refer readers to my previous work (Mosko 1983; 1985; cf. Seligmann 1910: 249-265; Hau'ofa 1981: chapters 5-6; Bergendorff 1996: 28-44, 70-73; Stephen 1974: 48-49). Justifications for presuming that these practices were indicative of the precontact era are elaborated in a separate monograph, still under development.

13. Seligmann's (1910) description of the colorful and resplendent dancing, drumming, and singing of *ufuapie* guests at death feasts is collective *bakai* courting in this sense; see also Hau'ofa (1981), Guis (1936), Bergendorff (1996: 66-70), and Mosko (2001b; 2002a; 2002b) for more recent descriptions of essentially the same practice.

14. The conduct of intertribal warfare (*aoao* or *uani*) is categorically distinct from the fighting between clans of the same tribe (*pipaini*), involving different weapons and quite different ritual protocols (see Seligmann 1910; Mosko 1985: 86-90; 1992; 1994a; cf. Stephen 1974: 107-111).

15. A fuller accounting of these practices and the complementation of the genders is contained in Mosko (1983; 1985: chapters 3-5).

16. According to Nigel Oram (personal communication), the reported outbreak of smallpox estimated between the years between 1851 and 1870 may have been chicken pox; according to Campbell McKnight (personal communication), however, it probably was smallpox.

17. It was this urgency for functional completeness which may account for the historical tendency for clan and subclan units to include lineage units of diverse ancestry (Seligmann 1910: passim; Mosko 1985: 118-123; Hau'ofa 1981: 34-40, passim; cf. Stephen 1974: 114) and, among the Biofa and Ve'e Mekeo, for the intensification of relationships internal to village units at the expense of the tribal autonomy (Hau'ofa 1981: 45-48).

18. Among all societies of Papua New Guinea, the Mekeo and their closely-related neighbors, the Roro, are supposedly the only societies where ritual specialists such as "sorcerers" are both hereditary officials and ranked structurally lower than "chiefs" (Mosko 1991b; 1994a; Hau'ofa 1981: 297; Godelier 1991: 301-303).

19. In precolonial times, such thefts of corpses by sorcerers constituted another context of the intratribal exchange of female-bloods.

8

AFTERWORD

Order is What Happens When Chaos Loses Its Temper

Roy Wagner

Heuristic Modeling and the Self-Validation of Deception

The so-called "chaos theory" implications of fractal mathematics came into vogue at a time when the artifice of modeling itself came to be more important than its subject, *what* was modeled in it, and even more important than the "why?" The term "science" is at least questionable in this application, for we are dealing with a broad-scale cultural phenomenon that has made itself well-nigh ubiquitous ("global," as they say), and pervades practically everything that its own application touches upon. What I have called "the true image of a false relationalism" (Wagner, 2001), and others have termed "quasification," turns the invention of culture into a self-conscious project, and invites the spectator or audience to participate (grandiloquently) in the scams that are being worked upon them. The results are very dramatic, and apt to be thoroughly misunderstood. "Information" modeled too closely upon itself becomes, in effect, information *about* information, self-advertisement; politics becomes a politics about politics, entertainment the mystification of its own proofs and special effects, personal relations become subtexts of the way one is persuaded to treat them. "Quasification," if that is the word, has become so nearly pervasive, even of its own analytic perspectives, that it would be impossible to single out a determinative factor or "independent variable." Information-technology, the Internet, education, self-confessional politics, moral insouciance, and abortive or dysfunctional interpersonal relations or irresponsible leadership are conspirators in a kind of covictimage. Publicly and privately, we dance to the theme of a "strange attractor." We are *unuwewe* (cf. Damon, chapter 4).

Everything in the world of power and knowledge, according to my Barok congeners in New Ireland, "works by means of a simple trick, however ingenious, and when you learn what that trick is, and why it is a fake, you stand, not at the end of knowledge, but at its beginning." Fractal mathematics and its many implications, most of them abstruse or irrelevant, would not have made much sense to us without the very practical reality (inherently Fractal) of "binary" digitalization in our computers. And until that very ingenious "coding" of thought-about-thought can be shown to be a fake—by some Kurt Gödel of the "hacker" world, or some super-virus—we are bound to live out its permutations in every aspect of our lives. It is the better mousetrap, and guess who are the mice.

The wisest philosophers of all are not the ones, like Aristotle, who reveal the truth, or at least pretend to, but those like Heraclitus, Plato, Jesus, and Wittgenstein, who make a *secret* of it, and then keep on making secrets. "We *picture* facts to ourselves" said Wittgenstein, meaning, among other things, that the fact of the picture is the picture of the fact. And if that self-grounding statement is a chiasmatic one, like the canonic formula of Lévi-Strauss, then Mandelbrot and Feigenbaum belong in that company as well.

The best-kept secrets, it is said, are those that keep themselves. There are no single solutions to paradoxes of the Epimenides type ("All Cretans are liars, and I tell you this in all honesty, for I myself am a Cretan"), which are true when proven false, and false when proven true, and so conceal their own agency within the means of its revelation. If all chiasmatic formulations, like the Canonic Formula, are variations on this "disinformational" schema, then even the wisest of them, like Heraclitus's "We live the Gods' deaths, and they live ours" both are very simple in their profundity, and profound in their simplicity.

"An aphorism," said the Viennese aphorist Karl Kraus, "is either half-true or one-and-a-half times true." The civilization or ("global") world economy that invested its financial or intellectual resources in a program of this sort would not have to decline, like Gibbon's Roman Empire, or exhibit the cyclical patterning made famous by Spengler and Toynbee. It would simply "max out," like a credit card.

So the "scientific" aspects of fractal modeling can be understood much more simply than the Chaos theorists would have us believe. We not only *rationalize* to determine the agency of cause-and-effect in the data, but actually *rationalize the fact that we rationalize*, hence overdetermine the effects of the modeling process by *underdetermining* our own agencies in doing so. The result is an evidential representation of a "strange attractor" that need have no counterpart existence in the real world, being an unaccountable consequence of the modeling process itself, and that finds its closest parallel in the "disinformation" of modern counterespionage agencies.

"We have met the enemy and he is us." If "underdetermination" means literally "being put in the denominator," then the rationalization of motion as *linear time* is compounded upon itself, rationalized once again in determining the quality called "acceleration" (velocity x velocity, or unit space per unit time squared), *motion* comes into its own as an independent variable. Hence the phenomenon of "gravity," the keystone of Newtonian mechanics, was science's first and most influential example of a strange attractor. When linearized on the model of cause-and-effect and the spatiotemporal "measurements" that make up its equation, gravity becomes an explanatory disaster, giving rise not only to the "three body problem" and the "direct action at a distance" that so vexed Newton, but also to enormities such as "gravity-waves" and particles of gravity, all of them inherently disinformational. A "black hole" is gravity's underdetermination of its own existence, and a very good example of what a strange attractor does to those who go looking for it. It is nature's way of "understanding" what we mean by it.

Fractality measures itself by itself, and so models the opposite of the factuality by which its effects—like the strange attractor—might be rationalized. In that respect the "cultures" modeled in this volume are neither descriptions of "how the natives think" nor evidences of how the anthropologists think *about* them, but secrets developed around an enigma that attracts all those who might elicit it. Peoples (and this includes anthropologists) do not *have* their myths, rituals, or worldviews because they *understand* them, but precisely because they fancy they might *be understood in them*, measured or tested by exotic departures from the familiar and the understandable. History, too, finds its best justification, its own "anthropology," in the *events* that happen to its own self-conception, which are then recoded in the data as "a new view of the past."

Imagine the future as *the past that did not happen*, the culture as *the way the people cannot think*, and you will get some idea of why event itself is a strange attractor. What Marshall Sahlins calls "the structure of the conjuncture" (what else is "gravity," for example?) is in that way a good example of the "interference-patterning" by which radically different cultural perspectives come to imitate one another's expectational designs, project a kind of hologram, an imaginably solid object called "history," out of the *boundary conditions* for cultural conceptualization, rather than its essences. Then the (historical) happening of culture and the (ahistorical) culture of *happening* itself, our potential understanding of what "event" would have to mean or be, become differential *iterations* of a scale-invariant procedure. We *rationalize* (events), and then *rationalize the fact that we rationalize*, and so underdetermine our purpose in inquiry. No wonder what we like to think of as "the news" is not the truth, and what we like to imagine as the "truth" is not news: they are inverse *quasifications* of one another.

The representation of credibility and the credibility of representation become one and the same thing. Seeing is believing; the advertisement that proves itself through what is called "entertainment value" makes the product or logo ancillary to its own designs. Hearing is understanding; the pioneer work on *acoustic* fractality was done six decades before Mandelbrot's discovery, by a German musicologist named Heinrich Schenker (see Zuck-erkandl 1956 and 1973). Schenker demonstrated conclusively that any work of traditional classical music (written "in a key") can be reduced to an interference-patterning between a single "germinal motif" and its various (structural) iterations. We "understand" a hologram in the great classical masterpieces, but recode it in our feelings—much as Americans with ethical dilemmas in anthropology—as emotional profundity. The Schenker effect is made so immediately obvious in contemporary "pop" music genres—virtually an interference-patterning with "life-style" body rhythms—that one need only to perform a simple experiment to find out why. Cut off the sound in *any version* of the ubiquitous "illuminated screen" spectacle, and you will wonder forever where the motivation has gotten.

Kissed to death by the eye? Fractality was forced into the semblance of a mathematical (read "visual") project—an interference-patterning of equations and their printouts—for the same reason that *Reason* had to be invented by Enlightenment philosophers, as the only viable antidote to conceptual castration. (Reading Kant aloud is the *opposite* of an aphrodisiac.) Among the many advantages of written representation, the one most nearly missed (and practically every time) is the aplomb or smartness-of-motion, the tact it engenders via the interference-patterning of thought and thing. What amounts to an equipoise in the sublimation of spoken resonance, a veritable succubus or fractal coefficient of the agency of speaking, could be obtained in no other way, *contains* the sensuality of experience rather than broadcasting it. Writing "prints in" what the fractal iteration prints *out*.

Most of the *agency* attributed in science, or *as* science, has no empirical basis at all, but simply reiterates the capture-mode of its articulative protocols. It is as though "the data" were hard at work studying our means of interrogating it—from time to time it publishes its findings—and the figure-ground reversal implicit in "Chaos" thinking became inevitable as a de-crypting of its feedback-loop. What gravity attracts most is its own description as such; what "natural selection" selects for is its own attribution to a strange attractor called "nature." It is not necessary to prove premises that become their own data in the course of eliciting them.

Representation of *any* kind entails taking the fullness of sense out of its subject and making up the deficit with some modeling of order; fractality is the *reductio ad absurdum* of abstraction. It marks out the *internal limit* of the sense it would have to make, and the external one goes begging. Just as taking *fact* out of context and relocating or remodeling it undercuts the whole rationale of the computer world, including the "media" and the news, so the (quasificational) supplementation of artificial sensing (such as sound-cues, background noise or music, contrived "personality") finds its charge in "making it real again." Fractality, paradoxically, is *more* dependent upon the sensual factor in modeling its arguments than even straightforward experimental science. To even begin to understand what fractality attributes to itself, it is necessary to flesh it out in more palpable exemplifications, like tracing out the interminable coastline of a real place called "England," quasifying the scale-invariant iterations of a fractal expression by adding false color, and trimming it to the dimensions of the screen or printed page—"advertising" Chaos or making a theme park of it.

The more surprising implication of this is that quasification, in and of itself, can sustain the kind of authoritarian hegemony that Thomas Kuhn (1970) has termed a "paradigm," and that passes, for most people, as the factual basis of a scientific discipline. Paradoxically, it is only when the basic model that underwrites a scientific ideology has been *disproven* or critically faulted in some significant way that scientific pundits who are "in on the secret" of that disqualification can find the assurance of "testing" it and using it as a background for "further research." From then on the "standard example" experiments that had led to the model's original prominence are performed regularly by students as part of their training, with the likelihood that they, too, might internalize the flaw, and so become initiates in the "paradigm." Though it works in a manner exactly opposite to what Kuhn proposed as "the structure of scientific revolutions," short-circuiting the scientific method, there are abundant examples of quasification as the secret of scientific precedence. After proposing, with Niles Eldridge, the most compromising riposte to Darwinian axiomatics in the theory of "punctuated equilibrium," Stephen Jay Gould spent the rest of his career writing grandiloquent essays on the basic soundness of the Darwinian approach. As though it were far better to be wrong in the right way than right in the wrong way.

It would be difficult, otherwise, to gauge the significance of Chaos science, or see its counterintuitive implications in a positive light, for, as Gödel's Proof did for mathematics, fractality laid bare the quasification necessary to establish all of scientific thinking as a paradigm. So it is not as though hard work, refined research techniques, and self-aware critical diligence were the problem, nor that scientists may be uniquely gullible, but rather that the "explanatory" function of heuristics was the "wild card" all along. We rationalize, and then rationalize the fact that we rationalize, and so, like Epimenides' Cretan, give the lie to our own truths.

We see the effects of telescopic magnification *as* the cosmos, those of our micro-magnification in biology or subatomic particle-physics as the facticity of the very small, and forget that, in both cases, the very same sort of exaggeration is going on. And when we underdetermine the time-scale of geological, evolutionary, or historical events, that is *minify* the human scale in determining our place in it, we deign to imagine ourselves and our world as *products* of the exercise. If the only real standard of comparison is scale-invariance—the (necessarily fractal) representation of representation to itself—no wonder that scientific paradigms are ultra-conservative, using "theory" to make up for what cannot be represented, and that scientists feed upon their own cynicism. Chaos theory does not show us what the world is like, or what thought or even representation may be like; it only shows us *how* they are like themselves.

Introduction (Mosko)

Sensitivity to initial conditions relates primarily to these natural sciences involved with prediction and the close study of behavior, areas that did not concern anthropologists like Bateson and Lévi-Strauss at all, and only served Karl Marx as an independent corroboration of theories that were hardly behavioral. Very few anthropologists, and no major theorists in the discipline, are concerned with prediction, replication of results, and the material or statistical realities of the societies they study. And for a very good reason: they do not study society at all, but the *representation* of society.

This is a crucial point for the elaboration of fractal or quasi-fractal analogical structures in anthropological theory. Not one of the theorists mentioned in Mosko's fine elucidation of self-scaling or scale-retentive concordances in social theory has ever *seen* a society, experienced a culture, or in fact examined a people without recourse to its representation in one form or another. An "event" is a representation of its "happening" to other such events; language itself, or any other means of comprehension, is a representation of and through itself of what it is supposed to mean. But anything that "represents" itself by and through its representation of something else, and vice versa, is, by virtue of that fact, nonlinear and implicitly fractal (e.g., an example of what I have called "a symbol that stands for itself"). To understand such an all-encompassing phenomenality (an order *made of* order) as being *merely* recursive or reflexive, as many "postmodern" authors have done, is to skim the surface, abandon the inquiry to self-gratifying ethical or political agendas.

Likewise, any special argument made for the *universality* of content—Lévi-Strauss's, Van Gennep's, or Victor Turner's formulae for ritual structure, the incest taboo, a "science of the concrete," Marx's or Evans-Pritchard's social theory, reciprocity, exchange, or classification—must necessarily derive its force from the representational *means* by which that content was elucidated or discovered. Self-scaling would have to mean that content and form feed upon one another, exactly as one might expect in a subject area (and this could mean, as per Mosko's discussion of Feigenbaum, *any* subject area) wherein the means of representation and the facticity of the represented echo one another. Feigenbaum's Constant ("for turbulence," as it is often put, "in *any* medium") would not register either a "natural law" or a "cultural order," but an established *resonance* between different orders of representation.

What has "universality" to do with a resonance of this sort? "Incest," we are told, on no uncertain authority and with little respect for its precise definition, is universally prohibited, and surely it is *represented* that way. But as a representation of "sexual activity," we have come to learn in recent years, it is *practiced* to a far greater extent than had been expected, and its practice is possibly ubiquitous in human social orders. One might indeed argue that the practice of incest and its prohibition both require and contradict one another at the same time, that a kind of resonance or turbulence is set up that makes natural and cultural orders components of a mutual representation.

Considered in this light, that of the representation of representation, "resonance" would seem to have a direct correspondence, basic to the so-called "complexity theory," with the problems of scale-change and scale-invariance. Anthropologists characteristically exemplify "small scale" societies in the context of larger ("universal," nowadays "global") issues, and often enough subsume the differences of scale within their conclusions. We want to be the figure as well as the ground. Startling conclusions, like that "modern, transnational, globalizing economies are the most primitive of all," or that "hunter gatherers do not have to work for a living, but have the most complex classificational systems" are, however untrue or provocative, no strangers to us. The problem, as Mosko suggests, would not be that of *introducing* fractality to anthropologists, but that of *educing* it from that which they already know and do.

But we are rank amateurs in this regard compared to the molecular biologists, brain specialists, cosmologists, astrophysicists, and students of thermodynamics, those whose theoretical formulations depend largely on the extremes of differentiation and similarity inherent in the magnificational process. Why consider the molecular, the cellular, or the subatomic at all, save in the context of the very large, or indeed contemplate the wholeness of things apart from the nice subdivision that theory makes of it? What is a galaxy without its atoms, a brain without its neurons, or, for that matter, a dog without its fleas? Why indeed, when most of the galaxies we can detect are perceptually smaller than germs, project their size, distance, and probable evolution on an astronomical scale? "Scientists," as the joke goes, "have just discovered the gene that makes one want to discover genes." We represent ourselves accordingly.

Chapter 2 (Morava)

What Morava calls "quantification," and an anthropologist might want to call "objectification" or even "modeling," amounts to the self-validating function of mathematical abstractions, as in the ancient Greek significance of the *ratio*. In that respect, and for most people, the "sense" or meaning of number is established by a ratio called "counting," in which the various numerical values are set in correspondence with an appropriate collection of countables, and so with one another. But mathematics as such can only be said to come into its own when this validating function is mapped (modeled) back upon itself, so that number counts number, as in the standard operations of "number-theory." The *equation*, so to speak, sets the standard of the human scale, a magical point of balance or equilibrium, like those small bones within the ear, or like our upright posture, so that we can "go straight."

But is it possible to have a "downright posture," and still go straight? The use of number to model numericity itself raises the intriguing possibility that there might be systems of denumeration that are *mathematical* but not *quantifactional*, such as the one in use by the Daribi people of Papua New Guinea as late as the 1960s. Numerical authenticity was based neither on quantification ("counting"), nor on the straightforward modeling of numericity upon itself, but on a peculiar sort of ratio established between duality (or scission) and itself. Hence the number *si* (equivocally translatable as either "two" or "half") was both sufficient and insufficient to its own "marking" function, and its ratio (to itself) or self-validation must be expressed by the formula *sidari-si*, the "two-together-two" or "half-together-half." But since this might also, and *equally,* mean "two-together half," or perhaps "half-together two," the formula was self-similar for the very mathematical reasons that its centrality to the system disallowed. Because duality *is* ("equals") scission, and scission is duality, ratio in theory is ratio in fact, *sidari-si* not only *de-coupled* (the term is advised) numericity from counting, but also compromised the possibility of *even numbers*, and thereby numerical comparisons. Traditional Daribi "recognized" only three numbers, 1, *si*, and 3 (or *si* plus or minus its own being there), which happen, and not by accident either, to be the only three primes in series. Unlike many other New Guinea peoples, Daribi *understood* the use of body parts to give a recognizable shape to the counting of things, but they did not universalize the practice.

Care to imagine what Daribi *marriage* is like? I once asked a Daribi informant whether *sidari-si* had anything to do with *balance*. "Oh yes," he replied, "we call that thing *usu si si* (e.g., "sufficient two-two"), and it is so that you can *go straight*." Numerical valuation, *if it could exist for the Daribi* would do so on a line *perpendicular* to our number-scale, and not even the zero could rival its gyroscope-like prowess in establishing place-value. Missing its ratio ("to what? Its own being-there?"), the ancient Egyptians did not need the zero either, but took the opposite tack on fractal place-value.

The first outsider to acquaint the ancient Egyptians with the zero would probably have been killed as someone of no account ("another one of those horrendous Mesopotamian mistakes, like the wheel"). But the first outsider to acquaint the Daribi with the zero might be given a wife, to teach him the finer points of division-by-duality, or at least how the Daribi *multiply*.

At the very root of any problem or systemic formulation in physics or mathematics is the question of how *seriously* it is to be taken, or else, to the

contrary of its prepositional integrity, how suavely its inherent humor-
ousness (read "fractality") is to be finessed. The significance of Heisen-
berg's Uncertainty Principle has yet to be determined. Is it a joke, or a
myth? Myth is canonical, at the bottom line, because the canonic formulations of science and mathematics (Morava's "concepts of art," Tennyson's
"fairy tales of science") are inherently mythical. They are "stories of a certain kind," but then so is a joke.

What is the *difference* between the self-limiting seriousness of the canon
and the self-propelling contagiousness of the humorous? Myth (of whatever kind, to whatever purpose) is fundamentally different, in its propositional structure, to that of the joke (used here as simply the most literal
example of what humor portends). The contingency of the joke is that it
breaks the frame of relevance for the initial scenario (or "thought-pic-
ture") that is set up in its telling; the contingency of the myth (and oper-
ant value of the canonic formula) is that it uses the very means of
breaking the initial frame to set up a new one, and its very credibility
depends on how this is done. Jokes are *triangular*, setting up the *ratio* or
metaphoric covalue of two points, and then subverting that value with
the third point of the "punch line"—the "point" of the joke itself. Myths
are *quadrilateral* or double-proportional because the initial ratio or
metaphor set up in the telling is suborned or supplanted by a final one
(which must, as Lévi-Strauss has pointed out, in some significant way
contain the initial one).

From this (propositional) standpoint, the secret of humor is that it does
not supply the means of its own understanding, but only petitions it. Once
the expectational frame set up in its telling has been broken, there is *no
telling* what sort of relevance should replace it, and the issue becomes very
personal. And since the most personal frame of relevance is that of the
body itself, some abrogation of its usual equipoise (sneer, snicker, chortle,
belly laugh) is the usual response.

The problem with this nice analytical separation, however, is that,
whatever its strictly formal appeal, things do not always work out that
way. Depending on how the *breaking of the frame* is weighted or valued,
and what part it plays in the outcome, one can laugh at a myth or take a
joke quite seriously. In other words, the very difference between the joke
and the myth can form a relation, or acquire a prepositional status, in and
of itself. In more general terms, *the joke of the myth is the myth of the joke*.
The myth of the joke is that it must be humorous; the joke of the myth is
that it may not be authentically serious at all. Hence the analytic strategy
of what I have called "obviation" uses the two inverse "propositional"
triangles (one inscribed within the other) to demonstrate how and why
"a myth is the joke of a joke." Contrariwise, but to the same analytical
end, Lévi-Strauss's canonical formula is not *simply* a double-proportional
statement, but an inverse one, that "catches itself" in its own narrational
format ("a joke is the myth of a myth"). To distinguish the one from the

other, one must learn the difference between them, how duality forms a "singularity."

Humor is *edged* (e.g., "cutting") and belongs, like obviation, to the family of fractal expressions called "Sierpinski triangles," whereas myth, like Epimenides' or Russell's paradox, expresses propositions that "keep their scale" by making their own articulation recursive to itself. Hence Daribi speak of *porigi po*, the "power-talk" of political leadership, as *po begerama pusabo po*, "the talk that turns back upon itself as it is spoken." In his book *The Main Stalk* (1984), John Farella grounds the whole of Navajo religion in the epigraphic relation *Sa'a naghai / Bik'e hozhǫǫ*, which may be glossed, somewhat simplistically, as "Lifetime recursive / Referred again to itself in excellence."

Chapter 3 (Piot)

What Piot characterizes as a "recursive logic" among the Kabre is perhaps best exemplified through the representational force of what he calls "duality." Duality is itself "represented" through that which it represents, and thereby organizes, so that the duality is not necessarily binary save in its iterations, nor are they themselves binary save in relation to *it*. Duality is to that which it models, as that which it models is to itself, and as a further example of the modeling process. This is expressed in Piot's first example: M:F :: F(m): M(f). The self-similarity of a "proportion" whose only comparative utility rests upon its reproduction within itself suggests a resonant line from the works of the science-fiction author Ursula LeGuin (1969): "Light is the left hand of darkness, and darkness the right hand of light." The internal cohesion of the expression resists its own sequence. But then, as Piot remarks apropos of Kabre historicity, the sequence also resists that cohesion.

Nonetheless (and I think that Piot would agree with me), it is very important to understand that this is *not a paradox*, and not to be dismissed as one. It is an epigraphically *constitutive* relation in which gender engenders itself, that is, forms a kind of hologram out of the interference-patterning generated by its bi-valent usage in both the "modeling" and "modeled" roles. By the same token, LeGuin's remarkable *perception* of a nonlinear relation between darkness and light (via *laterality*) both conceals and reveals the plot structure of her novel about a planet where the inhabitants are without permanent gender, and about the political and historical implications of that situation.

In their normal, ungendered state, the Gethenians in that novel are neither males nor females but integrals—human beings for whom the condition of maleness or femaleness would be irrelevant. And Piot notes that, among the Kabre, "… the recursive logic that constitutes what men and women are emerges from an unambiguous single-sex state and is processually constituted." It is, in that sense, neither dual nor dualistic, and dualism or even our commonplace notion of what gender ought to be has very little to do with it.

For what are we to make of a condition where a man can be not simply a member of "Female Clan," but in some hyper-mortal sense a *woman* because of it, or a woman be a *man* on the appositive side of it? Even the Gethenians, or I think especially the Gethenians, would have a problem with that. Who among us has ever had a *linear* love-affair, or raised (God forbid) a linear child?

Just how many "nonlinear" resonances of what we take to be a simple duality, coordinated, at best, with biology and social role, have had to be disguised or sublimated within our own concerns with "social problems," familial dysfunction, and politico-economic hierarchy and dominance? Might we have to reinvent a planet like Gethen for ourselves, or take a closer look at Piot's work on the Kabre, to get our own anthropology straight?

A recent discovery in biogenetic research suggests (but only suggests, since DNA is notoriously disinformational) some intriguing supplements to Piot's conclusions. We had generally known that the X chromosome must redouble itself (XX) to effect its own self-similarity (produce a female) in the offspring, and the Y chromosome must divide the field of its conquest (XY) to produce a male. We have just learned that the Y chromosome, previously thought to be a zero-term (e.g., largely devoid of chemical "information"), is actually counteragentive. It seems to *work chemically upon itself* to produce a kind of cascade-breakdown effect, called Mitchell's Ratchet, in the surrounding genetic material, and thus to obviate the possibility of deleterious genetic recombinations.

Genetically as well as organismically, woman *incorporates* the reproductive process on a part-for-whole basis, whereas man, in those same terms, disincorporates (de-contains) it. To understand what Piot calls the "recursive logic" in this, we need to turn to the sets of relational terms that make recursive self-similarity a possibility for the Kabre—most importantly the issue of social incorporation that highlights his discussion. Piot speaks of an obviational collapse of hierarchy *into* itself as a sort of auto-mimetic copy of the dualities upon which it is built: "if the logic of the tropic relation is recursive/bisecting, then fractal iteration ipso facto leads to a reversal and obviation of the original set of terms. One would expect, then, on purely logical grounds, an almost interminable fractal doubling and redoubling—and this is what occurs in the Kabre case." Now this is eloquent to our purpose, for otherwise we should have to say something very cumbersome like "the totality encompassed by Kabre life—from the chromosomal basis of its scission through the functioning of the organism to the political and ritual permutations of the social whole—divides itself *by* itself in its redoubling, and then redoubles itself again in its own self-division."

Of course the totality of which Piot speaks is much larger than that, and includes in its fractal iterations not only the molecular, organismic, and social, but also the territorial massif upon which Kabre calendric ritual life is grounded, climate, weather, growing conditions, and much more besides. It is questionable whether any of the standard rubrics as to what anthropological inquiry is supposed to be about, the organismic life-process, the integrational social, economic, psychological, political, or religious synthesis, the intersocietal or crosscultural, even the cosmic, would apply here. There is too much integral unity to make a division among them.

So we might best start with social incorporation, which is after all what women do—with themselves, their children, and with strangers or outsiders to Kabre life in general. Kabre recode this function and the gender represented in it as part of their clan structure, as female Clan in relation to other, coordinate fractionings of the life-totality. Understood fractally, in this way, Woman Clan is *even more female* than women themselves are because it encompasses both women and men within its overreaching similarity to itself. Then the very interference-patterning set up by their opposition would show that Male Clan would have to be its equal-but-opposite vector, that is even *less* male than men themselves are, *divided* by its self-similarity (e.g., its inclusion of women as well as men, as in the XY male pattern) rather than being enhanced by it. In that case the molecular-organismic antinomy ("gender") would retain its scale within the metaphorical extension ("society") that determines its own positioning in the world through the arbitration of boundaries. This means that a double-proportional expression of social distinctiveness:

indigenous Kabre		MORE-THAN-FEMALE CLAN
LESS-THAN-MALE CLAN	::	outsiders

gains its advantage in the adjustment of internal to external affairs at the cost of reproducing a discontinuity in gender-connection (More Than Female times Less Than Male equals ... ?), or in other words an antisocial monstrosity.

The fact that we have something very much like this—virtually a social-estrangement virus—in the "normative" (that is compulsive and effectively compulsory) *middle-class* emulative structure of our own society:

Real Americans		MORE THAN FEMALE ("SOCCER") MOM
LESS THAN MALE ("CORPORATE") DAD	::	Foreign Terrorists

might serve to whet our appetites for what an actually *social* human aggregate might be. For our own ("Western") legacy, from Hobbes's *The Leviathan* through Rousseau's *Essay on the Origins of Inequality*, has been a litany of the antisocial monstrosity, of the *need to civilize*, as a sort of quasi-functional apologia for whatever might be done on its behalf. If Corporate Dad and Soccer Mom could only reproduce the socially diffident cross-product (call it Hard Rock Kid) that Bruno Latour might want to call a "hybrid," then how might Kabre sociality reproduce itself in kind?

Recoding or representing gender as (though it were) sociality makes it necessary to register the inherent self-differentiation of the genders in the result (more properly *as* the result), so that gender keeps its scale at the expense of social mediation. The only possible redress would be to overdetermine the exigency of mediation itself in the same way that the respective "plus" or "minus" of the genders have been exaggerated in representing them socially, to create a "third term" modality that is equal to the equality of the genders, and hence both more than and less than equal to itself—the perfect social catalyst. Kabre call their version of this Chachararada, and the clan of that name plays an important role in the calendric ritual system by managing the transitions between the (female) wet and (male) dry seasonal nodes.

Though it is difficult to imagine how Westerners might engineer such a catalyst as an antidote to their centuries-long drama of the antisocial Monstrosity, the name alone has certain advantages. High-profile liberals might want to adopt it as a mascot (as they have done with "equality"); and Hard Rock Kid might fancy it ("Chacha! Cha ... cha ... cha! Hey, *cool!*") a new rock group.

Chapter 4 (Damon)

Damon's essay begins with a most acute example of fractality in the crisis of its own representation—how it means what it means and why—and does so by zeroing in on the *objectivity* of emotion. What amounts to *the* Melanesian choice in representing the unerring reality of any situation, the way in which feeling "informs on" (e.g., "represents") itself, turns into a self-destructive whirlwind, the self-interdicting and self-consuming agency called *unuwewe*, in the Kalauna myth of Honoyeta. Totally frustrated in his attempts to live socially, as a human being, the superbeing Honoyeta "goes *unuwewe*," accedes to a kind of divine madness (likened to the Passion of Jesus Christ by the Kalauna) when his efforts to inform his motives of their own reality come to feed on themselves. The results are cataclysmic, ultimately transforming the merely social death of this immortal being into something like a localized version of the El Niño condition.

If what we call "emotion" is inevitably a sort of postmortem on itself, then *unuwewe* would seem to be more the rule than the exception, cleverly masked in most of us by more objective concerns. We are mad, mostly, in thinking ourselves to be sane. And if *representation* ("of the self to the self") plays a key role in this, it is difficult to see why its more objective applications could be unaffected, or why "the thought that turns back on itself as it is cognized" should not be implicated in "worldview" as well.

In the most extreme case, the efforts of an indigenous people (or their anthropologist) to structure their gardening-schemes, localize their cosmology, or optimize their standing in an exchange-system, might betray an underlying *unuwewe* as well. A civilization that is overautomated, totally compromised by unerringly accurate "self-guidance" systems ("too much precision in all the wrong places"), might likewise feed on itself, find itself "guided" in all directions at once. What happens, really, when "intelligence" outstrips its own usefulness? "I am dead certain that we have one of these," said a close Daribi friend in the year 2000, after I had spent several days demonstrating to him, with some very concrete examples, just exactly what I mean by a "holographic world-perspective," "I just cannot think of what it is." His problem had nothing to do with incomprehension; he had, as a matter of fact, "understood" me all too well.

The modeling of a world, or of a world-perspective, in which one happens to be largely immersed, presumes that one be able to stand aside from it. We could not know the spherical shape of our own planet if we did not take a "cosmic perspective" on it, that is be able to imagine ourselves emotionally as well as intellectually to be off of it.

Chapter 5 (Kelly)

Kelly's remarkable synthesis of Amazonian spatial ("relational") heuristics—the ethnographic type-case for all that we call "structuralism"—caught me up in a strange reverie. For it seemed to me that the active/passive potential of what is basically a fractalizing ratio holds the key to much of the intriguing cultural variation in that region. Do the Araweté gods resubject themselves, or does Jaguar, in some ergative way by subjecting (preying upon) others? Is the passive/active ratio a scale-invariant determiner or behind-the-scenes operator in the jaguar-infested cosmologies of South America?

If we take the premise that human beings are not only major predators, but also inventors of the *idea* (as against the reality) of predation, then what difference would an other predator make? Can the cunning of the jaguar be matched with that of the human being? In outthinking the jaguar does not the human being outthink itself? How would the absence of such a perfect foil affect Melanesian cosmological views, or even their animating social operations and connections?

It is easy enough to find parallels and contrasts between the two regions, but far more difficult to make sense of them. Identity-capture, for instance, can easily be shown to be the motivating factor in much of New Guinea (as well as Amazonian) headhunting. It was vitally significant for both the Iatmul (Sepik River) and Marind-Anim (Papuan south coast) headhunters to secure the identity (both the head itself and the personal name) of the victim before departing with their trophies. For those of the Papuan south coast, at least, this was premised on the idea that there is a one-to-one correspondence between persons entering the world and those leaving it, and they wanted to clear the way for their own progeny.

The need to *control* others as well as oneself, predator and prey, is uppermost in this as in all other considerations of human interaction. And so that control is a contagious factor infecting ethnographer and data alike, and we had best be careful. Even in reverie: is their inability to control Jaguar a significant factor in the Amazonians' efforts to control one another and ultimately themselves? Is the *lack* of such a savage and magnificent Other, for Melanesians, somehow involved in what looks like an inherent predisposition to violence, their amazing ethnic and linguistic diversity, or even their ethnographers' manic obsession with reciprocity? Do Amazonians use their inability to control jaguar to force the hand of social control, and Melanesians try too hard to control one another for lack of such a scapegoat?

Clearly the kinds of on-the-surface relations that Dumont called "ideology" and Lévi-Strauss "structures" are going to be of little help in making the right contrasts and comparisons. One has to step back, as Kelly suggests, to detect the point of fractality or scale-invariance that unifies the differences and similarities among them. Otherwise it might be difficult enough to separate not only Amazonians from Melanesians, but ethnographers from their subjects as well. How many of even the most famous ethnographic exemplars—the Nuer, the Trobrianders, the Yanomamo, Bororo, or Mount Hagen peoples—used an obsessive interest in their customs and practices to control the weirdness of the world around them? Like someone else's jaguars, they resubjected themselves by preying on others, and had nothing else to do with primitivity, the wild, and the ostensible "construction" of human realities.

Spatial heuristics (e.g., what I have called "imaginary spaces," Wagner, 2001) such as structuralist diagrams or even the "relationships" promoted by psychologists are both extremely vulnerable and synthetically rewarding, as one might expect from any sort of learning procedure. They are on one hand guides to obsessiveness, as in the countless personal and familial relations demolished by "therapeutic" overexamination, and on the other hand keys to a gigantic leap forward in the comprehension of social meaningfulness. In this sense scale-change is the degree of freedom that allows one to conceptualize a whole range of cosmological or epistemological operations as variations on a single theme. What we have is a single ratio (in Morava's sense) both determining and being determined by variables fed into the "denominator" function. Hence Kelly: "When we zoom, out, so to speak, and look at this from a different scale we note that both captive enemy and the killer are operators in the relations between the generic positions of Wari and others."

The link between fractal ("dividual") personhood and personal (e.g., "mental") fractality—the "idea" of the person and the impersonation of the idea—would have to be a form of passive agency expressible mathematically as a fraction with unity in the numerator. "Agency" would then be a retrofunction of whatever quantity would occur in the denominator, so that only in the rather special case that the denominator happened to be *one* would the corresponding action be perceived as taking place in a *linear* or rationally cause-and-effect manner. Hence the anthropologist's trump card, the so-called "self-reflexive" or ironical logic of ritual, sacrifice, and sociocosmological transformation, is never really "temporal" in an ordinary scientific sense. It *surprises* time, eliciting cries of outrage, synchronicity, cyclicality, or worse from witnesses, sells few books, and makes very little profit.

Self-similarity takes on a special and more emphatic role when separated from the immediate context and treated as a lesson in itself, what the Tolai people of New Britain as well as the Barok of New Ireland call a *pidik*. "When you see that the foliage of a tree cuts out the shape of a human face against the sky, and then go back and forth between the two images, tree and face, without settling on either, that is a *tabapot*. Man is a *tabapot*." This Tolai view of our self-similarity in respect of the world around us is both subjective and objective at once, defining our selfness and otherness and so likewise our mortality and immortality, in terms of one another. When I explained it to my Barok congeners in New Ireland, they exclaimed, "Ah, we call that *pire wuo* (literally "the reciprocity of perspectives"); it is how you put power in art." Figure-ground reversal is a model of itself, a "take" on its own take on things, effectively canceling out all the agonizing about what representation is and what it does. Both self-absorbed and self-compromising at the same time, more or less like the contemporary personality-structure, it permits wild insights into the very core of the meaningful and then destroys their validity in the blink of an eye. What is the real significance of "self" and other, or mortality and immortality, for instance, once it is realized that each term in the pair is the result of false claims made upon the other?

Shall we blame "society" for the symptoms of individuals diagnosed as "bipolar" or perhaps "latent schizophrenic," and then clinch the diagnosis by proving that the society in question was defined by a conspiracy of similarly afflicted individuals? What passes in the literature for the steadfastness or self-consistency of a cultural pattern endlessly reproducing itself may simply be a reflection of the fact that Melanesian anthropology has not advanced one jot beyond the "schismogenesis" model proposed by Gregory Bateson in the 1930s (Bateson 1958[1936]), while its Amazonian twin is still bemused, trying vainly to "reciprocate" (if that is the word) the dualities projected by Lévi-Strauss in the 1940s. End of reverie: the reader will perhaps forgive me if the practical side of this dilemma reminds me of the "concentration camp" joke of the 1940s "We do the concentrating, you see, and the Natives do the camping." And if the epistemological side reminds me of a political cartoon I saw in the 1970s. There was George Washington, with his cherry tree and his hatchet, saying "I cannot tell a lie," and then there was Richard Nixon, with his Watergate tapes, saying "I cannot tell the truth." And then there was the current incumbent President, with his arms outstretched, saying "*I* cannot tell the difference."

Telling the *difference* is what we are all about.

Chapter 6 (Taylor)

Taylor reminds us at the outset that the most dangerous and difficult aspect of scientific modeling is that, the more powerful and "predictive" it becomes, the more it gets in the way of its own usefulness. Like the Newtonian paradigm for mechanics and physical reality, and like Darwinian "natural selection," it tells us more about the "data" than the data could ever tell about it. Science overdetermines its object, and its objectivity, by underdetermining the subject. Fractality, one would like to hope, does the opposite, makes a special virtue of what John Keats called our "negative capability" in things.

This calls attention to what is perhaps the most heuristically valuable insight of the fractal theorists—that what appear to us as patterns, images, concrete values, or metaphorical insights are not the aids to comprehension they appear to be, but actually the swirls and filigrees of a dimensionality that cannot be cast into the fullness of perspective. Fair enough, though "dimensionality" has become a tired trope by this time, the snake oil of desperate mathematical speculators, and the eye candy of Einstein's relativistic purview; what it destroys may yet be more valuable than what it allows us to perceive. Is it possible that, in their efforts to add supernumerary "dimensions" in the aid of an (overvalued) cosmic visualization, the speculators have only managed to subdivide the ones that we are certain of?

It was a composer, Jan Sibelius, who likened the amazingly intricate fractality of landscape (a *riverbed* in his case; otherwise of course the coastline of England) to the motion and behavior of fluids. It is a "printout," so to speak, of the motion of the water it contains, and that must, in a very special sense, contain *it*. And though Sibelius was alluding in a very fancy way to the paradox of symphonic form in its composition, his analogy speaks volumes about an aspect of fractality that only the physicist David Bohm seems to have noticed—its *dynamic* quality, or containment of and by *motion*.

What is the *dimensionality* of motion, given that its swirls and filigrees control what an earlier generation might have called the "structure" or the "function" of Rwandan life? Not only bodily fluids, in their motion and interchange, their flow and blockage, but other, extraneous and partial confluences, other fluids and even the rivers of the land itself, and, by Sibelius, the shaping of the landforms, configure a personage that is never completely either individual or collective, never an object of study without being, at the same time, a subject. To sculpt a "dimension" of it would be sacrilege.

Hence "flow" and "blockage" are but diffident intercepts, fractalized "iterations" of a fused containment and decontainment of motion that Rwandans label as *isibe*. Both highly volatile and completely static or passive, uniting and simultaneously dividing such diverse interests as cosmology, health and nutrition, kin relation, marriage, political ideology, and decision-making, the Rwandan fractality matches adroitly with the *sozogo*, the "forked branch" holography discovered by Arve Sørum among the Bedamini speakers of lowland Papua New Guinea. The inherent pattern of each individual tree or leaf is reiterated in the intricate tracings of the river systems that nourish and support them, *and* in the genealogies, marriages, political schisms and alliances, and even the circulatory and neural nets of the people that live along their banks. At each point of juncture, called *adimi*, in the *sozogo*, a new entity is generated, more or less as the veins of a leaf join to form a tree, or the effluence of two parents seed a lineage, yet it is the downstream pull or flow, the motion, that controls the pattern itself.

What is modeled in the Rwandan *isibe* and the Bedamini *sozogo* is not a "picture" or view of the World, but rather the making of the picture, or the focus from which it is made. It is not just a model of "happening," or event, in real time and space, but also, as a veritable incorporation of that which it demonstrates, likewise a *happening of the model*, or the act of modeling itself. We *detect* motion or agency, even in our own bodies, by the traces it leaves behind, but *know* it by anticipating its action. But the agency of fractal *iteration* (the way that the model "works" or "moves") is undetectable as ordinary movement for the simple reason that it *is* the traces it leaves behind, and "anticipates" itself in their very expression. "Moving in a sacred manner," as Native Americans would call this, is very much in evidence in the world around us, but intransigent to our ordinary experiences of motion. It bears a different character to the purely reactive or consequential (read "structural") chains of reasoning that we normally substitute for the agentive, and lays bare the surprise of a spontaneity that might otherwise be attributed to "consciousness." It is evident in the so-called "phase-locking" of a flock of starlings, that will wheel suddenly in mid-flight, unanimously and without the time-lapse necessary for the individual birds to "decide" or communicate. More significantly for the social sciences, it is the likely suspect in Sigmund Freud's

attribution of a "subconscious" agency to the genital organs and disposi-
tions of the body, which seem to move of their own accord and contrary to
the general habitus of the organism, even taking it over in the movements
of consummation and parturition.

The quasification of sui-generis agency (that which "happens" by itself)
as *either* spontaneity or consciousness suggests something far more intriguing than an "automation" of natural phenomena or preternatural forces at
work in mating and procreation. It brings forth the possibility of a synchronicity or phase-locking between the *thought of motion* and the *motion of
thought* itself, a coagentive modeling of perceiver and perceived so identical with its own exemplification that what we normally conceive of as
"motion," or understand through the cause-and-effect linearity of physical
mechanics, would be significant only insofar as it witnesses its absence.

Chapter 7 (Mosko)

> "Here nothing points; to choose between art and science the
> budding genius would have to spin a stick."
>
> —W.H. Auden, *Plains*

Recapitulative ethnography, even to the extent indulged in here, would
have to be a diagnostic feature of a folk like the North Mekeo. A social
order or pattern of relationships built upon the very structure of analogy
itself—constituted by the *facts* of comparison—makes any other form of
comparison, such as that between idealized model and empirical data,
irrelevant. A regimen of thought or meaning that incorporates the very
sense that would make sense of it is not the sort of environmentally or
socially challenged "primitivity" that hard-core rationalists would expect
to find in New Guinea. Neither primitive nor civilized and neither natural nor cultural, evolutionary or revolutionary, collective or individualist,
it eschews any form of hierarchy: hierarchy is *integral* to it rather than
integrity (or even "integration") being hierarchical. Just the sort of thing to
turn those who live by cheap ethical or economistic rationalizations to
Zen, missionaries to the bottle, anxious administrators to shooting pigs for
want of any other form of recognition. ("They were messing up the center
of the village:" "Don't be silly, your Honor, anything in that 'belly' of the
village is actually *outside* of the village.")

Just what does it *not* do? Let us start with the cold, hard facts in answer-
ing this; a unity (what else could we call it, though "diversity" would
work just as well) compounded of its own self-similarity, that disappears
even the difference between subject and object into its own entity, faces an
insoluble dilemma when confronted with anything that is not of its own
ilk. How else might a "world-in-itself," or a beauty gazing into a mirror to
know better her own designs, face the world? Lacking any real contrast or

opposition within its seamless encompassment of things, it must perforce rehearse every single detail of its design and constitution in order to tell anything about anything at all.

It is self/other dyslexic, having, as Mosko himself seems to have deduced, determined itself so completely upon condition #2 of the canonic formula (the comprehensive mutual inversion of terms and functions) that condition #1 ("that one term be replaced by its opposite") has no edge in it. To illustrate what this may mean in more concrete (e.g., formal) terms, I shall take a cue from Mosko's own discussion, and use Marshall Sahlins's interpretation of "The Apotheosis of Captain Cook" (1985) as a foil. It is the question of whether the Hawai'ans' dispatching of Captain Cook was an episode involving a "structure of the conjuncture," a sort of working misunderstanding between two mutually encompassing worldviews, or merely a *juncture of the construction*, a self-agentive *contrast* at work at all levels, that is at issue. For a real structuring of the conjuncture, a violation of condition #1 of the Formula, would mean that culture is fully hermetic, "hermeneutical," as Geertz and the so-called postmodernists claim it to be, and so dyslexic of otherness in any form.

Is there a *stricture of the conjecture* at work here as well? Where *else* in the history of Pacific encounters do we meet with something like the Cook Debacle? It *almost* happened to Captain Bligh and his party after they were put off the Bounty and given the ship's cutter in recompense. Remember? Making landfall on a nearby Polynesian island a while thereafter, they thought it bad publicity to advertise the differences among Bounty's crew, and so invented a story about how the big ship had gone down at sea. Thereupon things got rather ugly fast; the crowd that had gathered on the beach drew closer and began striking rocks together in a menacing fashion, eventually chucking them at the outsiders (one of whom was killed as he pushed the cutter off into the surf). What had happened? We do not know, and probably will never know for certain the full extent of the belief, reported by Gunnar Landtman (1927) and others for the south Papuan coast and the Torres Straits region, that those who are shipwrecked at sea become automatically "strangers to the land," or in other words *demons* who *must* be killed by anyone encountering them. If that idea were part of a general legacy carried across the Pacific to such far-flung reaches as Tahiti or Hawaii, the paranoia that settled upon Bligh and his men after their first landfall could be easily explained.

And the so-called apotheosis of Captain Cook betrays a trap so diabolically clever that even the most enlightened sea captain might never accredit it to the Hawai'ans. For in stealing his ship's cutter and obliging him to make for shore to negotiate its release, the Hawai'ans might well have "set up" the good Captain in a categorical opposite to the proverbial shipwreck at sea, and so *demonized* their Lono. (Had they had ordnance, they might have "canonized" him as well.) Unable to locate his cutter, running from one place to another, the Captain would have been "*land-*

wrecked," made a de facto "stranger to the sea," easily enough dispatched (as of course happened) once he reentered the shallows.

We may never know whether or not Hawai'ans of the time regarded this as a joke, and begrudged its details so as to avoid giving their game away. But regardless of what had happened on that first Kill A Haole Day or its subsequent reverberations, we are not going to get the point of its Canonic significance, nor its diacritical commentary upon Mosko's and Sahlins's understandings of "structure," until we register its details in formal terms.

We need, in other words, to "justify" the *ratio* between the two conditions set forth by Lévi-Strauss for the canonic formula by "drawing them" to the scale of the expression they describe, that is actually *inserting* the ratio within the double-proportional statement that generalizes its application. Given the ratio as:

$$\frac{\text{opposition of terms}}{\text{mutual inversion of terms and functions}}$$

and both suitably inverting its terms and opposing them respectively within the two sides of the analogy, we get:

$$\frac{\text{fooling the divine}}{\text{mutual inversion of terms}} :: \frac{\text{divining the fool}}{\text{opposition of terms and functions}}$$

"Fooling the divine" would be the traditional Hawai'an ritual effort to lure the god Lono ashore, by means of sexual enticements (the Hula, etc.), so as to ensure his annual circuit of the land, dispensing plenitude and fertility throughout the realm.

"Mutual inversion of terms and functions" would be the structure of the whole analogy expressed as part of itself—a sort of "cookie-cutter" microcosm in which the advent of Cook and his crew and the shape of Lono's annual visit bear each other's imprint, more or less as the cutter itself, or "captain's gig," is a small but effective version of the ship it came on.

It is then the ratio between the Lono ritual and its microcosmic sub-version (!) that finds its echo and its completion in the parallel one set up between the stratagem of the Hawai'ans and its outcome. For "divining the fool" would be the testing of Cook's divine mettle, determining whether he might see through the ruse offered him and retain his kinship between land and sea, or else succumb to it as a "stranger to the sea." And so the "opposition of terms" determines the actual outcome of the stratagem, like the choice made between two coequivalent and equipotential factorial "roots" (a positive and a negative) in opting for a solution to a quadratic equation.

Because the double-proportional basis of social meaningfulness for the North Mekeo might likewise be literalized as a virtual "quadratic equation," one is tempted to ask what difference (or what kind of difference) condition # 1 of the formula would make to its articulation. A clue to the significance of its "double twist" is suggested in Hau'ofa's remarks about the more or less perpetual ambivalence at work in the day-to-day continuity of Mekeo life. Would that mean that a "negative" root or optation would deny the significance of the double twist itself, obviating the choice in the act of choosing it, whereas a "positive" one would instantiate choice itself as an active (and hence destabilizing) movement of the analogy? Is a structure of this sort positively historicized (as Hegel might have noted) by asymmetries in its ongoing dialectic? Mosko has often observed that at any given time, at least some of the essential offices in the Mekeo core structure remain unfilled, and that, at least by implication, structure is the negative of history. And its double twist reminds one hauntingly of the behavior of Americans in a contemporary presidential election (only one shot, but two turkeys to shoot at), in which one avoids total commitment by voting against the least-favored candidate.

Captain Cook, by contrast, was a real historical figure.

Quasification as Reality

Already Tlön's (conjectural) "primitive language" has filtered into our schools; already the teaching of Tlön's harmonious history (filled with moving episodes) has obliterated the history that governed my own childhood; already a fictitious past has supplanted in men's memories that other past, of which we now know nothing certain—not even that it is false.

—Jorge Luis Borges, "Tlön, Uqbar, Orbis Tertius."

Borges's account of how and why a purely invented planet called Tlön came to take the place of our familiar Earth tells a better story about science than science could tell about it. If the description of any reality is no more and no less than the reality of the description itself, then any of the human worlds described in literature or anthropology is ipso facto an unacknowledged description of our own. Nothing is "discovered" but that science has described it with a more obsessive intensity, and so exaggerated its reality (gravity has never been witnessed, or isolated, in its "pure" form). Just the right finesse, in Borges's terms, might serve to tip the balance between the familiar and the exotic, but how many times, even in our own terms, has Robinson Crusoe's island actually become the mainland?

Borges's novelty, and its lesson, are not lost on fractal thinking. It would be possible, using an appropriately powerful "imaging" technology, to create a Tlön of one's own, using a single fractal expression to finesse the reality coefficient of what we call "detail," and so, in a sense, outprove the empirical. For "detail" controls the veracity of the imaging-process itself (e.g., even the "real" is imaged in its terms), as well as that of what is imaged in it. In point of fact every aspect of a planet—the semblance of its shape and constituent features from without and within, the "events" that made it so, the patterns of its weather and its continents, its histories and indiscretions, the items of its philosophies, and the habits, literatures, calligraphies, and dialects of its peoples—is a prima facie instance of its preponderance. To control or determine, not the generality but the specificity of occurrence to the extent that the simplifying abstractions of science are stupefied in the result, obliterate the distinction between the natural and the artificial, is to turn seeming into being, micromanage the "God that lives in the details," acquire a new past. To do so through the agency of a single fractal equation, substitute its self-similar retention of scale for "randomness," or whatever else may have been there before, is to make chaos rage, invert the logic as well as the expectational fantasy of cause-and-effect.

As in the case of Borges's (apocryphal) Tlön, a planet conceived on that basis would gradually come to supplant our own familiar earth, leak the more acutely modeled details of its descriptional strategy into the power vacuum left by our own (scientific) obsession with generic order and principle. For standardized scientific modeling actually disempowers itself by obliging a change of model (and hence degree and kind of detail) as one encounters differing levels of magnification (abstraction), whereas a fractal model would show the same degree of detail and patterning of detail at every level, concretize and unify the sense-value of the whole rather than sensing its valuation into "kinds" and "types."

"Real" earth gives way to the wonders of chemistry or the mysteries of subatomic particle physics when magnified beyond the tolerance limits of our commonplace understanding of things; fractal earth is isomorphic through and through, manipulates our facts to fit its designs instead of the reverse. A world, however "virtual," whose imageries for the saying and thinking of things have been predetermined by a single equation, could not veridically "work" or operate in terms of mechanical, energetic, chemical, or biogenetic processes. And if it could only reiterate its self-iteration, the kinds of agency upon which scientific thinking depends for its credibility, then the real critical value of fractal reality is that of the foil it presents to the "how it works" criteria of conventional scientific explanation.

An "explanation" of whatever kind, to whatever purpose, treats the details of a metaphor as though they were a picture of that which is to be explained; fractality treats the picture as though it were a metaphor. If a metaphor is an image, neither of a concrete thing nor of an abstraction, but of the attempt to form an image, then one might think of trope in all of its various guises as fractalized language. Metaphor does not "explain" language any more than language can explain metaphor, and the attempt to do either omits the parts that would make sense of the whole. So one is forced to the conclusion that fractality is neither a defect of explanation, nor an incomplete form of it, but rather the opposite of what it attempts to do.

Without the quasi-explanatory values of its metaphors, called "hypotheses" and sometimes "theories," science would lack any purchase over the redundancy of the empirical world, its "being the way it is." But without the literalization of those metaphors, turning their details into the pictures we call "facts," it would want for the solidification of ideas into things that serves as a foundation for belief. Fractality measures the uncertainty that metaphor, in effect, misrepresents, for a fractal expression "scales" itself upon itself, makes a "content" of its formal means while simultaneously expressing that content as a form. It undercuts the significance of representation itself.

All representation depends on boundaries, the outlines drawn by its figures, words, categories, or concepts around that which they represent, and thus presumes upon the supposition that what it so demarcates is real or important. No essence, no demarcation / no demarcation, no essence. This poses a kind of double jeopardy for the project of knowledge itself, for one could not know the content of what is represented in it for the boundaries that delimit it, but likewise not see the boundaries or limits for the "facts" that would seem to justify them. This means that scientific explanation, or at least the attempt to confirm or prove it, meets itself coming back, that the test of the metaphor is the metaphor of the test.

None of our conceptual worlds are real, and so none of our real worlds are conceptual. We could not possibly experience or organize what is fondly imagined as a "social construction of reality" for the simple reason that we are not that good, and do not have "the right stuff." No one has ever known or understood the precise content or "meaning" of even a single word or perception, let alone the eclipsing of one by another that we call "metaphor," or their extension and concatenation into an objectifiable surround of experience. We obsess upon details alone, like the inventors of Borges's Tlön, and pretend realities to suit them.

Stacking the Deck

Fractality makes the relation of a thing to itself transitive; turns the tautology of "a thing as itself" inside out, and so represents by the very fact of its own representation. In that respect the most basic regularities by which physical reality is "measured" (e.g., objectified—qualified or quantified) have very little to do with the phenomena-like light, or motion, or distinctive "properties"—that they are supposed to be "about." They represent instead the rules or standards (e.g., agreements or conventions) for how we behave in taking account of the world around us. When we speak of the velocity of light, the acceleration of gravity, or Planck's Constant for the quantification of energy, we are talking about a self-scaling or scale-retentional agency that might better be expressed in fractal terms, but had to be physicalized at the time of its discovery because fractality was not yet known. Otherwise, and for all we might know, the progression of light might well be instantaneous, and the quality of "motion" might be something altogether different to what we intuit as such.

What "physics" measures is its own interference with the data; we do not measure time, for instance, except that we time the measures for it. Time, whatever that might be, exists outside of the measures we construct for its recognizance, and only coincidentally within them. It "times" us in our timing of it, and so, along with other time-related propositions (such as the velocity of light, Planck's constant, or the acceleration of gravity), acquires a value that has more to do with proportion than with something that might be confused with reality. How we may be redundant to ourselves in seeking these measures is not necessarily the same thing as how "the universe" may be redundant to itself.

Apart from the models we use to evoke, educe, or distinguish them, there are no inherent differentiations or unifications, no quantities or qualities, in the nature of things. The numbers that count are the ones that we count; the processes that work are the ones that we work. But if one always knew this to be true, and were only uncertain as to how to say it, or lacked the social courage to maintain it, one would have to acknowledge that there are no "parts" and "wholes" in the real world either. How we cut the cards is part of the game, not part of the cosmos.

There are no wholes in our thinking or modeling of the world that are not parts of something else, and no parts that cannot be conceived as whole in themselves. If the DNA that supposedly organizes (the word is advised) life itself (including, of course, the ability to think about it) is composed of only four distinctive molecular fragments, then how could one tell, without a lot of circuitous and ad hoc rationalization, where one "gene" begins and another leaves off? Would this not mean that the structure of life itself is composed, like the modeling that tells us what it is, of disparate chains of (often spurious) reasoning? Just what part does the macroenvironment, agencies beyond the purview of genetic material and its supporting chemical infrastructures, play in the control, distribution, and even the definition of the genome? Where would science be without its artificially and automatically imposed hierarchies?

Like the traditional "great chain of being" arguments, hierarchical models substitute significant differences of scale, and hence the supposed efficaciousness of "emergent" orders of reality for cause-and-effect in explaining the working of things. The world of subatomic physics works on altogether different premises to those of everyday practical experience, and other, "emergent" factors come into play when we consider stars and galaxies. But it is precisely this dependence upon scale-change and "emergent" facticity that the special applications of fractality called "Chaos science" or "complexity theory" serve to correct for, and they do so by using scale-retentive models to give the game away.

So the question "how might science develop a better strategy for predicting, and thus understanding, the nature of reality?" goes to the issue of "developmental process" itself, and of the hegemonic role it has come to play, along with "evolution," in our generalized scientific schema. Fractal models do not develop; they iterate, and what they iterate is their own version of themselves. They exist, in other words, very much like the concept of "species" in biology, "essence" in philosophy, or "meaning" in epistemology, all of which turn out to be very difficult to define, and perhaps even too simple to understand in all but naive terms. For if "species" kept its scale absolutely, nothing would evolve; if "essence" kept its scale in that way, comparatives would be impossible; and if "meaning" were in that way scale-retentive, discourse, dialogue, and conversation would be impossible. Redundancy, in all cases, would lack for a palliative.

"Nature," or, more properly speaking, the so-called "environmental niche" to which an evolving life-form is commonly said to "adapt," does not come into being—or even "exist" as a possibility until that life-form has acquired the requisite traits of form, habitus, and character. The theory, or rather the expectational set, of evolution has it exactly backwards. But so does the physics that, ever since the completion of the Maxwell equations, has sought to define the qualities of matter and energy processually according to the extensional properties ("fields," "orbits," even "particle strings") of the surrounding "medium." Is mass a function of gravity, or is gravity a function of mass? Are they both, in some very clever way, introverted counterparts of the sort of extensiveness ("dimensionality") that we identify with space? Has nonlight, or rather the absence of electromagnetic energy, a constant nonvelocity, a robust cosmic immobility that might well account for the preeminence of "cold dark matter"? Is the (largely intuitive) concept of "energy" even defensible, given the fact that what we pretend to know by this term cannot be detected, observed, defined, formulated, or understood without basically turning one distinctive kind of energy into another?

Concealed behind the diagnostic quandaries and problem-areas that are the legacy of nineteenth-century science (wave/particle, nature/history, organism/environment) is a fundamental uncertainty or indeterminacy with respect to figure and ground. There is the "figure" of knowledge, numerical, perhaps, as in an equation, the algorithm, hypothesis, or stated proposition, the imaginal diagram or printout, and then there is the "field" or background, the environment or continuum of its epiphenomenal placement. There are cause and effect, each serving, under the appropriate explanatory circumstances, to foreground or background the other. If separating figure and field in any of these considerations corresponds to the crucial action of definition itself, then conflating the two in some elemental way would be the mark of chaos.

And, of course, of implicit quasification. Does our insight, and even our application of scientific ideas and principles represent the true description of factual reality, or only the reality of description itself? Do we describe laws or inherent orders of nature, or only the nature of laws and orders? The fact that the necessarily visual (and visually necessary) iteration of a fractal expression is self-containing and self-contained in that respect (e.g., it grounds its own figure and figures its own ground) suggests that the (veridical) description of reality and the reality of the description itself are distributive functions of the same basic relation.

The so-called "strange attractor" is the cause-and-effect intercept, or logical equivalent, of the self-scaling (fractal) expression, in that it stands at the center of the causative relation—the "linkage" that is neither active nor passive; but only conjunctive. In the same way, the "printout" or visual iteration of a fractal expression is neither humorous nor seriously purposeful, but "poised," as it were, between causative irony and ironical causation. As though to remind us that the funniest (or most original) jokes are the ones we take most seriously, whereas the most serious matters of all are often the most inadvertently (and inadmissibly) funny.

For the joke, as the most succinct and tractable expression of humorous portent, owes most of its charm and power to the fact that it is a viable inversion of the cause-and-effect relation that we disguise as "logic," common-sense reasonableness, and even pragmatic purpose or value. (The much-prized notion of "origins" or beginnings is a kind of exaggeration of this value.) The effect, or scenario of the joke's initial proposition, comes first and amounts to the "setting-up" the (humoring or patronizing) of its own, later-to-be-revealed cause, in the so-called "punch line." In that sense, and for all the fact that the sort of irony that we identify with humor comes in an indescribable array of variant-forms, what we know as "agency" amounts to a backwards-humor of "telling the serious."

Easily traceable to its sources, which by definition must have been there for the principle to be known and operative at all, cause-and-effect is always derivative, predictable, easily locatable if you know where to look, and always right. Humor, by contrast, is untraceable as to its roots or origins, unpredictable, indeterminate, apparently original, and makes rather a circus of its irrelevance to the matter or purpose at hand. Technology and the science that is grounded in its examples misses the point of this fundamental difference ("Between itself and what?" asks the humorist) by taking it literally and getting it all too well. The irony that is automatically elicited by this sort of artificial certitude, more or less like a discharge of static electricity, does the opposite: it "gets the point" of its own ostensible purpose or relevance by not getting it at all, betraying its own quasificational antilogic.

In a sort of summary judgment about the effects of his prodigy, fractal mathematics, Benoit Mandelbrot (1982) is said to have remarked that he had finally gotten mathematicians to looking at pictures again. In a manner that recalls Wittgenstein ("We picture facts to ourselves." "A proposition is significant only insofar as it is a picture."), Mandelbrot revealed more to mathematicians about their craft than they might want to know. What fractality restored to the mathematical imagination, the acid humor behind Mandelbrot's observation, was the same thing that Wittgenstein restored to philosophy—the paramount fact that no abstraction of any kind, however telling its formulation, is any better than the concrete imagery necessary to make sense of it.

This may help, through the very ambivalence of order and chaos to one another, our understanding of why the self-iterative character of fractality seems to express ("arbitrate") both order and chaos through the same figurative patterning. For the design that models only itself, that grounds its own figure and figures its own ground, likewise integrates the purpose of irony and the irony of purpose within the same patterned intercept. Like the trope or metaphor, the squiggle that stands for itself has a solely meditative function, in that all or its potential implications or applications are consequences of its own self-modeling.

Cause-and-effect depends, for its very usefulness or "predictive" efficacy, upon a purely arbitrary division or distinction imposed upon a unitary action, so as to project the "working illusion" that one part of it is anterior ("causal") or antecedent to the other. Humor makes light of this fact, and light itself makes a humor of it. The effect of a joke or other ironic expression (anecdote, epigram, aphorism) is its cause, or conditional priority, but the cause of an agentive (e.g., cause-and-effect) sequence as it collects into the multiphasic innovational precedence of a technos, is its "effect" (q.v. "necessity is the mother of invention"). So in fact the tension of doubt, disbelief, and wry, erratic humor that surrounds any serious experiment or testing of a prototype-model is hardly incidental; it is the equilibrial foil of the invention ("hypothesis") itself and its "cracking" of empirical reality. It is how the joke is told, the "timing" and precision of its innuendo, that makes the difference of its "funny," but, conversely, it is how the invention tells (informs) you, refigures the conceptual drama of agency, that determines its serious purpose.

What we have in the "normal" interplay between the humorous and the agentive—the fact that jokes, on one hand, and inventions on the other, seem to arise of their own accord—is a figure-ground reversal that controls the realm of human thought and action instead of being controlled by it. The normative human condition is subjected by a cause-and-effect dyslexia, a self-paradoxical perplexity (usually equated with subjectivity itself) in which the ironic and the agentive or effectual threaten to take over one another. Overdramatized in opera, underdetermined ("subconsciously") in what we like to pretend as a psychology, the dyslexia is Nature's own way of joking about inventions, and of inventing jokes. (Only a fundamentally dyslexic species could bring itself to wonder whether crop circles are fraudulent or real.)

Upon such premises, then, the culture or tradition that made the truth of humor the goal of its quest for knowledge would find itself inundated with an otherwise inexplicable superfluity of miniscule and incredibly effective "inventions"—diabolically clever and much better mousetraps (that "beat a path to your door" of their own accord), pencil sharpeners that work with 120 percent efficiency (so that all you have left is the eraser); and computers that are actually useful (instead of insidiously distractive, or insistently destructive of the purpose of human life and its humors). And as for crop circles, let's put it this way: we human beings have worked so hard and so long—virtually since the times of Stonehenge and the Lay Lines—at reconfiguring the earth in terms of our own geometries, that it is high time that Earth ("Nature") took a hand in it, imitated us back by refiguring our geometries in its terms.

Does Nature itself exist solely by the reimitation of our efforts to make sense of it, our designs, more or less like those Indian tribes in the United States that have been so consistently imitated by anxious appropriators that they are forced to imitate themselves all over again so as to counterfeit a certain desperate autonomy? Is it fair to treat so pathetic an effort ethically, in terms of a new anthropology of false pathos, using rhetorics that give the lie to their own efficacy, or understand crop circles in terms of ecology and environmental damage? "Stacking the deck" of anthropological designs and purposes in that way invites a reconsideration of language as the fundamental root and arbitrator of our dyslexic being.

Consider the first three assertions of proposition 4.121 in Wittgenstein's Tractatus Logico-Philosophicus (tr. Pears and McGuinness, 1961):

> "Propositions cannot represent logical form; it is mirrored in them."
> "What finds its reflection in language, language cannot represent."
> "What expresses itself in language, we cannot express by means of language."

Language is the fact of its own picturing, a jeweled inscription of the worlds of thought, pattern, and reality that may be elicited, but never defined, through its devices. It appears to us already formed and made, as our consciousness does, or as the moon's reflection in the sea, and so seems to have a consciousness of its own, or a primary luminary source located somewhere outside of our world. We do not learn it, but talk back to it, and teach ourselves to it. Even the rules or orders, the descriptions or logics by which language may be said to exist as such belong to a larger scale of iteration than the phenomenon they describe. Thus the cause-and-effect logic that is inadvertently intended in the propositional representation of a language—the derivation of its words and its grammatical, syntactical, or phonological forms—is as vulnerable to dyslexic inversion or ironical figure-ground reversal as anything in the realms of physics, mechanics, or perspective. This means that practically every proposition in Wittgenstein's Tractatus could be turned inside out and make as much sense as the original. Facts picture us to themselves, carry a little image of the one who imagines them as a function of their form and meaning. "Reality" is a fractal coefficient of our ability to imagine it (like consciousness itself), one that "constructs" its imaginer quite as much as that one might construct it, so that the fact or proposition is not the picture of reality we mean it to be, insofar as reality depicts it, and its inscription in reality is what makes it a fact.

Agency has less to do with time than time has to do with it, especially when we consider that the whole generality of what we mean by that term, "time," or the temporal matrix, is at best a miragelike apparition of our own agentive dyslexia. In that case "futurity," the effect of temporal agency, expands ironically into an immensity of experiential relation and detail behind us, so that what we collect in moving forward in our moments and actions is a ghostly vision of its precedence called "past" or "memory." The whole lexicality of language, all that is shown in it, is something that it tries in vain to escape. For it is no illusion at all that everything that we can ever know, remember, recover, or reconstruct about the past, all that informs our knowledge of who we are and what we are doing, lies in the future of the present moment. What is in fact a mutual mirroring of two self-reflexive and otherwise unaccountable perversions of agency, past-in-its-own-future and future-in-its-own-past, has less to do with time or how it may "work" than with the fundamental paradox of agency, the "chaos," as it were, of the temporal.

Forget time, pay attention to the timer. "Using logic, this hypothesis cannot be proven to be true." In one form or another—Gödel's Proof, Russell's Paradox, or Epimenides' version of the same thing—the self-referential syllogism uses irony or what might be termed propositional figure ground reversal to demonstrate the antilogical framing of what we like to think of as the logical. Or the agentive: think of the doorbell buzzer, a device that "works" by breaking its own circuit so as to set it up again, setting up its own response to itself, and so creates an irritating rattle. The effect is presented first, as in a joke, and then, alarmed by what is in fact our most familiar version of the Strange Attractor, one goes to the door in hopes to discover the Attractive Stranger.

The imitation of reality, the modeling of a subject-matter upon the cause-and-effect propositional structure that rationality claims for its own, is no more and no less than the reality of imitation itself, a kind of ironical mimicry of the ability to represent. We rationalize, in other words, and then rationalize the fact that we rationalize, in a droll imitation of the ability to imitate. Consider the dramatic self-representations, say, of Hamlet and of Jesus—the son of a king who acted himself mad for the sake of truth, and the Son of Man who acted himself divine for the sake of humanity—but with such unanimity of means that their epitaphs or last words could well be exchanged for one another: "And flights of angels sing thee to thy rest" for "My Lord, my Lord, why dost Thou forsake me?"

Success models itself so well upon its failures, or failure upon its successes, that the object of the modeling becomes the subjectivity of its attainment; of the Prince who succumbs to his own succession, the prophet crucified by his attempt to know God. In that respect the "stacking" of the deck that built the library up, and the blow that brings down its house of cards, "decking the stacks," are not all that different either.

Decking the Stacks—The Joke That Brings the Library Down

> "A sentence is what a word would look like if it were made up by a committee."
>
> —R. Wagner, 2002

Just as metaphor (trope), created wholly out of disjunctions ("between words") in the lexical design of our thought, forms the seamless continuity of another language within our own, so the whole continuity of "energy" (concept as well as application) owes its facility to discontinuities between the various kinds of energies that empiricism forces us to categorize. There are, of course, many kinds of energy, including the "mental" energy of the one who is observing or understanding the phenomenon, but because one must see what one sees or know what one knows only through the transformational process that masks its own reality in this way, we know what energy is through the machinery of its changes alone. As long as the "energies" of the dictionary (or library) are used to keep its lexicality (definitions) in place, the physical reality of energy will remain metaphorical, and as long as the metaphor of "energy" retains its factual status, the imagery of thought itself will mimic that of the machine.

It will form the seamless design of a categorical "mind" within the physical body, and that of a wholly metaphorical, or "energic" body within the mind-each beholden to the other for its "energy" and corroborative reality. Deeply suspicious or fundamentally unaware of its own incongruities in this regard, contemporary social science performs a classic figure-ground reversal to exorcise its own worst nightmare, subjectifying its object by objectifying its own subjectivity in a kind of reprojective déjà vu called "the social (or "symbolic") construction of reality." What passes itself off as an "interpretive" or perhaps "hermeneutical" approach to anthropological knowledge, a reflexivity honed on "intersubjective" (e.g., the self-privileging of the "observer") means, is in fact the authoritative counterpart of what used to be called the "native worldview." Behind all the nostalgic attempts to reconstitute the determinism of social scientific theory—the substantialism of economic, kin-relational, psychological, political, and even semiotic approaches—lies a basic inability to get beyond the foregrounding facticity that serves categorization as its mask, its "Mr. Data" android. The fact of (cultural) relativity is the (natural) relativity of fact, but in fact the conditional role of irony in reaching ("determining") even this conclusion makes a kind of moto perpetuo redundancy of its cause-and-effect fetishism. Hamlet himself must have gotten so lonely in his mad act, the (schizophrenic) solipsism of figuring out his own design (so much like the bogus "self-interest" of postmodernist thinking) in every person and situation he met, that death would have seemed a positive reprieve. Postmodernism, or at best "hermeneutical" social science, is an epitaph for a science that never existed.

Was Hamlet, too, destroyed by the ironical redescription of his actions, like a nightmare-of-himself haunting himself (forget the ghost—"To sleep, perchance to dream; aye, there's the rub")? The ironical and the causative, or rational, both describe the same content, but do so from alternative or "staggered" positionings. It is their simultaneity, or in other words the actuality of their mutual content, that is difficult to account for subjectively. What we dream is necessarily effect-causal rather than cause-effectual because no one knows for certain what causes dreaming itself, so that the attempt to recall, retell, or explain the dream is always guesswork aimed at some sort of "punch line," some after-the-fact explanation of how the dream happened. In effect, why that particular dream happened becomes a concrete substitutional proxy for why any dream ever happens. What happens in ordinary, day-to-day waking perception gives the clue to this, for it assumes (—is constituted through the fact that) any perception is caused by the happening of the (perceived) event a very short time beforehand. But since we depend upon perception itself to know what we know about anything—including, of course, causation—the opposite of this is true, and perception precedes the event by the very act of imagining it to have come beforehand. Hence the fact that we seem to dream ourselves awake is the real cause of our need to sleep at night, and the simple but profound inversion involved in coming to terms with this provides all the irrationality or cognitive static necessary to imagine a "subconscious."

What ad-hoc conceptions like the "subconscious" or "unconscious" repress is their own fully conscious and hyperrational strategy—they hide their schemes in madness like Prince Hamlet. What they conceal is not some enormity of intent or motivation, but the far more radical disjunction that authorizes their neurotic manifestations, the figure-field inversion of subject and object that Freud termed "the transference." The turnabout effect of the diagnosis itself is the diagnostic feature, the "therapy" in which the analyst takes on the patient's symptoms whereas the patient acquires the analytic potency of recognizing and dealing with them. Carried to term in its full analogic portent, this means that the effect of modeling is turned back upon itself so that, as in chaos theory, the "data" models one's attempts to comprehend it better than any hypothesis might. (This also explains why the fictional android, "Mr. Data," in the Star Trek the Next Generation series, could never get the point of a joke. In a word, he was it—the joke of the person in the personification of the joke, and the closest one could ever come to the joke-on-itself.)

Understood in fractal terms, the secret of Freud's discovery has more to do with the scale-retentive possibilities of explanation—the basic contagion in what we mean by that term—than with anything about the human psyche. Explanation takes on a life of its own, enters its own reality, in masterpieces of what used to be called "scientific reasoning" like the principle of gravity and natural selection, where the focus of understanding is turned back upon itself with such finesse that its ordinary purpose in fostering empiricism is likewise inverted, and the "data" itself comes to serve as a sort of apology for its existence.

Or else a surreptitious art-form, poaching in the preserves of objectivist patterning. The effect of interchanging personal presence that Freud called "the transference" finds its objective equivalent in a refinement of artistic perspective that was almost the exclusive preserve of Jan Vermeer's later paintings. There are many ways of appreciating what is effectively a perspectival prism, some of them more illuminating than others, but what Vermeer seems to have perfected was a capturing of its action in perfect stillness, in which the personal space of the object and the objective space of the person execute a subtle transformation.

Interestingly, Vermeer's exteriors (the "view of Delft," etc.) share this quality as well, and psychoanalysts often enough project as well as introject the symptoms of their patients. On retrospect, Vermeer's art was a more or less "personalized" precognition of that of M.C. Escher, and Freud's science an anticipation of Einstein's or Franz Boas's objectified relativism. It is as though "the data" themselves painted Vermeer's inverted optical perspectives, his camera obscura view of the world, and the subject-object interchange that made this possible ventriloquized the "talking cure" of Sigmund Freud, and took an active role in the exteriorized "points of view" of Albert Einstein and Franz Boas.

The reason Vermeer's pictures are difficult to decrypt (they dazzle and disarm the viewer with a deeply obscure intimacy), Freud's "therapies" are unsafe and unlikely cures for anything, Einstein's universe and Boas's cultures impossible to objectify with any kind of certitude, has little enough to do with truth, depth, intellectual profundity, or scientific accuracy. It is because they threaten to take us over, and we must stop them, more or less as the Egyptians may have mummified cats—not for obscure reasons of sacredness and afterlife, but simply to make sure they stayed dead, and keep them from reincarnating all over the place. Was it not, likewise, to keep a plague of ill-defined and purely subjective Boasian "cultures" from pullulating and running amok in the streets (look at us now) that Colonialism disempowered and exploited their identifiable peoples, and the insidious monstrosity called "postmodernism" poisoned their credibility in the minds and hearts of the multitudes?

In the way that cats were most likely small, wild, fuzzy predators skulking about the north African deserts until the ancient Egyptians "domesticated" them and gifted them with their most characteristic product—the really, REALLY objectified death, so the essence of the joke may once have fueled and provoked the whole imagination and life-energy of the human species (possibly Shakespeare's works were a reversion-to-type of that era). Language and/or culture would have come onto the scene as a somewhat misguided attempt to temper and control—mummify with words, contain with concepts-and in the end disqualify what threatened to become a supersentient, world consuming stroke of madness. It is not for nothing that we call our most felicitous reaction to humor catalepsy, though for most purposes mere laughter will show what disqualification really means, that invention of an antilanguage that makes us weak in the knees, prone to doubt and suspicion, that threatens the very uprightness of the race. (Cat got your tongue? Just how many human tongues did those fuzzy predators dispense with, out there in the cool of the desert nights, before the Egyptians got to them with their shrouds and incantations?)

If cats can laugh, they must do so on the inside, in the camera obscura of their thoughts; they get tongues, not jokes. If it is difficult enough for us to even think about humor without its public contagion invading the privacy of our thoughts, the rabid, pandemic invasiveness of the cause-and-effect virus has a far more deleterious effect. It hides itself in the seriousness of what we call "meaning," pretends arbitrary continuities of its own into the workings of the machine, the ostensible natural "process," and the evocative potentialities of language. It shows us (cats would be very jealous, positively green-eyed with envy) more cognitive detail in the world of purposiveness and order than could ever possibly be there.

Automimetic Agency

> "The trouble with you, Robert, is that you make the visible world
> too easy to see."
>
> —Wallace Stevens to Robert Frost

And the trouble with that memory-virus, or fractal coefficiency of mind-in-its-representation that Richard Dawkins has called the "meme," is that it makes the invisible world impossible to miss. "Virus" is perhaps too sanitary a term for what Dawkins has in mind, and "mirror-reflection" a bit too opaque, for a function that imitates itself in every way that one may choose to imitate (that is choose to copy out, in our thoughts and ideas) it, is the ultimate diacritical (critique) on the cause-and-effect mode of continuity that underlies every form of reason or logic. Closely related to the cat-genus, which evolved by a stalking-strategy of pretending itself as "no-cat" to its prey, it hides the cause in the effect, and is a cousin at least to the joke, and the enigmatic "auto-immune system," which is virtually impossible to locate in the body.

What is more immune, even to itself, than a cause that hides itself in its effects? If the whole outline of the rational, the continuity of logic, and hence of a procedural order in things, is based on an imaginary cut made between assigned cause and follow-up effect, and thus essentially wrong, then that of its ironical, effect-and-then-cause opposite, is not only doubly wrong, but makes a positive virtue of that fact. The meme that controls both of them is neither right nor wrong, logical nor irrational, subjective or objective, or even real or fraudulent. No-cat determines the existence, personal or evolutionary, of the cat, but the cat itself determines, in its ongoing play or hunting strategy, the presence or absence of no-cat. If the only similarity between the two (cat and no-cat) lies in their complete and total differentiation from one another, so that their major difference is their similarity, then the meme that controls both of them (the self-similarity of cat/no-cat) would be that of self-imitating survival/extinction, or the Schrödinger-Heisenberg catalysis. (Cats sometimes make quantum-leaps, but if you know the cat's location with perfect accuracy, you cannot guess its intentions, and if you know those intentions well enough, you will never determine its location. If you do not either, you will have a cataleptic fit yourself.)

The pun, progenitor of ironies, is not the Godfather but the veritable Gross-father of language. So it would be the "copy-cat" or automimetic strategy of this argument, the fact that its exemplification of cause-in-effect ironies is not necessarily commutative in any straightforward "linear" sense, that might pose major problems for the reader. Just as a joke cannot be explained at all without making another joke of the attempt to explain it, so the very effort to build an argument around these premises falls victim to its own self-recursive subterfuge, becomes the copy-cat antithesis or jocular twin of its seeming-to-be-there. (The meme lives in its Echo, or drowns like Narcissus in being spurned by her.) No wonder Lévi-Strauss exchanged winks with a cat, and then moved from cat-and-mouse games with exchange itself to the role of geminate (e.g., twinned, dualistic) agencies in the logic of myth.

What might we not learn from the contretemps of two distinct species that are more closely unrelated to one another than most others are interrelated among themselves? What language does for human beings, cats do with presence and absence (e.g., they naturally select themselves). So nothing as crude as domestication, "petting" (do we not, sometimes, adopt "pet languages"?) or even marriage is at issue here, but rather that "each has defined itself as superior to the other," as a good friend of mine once put it, "and that makes a bond stronger than love."

Language, in other words, did not have to originate, or even evolve, but simply define itself (in its own terms, of course) as superior to anything that lies outside of it, or came before it, and from that point onward it was only concerned with where it was going, and never with where it had been. (Cats do not originate or evolve either, but simply imitate the process, appearing or disappearing as it suits their convenience, and likewise need only imitate human speech to get what they want. They only sing on matters of the heart, so we use their guts to make music.)

Might it then be the cat-like quality, or self-dis-similarity, of language to its human congeners that holds the key to our own specific self-similarity, how we construe our relatedness to one another? The question, posed in this way, goes well beyond the purview of so-called "interdisciplinary" connections, and straight to the heart of anthropology's foundation. As a kind of quasi-autonomous felicity that we like to imagine "culture" itself to be—a categorical inventory of the world that only incidentally includes the one who is speaking or using it—language realizes its own agency in the kind of closure-upon-itself that we know as "metaphor" or "trope." This is highly problematic in that the items of the inventory acquire a quite unexpected agency (e.g., a power of representing or standing-for themselves) along with that of the language that fosters them, so that a sort of trade-off exists between them. The more suspect "language" itself becomes (in the undermining of credibility in its words and phrases, its concepts and ethnic background, its very authority), the greater the tendency to attribute weird and highly inappropriate autonomies to the items of its inventory, invent "cultures," "symbolic constructions of reality," and even spiritual insights to explain them.

Whether or not it approximates to the definitions that the philologist Max Müller gave to myth as a "disease of language," the autonomizing of the inventory (what is said or shown in it) grants enough distance from the phenomenon to throw the more interesting part of the issue, the actual self-similarity of language, into sharp relief. Turning to the more holistic understanding of language fostered by "sociolinguistic" approaches, the integration of language, person, and social context, we find the invention of culture (e.g., the analogical relation of language to its inventory) to stand in a larger, homological correspondence with the set of human speakers. In effect, the actual self-similarity of language is neither the extensive, analogical expansion of the inventory that makes "imagery" and cultural meaning possible, nor the restrictive, homological socialization of that meaningfulness into a relational community of speakers, but in fact a kind of relation between the two.

Anthropologists have long known that the so-called "classificatory" categorical or terminological aspect of kinship constitutes a subject in it own right, one that has hardly anything to do with biogenetic substance, human reproduction and its consequences, or even the "relationships" that have become the favorite sport of modern-day subjectivists. This is kinship without substance, and its senseless commitment to classification becomes a (comparativist) end in itself and a worthy counterpart to the substance without kinship of the cultural materialists, the need to rescue the credibility or viability of the "mere symbolism" by ballasting it with Marxian, utilitarian, or other forms of materialist argument.

Both sides of what has become an interminable academic debate (called simply "theory") are part of a much larger historical phenomenon (call it "liberation"). The whole world of high-relief, self-conscious "social relationships" that we have come to take for granted—overdetermined family life, predatory advertising and political propaganda, the rage over social justice and psychological self-liberation, even the "media" and entertainment—belongs to an interference-patterning between the homological and analogical components of language's similarity to itself. Social relations and relational society have not always existed; they are as much an innovation of the present era as the idea of "society" itself was an invention of the age of Hobbes, Locke, and Rousseau. Human self-consciousness had to be "socialized" before it could be "relativized."

Speculative anthropology is ageless, something that antedates recorded history by millennia and rivals espionage and prostitution in the "second oldest profession" category. To become properly professional or institutional (e.g., degree-granting, guildlike, begrudging of its insights to all but the initiated) anthropology had to reflect in its own agendas and organization the basic schismatic of its age. Professional anthropology began as a "double cross" between the analogical and homological aspects of what is basically a "Chaos" problem. Hence the concept of "culture" that embodies the extensive properties of human sentience and formed the basis of American (particularly Boasian) cultural anthropology, took its impetus from E.B. Tylor's Primitive Culture, published in England in 1871. The concept of "kinship" that focused the restrictive basis of human aggregation and fostered the development of British Social Anthropology drew its (distinguished) pedigree from Lewis Henry Morgan's Systems of Consanguinity and Affinity in the Human Family, published in the United States in 1870. Anthropology has not been a whole, or self-similar discipline since.

Nor has society, trapped in what amounts to the same dilemma, obliged it very much. One is reminded once again of Captain Cook, another rationalist trapped by his own initiative in much the same way, and his doomed effort to "… by indirection find directions out." Might not the Canonic Formula, parallactic displacements and all, help us to chart a course through the interference-patterning of language's self-similarities?

We may begin with a simple proportion, between the self-similar autonomy of language, the relationship of language to itself in the shape of its extensive inventory of tropes, and the language of relationship in itself, the virtual homology of speakers relative to that inventory (e.g., "kinship"), that inverts the terms and functions of what could be called the "sentience" or the autonomy of the human species.

$$\frac{\text{relationship of language to itself}}{\text{language of relationship in itself}}$$

What we find is that the inversion of terms and functions in this proportion matches exactly with the conclusions drawn about human social/conceptual differentiation in Lévi-Strauss's study of Totemism to the effect that it is precisely (and counterintuitively) the differences among the (analogously defined) totemic species that correspond to the differences among (homologously determined) human aggregates. Remarkably then, "autonomy of the species" combines analogy and homology in a single, linear statement, but to satisfy Condition #1 of the Canonic Formula, its inclusion must be set in relation to another, self-oppositional (what Mosko calls the "double-twist") counterpart, one that is very specific (to honor the totemistic derivation of the point). What we need is a species (guess which one) that is not only closely unrelated to our own, since it is the differences that count most, but also closely differentiated from its own presence.

What would, in purely comparative terms, amount to a second proportion to counterbalance the first,

$$\frac{\text{autonomy of the species}}{\text{the species of autonomy}}$$

completes the design of the formula by a "double twist" of its tale. For if "autonomy" means a kind of self-reliant containment, the species of autonomy could only be the exogenous (exo-genetic) cat, that encompasses appearance and disappearance sub specie aeternis within its own being.

Reapportioning the two ratios ("cutting the deck") in an overall accordance with the inversion of terms and functions, we get:

$$\frac{\text{Autonomy of the species}}{\text{relationship of language to itself}} :: \frac{\text{language of relationship in itself}}{\text{No cat}}$$

Multiplying the means and the extremes of the expression together, and setting the products equal to one another in order to "prove" this formula, we get that: (the relationship of language to itself), or the "what is shown in language" sentience of the human race TIMES (the language of relationship in itself) or the relational set of "kinship" IS EQUAL TO the autonomy, or metaphorical self-definition of the species (that invented species) TIMES the cat's metaphorical abnegation of itself, or, in other words, ZERO.

Metaphorically speaking, of course. In other words, not only does this prove David M. Schneider's famous contention that there is "no such thing as kinship" in the over-polite rhetoric of mathematics, but, because there is no such thing as "no cat" either (or else what are cats, and even metaphors, all about?) it goes a fair way to explaining the earlier query that was germinal to Schneider's conclusion, that of "what is kinship all about?" For a zero, taken in and of itself, is really nothing, but taken in the full implication of what denumeration really means, it constitutes the sine qua non of a place-value system.

What kinship is all about may be far from obvious without the zero-term through which its possibilities are realized. No-kinship is the bottom line, the only basis upon which the homological constitution of "kin relation" might be raised. Beyond this the implications go far beyond the constraints of academic discourse. Normally social scientists have had recourse to "social justice" or "pathetic ethnicity" arguments as a mere foil ("poor man's whiskey," Malinowski would have called it) to pique the interest of readers already dead on their feet from the sheer inconclusiveness of what we pretend as a science (when the technique backfires, of course, we find ourselves equated with the United Nations, the Girl Scouts, the Red Cross, and perhaps the United States Congress). Under what conditions might the conclusion "there is no such thing as kinship" remark upon a more general truth of its times, by a symptom, as it were, of the venue in which the diagnosis was made?

What I have earlier called "quasification" may be a case in point, a regimen in which distinctive (homological) relational boundaries of any kind are overwhelmed and taken over by a hypertrophy of the "relational" mind-set. The relational basis of human aggregation merges with the sum aggregate basis of relational possibilities, and this makes the distinctions of kinship tautologous to their purpose. Despite the precautions, there is no kinship on the psychiatrist's couch, or in the courtroom, and despite the "family values" products, love-charms, and lingerie on sale there, the only kinship in a shopping mall is imaginary. Drug addiction, family dysfunction, functional illiteracy, and crime in the streets are nothing to the virtual anomie (social chaos) that has scared so much of the world's population into the various fundamentalisms—the sociopolitical (fascist), the intellectual (deconstructionist), the economic (socialist), and the religious (no holds barred). We live in anthropologically challenged times.

Everybody comprehends everything; it is only when we begin to differ (fundamentalists beg to differ) that things get interesting. To comprehend is one thing, but to communicate or act upon that comprehension, understand it, is quite another. The ways in which "kinship" might actually connect with the details of human reproduction or interrelationship (that is "naturalize" or "socialize" itself) add a touch of realism, a kind of "special effects" imagery, to its homological engenderment of human presence. On the counterintuitive or "cat" side of the ledger, sex is the fundamental force in driving people apart. Homologically speaking, all "relationships" are fundamentally alike, quintessentially undifferentiated as an inalienable property of their cohesive intent, and it is only their analogical connections with other things that serve to interfere with this patterning, fractalize its similarity to itself. So many origin-accounts of the greater Australasian region (the third, or fractalized projection of earth's land-mass into the southern hemisphere) say the same thing: that humanity was undifferentiated from itself or its surroundings, until some analogic agency or cookie-cutter device arrived to cut them apart into the shapes and distinctions to which they belong.

But since this describes language or description, the shaping of things in the understanding of them, arguably better than it does relationship, the question of what kinship may be all about transforms itself as though by contagious magic into another one, that of what language itself may be all about.

We may take the cat's cross-cousin, "no-cat" or the missing lynx, as a key in this transition. Whatever their significance, genetic studies show that the cat family has more DNA similarity in common with the human than any other order outside of the primates, and by a considerable margin. But the real connection seems to be more a matter of vocation ("calling"). Nietzsche once observed that cats can lie (with their bodies, intentions, etc.) in ways that human beings might never suspect. But human beings, for their part, can tell truths in ways (politically, economically, scientifically) that put the lie to the cat's deviousness (we might deserve the no-bell cat prize for soothsaying). So the two species are not so much related or even "married" by affinity with one another as they are well matched (they strike fire, throw sparks, generate a negative charge). No cat/no primate. Language and its contents give way to voice in forging the links between them, setting up the ways in which each stands as a sort of (foxy) proxy for the other.

It was the precocious (and still underappreciated) discovery of Jerome Laitman that the human larynx undergoes a progressive lowering into the throat cavity between the ages of about eighteen months and two years. This allows us, uniquely among animal species, to articulate vowel sounds in the throat and also choke to death on food (something that a cat might find hard to swallow, given the ambiguity: "Oh, I thought you said 'ventriloquate BOWEL-sounds'"). There is an analogous but probably dissimilar laryngeal transformation in the cat family, one that turns the purring of smaller felines into the roar of the larger ones (and that made Jaguar famous). It would be difficult to exaggerate the difference this makes, or indeed find its analogy to human hunting prowess (most of the food that humans choke to death on is unchewed muscle-fiber), however, without using another analogy to contain it.

In other words the ratio of contained (pussycat) to containing (big cat) vocation becomes pragmatic (does work, as a vocation should) as a radical figure-ground reversal, more or less as the combustion that drives a piston or reciprocating engine is contained in its mechanism, whereas the mechanism (turbine and compressor) of a jet engine is contained by the explosion it generates. Then, by analogy, a species in which Laitman's transformation is only incipient (as skeletal correspondences indicate for Homo erectus) would exhibit the contained vocality of the smaller feline species, whereas the full-bore or extended throat capacity of Homo sapiens would approximate to the encompassing, jungle-compelling roar of the larger species.

Despite anatomical and perhaps evolutionary differences, the ratio

$$\frac{\text{containment of voice}}{\text{voice of containment}}$$

works for both kinds of creatures, inverting terms and functions. But to round out the analogy, and add the distinction of contrast that marks out its precision, we need another. And since we are not howler monkeys, a trade-off, syllables for decibels ("order is what happens when chaos loses its temper") would have to be incorporated to distinguish our kind from the great Pavarotti of the feline famiglia. So a second-order ratio like

$$\frac{\text{order of Primates}}{\textit{the} \text{ primate of order}}$$

would promote the distinction well enough, but not the discretion. We are not simply the primates of order (as Mark Twain, for instance, maintained that he was not an American, but the American) but actually PRIMA DONNAS OF DISTINCTIVENESS ITSELF, the ones who can digitalize, say "no" and really mean it.

We are the no primates, so that, by default,

$$\frac{\text{Order of Primates}}{\text{containment of voice}} \quad : \quad \frac{\text{voice of containment}}{\text{no primate}}$$

We are the "know" primates, the species that invented species, encompassing the whole world of creatures in a fold in the throat, and so, by the very action of doing so, generalizing ourselves out of the comparison.

Curiosity, they say, killed the cat. What does the curious "anti-logic" of these examples—the brash (and the quite uncalled-for) displays of humor, the counterintuitive dialectic between (that) irony and cause-and-effect order that has been my main point all along—really show? How is the Canonic Formula related, if not through the "structuralism" that Lévi-

Strauss and others have pretended for its convenience, to the self-similarity and scale-retentiveness that are the hallmarks of fractality and its "Chaos" derivations?

Just what was in that wink that Lévi-Strauss exchanged with the cat? In the guise of analogy the canonic formula, too, winks at us from the most obscure places, like the "look" (Blick) that "wanders here and there" in Rilke's poem "The Window-Rose." Notice that the image-structure of the fragment I have isolated here inverts itself perfectly according to the designs of the Formula, and then supplies Condition #1 in a most un-Captain-Cook-like Apotheosis (translated chaotically, but with joy, by the author)

just as if one of the cats would take
the look that wanders here and there
powerfully into its own eye

and if that eye, seemingly at rest,
would open and then slam shut in rage
pulling the image into the red blood

So once the great rose-windows would seize
a heart out of the cathedral's darkness
and pull it straight into God.

ADDENDUM

June 17, 2003

Dear Fred and Mark,

A few words about why the argument of this conclusion might seem problematic to you. All three of us (and, I would argue the other contributors as well) have faced a situation in our own research in which the data, or imagery to be explained (North Mekeo, Barok, and your tree stuff from Muyuw, Fred), appears to be more powerful, compelling, and eloquent to the purpose than the models (or rhetorical imageries) used to explain it, and either threatens to take it (us) over, or at least engages in a kind of moot competition with it. It is as though two different senses of humor were at war, each trying to make a joke of the standpoint of the other ("stacking the deck," "decking the stacks," "the joke that brings the library down.") Borrowing a phrase from the technology of hologram-projection, one could say that the medium of representation (e.g., description, explanation) and that of the represented or modeled are automatically engaged in an interference-patterning with one another, and that patterning of interference acquires an autonomy of its own, one that is scale-invariant — it "keeps its own scale" regardless of whatever we try to do with it. It is a fractal, and a Chaos problem.

What medium of representation shall we use to represent that which represents itself better than we can represent it, that automimetic quality that Richard Dawkins has called the "meme" (The cat family seems to have evolved by "stalking"— imitating its own nonpresence to its prey, so I have used it here as a totem for the automimetic; Hamlet ("To be or not to be") is the automimetic hero of our literature. Wittgenstein ("we picture facts to ourselves") was the philosopher of the meme, Borges's short story Tlön, Uqbar, Orbis Tertius shows what happens when history itself acquires an automimetic autonomy. Language itself acquires a self-similarity when it mimes the things of which it speaks, and because that self-similarity is both tighter than logic and looser than fiction, much of my prose seems to be about itself in a kind of free-associational word-play. It is not. It is about Chaos.

To rescue a sense of proportion in this, as the Canonic Formula does with myth, I have proposed a kind of dialectic between the ironic, or humorous on one hand ("effect and then revealed cause") and that of positional cause-and-effect logic upon which all of our explanatory prowess depends. These two are configured together in the Canonic Formula, so I have used it as a handy tool or arbiter in bringing the essay to a close.

Good luck, and good wishes.

BIBLIOGRAPHY

Abraham, F.D. 1995. "Dynamics, Bifurcation, Self-Organization, Chaos, Mind, Conflict, Insensitivity to Initial Conditions, Time, Unification, Diversity, Free Will, and Social Responsibility." In *Chaos Theory in Psychology and the Life Sciences*, Robin Robertson and Allan Combs (Eds.), Mahwah, NJ: Lawrence Erlbaum Associates, pp. 155-173.

Abrahams, R. 1990. "Chaos and Kachin." *Anthropology Today*, vol. 6, no. 3: 15-17.

Allen, N. 2000. *Categories and Classifications: Maussian Reflections on the Social*. New York: Berghahn.

Allen, P.M. and W.C. Schieve (Eds.) 1982. *Self-Organization and Dissipative Structures*. Austin: University of Texas Press.

Anderson, E.N. 2000. "Maya Knowledge and 'Science Wars.'" *Journal of Ethnobiology*, vol. 20, no. 2: 129-158.

Appadurai, A. 1990. "Disjuncture and Difference in the Global Cultural Economy." *Theory, Culture & Society*, vol. 7: 295-310.

_____, 1996. *Modernity at Large: Cultural Dimensions of Globalization*. Minneapolis: University of Minnesota Press.

Arrigo, B. and C. Williams. 1999. "Chaos Theory and the Social Control Thesis: A Post-Foucauldian Analysis of Mental Illness and Involuntary Civil Confinement." *Social Justice*, vol. 26, no. 1: 177-207.

Arrigo, B. and T. Young. 1998. *Chaos and Crime: From Criminal Justice to Social Justice*. Albany: State University of New York Press.

Asad, T. (Ed.) 1973. *Anthropology and the Colonial Encounter*. New York: Humanities Press.

Axtell, R. and J. Epstein. 1997. *Growing Artificial Societies*. Boston: MIT Press.

Baldwin, B. 1946. "Usituma! Song of Heaven." *Oceania*, vol. 15, no. 3: 201-238.

Barraud, C., D. de Coppet, A. Iteanu, and R. Jamous (Eds.) 1994. *Of Relations and the Dead: Four Societies Viewed from the Angle of Their Exchange*. Oxford: Berg.

Bateson, G. 1958[1936]. *Naven: A Survey of the Problems Suggested by a Composite Picture of the Culture of a New Guinea Tribe Drawn from Three Points of View*. 2nd edn. Stanford: Stanford University Press.

_____, 1972. "Style Grace and Information in Primitive Art." In *Steps to an Ecology of Mind*. New York: Ballantine Books.

Battaglia, D. 1992. "Displacing Culture: A Joke of Significance in Urban Papua New Guinea." *New Literary History*, vol. 23: 1003-1017.

Belshaw, C.S. 1951. "Recent History of Mekeo Society." *Oceania*, vol. 22: 1-12.

Benedict, R.F. 1946. *The Chrysanthemum and the Sword: Patterns of Japanese Culture*. Boston: Houghton Mifflin.

Bergendorff, S. 1996. *Faingu City: A Modern Mekeo Clan in Papua New Guinea*. Lund Monographs in Social Anthropology, Lund, Sweden: Lund University Press.

Best, S. 1995. "Chaos and Entropy: Metaphors in Postmodern Science and Social Theory." *Science as Culture*, vol. 11: 188-226.

Bevan, T.F. 1890. *Toil, Travel and Discovery in British New Guinea*. London: Kegan, Paul Trench Trubner.

Bickler, S.H. 1998. "Eating Stone and Dying: Archaeological Survey on Wood." Dissertation, University of Virginia.

Bickler, S.H. and B. Ivuyo. 2002. "Megaliths of Muyuw (Woodlark Island), Milne Bay Province, PNG." *Archaeology in Oceania*, vol. 37: 22-36.

Blier, S. 1987. *The Anatomy of Architecture: Ontology and Metaphor in Batammaliba Architectural Expression*. Cambridge: Cambridge University Press.

Bloch, M. 1992. "What Goes Without Saying: The Conceptualization of Zafimaniry Society." In *Conceptualizing Society*, A. Kuper (Ed.), London and New York: Routledge, pp. 127-146.

Bourdieu, P. 1973. "The Berber House." In *Rules and Meanings: The Anthropology of Everyday Knowledge, Selected Readings*, M. Douglas (Ed.), Harmondsworth: Penguin, pp. 98-110.

_____, 1977. *Outline of a Theory of Practice*. Cambridge: Cambridge University Press.

_____, 1990. *The Logic of Practice*. Stanford, CA: Stanford University Press.

Braeckman, C. 1994. *Rwanda. Histoire d'un genocide*. Paris: Fayard.

Bricmont, J. 1996. "Science of Chaos or Chaos in Science?" In *The Flight from Science and Reason*, P. Gross, N. Levitt, and M. Lewis (Eds.), *Annals of the New York Academy of Sciences*, vol. 775, pp. 131-175.

Briggs, J. and F. Peat. 1989. *Turbulent Mirror*. New York: Harper and Row.

British New Guinea Annual Report (BNGAR) 1890a. "Despatch in Further Reference to Visit of Inspection to the St. Joseph River District." In *British New Guinea Annual Report for the Year 1889-90*. Brisbane: Queensland Parliamentary Papers, pp. 76-83.

_____, 1890b. "Despatch in Further Reference to Visit of Inspection to the St. Joseph River District." In *British New Guinea Annual Report for the Year 1889-90*. Brisbane: Queensland Parliamentary Papers, pp. 87-91.

_____, 1893. "Report of the Government Agent for the Mekeo District." In *British New Guinea Annual Report for the Year 1891-92*. Brisbane: Queensland Parliamentary Papers, pp. 90-91.

_____, 1894a. "Despatch Report on Visit to Country West of Port Moresby, as Far as Freshwater Bay." In *British New Guinea Annual Report for the Year 1892-93*. Brisbane: Queensland Parliamentary Papers, pp. 15-20.

_____, 1894b. "Despatch Report Visit of Inspection to the Mekeo District." In *British New Guinea Annual Report for the Year 1893-94*. Brisbane: Queensland Parliamentary Papers, pp. 36-38.

_____, 1896. "Despatch Reporting Visit of Inspection to the Mekeo District." In *British New Guinea Annual Report for the Year 1894-95*. Brisbane: Queensland Parliamentary Papers, pp. xv-9.

_____, 1898a. "Central Division." In *British New Guinea Annual Report for the Year 1897-98*. Brisbane: Queensland Parliamentary Papers, pp. xxii-xxiv.

_____, 1898b. "Report of the Resident Magistrate for the Central Division." In *British New Guinea Annual Report for the Year 1896-97*. Brisbane: Queensland Parliamentary Papers, pp. 51-53.

_____, 1898c. "Report of the Resident Magistrate for the Central Division." In *British New Guinea Annual Report for the Year 1897-98*. Brisbane: Queensland Parliamentary Papers, pp. 86-93.

_____, 1898d. "Sanitary." In *British New Guinea Annual Report for the Year 1897-98*. Brisbane: Queensland Parliamentary Papers, pp. xxxiv-xxxvi.

_____, 1899. "Report of the Resident Magistrate for the Central Division." In *British New Guinea Annual Report for the Year 1897-98*. Brisbane: Queensland Parliamentary Papers, pp. 66-71.

_____, 1900. "Report of the Resident Magistrate for the Central Division." In *British New Guinea Annual Report for the Year 1898-99*. Brisbane: Queensland Parliamentary Papers, pp. 68-71.

_____, 1901a. "Medical." In *British New Guinea Annual Report for the Year 1899-1900.* Victoria: Parliament of the Commonwealth of Australia, pp. xxiv-xxv.

_____, 1901b. "Report of the Chief Medical Officer, Port Moresby." In *British New Guinea Annual Report for the Year 1899-1900.* Victoria: Parliament of the Commonwealth of Australia, pp. 111-112.

_____, 1902. "Medical and Sanitary, &c." In *British New Guinea Annual Report for the Year 1st July, 1900, to 30th June, 1901.* Victoria: Parliament of the Commonwealth of Australia, pp. xlvii.

_____, 1904a. "Chief Medical Officer's Report." In *British New Guinea Annual Report for the Year 1902-03.* Victoria: Parliament of the Commonwealth of Australia, pp. 40-42.

_____, 1904b. "Report on Central Division." In *British New Guinea Annual Report for the Year 1902-03.* Victoria: Parliament of the Commonwealth of Australia, pp. 16-18.

_____, 1907. "Assistant Resident Magistrate's Report for the Mekeo District of the Central Division for the Year 1906." In *British New Guinea Annual Report for the Year 1905-06.* Brisbane: Queensland Parliamentary Papers, pp. 16-18.

British New Guinea Colonial Reports (BNGCR) 1898. "Report of Resident Magistrate of Central Division." In *Annual Report for 1896-97 (No. 237).* London: Colonial Reports, pp. 26-27.

_____, 1899a. "Remarks on Climate and Diseases Existing in the Possession." In *Annual Report for 1897-98 (No. 258).* London: Colonial Reports, pp. 58-59.

_____, 1899b. "Report of the Resident Magistrate for the Central Division." In *Annual Report for 1897-98 (No. 258).* London: Colonial Reports, pp. 39-40.

_____, 1900. "Report of the Resident Magistrate of the Central Division." In *Annual Report for 1898-99 (No. 292).* London: Colonial Reports, pp. 19-26.

_____, 1901. "Medical." In *Annual Report for 1899-1900 (No. 336).* London: Colonial Reports, pp. 40-41.

Brown, T. 1997. "Nonlinear Politics." In *Chaos Theory in the Social Sciences: Foundations and Applications,* D. Kiel and E. Elliot (Eds.), Ann Arbor: University of Michigan Press, pp. 119-137.

Burridge, K. 1969. *New Heaven, New Earth: A Study of Millenarian Activities.* Oxford: Blackwell.

Butz, M. 1997. *Chaos and Complexity: Implications for Psychological Theory and Practice.* Bristol, PA: Taylor and Francis.

Byrne, D. 1998. *Complexity Theory and the Social Sciences: An Introduction.* London: Routledge.

Carnap, R. 1958. *Introduction to Symbolic Logic and its Applications.* Translated by W.H. Meyer and J. Wilkinson. New York: Dover.

Carneiro da Cunha, M. 1978. *Os Mortos e Os Otros.* São Paulo: Editora Hucitec.

Chalmers, J. 1887. *Pioneering in New Guinea.* 2nd edn, London: Religious Tract Society.

Cheater, A. 1995. "Globalisation and the New Technologies of Knowing: Anthropological Calculus or Chaos?" In *Shifting Contexts: Transformations in Anthropological Knowledge,* M. Strathern (Ed.), London: Routledge, pp. 117-130.

Chrétien, J-P. 1995. *Rwanda: Les médias du genocide.* Paris: Karthala.

_____, 1997. *Le Defi de l'Ethnisme: Rwandan et Burundi 1990 -1996.* Paris: Karthala.

Clifford, J. 1988. *The Predicament of Culture: Twentieth Century Ethnography, Literature, and Art.* Cambridge, MA: Harvard University Press.

Clifford, J. and G. Marcus (Eds.) 1986. *Writing Culture: The Poetics and Politics of Ethnography.* Berkeley/Los Angeles: University of California Press.

Cohen, J. and I. Stewart. 1994. *The Collapse of Chaos: Discovering Simplicity in a Complex World.* New York: Viking.

Comaroff, J. and J. 1992. *Ethnography and the Historical Imagination.* Boulder, CO: Westview Press.

Contini-Morava, E. 2003. *Noun Classification in Swahili*. [online]
http://jefferson.village.virginia.edu/swahili/swahili.html, University of Virginia,
accessed December 2003.

Conway, J.H. and D.A. Smith. 2003. *On Quaternions and Octonions*. Natick, MA: A K Peters,
Ltd.

Cornevin, R. 1962. *Histoire du Togo*. Paris: Berger-Levrault.

_____, 1981. *La République Populaire du Benin: Des Origines Dahoméennes à Nos Jours*. Paris:
Maisonneuve & Larose.

Côté, A. 2001. "The Set of Canonical Transformations Implied in the Canonical Formula for
the Analysis of Myth." In *The Double Twist: From Ethnography to Morphodynamics*, P.
Miranda (Ed.), Toronto: University of Toronto Press, pp. 199-221.

Coveney, P. and R. Highfield. 1995. *Frontiers of Chaos: The Search for Order in a Chaotic World*.
London: Faber and Faber.

Crosby, A.W. 1976. "Virgin Soil Epidemics as a Factor in Aboriginal Depopulation in
America." *The William and Mary Quarterly*, vol. 33: 289-299.

D'Albertis, L.M. 1881. *New Guinea: What I Did and What I Saw*. 2nd edn, Boston: Houghton.

Damon, F.H. 1979. "Woodlark Island Megalithic Structures and Trenches: Towards an
Interpretation." *Archaeology & Physical Anthropology in Oceania*, vol. 14: 195-226.

_____, 1980a. "The Kula and Generalised Exchange: Considering Some Unconsidered
Aspects of the Elementary Structures of Kinship." *Man* (n.s), vol. 15, no. 2: 267-293.

_____, 1980b. "The Problem of the Kula on Woodlark Island; Expansion, Accumulation,
and Overproduction." *Ethnos*, vol. 45, no. 2: 176-201.

_____, 1982. "Calendars and Calendrical Rites on the Northern Side of the Kula Ring."
Oceania, vol. 52, no. 3: 221-239.

_____, 1983a. "Muyuw Kinship and the Metamorphosis of Gender Labour." *Man* (n.s), vol.
18, no. 2: 305-326.

_____, 1983b. "What Moves the Kula: Opening and Closing Gifts on Woodlark Island." In
The Kula: New Perspectives on Massim Exchange, J.W. Leach and E.R. Leach (Eds.),
DeKalb: Cambridge University Press, pp. 309-342.

_____, 1989. "The Muyuw Lo'un and the End of Marriage." In *Death Rituals and Life in the
Societies of the Kula*, F.H. Damon and R. Wagner (Eds.), DeKalb: Northern Illinois
University Press, pp. 73-94.

_____, 1990. *From Muyuw to the Trobriands: Transformations Along the Northern Side of the Kula
Ring*. Tucson: University of Arizona Press.

_____, 1993. "(Notes On The) Representation and Experience in Western and Kula
Exchange Spheres, or Billy." *Research in Economic Anthropology*, vol. 14: 235-254.

_____, 1997. "Cutting the Wood of Woodlark: Retrospects and Prospects for Logging on
Muyuw, Milne Bay Province, Papua New Guinea." In *The Political Economy of Forest
Management in Papua New Guinea*, C. Filer (Ed.), NRI Monograph 32, Hong Kong:
National Research Institute.

_____, 1998. "Selective Anthropomorphization: Trees in the Northeast Kula Ring." *Social
Analysis*, vol. 42, no. 3: 67-69.

_____, 2002. "Kula Valuables, the Problem of Value and the Production of Names."
L'Homme, vol. 162, April-June: 107-136.

D'Andrade, R. 1995. "Moral Models in Anthropology. Commentary in 'Objectivity and
Militancy: A Debate.'" *Current Anthropology*, vol. 36, no. 3: 339-408.

De Barros, P. 1985. "The Bassar: Large Scale Iron Producers of the West African Savanna."
Dissertation, University of California Los Angeles.

de Coppet, D. 1985. "The Life-giving Death." In *Mortality and Immortality: The Anthropology
and Archaeology of Death*, S. Humphrey and H. King (Eds.), New York: Academic Press,
pp. 175-204.

de Heusch, L. 1966. *Le Rwanda et la civilisation interlacustre*. Brussels: Université Libre de
Bruxelles.

_____, 1985. *Sacrifice in Africa*. Manchester: Manchester University Press.

Denoon, D., P. Mein-Smith, and M. Wyndham. 2000. "Depopulation." In *A History of Australia, New Zealand and the Pacific*, D. Denoon, P. Mein-Smith, and M. Wyndham (Eds.), Oxford: Blackwell, pp. 72-79.

Descola, P. 1997. *The Spears of Twilight: Life and Death in the Amazon Jungle*. London: Flamingo, HarperCollins.

d'Hertefelt, M. 1971. *Les clans du Rwanda ancient*. Serie in 8, Sciences Humaines, Tervuren, Belgium: Musee Royal de l'Afrique Centrale.

d'Hertefelt, M. and A. Coupez. 1964. *La royauté sacrée de l'ancien Rwanda*. Série in-8o, Sciences Humaines, no. 52, Tervuren: Musée. Royal de l'Afrique Centrale, Annales.

Douglas, M. 1966. *Purity and Danger: An Analysis of Concepts of Pollution and Taboo*. London: Routledge.

_____, 1970. *Natural Symbols: Explorations in Cosmology*. New York: Random House.

Downey, G. and J. Rogers. 1995. "On the Politics of Theorizing in a Postmodern Academy." *American Anthropologist*, vol. 97, no. 2: 269-281.

Drucker, P.F. 1989. *The New Realities*. Oxford: Heinemann.

Dumont, L. 1980. *Homo Hierarchicus*. 2nd edn. Chicago: University of Chicago Press.

_____, 1985. "On Value, Modern and Nonmodern." In *Essays on Individualism: Modern Ideology in Anthropological Perspective*. Chicago: The University of Chicago Press.

Dupeyrat, A. 1935. *Papouasie: Histoire de la Mission (1885-1935)*. Paris: Dillen.

Durkheim, E. 1893. *The Division of Labor in Society*. New York: Macmillan.

_____, 1915. *Elementary Forms of the Religious Life*. London: Allen and Unwin.

Durkheim, E. and M. Mauss. 1963. *Primitive Classification*. Translated by R. Needham. London: Cohen & West.

Egidi, V. n.d. "Mekeo Genealogies." Unpublished mss, Sacred Heart Mission.

Evans-Pritchard, E. 1940. *The Nuer: A Description of the Modes of Livelihood and Political Institutions of a Nilotic People*. Oxford: University of Oxford Press.

_____, 1962. *Social Anthropology and Other Essays*. New York: The Free Press.

Eve, R., S. Horsfall, and M. Lee. (Eds.) 1997. *Chaos, Complexity and Sociology: Myths, Models and Theories*. Thousand Oaks, CA: Sage.

Fabian, J. 1983. *Time and the Other: How Anthropology Makes its Object*. New York: Columbia University Press.

Farella, J.R. 1984. *The Main Stalk: A Synthesis of Navajo Philosophy*. Tucson: The University of Arizona Press.

Fausto, C. 2000. "Of Enemies and Pets: Warfare and Shamanism in Amazonia." *American Ethnologist*, vol. 26, no. 4: 933-956.

Firth, R. 1970. "Sibling Terms in Polynesia." *The Journal of the Polynesian Society*, vol. 79: 272-287.

Fiske, A. 1991. *Structures of Social Life: The Four Elementary Forms of Human Relations*. New York: Free Press.

Fortes, M. 1936. "Ritual Festivals and Social Cohesion in the Hinterland of the Gold Coast." *American Anthropologist*, vol. 38: 590-604.

_____, 1945. *The Dynamics of Clanship among the Tallensi*. Oxford: Oxford University Press.

_____, 1949. *The Web of Kinship Among the Tallensi*. Oxford: Oxford University Press.

_____, 1970. "Time and Social Structure: An Ashanti Case Study." In *Time and Social Structure and Other Essays*, M. Fortes (Ed.), London: Althone, pp. 1-32.

Fortes, M. and E. Evans-Pritchard (Eds.) 1940. *African Political Systems*. Oxford: Oxford University Press.

Foucault, M. 1975. *Discipline and Punish*. New York: Vintage Books.

Fox, J.J. 1973. "On Bad Death and the Left Hand: A Study of Rotinese Symbolic Inversions." In *Right and Left: Essays on Dual Symbolic Classification*, R. Needham (Ed.), Chicago: University of Chicago Press, pp. 342-368.

_____, 1975. "On Binary Categories and Primary Symbols," In *The Interpretation of Ritual*, R. Willis (Ed.), London: Malaby, pp. 99-132.

_____, 1989. "Category and Complement: Binary Ideologies and the Organization of Dualism in Eastern Indonesia." In *The Attraction of Opposites: Thought and Society in a Dualistic Mode*, D. Maybury-Lewis and U. Almangor (Eds.), Ann Arbor: University of Michigan Press, pp. 33-56.

_____, 1993. "Comparative Perspectives on Austronesian Houses: An Introductory Essay." In *Inside Austronesian Houses*, J.J. Fox (Ed.), Canberra: Department of Anthropology in association with the Comparative Austronesian Project, Research School of Pacific Studies, Australian National University, pp. 1-29.

Friedman, J. 1987. "Beyond Otherness or: The Spectacularization of Anthropology." *Telos*, vol. 71: 161-170.

Friedrich, P. 1988. "'Eeerie Chaos and Eeerier Order,' Review of *Chaos: Making a New Science* by James Gleick." *The Journal of Anthropological Research*, vol. 44: 435-444.

Fujimura, J. 1998. "Authorizing Knowledge in Science and Anthropology." *American Anthropologist*, vol. 100, no. 2: 347-360.

Geertz, C. 1980a. "Blurred Genres." *American Scholar*, vol. 49: 165-179.

_____, 1980b. *Negara*. Princeton, NJ: Princeton University Press.

Gell, A. 1992. *The Anthropology of Time: Cultural Constructions of Temporal Maps and Images*. New York: Berg.

_____, 1993. *Wrapping in Images: Tattooing in Polynesia*. Oxford: Oxford University Press.

_____, 1999. "Strathernograms or the Semiotics of Mixed Metaphors." In *The Art of Anthropology: Essays and Diagrams*, E. Hirsch (Ed.), London: The Athlone Press, pp. 29-75.

Giddens, A. 1990. *The Consequences of Modernity*. Stanford: Stanford University Press.

Gleick, J. 1987. *Chaos: Making a New Science*. New York: Penguin.

_____, 1988. *Chaos: Making a New Science*. Reprint Edition. New York: Penguin.

Gluckman, M. (Ed.) 1964. *Closed Systems and Open Minds: The Limits of Naivety in Social Anthropology*. Edinburgh: Oliver and Boyd.

Godelier, M. 1975. "Modes of Production, Kinship, and Demographic Structures." In *Marxist Analyses and Social Anthropology*, M. Bloch (Ed.), ASA Studies 4, New York: Wiley & Sons, pp. 3-28.

_____, 1991. "An Unfinished Attempt at Reconstructing the Social Processes which May Have Provided the Transformation of Great-man Societies into Big-man Societies." In *Big Men and Great Men: Personifications of Power in Melanesia*, M. Godelier and M. Strathern (Eds.), Cambridge: Cambridge University Press, pp. 275-304.

_____, 2000. "Is Social Anthropology Still Worth the Trouble? A Response to Some Echoes from America." *Ethnos*, vol. 65, no. 3: 301-316.

Goerner, S. 1994. *Chaos and the Evolving Ecological University*. Langhorne, PA: Gordon and Breach Science Publishers.

Goertzel, B. 1995a. "Belief Systems as Attractors." In *Chaos Theory in Psychology and the Life Sciences*, Robin Robertson and Allan Combs (Eds.), Mahwah, NJ: Lawrence Erlbaum Associates, pp. 123-134.

_____, 1995b. "A Cognitive Law of Motion." In *Chaos Theory in Psychology and the Life Sciences*, Robin Robertson and Allan Combs (Eds.), Mahwah, NJ: Lawrence Erlbaum Associates, pp. 135-154.

Goldman, I. 1957. "Status Rivalry and Cultural Evolution in Polynesia." *American Anthropologist*, vol. 57: 680-697.

_____, 1970. *Ancient Polynesian Society*. Chicago: University of Chicago Press.

Goody, J. 1956. *The Social Organisation of the Lowiili*. London: Her Majesty's Stationary Office.

_____, 1978. "Population and Polity in the Voltaic Region." In *The Evolution of Social Systems*, J. Friedman and M.J. Rowlands (Eds.), Pittsburgh: University of Pittsburgh Press.

Gregory, C. 1982. *Gifts and Commodities*. London: Academic Press.

_____, 2001. "Ramistic Commonplaces, Lévi-Straussian Mythlogic and Binary Logic." In *The Double Twist: From Ethnography to Morphodynamics*, P. Maranda (Ed.), Toronto: University of Toronto Press, pp. 177-195.

_____, n.d. *Decoding the Canonic Formula*. Preprint.

Griaule, M. 1965. *Conversations with Ogotemmeli*. Oxford: Oxford University Press.

Griaule, M. and G. Dieterlen. 1965. *Le Renard Pale*. Paris: Institut de Ethnologie.

Gross, P. and N. Levitt. 1994. *Higher Superstition: The Academic Left and Its Quarrels with Science*. Baltimore: John Hopkins University Press.

Guastello, S.J., T. Hyde, and M. Odak. 1998. "Symbolic Dynamics of Verbal Exchange in a Creative Problem Solving Group." *Nonlinear Dynamics, Psychology and Life Sciences*, vol. 2, no. 1: 35-58.

Guille-Escuret, G. 1999. "Need Anthropology Resign?" *Anthropology Today*, vol. 15, no. 5: 1-3.

Guis, J. 1936. *La vie des Papous: cote sud-est de la Nouvelle-Guinee (Roro et Mekeo)*. Paris: Dillen.

Haddon, A.C. 1901. *Headhunters, Black, White, Brown*. London: Methuen.

Hage, P. and F. Harary. 1983. *Structural Models in Anthropology*. Cambridge Studies in Social Anthropology 46. New York: Cambridge University Press.

Hamel, J. 1999. "Le dilemme de la science en anthropologie et en sociologie: heur et malheur de la pensée postmoderne [The Dilemma of Science in Anthropology and Sociology: Pros and Cons of Postmodern Thought]." *Social Science Information*, vol. 38, no. 1: 5-27.

Hardt, M. and A. Negri. 2000. *Empire*. Cambridge: Harvard University Press.

Harris, M. 1997. "Comment on T. O'Meara 'Causation and the Struggle for a Science of Culture,' CA Forum on Theory in Anthropology." *Current Anthropology*, vol. 38, no. 3: 410-418.

Hart, R. 1996. "The Flight from Reason: Higher Superstition and the Refutation of Science Studies." In *Science Wars*, A. Ross (Ed.), Durham: Duke University Press, pp. 259-292.

Harvey, D. and M. Reed. 1997. "Social Science and the Study of Complex Systems." In *Chaos Theory in the Social Sciences: Foundations and Applications*, D. Kiel and E. Elliot (Eds.), Ann Arbor: University of Michigan Press, pp. 295-323.

Hau'ofa, E. 1971. "Mekeo Chieftainship." *Journal of the Polynesian Society*, vol. 80: 152-169.

_____, 1981. *Mekeo: Inequality and Ambivalence in a Village Society*. Canberra: Australian National University Press.

Hayles, N.K. 1990. *Chaos Bound: Orderly Disorder in Contemporary Literature and Science*. Ithaca, NY: Cornell University Press.

_____, (Ed.) 1991a. *Chaos and Order: Complex Dynamics in Literature and Science*. Chicago: University of Chicago Press.

_____, 1991b. "Chaos: More than Metaphor." In *Chaos and Order: Complex Dynamics in Literature and Science*, N.K. Hayles (Ed.), Chicago: University of Chicago Press, pp. 37-99.

Hertz, R. 1960[1909]. *Death and the Right Hand*. New York: Free Press.

Hogbin, I. 1930. "The Problem of Depopulation in Melanesia as Applied to Ontong Java (Solomon Islands)." *Journal of the Polynesian Society*, vol. 29: 43-66.

Hubert, H. and M. Mauss. 1964. *Sacrifice: Its Nature and Function*. Chicago: University of Chicago Press.

Hughes, G.E. and M.J. Cresswell. 1977. *An Introduction to Modal Logic*. London: Methuen.

Hugh-Jones, S. 2001. "The Gender of Some Amazonian Gifts: An Experiment with an Experiment." In *Gender in Amazonia and Melanesia: An Exploration of the Comparative Method*, T. Gregor and D. Tuzin (Eds.), Berkeley: University of California Press, pp. 245-278.

Humphrey, C. and J. Laidlaw. 1994. *The Archetypal Actions of Ritual: A Theory of Ritual Illustrated by the Jain Rite of Worship*. Oxford: Clarendon Press.

Iteanu, A. 1983. *La ronde des echanges. De la circulation aux valeurs chez le Orokaiva*. Cambridge: Cambridge University Press.

_____, 1985. "Levels and Convertibility." In *Contexts and Levels: Anthropological Essays on Hierarchy*. JASO Occasional Papers No. 4, R.H. Barnes, D. de Coppet, and R.J. Parkin (Eds.), Oxford: The Anthropological Society, pp. 91-102.

Izard, M. 1985. *Gens du Pouvoir, Gens de la Terre: Les Institutions Politiques de l'Ancien Royaume du Yatenga*. Cambridge: Cambridge University Press.

Jacob, I. 1984. *Dictionnaire Rwandais-Français, Extrait du dictionnaire de l'Institut National de Recherche Scientifique*. Kigali.

Jamous, R. 1981. *Honneur et Baraka, les structures sociales traditionnelles das le Rif*. Cambridge: Cambridge University Press.

Jardine, N. and M. Frasca-Spada. 1997. "Splendours and Miseries of the Science Wars." *Studies in the History and Philosophy of Science*, vol. 28, no. 2: 219-236.

Jones, A.A. 1998. *Towards a Lexicogrammar of Mekeo: An Austronesian Language of West Central Papua. Pacific Linguistics*. Series C, 138., Canberra: Department of Linguistics, Research School of Pacific and Asian Studies Australian National University.

Kagame, A. 1947. 'Le code ésotérique de la dynastie du Rwanda." *Zaire*, vol. I, no. 4: 364-386.

Kantorowicz, E.H. 1957. *The King's Two Bodies: A Study in Mediaeval Political Theology*. Princeton: Princeton University Press.

Kapferer, B. 1988. *Legends of People, Myths of State*. Washington, DC: Smithsonian Institution Press.

Kauffman, S. 1993. *The Origins of Order: Self-Organization and Selection in Evolution*. New York: Oxford University Press.

Keesing, R.M. 1975. *Kin Groups and Social Structure*. Fort Worth: Holt Rinehart and Winston.

Kiel, D. and E. Elliot (Eds.) 1997. *Chaos Theory in the Social Sciences: Foundations and Applications*. Ann Arbor: University of Michigan Press.

Koertge, N. (Ed.) 1998. *A House Built on Sand: Exposing Postmodernist Myths About Science*. New York: Oxford University Press.

Kuhn, T. 1970. *The Structure of Scientific Revolutions*. 2nd edn, Chicago: University of Chicago Press.

Kuper, A. 1992. *Conceptualizing Society*. London: Routledge.

_____, 1994. "Culture, Identity, and the Project of a Cosmopolitan Anthropology." *Man* (n.s), vol. 29, no. 3: 537-554.

Kuznar, L. 1997. *Reclaiming a Scientific Anthropology*. Walnut Creek, CA: Altamira.

La Medaille-Nyiramacibiri. *Rwandan popular political magazine*.

Labinger, J. 1997. "The Science Wars and the Future of the American Academic Profession." *Daedalus*, vol. 126, no. 4: 201-220.

Lambek, J. 1958. "The Mathematics of Sentence Structure." *American Mathematical Monthly*, vol. 65: 154-170.

Landtman, G. 1927. *The Kiwai Papuans of British New Guinea: A Nature-born Instance of Rousseau's Ideal Community*. London: Macmillan.

Lansing, J.S. and J.N. Kremer. 1993. "Emergent Properties of Balinese Water Temple Networks: Coadaptation on a Rugged Fitness Landscape." *American Anthropologist*, vol. 95, no. 1: 97-114.

Lansing, J.S., J.N. Kremer, and B.B. Smuts. 1998. "System-dependent Selection, Ecological Feedback and the Emergence of Functional Structure in Ecosystems." *Journal of Theoretical Biology*, vol. 192: 377-391.

Law, R. 1989. "Slave-raiders and Middlemen, Monopolists and Free-traders: The Supply of Slaves for the Atlantic Trade in Dahomey c. 1715-1850." *Journal of African History and Anthropology*, vol. 30: 45-68.

Lawton, R. 1980. "The Kiriwinan Classifiers." M.A. Thesis, School of General Studies, Australian National University.

Leach, E. 1954. *Political Systems of Highland Burma: A Study of Kachin Social Structure*. London: London School of Economics and Political Science.

_____, 1961a. *Rethinking Anthropology*. LSE Monographs on Social Anthropology, London: Althone.

_____, 1961b. "Two Essays Concerning the Symbolic Representation of Time." In *Rethinking Anthropology*. LSE Monographs on Social Anthropology, London: Althone, pp. 124-136.

_____, 1970. *Claude Levi-Strauss*. New York: Viking Press.

_____, 1976. *Culture and Communication. The Logic by Which Symbols Are Connected.* Cambridge: Cambridge University Press.

Leach, J.W. and E. Leach (Eds.) 1983. *The Kula: New Perspectives on Massim Exchange.* Cambridge: Cambridge University Press.

LeGuin, U. 1969. *The Left Hand of Darkness.* New York: Ace Books.

Levine, G. 1996. "What Is Science Studied for and Who Cares?" In *Science Wars*, A. Ross (Ed.), Durham: Duke University Press, pp. 123-138.

Lévi-Strauss, C. 1955. "The Structural Study of Myth." *Journal of American Folklore*, vol. 68: 428-444.

_____, 1958. *Anthropogie structurale.* Paris: Plon.

_____, 1962. *La pensée sauvage.* Paris: Plon.

_____, 1963a. "Do Dual Organizations Exist?" In *Structural Anthropology*, translated by C. Jacobson, vol. 1, New York: Basic Books, pp. 128-160.

_____, 1963b. *Structural Anthropology.* Translated by C.J. and B.G. Schoepf. New York: Basic Books.

_____, 1963c. "The Structural Study of Myth." In *Structural Anthropology*, translated by C. Jacobson, vol. 1, New York: Basic Books, pp. 202-228.

_____, 1966. *The Savage Mind.* Chicago: University of Chicago Press.

_____, 1969. *The Raw and the Cooked.* Translated by J. and D. Weightman, Chicago: The University of Chicago Press.

_____, 1969[1949]. *The Elementary Structures of Kinship.* Translated by J.H. Bell, J.R. von Sturmer, and R. Needham (Ed.), Boston: Beacon Press.

_____, 1973. *From Honey to Ashes.* Mythologiques No. 2. Translated by J. and D. Weightman. Chicago: University of Chicago Press.

_____, 1976. *Structural Anthropology, vol. II.* New York: Basic Books.

_____, 1978. *The Origin of Table Manners.* Mythologiques No. 3. Translated by J. and D. Weightman, London: Cape.

_____, 1981. *The Naked Man.* Mythologiques No. 4. Translated by J. and D. Weightman, New York: Harper & Row.

_____, 1988. *The Jealous Potter.* Translated by B. Chorier, Chicago: University of Chicago Press.

_____, 1995. *The Story of Lynx.* Chicago: University of Chicago Press.

Levtzion, N. 1968. *Muslims and Chiefs in West Africa: A Study of Islam in the Middle Volta Basin in the Precolonial Period.* Oxford: Oxford University Press.

_____, 1978. "Trade and Politics Among Dyula and Mossi-Dagomba." In *Cambridge History of Africa*, R. Gray (Ed.), vol. 4, Cambridge: Cambridge University Press.

Lewin, R. 1993. *Complexity: Life at the Edge of Chaos.* London: J.M. Dent.

Linden, I. 1977. *Church and Revolution in Rwanda.* New York: Manchester University Press.

Lombard, J. 1965. *Structures de Type 'Feodal' en Afrique Noire: Etude des Dynamismes Internes et des Relations Sociales chez les Bariba du Dahomey.* Paris: Mouton.

Lorenz, E.N. 1963. "Deterministic Nonperiodic Flow." *Journal of the Atmospheric Sciences*, vol. 20: 130-144.

_____, 1993. *The Essence of Chaos.* Seattle: University of Washington Press.

Louis, R. 1963. *Ruanda-Urundi, 1884 -1919.* Oxford: Clarendon Press.

Lyons, J. 1977. *Semantics.* Cambridge; New York: Cambridge University Press.

Lyotard, J. 1984. *The Postmodern Condition.* Minneapolis: University of Minnesota Press.

Macintyre, M. 1989. "The Triumph of the Susu: Mortuary Exchanges on Tubetube." In *Death Rituals and Life in the Societies of the Kula Ring*, F.H. Damon and R. Wagner (Eds.), DeKalb: Northern Illinois University Press, pp. 133-152.

Mainzer, K. 1994. *Thinking in Complexity: The Complex Dynamics of Matter, Mind, and Mankind.* Berlin and New York: Springer-Verlag.

Mair, L.P. 1970. *Australia in New Guinea.* 2nd edn, Carlton, Vic: M.U.P.

Makkai, M. and G. Reyes. 1977. *First Order Categorical Logic: Model-theoretical Methods in the Theory of Topoi and Related Categories.* Lecture Notes in Mathematics. Berlin: Springer.

Malinowski, B. 1966 [1935]. *Coral Gardens and Their Magic.* London: Allen & Unwin.

Mandelbrot, B. 1982. *The Fractal Geometry of Nature.* San Francisco: W.H. Freeman.

Manning, P. 1979. "The Slave Trade in the Bight of Benin, 1640-1890." In *The Uncommon Market: Essays in the Economic History of the Atlantic Slave Trade,* H. Gemery and J. Hogendorn (Eds.), New York: Academic Press.

_____, 1990. *Slavery and African Life: Occidental, Oriental, and African Slave Trades.* Cambridge: Cambridge University Press.

Maquet, J. 1954. *Le systéme des relations sociales dans le Ruanda ancien.* Tervuren, Belgium: Musée Royal de l'Afrique Centrale.

Maranda, E. 1971. "A Tree Grows: Transformations of a Riddle Metaphor." In *Structural Models in Folklore and Transformational Essays,* P. and E. Maranda (Eds.), The Hague: Mouton.

Maranda, P. (Ed.) 2001. *The Double Twist: From Ethnography to Morphodynamics.* Toronto: University of Toronto Press.

Maranda, P. and E. 1971. *Structural Models in Folklore and Transformational Essays.* The Hague: Mouton.

Marcus, G. and M. Fischer. 1986. *Anthropology as Cultural Critique: An Experimental Moment in the Human Sciences.* Chicago: University of Chicago Press.

Marshall, M. 1983. "Introduction." In *Siblingship in Oceania: Studies in the Meaning of Kin Relations,* M. Marshall (Ed.), Lanham, MD: University Presses of America, pp. 1-16.

Martin, E. 1987. *The Woman in the Body: A Cultural Analysis of Reproduction.* Boston: Beacon Press.

Martin, G. 2002. "Readings of the Rwandan Genocide." *African Studies Review,* vol. 45, no. 3: 17-30.

Marx, K. 1976. *Capital: a Critique of Political Economy, vol. 1.* New York: Vintage Books Edition.

Mauss, M. 1936. "Les Techniques du corps." *Journal de la Psychologie,* vol. 32: 3-4.

_____, 1967[1925]. *The Gift.* New York: Norton.

_____, 1979[1906]. *Seasonal Variations of the Eskimo: A Study in Social Morphology.* Translated by J.J. Fox. London: Routledge & Kegan Paul.

Maybury-Lewis, D. 1979. *Dialectical Societies: The Gê and the Bororo of Central Brazil.* Massachusetts: Harvard University Press.

McArthur, N. 1967. *Island Populations of the Pacific.* Canberra: Australian National University Press.

McArthur, N. and J.F. Yaxley. 1968. *Condominium of the New Hebrides: A Report on the First Census of the Population, 1967.* Sydney: Government Printer.

McClure, B. 1998. *Putting a New Spin on Groups: The Science of Chaos.* Mahwah, NJ: Erlbaum.

Merry, U. 1995. *Coping with Uncertainty: Insights from the New Sciences of Chaos, Self-organization, and Complexity.* Westport, CT: Praeger.

Milovanovic, D. 1997. *Chaos, Criminology, and Social Justice: The New Orderly (Dis)Order.* Westport, CT: Praeger.

Monckton, C.A.W. 1921. *Taming New Guinea: Some Experiences of a New Guinea Resident Magistrate.* New York: John Lane.

Monsell-Davis, M.D. 1981. "Nabuapaka: Social Change in a Roro Community." Ph.D. Thesis, Department of Anthropology, Macquarie University.

Montroll, E.W. 1987. "On the Dynamics and Evolution of Some Sociotechnical Systems." *Bulletin of the American Mathematical Society,* vol. 16: 1-46.

Morava, J. 2003. *On the Canonical Formula of C. Lévi-Strauss.* [online] http://arxiv.org/pdf/math.CT/0306174, Cornell University, accessed December 2003.

Morgan, L.H. 1870. *Systems of Consanguinity and Affinity of the Human Family.* Washington: Smithsonian Institution.

Mosko, M. 1973. "Leadership and Social Integration: A Prospectus for Ethnographic Research among the Roro." Unpublished mss. Department of Anthropology, University of Minnesota.

_____, 1983. "Conception, De-conception and Social Structure in Bush Mekeo Culture." In *Concepts of Conception: Procreation Ideologies in Papua New Guinea*, D. Jorgensen (Ed.), vol. 14, *Mankind* (special issue), pp. 24-32.

_____, 1985. *Quadripartite Structures: Categories, Relations and Homologies in Bush Mekeo Culture*. Cambridge: Cambridge University Press.

_____, 1989. "The Development Cycle Among Public Groups." *Man* (n.s), vol. 24, no. 3: 470-484.

_____, 1991a. "The Canonic Formula of Myth and Non-myth." *American Ethnologist*, vol. 18, no. 1: 126-151.

_____, 1991b. "Great Men and Total Systems: Hereditary Authority and Social Reproduction among the North Mekeo." In *Big Men and Great Men: Personifications of Power in Melanesia*, M. Godelier and M. Strathern (Eds.), Cambridge: Cambridge University Press, pp. 97-114.

_____, 1991c. "Yali Revisited: The Interplay of Messages and Missions in Melanesian Structural History." *Journal of the Polynesian Society*, vol. 100: 269-298.

_____, 1992. "Motherless Sons: 'Divine Heroes' and 'Partible Persons' in Melanesia and Polynesia." *Man* (n.s), vol. 27, no. 4: 697-717.

_____, 1994a. "Junior Chiefs and Senior Sorcerers: The Contradictions and Inversions of Mekeo Genealogical Seniority." In *Transformations of Hierarchy: Structure, History and Horizon in the Austronesian World*, M. Jolly and M. Mosko (Eds.), *History and Anthropology 7* (special edition), Cambridge: Harwood, pp. 195-222.

_____, 1994b. "Transformations of Dumont: The Hierarchical, the Sacred and the Profane." In *Transformations of Hierarchy: Structure, History and Horizon in the Austronesian World*, M. Jolly and M. Mosko (Eds.), *History and Anthropology 7* (special edition), Cambridge: Harwood, pp. 19-86.

_____, 1995. "Rethinking Trobriand Chieftainship." *Journal of the Royal Anthropological Institute* (n.s.), vol. 1, no. 4: 763-785.

_____, 1997a. "Cultural Constructs Versus Psychoanalytic Conjectures." *American Ethnologist*, vol. 24, no. 4: 934-939.

_____, 1997b. "Trobriand Chiefs and Fathers." *Journal of the Royal Anthropological Institute* (n.s.), vol. 3, no. 1: 154-159.

_____, 1999. "Magical Money: Commoditization and the Linkage of *maketsi* ("market") and *kangakanga* ("custom") in Contemporary North Mekeo." In *Money and Modernity: State and Local Currencies in Melanesia*, D. Akins and J. Robbins (Eds.), Pittsburgh: University of Pittsburgh Press.

_____, 2000. "Inalienable Ethnography: Keeping-while-giving and the Trobriand Case." *Journal of the Royal Anthropological Institute* (n.s), vol. 6, no. 3: 377-396.

_____, 2001a. "Self-evident Chiefs." Paper presented at *Property, Transactions and Creativity* conference, Cambridge.

_____, 2001b. "Syncretic Persons: Sociality, Agency and Personhood in Recent Charismatic Ritual Practices among North Mekeo (PNG)." In *Beyond Syncretism: Indigenous Expressions of World Religions*, J. Gordon and F. Magowan (Eds.), *The Australian Journal of Anthropology* (special issue), vol. 12, pp. 259-274.

_____, 2002a. "Melanesian 'Mod': Body Decoration, Love magic, and Western Clothing among North Mekeo (PNG)." Paper presented at colloquium, *Body Art and Modernity*, Pitt-Rivers Museum, Oxford.

_____, 2002b. "Totem and Transaction: The Objectification of 'Tradition' among North Mekeo." *Oceania*, vol. 73, no. 2: 89-109.

_____, n.d. "Black Powder, White magic: European Armaments and Sorcery in early Mekeo-Roro Encounters." In M. Jolly, D. Tryon and S. Tcherkezoff (Eds.), mss in preparation.

Munn, N.D. 1977. "The Spatiotemporal Transformations of Gawa Canoes." *Journal de la Société des Océanistes*, vol. 33, no. 54-55: 39-53.

_____, 1986. *The Fame of Gawa: A Symbolic Study of Value Transformation in a Massim (Papua New Guinea) Society*. Cambridge: Cambridge University Press.

Murdock, G.P. 1965[1949]. *Social Structure*. 2nd edn. Glencoe: Free Press.

_____, 1967. *Ethnographic Atlas*. Pittsburgh: University of Pittsburgh Press.

Murray, H.P. 1912. *Papua or British New Guinea*. London: T. Fisher Unwin.

Needham, J. 1970. *Science and Civilization in China*. Cambridge: Cambridge University Press.

Needham, R. 1962. *Structure and Sentiment*. Chicago: University of Chicago Press.

Nicolis, G. and I. Prigogine. 1989. *Exploring Complexity: An Introduction*. San Francisco: W.H. Freeman.

Obeyesekere, G. 1992. *The Apotheosis of Captain Cook. European Myth-making in the Pacific*. Princeton, NJ: Princeton University Press.

Ollier, C.D. 1978. "Tectonics and Geomorphology of the Eastern Highlands." In *Landform Evolution in Australasia*, J.L. Davies and M.A.J. Williams (Eds.), Canberra: Australian National University Press, pp. 5-47.

Olson, R.L. 1967. *Social Structure and Social Life of the Tlingit in Alaska*. University of California Anthropological Records, Berkeley.

Omaar, R. and A. de Waal (Eds.) 1996. *Rwanda: Killing the Evidence*. London: African Rights.

O'Meara, T. 1997. "Causation and the Struggle for a Science of Culture. CA Forum on Theory in Anthropology." *Current Anthropology*, vol. 38, no. 3: 399-410.

Oram, N. 1977. "Environment, Migration and Site Selection in the Port Moresby Coastal Area." In *The Melanesian Environment*, J.H. Winslow (Ed.), Canberra: Australian National University Press, pp. 74-99.

Ortner, S. 1981. "Gender and Sexuality in Hierarchical Societies: The Case of Polynesia and Some Comparative Implications." In *Sexual Meanings, the Cultural Construction of Gender and Sexuality*, S.B. Ortner and H. Whitehead (Eds.), Cambridge: Cambridge University Press, pp. 359-409.

_____, 1995. "Resistance and the Problem of Ethnographic Refusal." *Comparative Studies in Society and History*, vol. 37, no. 1: 173-193.

Papua 1909. "Central Division." In *Report for the Year ended 30th June, 1909*. Victoria: Government of the Commonwealth of Australia, pp. 14-17, 63.

_____, 1911a. "General Health." In *Report for the Year ended 30th June, 1910*. Victoria: Government of the Commonwealth of Australia, p. 33.

_____, 1911b. "Medical Department." In *Report for the Year ended 30th June, 1910*. Victoria: Government of the Commonwealth of Australia, p. 32.

_____, 1911c. "Native Labour." In *Report for the Year ended 30th June, 1910*. Victoria: Government of the Commonwealth of Australia, p. 65.

_____, 1912a. "Annual Report, Chief Medical Officer, 1911-12." In *Report for the Year ended 30th June, 1912*. Victoria: Parliament of the Commonwealth of Australia, pp. 164-165.

_____, 1912b. "Dysentery." In *Report for the Year ended 30th June, 1912*. Victoria: Parliament of the Commonwealth of Australia, p. 156.

_____, 1917. "Public Health." In *Annual Report for the Year 1815-16*. Victoria: Parliament of the Commonwealth of Australia, pp. 35-38.

_____, 1918. "Public Health." In *Report for the Year ended 30th June, 1917*. Victoria: Parliament of the Commonwealth of Australia, p. 45.

_____, 1919. "Public Health." In *Annual Report for the Year 1917-18*. Victoria: Parliament of the Commonwealth of Australia, pp. 56-60.

_____, 1923. "Native Population." In *Annual Report for the Year 1921-22*. Victoria: Parliament of the Commonwealth of Australia, p. 55.

_____, 1927. "Public Health." In *Annual Report for the Year 1925-26*. Victoria: Parliament of the Commonwealth of Australia, pp. 78-79.

_____, 1928. "Measles." In *Annual Report for the Year 1926-27*. Canberra: Parliament of the Commonwealth of Australia, pp. 78-79.

_____, 1933. "Medical." In *Annual Report for the Year 1931-32*. Canberra: Parliament of the Commonwealth of Australia, pp. 4-6.

_____, 1934. "Native Labour." In *Annual Report for 1932-33*. Canberra: Parliament of the Commonwealth of Australia, p. 11.

Papua New Guinea (PNG) 1929. "Report of Government Patrol to Nara and Kaebada, May 1929." Patrol Report, Kairuku Subdistrict, Bereina.

_____, 1931. "Report of Government Patrol to Roro and Mekeo, May 1931." Patrol Report, Kairuku Subdistrict, Bereina.

_____, 1932a. "Annual Report." Kairuku Subdistrict 1931-32.

_____, 1932b. "Report of Government Patrol to Bush Mekeo, November 1931." Patrol Report, Kairuku Subdistrict, Bereina.

_____, 1932c. "Report of Government Patrol to Nara and Kabadi, February 1932." Patrol Report, Kairuku Subdistrict, Bereina.

_____, 1932d. "Report of Government Patrol to Roro and Mekeo, November 1931." Patrol Report, Kairuku Subdistrict, Bereina.

_____, 1935. "Report, Mekeo Sorcery, 1934-35." Patrol Report, Kairuku Subdistrict, Bereina.

_____, 1941a. "Report of Government Patrol to Bush Mekeo, February 1941." Patrol Report, Kairuku Subdistrict, Bereina.

_____, 1941b. "Report of Outbreak of 'Vailala Madness,' February 1941." Patrol Report, Kairuku Subdistrict, Bereina.

_____, 1948. "Report of Government Patrol to Bush Mekeo, December 1947." Patrol Report, Kairuku Subdistrict, Bereina.

_____, 1949. "Village Population Register." Government Offices, Kairuku Subdistrict, Bereina.

_____, 1955. "Report of Government Patrol to Bush Mekeo, October 1954." Patrol Report, Kairuku Subdistrict, Bereina.

Percy, W. 1975. *The Message in the Bottle: How Queer Man Is, How Queer Language Is, and What One Has to Do with the Other*. New York: Noonday Press.

Petitot, J. 2001. "A Morphodynamical Schematization of the Canonical Formula for Myths." In *The Double Twist: From Ethnography to Morphodynamics*. P. Maranda (Ed.), Toronto: University of Toronto Press, pp. 267-311.

Piot, C. 1992. "Wealth Production, Ritual Consumption and Center/Periphery Relations in a West African Regional System." *American Ethnologist*, vol. 19: 34-52.

_____, 1996. "Of Slaves and the Gift: Kabre Sale of Kin during the Era of the Slave Trade." *Journal of African History*, vol. 37: 31-49.

_____, 1999. *Remotely Global: Village Modernity in West Africa*. Chicago: University of Chicago Press.

Pitt-Rivers, G.H.L.F. 1927. *The Clash of Culture and the Contact of Races: An Anthropological and Psychological Study of the Laws of Racial Adaptability with Special Reference to the Depopulation of the Pacific and the Government of Subject Races*. London: G. Routledge.

Porush, D. 1991. "Prigogine, Chaos, and Contemporary Science Fiction." *Science Fiction Studies*, vol. 18, no. 3.

Price, B. 1997. "The Myth of Postmodern Science." In *Chaos, Complexity, and Sociology: Myths, Models and Theories*, R. Eve, S. Horsfall, and M. Lee (Eds.), Thousand Oaks, CA: Sage, pp. 1-14.

Prigogine, I. 1980. *From Being to Becoming*. San Francisco: W.H. Freeman.

Prigogine, I. and I. Stengers. 1984. *Order Out of Chaos*. New York: Bantam Press.

Prunier, G. 1995. *The Rwanda Crisis: History of a Genocide*. New York: Columbia University Press.

Rabinow, P. 1977. *Reflections on Fieldwork in Morocco*. Berkeley: University of California Press.

Racine, L. 2001. "Analogy and the Canonical Formula of Mythic Transformation." In *The Double Twist: From Ethnography to Morphodynamics*, P. Maranda (Ed.), Toronto: University of Toronto Press, pp. 33 - 55.

Radcliffe-Brown, A. 1931. "The Social Organization of Australian Tribes." *Oceania*, vol. 1: 43-63.

_____, 1952. *Structure and Function in Primitive Society*. London: Oxford University Press.

Rattray, R.S. 1932. *The Tribes of the Ashanti Hinterland*. Oxford: Oxford University Press.

Reulle, D. 1994. "Where Can One Hope to Profitably Apply the Ideas of Chaos?" *Physics Today*, vol. July: 24-30.

Reyntjens, F. 1999. *La guerre des grands lacs: alliances mouvantes et conflits extraterritoriaux en Afrique centrale*. Paris: Harmattan.

Rivers, W.H.R. 1922. *Essays on the Depopulation of Melanesia*. Cambridge: Cambridge University Press.

Rivière, P. 1984. *Individual and Society in Guiana*. Cambridge: Cambridge University Press.

_____, 1994. "WYSINWYG in Amazonia." *Journal of the Anthropological Society of Oxford*, vol. 25, no. 3: 255-262.

Robbins, B. 1998. "Science-envy: Sokal, Science and the Police." *Radical Philosophy*, vol. 88, March/April: 2-5.

Roberts, S.H. 1927. *Population Problems of the Pacific*. London: Routledge.

Romilly, H.H. 1889. *From my Verandah in New Guinea: Sketches and Traditions*. London: D. Nutt.

Ross, A. (Ed.) 1996. *Science Wars*. Durham: Duke University Press.

Rosser Jr, J.B. 1997. "Chaos Theory and Rationality in Economics." In *Chaos Theory in the Social Sciences: Foundations and Applications*, D. Kiel and E. Elliot (Eds.), Ann Arbor: University of Michigan Press, pp. 199-213.

Rowley, C.D. 1966. *The New Guinea Villager: The Impact of Colonial Rule on Primitive Society and Economy*. New York: Praeger.

Ruelle, D. 1993. *Chance and Chaos*. London: Penguin Books.

Sagir, B.F. 2003. "The Politics and Transformations of Chieftainship in Haku, Buka Island, Papua New Guinea." Ph.D. Thesis, Department of Anthropology, Research School of Pacific and Asian Studies, Australian National University.

Sahlins, M. 1958. *Social Stratification in Polynesia*. Monographs of the American Ethnological Society; no. 29., Seattle: University of Washington Press.

_____, 1976. *Culture and Practical Reason*. Chicago: University of Chicago Press.

_____, 1981. *Historical Metaphors and Mythical Realities: Structure in the Early History of the Sandwich Islands Kingdom*. Ann Arbor: University of Michigan Press.

_____, 1985. *Islands of History*. Chicago: University of Chicago Press.

_____, 1991. "The Return of the Event, Again; with Reflections on the Beginnings of the Great Fijian War of 1893 to 1855 Between the Kingdoms of Bau and Rewa." In *Clio in Oceania*. A. Biersack (Ed.), Washington, DC: Smithsonian Institution Press, pp. 37-99.

Said, E. 1979. *Orientalism*. New York: Random House.

Salmond, A. 1991. "Tipuna - Ancestors: Aspects of Maori Cognatic Descent." In *Man and a Half: Essays in Pacific Anthropology and Ethnobiology in Honour of Ralph Bulmer*, A. Pawley (Ed.), Memoir 48, Auckland, New Zealand: Polynesian Society, pp. 343-356.

Sapperstein, A. 1997. "The Prediction of Unpredictability: Applications of the New Paradigm of Chaos in Dynamical Systems to the Old Problem of the Stability of a System of Hostile Nations." In *Chaos Theory in the Social Sciences: Foundations and Applications*, D. Kiel and E. Elliot (Eds.), Ann Arbor: University of Michigan Press, pp. 139-163.

Schepper-Hughes, N. 1995. "The Primacy of the Ethical: Propositions for a Militant Anthropology. Commentary in 'Objectivity and Militancy: A Debate.'" *Current Anthropology*, vol. 36, no. 3: 409-420.

Schlee, G. 2002. "Regularities dans le chaos: traits recurrents dans l'organisation politico-religieuse et militaire des Somali." *L'Homme*, vol. 161, January-March: 17-50.

Schneider, D. 1969. "Kinship, Nationality and Religion in American Culture: Toward a Definition of Kinship." In *Forms of Symbolic Action. Proceedings of the 1969 Annual Spring*

Meeting of the American Ethnological Society, R.F. Spencer (Ed.), 2nd edn, Seattle: University of Washington Press, pp. 116-125.

_____, 1980. *American Kinship: A Cultural Account*. 2nd edn. Chicago: University of Chicago Press.

Schwimmer, E. 2001. "Is the Canonic Formula Useful in Cultural Description?" In *The Double Twist: From Ethnography to Morphodynamics*, P. Maranda (Ed.), Toronto: University of Toronto Press, pp. 56 - 96.

Scott, G. (Ed.) 1991. *Time Rhythm and Chaos: In the New Dialogue with Nature*. Ames: Iowa State University Press.

Scragg, R. 1977. "Historical Epidemiology in Papua New Guinea." *Papua New Guinea Medical Journal*, vol. 20: 102-109.

Scubla, L. 2001. "Hesiod, the Three Functions, and the Canonical Formula of Myth." In *The Double Twist: From Ethnography to Morphodynamics*, P. Maranda (Ed.), Toronto: University of Toronto Press, pp. 123-155.

Seeger, A., R. Damatta, and E. Viveiros de Castro. 1979. "A construção da pessoa nas sociedades indígenas brasileiras." *Boletim do Museo Nacioanl – Antropología*, vol. 32: 1-20.

Segerstråle, U.C.O. 2000. *Beyond the Science Wars: The Missing Discourse About Science and Society*. Albany: State University of New York Press.

Seligmann, C.G. 1910. *The Melanesians of British New Guinea*. Cambridge: Cambridge University Press.

Shankland, D. 2001. "Putting the Science Back in." *Anthropology Today*, vol. 17, no. 2: 1-2.

Shugart, H.H. 1998. *Terrestrial Ecosystems in Changing Environments*. Cambridge: Cambridge University Press.

Siemens, S. 1991. "Three Formal Theories of Cultural Analogy." *Journal of Quantitative Anthropology*, vol. 3: 229-250.

Singleton, M. and S.P. Reyna. 1995. "Comment: Science - Artichoke or Onion?" *Journal of the Royal Anthropological Institute* (n.s), vol. 1, no. 3: 628-31.

Smith, P. 1970. "La Forge de l'intelligence." *L'Homme*, vol. X, no. 2: 5-21.

_____, 1975. *Le recit populaire au Rwanda*. Paris: Armand Colin.

_____, 1979. "L'efficacité des interdits." *L'Homme*, vol. XIX, no. 1: 5-47.

Sokol, A. 1996. "Transgressing the Boundaries: Toward a Transformative Hermeneutics of Quantum Gravity." *Social Text*, vol. 46/47: 215-252.

Sokol, A. and J. Bricmont. 1998. *Intellectual Impostures: Postmodern Philosophers' Abuse of Science*. London: Profile Books.

Sornette, D. 2003. *Why Stock Markets Crash: Critical Events in Complex Financial Systems*. Princeton: Princeton University Press.

Spencer, H. 1873. *The Study of Sociology*. New York: Appleton.

Spiro, M. 1986. "Cultural Relativism and the Future of Anthropology." *Cultural Anthropology*, vol. 1, no. 3: 259-286.

_____, 1996. "Postmodernist Anthropology, Subjectivity, and Science: A Modernist Critique." *Society for Comparative Study of Society and History*, vol. 38, no. 4: 759-780.

Stannard, D. 1989. *Before the Horror: The Population of Hawai'i on the Eve of Western Contact*. Honolulu: University of Hawaii Press.

Stephen, M. 1974. "Continuity and Change in Mekeo Society, 1890-1971." Ph.D. Thesis, Department of Pacific History, Research School of Pacific Studies, Australian National University.

_____, 1977. *Cargo Cult Hysteria: Symptom of Despair or Technique of Ecstasy?* Occasional Paper, Research Centre for Southwest Pacific Studies; no. 1., Bundoora: La Trobe University.

_____, 1979a. "An Honourable Man: Mekeo Views of the Village Constable." *Journal of Pacific History*, vol. 14: 84-99.

_____, 1979b. "Sorcery, Magic and the Mekeo World View." In *Powers, Plumes and Piglets: Phenomena of Melanesian Religion*, N.C. Habel (Ed.), Bedford Park, Australia: Australian Association for the Study of Religions, pp. 149-160.

_____, 1987a. "Master of Souls: The Mekeo Sorcerer." In *Sorcerer and Witch in Melanesia*, M. Stephen (Ed.), Melbourne: Melbourne University Press, pp. 41-80.

_____, 1987b. *Sorcerer and Witch in Melanesia*. Carlton, Vic: Melbourne University Press in association with La Trobe University Research Centre for South-West Pacific Studies.

_____, 1995. *A'aisa's Gifts: A Study of Magic and the Self*. Studies in Melanesian Anthropology; 13. Berkeley: University of California Press.

_____, 1996. "The Mekeo 'Man of Sorrow': Sorcery and the Individuation of the Self." *American Ethnologist*, vol. 23, no. 1: 83-101.

_____, 1998. "A Response to Mosko's Comments on 'The Man of Sorrow.'" *American Ethnologist*, vol. 25, no. 4: 747-749.

Stewart, I. 1989. *Does God Play Dice?: The Mathematics of Chaos*. Cambridge, MA: Blackwell.

_____, 1997. *Does God Play Dice?: The Mathematics of Chaos*. 2nd edn, Cambridge, MA: Blackwell.

Strathern, A. 1966. "Despots and Directors in the Highlands of New Guinea." *Man*, vol. 1, no. 3: 356-367.

_____, 1982. "Two Waves of African Models in the New Guinea Highlands." In *Inequality in New Guinea Highlands Societies*, A. Strathern (Ed.), Cambridge Papers in Social Anthropology; no. 11, Cambridge: Cambridge University Press, pp. 35-49.

Strathern, A. and M. 1971. *Self-decoration in Mount Hagen*. London: Duckworth.

Strathern, M. 1979. "The Self in Self-decoration." *Oceania*, vol. 49: 241-257.

_____, 1988. *The Gender of the Gift: Problems with Women and Problems with Society in Melanesia*. Berkeley/Los Angeles: University of California Press.

_____, 1991a. "One Man and Many Men." In *Great Men and Big Men: Personifications of Power in Melanesia*, M. Godelier and M. Strathern (Eds.), Cambridge: Cambridge University Press, pp. 159-173.

_____, 1991b. *Partial Connections*. Savage, MD: Rowman and Littlefield.

_____, 1992a. "Parts and Wholes: Refiguring Relationships in a Post-plural World." In *Conceptualizing Society*, A. Kuper (Ed.), London: Routledge, pp. 73-104.

_____, 1992b. "Qualified Value: The Perspective of Gift Exchange." In *Barter Exchange and Value: An Anthropological Approach*, C. Humphrey and S. Hugh-Jones (Eds.), Cambridge: Cambridge University Press, pp. 169-191.

_____, 1995. *The Relation: Issues in Complexity and Scale*. Cambridge: Prickly Pear Press.

_____, 1999. *Property, Substance and Effect: Anthropological Essays on Persons and Things*. London: Athlone.

_____, 2000. "Environments Within: An Ethnographic Commentary on Scale." In *Culture, Landscape and the Environment: The Linacre Lectures 1997*, K. Flint and H. Morphy (Eds.), Oxford: Oxford University Press, pp. 44-71.

_____, 2001. "The Patent and the Malanggan." *Theory, Culture & Society*, vol. 18, no. 4: 1-26.

Swaddling, P., L. Aitsi, G. Trompf, and M. Kari. 1977. "Beyond the Early Oral Traditions of the Austronesian Speaking People of the Gulf and Western Central Provinces." *Oral History*, vol. 1: 50-80.

Tait, D. 1961. *The Konkomba of Northern Ghana*. London: Oxford University Press.

Taussig, M. 1993. *Mimesis and Alterity: A Particular History of the Senses*. New York: Routledge.

Taylor, A.C. 1996. "The Soul's Body and Its States: An Amazonian Perspective on the Nature of Being Human." *Journal of the Royal Anthropological Institute* (n.s.), vol. 2, no. 2: 201-216.

Taylor, C. 1992. *Milk, Honey and Money*. Washington, DC: Smithsonian Institution Press.

_____, 1999. *Sacrifice as Terror*. Oxford: Berg Press.

_____, 2002. "The Cultural Face of Terror in the Rwandan Genocide of 1994." In *Annihilating Difference: The Anthropology of Genocide*, A.L. Hinton (Ed.), Berkeley: University of California Press.

Tcherkezoff, S. 1987. *Dual Classification Reconsidered: Nyamwezi Sacred Kingship and Other Examples*. Cambridge: Cambridge University Press.

Thom, R. 1975. *Structural Stability and Morphogenesis: An Outline of a General Theory of Models*. Translated by D.H. Fowler. Reading, MA: Benjamin.

_____, 1990. *Semio Physics: A Sketch*. Translated by D.H. Fowler. Boston: Addison-Wesley Publishing Company, Inc.

Thomas, L. 1983. *Late Night Thoughts on Listening to Mahler's Ninth Symphony*. New York: Viking Press.

Thomas, N. 1986a. "Gender and Social Relations in Polynesia: A Critical Note." *Canberra Anthropology*, vol. 9, no. 1: 78-89.

_____, 1986b. *Planets Around the Sun: Dynamics and Contradictions of the Fijian Matanitu*. Oceania Monographs 31. Sydney: University of Sydney Press.

_____, 1989. *Out of Time: History and Evolution in Anthropological Discourse*. Cambridge and New York: Cambridge University Press.

Thune, C. 1989. "Death and Matrilineal Reincorporation on Normanby Island." In *Death Rituals and Life in the Societies of the Kula Ring*, F.H. Damon and R. Wagner (Eds.), DeKalb: Northern Illinois University Press, pp. 153-179.

Tresch, J. 2001. "On Going Native: Thomas Kuhn and Anthropological Method." *Philosophy of the Social Sciences*, vol. 31, no. 3: 302-322.

Turner, T. 1969. "Oedipus: Time and Structure in Narrative Form." In *Forms of Symbolic Action*, R.F. Spencer (Ed.), Seattle: University of Washington, pp. 26-68.

_____, 1977. "Transformation, Hierarchy and Transcendence: A Reformulation of van Gennep's Model of the Structure of Rites de Passage." In *Secular Ritual*, S. Moore and B. Myerhoff (Eds.), Assen/Amsterdam: Van Gorcum, pp. 53-70.

_____, 1995. "Social Body and Embodied Subject: Bodiliness, Subjectivity and Sociality Among the Kayapo." *Cultural Anthropology*, vol. 10, no. 2: 143-170.

Turner, V. 1966. "Colour Classification in Ndembu Ritual: A Problem in Primitive Classification." In *Anthropological Approaches to the Study of Religion*, M. Banton (Ed.), London: Tavistock, pp. 47-84.

_____, 1969. *The Ritual Process: Structure and Anti-structure*. Chicago: Aldine.

Tylor, E.B. 1891. *Primitive Culture: Researches into the Development of Mythology, Philosophy, Religion, Language, Art, & Custom*. 3rd edn, London: J. Murray.

Umurangi. *Rwandan popular political magazine*.

Valeri, V. 1985. *Kingship and Sacrifice: Ritual and Society in Ancient Hawaii*. Chicago: University of Chicago Press.

_____, 1991. "The Transformation of a Transformation: A Structural Essay on an Aspect of Hawaiian History (1809 to 1819)." In *Clio in Oceania: Toward a Historical Anthropology*, A. Biersack (Ed.), pp. 101-164.

Van Gennep, A. 1960. *The Rites of Passage*. Chicago: University of Chicago Press.

Van Peer, W. 1998. "Sense and Nonsense of Chaos Theory in Literary Studies." In *The Third Culture: Literature and Science*, E. Shaffer (Ed.), Berlin: Walter de Gruyter, pp. 40-48.

Vansina, J. 1967. "L'évolution du royaume Rwandais des origines B 1900." *Cahiers Internationaux de Sociologie*, vol. XLIII: 143-158.

_____, 1983. "Is Elegance Proof? Structuralism and African History." *History in Africa*, vol. 10: 307-348.

_____, 2001. *Le Rwanda ancien: le royaume nyiginya*. Paris: Karthala.

Vilaça, A. 1992. *Comendo como Gente: Formas do canibalismo Wari*. Rio de Janeiro: Universidad Federal do Rio de Janeiro.

_____, 1997. "Christians Without Faith: Some Aspects of the Conversion of the Wari (Pakaa Nova)." *Ethnos*, vol. 62, no. 1-2: 91-115.

Vincke, E. 1991. "Liquides sexuels féminins et rapports sociaux en Afrique centrale." *Anthropologie et Sociétés*, vol. 15, no. 2-3: 167-188.

Viveiros de Castro, E. 1992. *From the Enemy's Point of View*. Chicago: Chicago University Press.

_____, 1993. "Alguns aspectos da afinidade no dravidianato amazônico." In *Amazônia: etnologia e história indígena*, E. Viveiros de Castro and M. Carneiro da Cunha (Eds.), São Paulo: NHII-USP/FAPESP, pp. 365-431.

_____, 1998. "Cosmological Deixis and Amerindian Perspectivism." *Journal of the Royal Anthropological Institute* (n.s.), vol. 4, no. 3: 469-488.

_____, 2002. *A Inconstância da Alma Selvagem*. São Paulo: Cosac & Naify.

Wagner, R. 1978. *Lethal Speech: Daribi Myth as Symbolic Obviation*. Ithaca, NY: Cornell University Press.

_____, 1981. *The Invention of Culture*. Chicago: University of Chicago Press.

_____, 1986a. *Asiwinarong: Ethos, Image and Social Power among the Usen Barok of New Ireland*. Princeton: Princeton University Press.

_____, 1986b. "The Fractal Person." Paper for the symposium on Great Man and Big Man Societies.

_____, 1986c. *Symbols that Stand for Themselves*. Chicago: University of Chicago Press.

_____, 1991. "The Fractal Person." In *Big Men and Great Men: Personifications of Power in Melanesia*, M. Godelier and M. Strathern (Eds.), Cambridge: Cambridge University Press, pp. 159-173.

_____, 2001. *Anthropology of the Subject: Holographic Worldview in New Guinea and its Meaning and Significance for the World of Anthropology*. Berkeley: University of California Press.

Waldrop, M.M. 1992. *Complexity: The Emerging Science at the Edge of Order and Chaos*. New York: Simon & Schuster.

Wallace, A. 1956. "Revitalization Movements." *American Anthropologist*, vol. 58: 264-281.

Wallerstein, I. 1993. "The World-System after the Cold War." *Journal of Peace Research*, vol. 30, no. 1: 1-6.

Weil, A. 1969[1949]. "On the Algebraic Study of Certain Types of Marriage Laws (Murngin system)." In *The Elementary Structures of Kinship*, C. Lévi-Strauss (Ed.), Boston: Beacon Press, pp. 221-227.

_____, 1991. "Sur quelques symétries dans l'Iliade." In *Miscellanea Mathematica*, P.J. Hilton, F. Hirzebruch, and R. Remmert (Eds.), Berlin: Springer Verlag, pp. 305 - 309.

Weiner, A. 1977. *Women of Value, Men of Renown*. Austin: University of Texas Press.

Weiner, J. 1988. *The Heart of the Pearl Shell*. Berkeley: University of California Press.

West, F.J. 1968. *Hubert Murray: the Australian Pro-consul*. Melbourne: Oxford University Press.

Weyl, H. 1952. *Symmetry*. Princeton, New Jersey: Princeton University Press.

Wilks, I. 1976. "The Akan and Mossi States: 1500-1800." In *History of West Africa*, J.F.A. Ajayi and M. Crowder (Eds.), New York: Columbia University Press.

Willis, R.G. 1967. "The Head and the Loins: Levi-Strauss and Beyond." *Man* (n.s), vol. 2, no. 4: 519-534.

Winterhalder, B. 1994. "Concepts in Historical Ecology." In *Historical Ecology: Cultural Knowledge and Changing Landscapes*, C. L. Crumley (Ed.), Santa Fe, NM: School of American Research Press, pp. 17-42.

Wittgenstein, L. 1961. *Tractatus Logico-Philosophicus*. Translated by D.F. Pears and B.F. McGuinness. London: Routledge and Kegan Paul.

Yengoyan, A.A. 1968. "Demographic and Ecological Influences on Aboriginal Australian Marriage Systems." In *Man the Hunter*, R.B. Lee and I. DeVore (Eds.), Chicago: Aldine Pub. Co, pp. 185-199.

_____, 1970. "Demographic Factors in Pitjandjara Social Organization." In *Australian Aboriginal Anthropology: Modern Studies in the Social Anthropology of the Australian Aborigines*, R.M. Berndt (Ed.), Perth: University of Western Australia Press, pp. 70-91.

Young, M. 1971. *Fighting with Food: Leadership, Values and Social Control in a Massim Society*. London: Cambridge University Press.

_____, 1983a. "Ceremonial Visiting in Goodenough Island." In *The Kula: New Perspectives on Massim Exchange*, J.W. Leach and E.R. Leach (Eds.): Cambridge University Press, pp. 395-410.

____, 1983b. *Magicians of Manumanua: Living Myth in Kalauna*. Berkeley: University of California Press.

____, 1983c. "The Theme of the Resentful Hero: Stasis and Mobility in Goodenough Mythology." In *The Kula: New Perspectives on Massim Exchange*, J.W. Leach and E.R. Leach (Eds.): Cambridge University Press, pp. 383-384.

Young, T. 1991a. "Chaos and Social Change: Metaphysics of the Postmodern." *The Social Science Journal*, vol. 28, no. 3: 289-305.

____, 1991b. "Chaos Theory and Symbolic Interactionism." *Journal of Symbolic Interaction*, vol. 14: 3-21.

____, 1992. "Chaos Theory and Human Agency: Humanist Sociology in a Postmodern Age." *Humanity and Society*, vol. 16: 441-460.

Zelenietz, M. 1981. "An Introduction." In *Sorcery and Social Change in Melanesia*, M. Zelenietz and S. Lindenbaum (Eds.), *Social Analysis* (special issue), vol. 8, pp. 3-14.

Zelenietz, M. and S. Lindenbaum (Eds.) 1981. "Sorcery and Social Change in Melanesia." *Social Analysis* (special issue), vol. 8.

Zirikana. *Rwandan popular political magazine.*

Zuckerkandl, V. 1956. *Sound and Symbol.* (Bollington Series,) Princeton University Press.

____, 1973. *Man the Musician.* (Bollington Series.) Translated by N. Guterman. Princeton University Press.

CONTRIBUTORS

Frederick H. Damon is Professor of Anthropology at the University of Virginia in Charlottesville, Virginia. He has conducted two sets of research in the Kula Ring of Papua New Guinea, one beginning in 1973 focused on exchange, production, and ritual, the other extending from 1991 to 2002 dealing with environmental issues. Among his publications are "The Kula and generalised exchange: considering some unconsidered aspects of The Elementary Structures of Kinship," *Man* (n.s) (1980); "Kula Valuables, the Problem of Value and the Production of Names," *L'Homme* (2002); *From Muyuw To The Trobriands: Transformations Along the Northern Side of the Kula Ring* (1990); and "Selective Anthropomorphization: Trees in the Northeast Kula Ring," *Social Analysis* (1998). Recent research and writing deal with the use and symbolism of flora and wooden objects. A central focus in this work concerns how sailing craft are dynamical, chaotic systems and provide well-formed models for such conceptions.

José Antonio Kelly works in the Amazon Center for the Research and Control of Tropical Diseases, Amazonas, Venezuela, and is associated with the Indigenous Transformations: Amerindian Regimes of Subjectivity withstanding History project at the Graduate Program in Social Anthropology, Museu Nacional, Federal University of Rio de Janeiro/Brazilian National Research Council. He earned a degree in Electronics Engineering in 1996 before turning to social anthropology, in which he completed his Ph.D. at the University of Cambridge in 2003. His doctoral research focused on the health system among the Venezuelan Yanomami as entry point into the wider issue of Indian-State relations. He is particularly interested in bringing anthropological knowledge drawn from traditional ethnographic settings to bear on Amerindians' contemporary relations with their respective nation-states.

Jack Morava is Professor of Mathematics and of Physics and Astronomy at the Johns Hopkins University in Baltimore. He studied at Oxford and received a Ph.D. from Rice University in 1968. He was a member of the

Institute for Advanced Study in Princeton, and he also held visiting positions at the Steklov Institute in Moscow and the Tata Institute of Fundamental Research in Mumbai. His early work concerned relations between stable homotopy and local number theory, but more recently he has been involved in the study of what physicists call topological gravity, which involves generalizing ideas from string theory to four dimensions. Among his publications are"Noetherian Localisations of Categories of Cobordism Comodules," *Annals of Math* (1985) and "Pretty Good Gravity," in *Advances in Theoretical and Mathematical Physics* (2001).

Mark S. Mosko is Professor and Head of the Anthropology Department in the Research School of Pacific and Asian Studies at the Australian National University. Over three decades he has conducted numerous ethnographic field studies of the North Mekeo peoples of Papua New Guinea and written comparatively on numerous other societies including hinterland Madang, Trobriands, ancient Hawaii, Micronesia, caste India, and the Mbuti of Zaire. His theoretical interests have covered a wide range of ethnological issues, from structuralism, symbolism and gift exchange to the historical potentialities of Pacific hierarchy and chieftainship, personhood, gender, body art, religious syncretism, and commodification. He is author of *Quadripartite Structures* (1985), coeditor (with Margaret Jolly) of *Transformations of Hierarchy* (Special Issue of *History and Anthropology*, 1994) and author of numerous journal articles and book chapters.

Charles Piot is Creed C. Black Associate Professor in the Department of Cultural Anthropology and the Program in African and African American Studies at Duke University. He does research on the political economy and history of rural west Africa. His recent book, *Remotely Global: Village Modernity in West Africa* (1999), attempts to retheorize a classic out-of-the-way place as within the modern and the global.

Dame Marilyn Strathern is William Wyse Professor of Social Anthropology at the University of Cambridge. Her ethnographic interests are divided between Melanesia and Britain, and latterly between Euro-American kinship, new reproductive technologies, intellectual property issues, and the audit culture. An abiding interest in comparison and its impossible premises led to some "complex" reflections in *Partial Connections* (1991) which constituted one first explicit attempt in social anthropology to draw upon the insights of chaos theory. Many of the ideas pioneered in *Partial Connections* have found their way into Strathern's other recent treatments of gender relations in Melanesia (*The Gender of the Gift*, 1988), the cultural revolution at home (*After Nature*, 1992), new birth technologies (*Technologies of Procreation*, 1993), and new views of persons and things (*Property, Substance and Effect*, 1999).

Christopher C. Taylor is Associate Professor and Chair of the Anthropology Department at the University of Alabama at Birmingham. He received his Ph.D. from the University of Virginia in 1988. His work on central Africa probes the nature of precolonial, colonial, and contemporary social order there drawing upon ethnomedical fieldwork experience in Rwanda. His publications include *Milk, Honey and Money* (1992), and *Sacrifice as Terror* (1999).

Roy Wagner, Professor of Anthropology at the University of Virginia, researches in and writes about work emanating from Highland Papua New Guinea, New Ireland, and, occasionally, indigenous North America. His general concern is with indigenous conceptual systems, more specifically the objective basis of subjective phenomena like thought imagery, representation, and symbolism. Much of this discussion here follows from *An Anthropology of the Subject* (2001). His household is dominated (chaotically) by three cats.

INDEX